SERIAL OFFENDERS

Current Thought, Recent Findings

Edited by
Louis B. Schlesinger, Ph.D.

CRC Press
Boca Raton   London   New York   Washington, D.C.

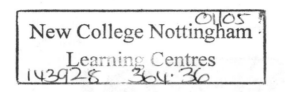
Library of Congress Cataloging-in-Publication Data

Schlesinger, Louis B.
   Serial offenders : current thought, recent findings / Louis B. Schlesinger, editor.
      p. cm.
   Includes bibliographical references and index.
   ISBN 0-8493-2236-7 (alk. paper)
   1. Recidivism. 2. Recidivists. I. Title.

HV6049 .S47 2000
364.3—dc21

00-040350

Visit the CRC Press Web site at www.crcpress.com

© 2000 by CRC Press LLC

No claim to original U.S. Government works
International Standard Book Number 0-8493-2236-7
Library of Congress Card Number 00-040350
Printed in the United States of America   3 4 5 6 7 8 9 0
Printed on acid-free paper

Foreword

As evidenced by the popularity of such "entertainments" as Robert Lewis Stevenson's *Dr. Jekyll and Mr. Hyde* in late 19th-century England and Thomas Harris' *The Silence of the Lambs* in late 20th-century America, few facets of criminal behavior capture the public imagination so tenaciously as serial murder, most particularly when sexuality also figures prominently as a governing motive. Each of these tales recounts a series of murders perpetrated by a physician in whom "the dark side" has rather inexplicably triumphed. From those fictional terminal points alone (and not to neglect the nonfictional *reportage* of Truman Capote's *In Cold Blood* or Joseph McGinniss' *Fatal Vision*), we can readily surmise that cleverly planned and brutally executed sequential homicides hold an endless fascination for the citizenry at large. When one adds journalistic accounts of the horrific slayings of a John Wayne Gacey, Jeffrey Dahmer, Ted Bundy, the Hillside Strangler of Los Angeles, the Atlanta Child Killer, and the Gainesville Slasher in the U.S. or the Yorkshire Ripper in England, there is little mystery as to why many in the reading and viewing public have come to believe that serial homicide constitutes the rule rather than the very rare exception, thereby mistaking the exotic for the normative.

Indeed, to counter such erroneous beliefs, federal officials complained to *New York Times* writer Sara Paretsky that serial murders account for less than 0.40% (four tenths of one percent) of the homicides committed in the U.S. annually — or, in whole numbers, 84 of a total of 21,000. With 60 or more video channels available in many major cities, it is likely that at least 84 serial killings are depicted in any given *week* in the programs offered on the television screen. The reasons are not difficult to discern. The exotica of cleverly planned and brutally executed sequential homicides, with or without sexual motivation as an added bonus but with riveting descriptions of the deceptions and evasions without which serial offending would not become serial, are ever more engrossing than the usual, "garden variety" homicide, typified by the slaying of one motorist by another (with perhaps both mildly inebriated) in a dispute over who properly had the right of access to a parking place. Fictional or cinematic depictions of homicide as it is actually committed are likely to elicit no more than a long yawn among a viewing public seeking a thrill a minute, and so the mythology grows.

While skepticism about the ubiquitous entertainment focused on serial homicide is surely justified on the basis of the data, there is a downside risk that such skepticism may generalize across other categories of criminal behavior so that the exotic may become confused with the normative or prototypical. For their part, whenever scholars or clinicians concerned with understanding or altering the dynamics of criminal behavior focus on serial offending, prototypically it is the serial killer toward whom attention is turned.

Quite in contrast to the picture with regard to homicide, as the distinguished criminologist Alfred Blumstein demonstrated two decades ago in his groundbreaking research on "career criminals," it is highly probable that a very small proportion of all those who have ever been convicted of a criminal offense (perhaps as few as 6%) are responsible for a very large proportion (perhaps on the order of 55%) of all criminal activity. When one considers "property" offenses (burglary, larceny, motor vehicle theft, embezzlement, etc.) in isolation from "violent" offenses (homicide, sexual assault, robbery, assault), the proportion of offenses attributable to repeat offenders increases dramatically.

If Blumstein is correct, it is thus paradoxically the case that serial offending indeed constitutes the rule rather than the exception in all categories of crime save homicide. That paradox becomes explicable only when we consider the rates at which apprehension, prosecution, and adjudication ensue when criminal offending is examined by specific category. Hence, the ratio between the incidence of homicide (which accounts for only about .2% of all crime reported nationally in a year) and subsequent apprehension ("clearance by arrest," in the inimitable lexicon of federal criminal justice recordkeeping) of the offender begins to approach 1:1, while the ratio between the incidence of burglary (accounting for something over 22% of all crime reported nationally in a year) and subsequent apprehension is only on the order of 1:8. To turn the matter slightly, the probability that apprehension will ensue following homicide inches close to 100% (indeed, perhaps because most homicides are of the garden variety, in which the offender is readily identifiable), while the probability that apprehension will ensue following burglary tops out at approximately 12.5%. In other words, it is about eight times more probable that a homicide offender will be apprehended than a burglar will be apprehended.

If we grant Blumstein his conjecture, it would seem to follow that the majority of recidivating offenders, especially property offenders, are never apprehended, prosecuted, or sanctioned. Because we can only rationally assume that it is universally their goal not merely to accomplish the instant offense but further to escape sanction, we can only regard such offenders as successful. To that extent, the "successful" serial burglar or serial thief may exhibit levels of cleverness in planning and brilliance in execution not unlike those that characterize the serial killer who eludes detection long enough for his or her behavior to be properly categorized as serial offending.

And therein lies the core strength of the present volume, which, at its heart, addresses the interplay between the exotic and the normative but does so beyond the confines of a single category of criminal behavior. Louis B. Schlesinger has brought together in a single source and, to the knowledge of this writer, for the first time spare and original analyses of serial criminal offending *across* types and categories of crime, with particular attention to offender and victim groups not often the focus of serious scholarly or clinical inquiry. In his Introduction, Dr. Schlesinger announces that the intent of this work is "to present current and inclusive information on serial offending in a clear and straightforward manner" in order to provide "in-depth understanding." That he and the contributors to this volume have brilliantly satisfied that intent is everywhere evident.

Nathaniel J. Pallone, Ph.D.
*University Distinguished Professor of
Psychology and Criminal Justice
Rutgers – The State University*

Introduction

Although the adjective "serial" has been used only recently to describe individuals whose crimes are repetitive, such offenders have been present since antiquity. In pre-modern times, when several bodies of brutally mutilated women were found in a particular area, the attack often was attributed not to a person but to the workings of a supernatural force, such as a werewolf or vampire. And, throughout the centuries, there have been numerous recorded cases of individuals committing multiple rapes or other repetitive antisocial acts, such as arson, peeping, or lewdness. There are also countless examples of offenders who served lengthy prison terms and then, when they were released or paroled, went on to commit the exact crime for which they were incarcerated.

Thus, repetitive-compulsive offenders, particularly those who repeat their crimes in a ritualistic manner, have vexed mental health professionals, law enforcement, and society for decades. What do we do with such individuals? How do we protect society from repeat offenders, and how do we prevent such individuals from behaving in this manner to begin with? Can these people be treated or cured? In the early 1950s, programs for the repetitive-compulsive (usually sexual) offender were established in almost every state; by the 1990s many had been abolished. In the meantime, the problem has not vanished. In fact, although crime in general has declined in the past decade, there is considerable evidence that many serial crimes may actually be increasing. Nevertheless, the courts, law enforcement officials, and the general public now tend to view such behavior not as evidence of a clinical disorder (with common signs, symptoms, course, and prognosis) but solely as a criminal problem where little distinction is made between the offender and the offense. Moreover, this purely legal approach deals only with the overt manifestations of the act. Many individuals who commit an offense that is sexual in nature may do so out of social, situational, or impulsive motives. Such individuals may not truly be serial compulsive-repetitive offenders whose crimes are an outgrowth of psychogenesis. Conversely, many overtly nonsexual offenses, such as arson and burglary, may have been sexually motivated but are never classified as such legally. The purely legal approach also fails to take into account the degree of dangerousness posed by the offender or the likelihood that the offender will repeat the criminal act or commit a related but more heinous crime. An offender without a psychogenically driven compulsion may present relatively little danger to society, whereas a sexually motivated burglar, for example, might eventually commit a sexual homicide.

The topic of serial offenders has clearly captured the interest of mental health and criminal justice professionals. However, these professionals often have failed to share the scientific knowledge they have accumulated about such offenders, and also have neglected to apply that knowledge in an effort to bring about an informed public policy. For too long, professionals in different disciplines worked independently of one another; mental health professionals rarely interacted with law enforcement and rarely informed legislatures of the state of knowledge about a particular type of criminal behavior. In the area of serial offenders, information is often scattered in different professional publications, such as journals of general and forensic psychiatry, clinical and forensic psychology, sociology, criminology, police and forensic science, criminal justice, and law.

Serial Offenders: Current Thought, Recent Findings represents a modest attempt to remedy this problem. A group of leading clinicians and researchers in the field, encompassing different professions and different points of view, have contributed chapters on various aspects of the serial offender. Divided into three general sections, this volume covers current theory and research on traditional serial offenders and also describes certain special populations and unusual aspects of serial offenders.

Part I presents current theory and thinking on serial offenders. Its five chapters cover serial homicide, child molestation, rape, arson, and the nonviolent serial offender. All provide new information and new perspectives on some traditional problems. Part II, on recent clinical and research findings, begins with a chapter on criminal investigative profiling — an area familiar to law enforcement but under-valued by the mental health community. As the chapter demonstrates, this approach has elicited a tremendous amount of information about the psychodynamics and psychopathology of serial offenders. Chapter 7 covers an important topic about which very little has been written — namely, neurobiological approaches to understanding serial offenders. Serial stalkers, and those individuals who develop pathological attachments toward others, are explored thoroughly in Chapter 8. Chapter 9 discusses the serial burglar — contrasting social, situational, and sexually motivated burglaries and their consequences. The final chapter in Part II is on serial sexual harassment, a topic frequently omitted in discussions of the serial offender.

The five chapters in Part III focus on several unusual aspects of serial offending and on special populations of offenders: female and adolescent serial offenders, the syndrome of infantophilia (attraction not to children but to young infants), serial offending by the clergy, and, finally, the victims and survivors of the serial offender.

Serial Offenders: Current Thought, Recent Findings is not just another book on forensic practice, or a compendium of traditional sex offenses, or a critique of subtle methodological nuances of various research studies. The intent is to present current and inclusive information on serial offending in a clear and straightforward manner. It is hoped that this volume will provide the reader with an in-depth understanding of the serial offender, a phenomenon that has been present for centuries but whose complexities we are only now beginning to unravel.

Louis B. Schlesinger

About the Editor

 **Louis B. Schlesinger, Ph.D.,** is Associate Professor of Psychology at John Jay College of Criminal Justice, City University of New York. He is a Diplomate in Forensic Psychology of the American Board of Professional Psychology and served as president of the New Jersey Psychological Association in 1989 and as a member of the Council of Representatives of the American Psychological Association from 1991 to 1994. Dr. Schlesinger was the 1990 recipient of the New Jersey Psychological Association's "Psychologist of the Year" award, as well as a recipient of the American Psychological Association's Karl F. Heiser Presidential Award (1993). He has testified in numerous forensic cases and has published many articles, chapters, and six other books on the topics of homicide, sexual homicide, and criminal psychopathology.

Contributors

Sharon K. Araji, Ph.D.
Professor of Sociology
University of Alaska
Anchorage, Alaska

Marian J. Borg, Ph.D.
Assistant Professor of Sociology
University of Florida
Gainesville, Florida

John M. Bradford, M.D.
Professor and Head, Division of
  Forensic Psychiatry
University of Ottawa
Ottawa, Canada

Ian Broom
Department of Psychology
University of Ottawa
Ottawa, Canada

A.J. Cooper, M.D., FRC Psych.
Professor of Psychiatry
University of Western Ontario
London, Ontario, Canada

Philip Firestone, Ph.D.
Professor of Psychology
University of Ottawa
Ottawa, Canada

Jack Green, Psy.D.
Isaac Ray Center
Rush-Presbyterian-St. Lukes
  Medical Center
Chicago, Illinois

David M. Greenberg, M.D.
Professor and Chair of
  Forensic Psychiatry
University of Western Australia
Nedlands, Australia

Thomas W. Haywood, MPH
Isaac Ray Center
Rush-Presbyterian-St. Lukes
  Medical Center
Chicago, Illinois

Meg S. Kaplan, Ph.D.
Director, Sexual Behavior Clinic
New York State Psychiatric Institute;
Associate Professor of Clinical
  Psychology in Psychiatry
Columbia University, College of
  Physicians and Surgeons
New York, New York

Robert D. Keppel, Ph.D.
Retired, Chief Criminal Investigator,
  Washington State Attorney
  General's Office;
President, Institute for Forensics
Seattle, Washington

Richard B. Krueger, M.D.
Medical Director
Sexual Behavior Clinic
New York State Psychiatric Institute;
Associate Clinical Professor
  of Psychiatry
Columbia University, College of
  Physicians and Surgeons
New York, New York

Robert Lloyd-Goldstein, M.D., J.D.
Clinical Professor of Psychiatry and
  Director of the Legal Issues in the
  Practice of Psychiatry Program
Columbia University, College of
  Physicians and Surgeons
New York, New York

Mary Mavromatis, M.D.
Director of Psychiatric Services
Jawanio, Inc.; private practice
Upper Nyack, New York

Adena B. Meyers, Ph.D.
Assistant Professor of Psychology
Illinois State University
Normal, Illinois

Laurence Miller, Ph.D.
Independent practice, Boca Raton;
Police Psychologist, West Palm
  Beach Police Department;
Psychology Department
Florida Atlantic University
Boca Raton, Florida

Wade C. Myers, M.D.
Associate Professor of Psychiatry
Director, Child Psychiatry
  and the Law Clinic
University of Florida
Gainesville, Florida

Craig T. Palmer, Ph.D.
Instructor of Anthropology
University of Colorado
Colorado Springs, Colorado

John B. Pryor, Ph.D.
Professor of Psychology
Illinois State University
Normal, Illinois

Randy Thornhill, Ph.D.
Regents Professor of Biology
University of New Mexico
Albuquerque, New Mexico

Table of Contents

Dedication

*This book is dedicated
to my son Gene*

"The history of human civilization shows beyond any doubt that there is an intimate connection between cruelty and the sexual instinct; but nothing has been done towards explaining the connection, apart from laying emphasis on the aggressive factor in the libido. According to some authorities this aggressive element of the sexual instinct is in reality a relic of cannibalistic desires — that is, it is a contribution derived from the apparatus for obtaining mastery, which is concerned with the satisfaction of the other and, ontogenetically, the older of the great instinctual needs. It has been maintained that every pain contains in itself the possibility of a feeling of pleasure. All that needs to be said is that no satisfactory explanation of this perversion has been put forward and that it seems possible that a number of mental impulses are combined in it to produce a single resultant."

—Freud (*Three Essays on the Theory of Sexuality*)

"Anyone who has once experienced this power, this unlimited control over the body, blood, and spirit of a man like himself, a fellow creature, his brother in Christ — anyone who has experienced the power to inflict supreme humiliation upon another being, created like himself in the image of God, is bound to be ruled by emotions. Tyranny is a habit; it grows upon us and, in the long run, turns into a disease. I say that the most decent man in the world can, through habit, become as brutish and coarse as a wild beast. Blood and power intoxicate, callousness and vice develop; the most abnormal things become first acceptable, then sweet to the mind and heart. The human being, the member of society, is drowned forever in the tyrant, and it is practically impossible for him to regain human dignity, repentance, and regeneration. One such instance — the realization that such arbitrary power can be exercised — can infect all society; such power is seductive."

—Dostoevsky (*The House of the Dead*)

Part I

Introduction to Part I

The five chapters in this section discuss current theory regarding various types of serial offending. In Chapter 1, Louis B. Schlesinger presents serial homicide from a historical perspective, beginning with the seminal contributions of Richard von Krafft-Ebing. Dr. Schlesinger then describes three components present, in varying degrees, in all serial homicides: sadism, fantasy, and a compulsion to kill. Also highlighted in this chapter are the significance of voyeurism and fetishism in the etiology of sexual murder; postmortem paraphilias, including cannibalism, vampirism, and necrophilia; personality characteristics of serial murderers; and several theories of causation. Dr. Schlesinger argues that serial murder must be recognized as a clinical disorder with a biopsychosocial etiology, as opposed to simply a criminal problem. He believes that such recognition will stimulate further scientific interest, research, and thinking in this important area.

In Chapter 2, Sharon K. Araji reviews and updates current thinking on the serial child abuser, whose acts may range from viewing, exhibitionism, touching, fondling, and oral sex to all types of intercourse. The empirical studies described in this chapter enhance our knowledge of demographic, social, and personality characteristics of child sexual abusers and help us understand the offender's thinking and behavioral patterns. Professor Araji includes a number of illuminating case examples and also mentions some recent trends — among them, child abuse via the Internet. The chapter concludes with a discussion of treatment, prevention, and necessary legislative action.

In Chapter 3, anthropologists Craig T. Palmer and Randy Thornhill offer a unique evolutionary perspective on serial rape. Such a perspective, they believe, can provide a more complete understanding of the serial rapist. The authors argue that a profound re-evaluation of the popular view that rapists are not motivated by sexual desires is necessary. Professors Palmer and Thornhill certainly do not regard rape as an evolutionary inevitability; in fact, their theory provides a framework for identifying environmental factors that contribute to rape. An understanding of these factors, they point out, can lead to prevention of its occurrence and repetition.

Chapter 4 provides a comprehensive review of serial arson and pyromania. In this chapter, Mary Mavromatis discusses various theories of repetitive firesetting, including sexually motivated pyromania and nonsexually motivated repetitive arson. Also discussed in this chapter are female and child firesetters, the prognostic significance of repetitive arson and its relationship to serial murder, investigative profiling, treatment issues, and biological and sexual motives for firesetting. Although classic pyromania, with overt sexual dynamics, may not be a common phenomenon, Dr. Mavromatis argues that it is a legitimate, valid, and useful diagnosis that helps us understand one class of potentially very dangerous serial offenders.

The final chapter in Part I, by Richard B. Krueger and Meg S. Kaplan, covers three nonviolent serial offenses: exhibitionism, frotteurism, and telephone scatologia. These seemingly less dangerous paraphiliac offenses frequently escalate to more aggressive forms of serial acting-out behavior and therefore can be instrumental in identifying or deterring future aggressive offenders. The chapter begins with definitions and then provides an overview of epidemiology and etiology of these behaviors. Drs. Krueger and Kaplan next discuss the meaning of multiple paraphilias among sex offenders, adolescents who engage in such acts, offender and victim characteristics, and treatment issues, with a goal towards prevention.

1 Serial Homicide: Sadism, Fantasy, and a Compulsion To Kill

Louis B. Schlesinger

CONTENTS

Although there is no universally agreed-upon definition of serial homicide in all its particulars (Keeney and Heide, 1995; McKenzie, 1995), the majority of researchers, investigators, and clinicians view serial murder as sexually motivated and as basically a sub-type of sexual homicide (e.g., Geberth and Turco, 1997; Grubin, 1994; Lunde, 1976; Myers et al., 1993; Ressler et al., 1988; Revitch and Schlesinger, 1981, 1989; Warren et al.,1996). Sexual homicide becomes serial when multiple victims are involved, usually in multiple locations, with a cooling-off period between murders.

Homicides with distinct manifestations of genitality are easily detected as sexual, as are cases where the offender's "control of his victim, and her pain and humiliation, become linked to his sexual arousal" (Grubin, 1994, p. 624). However, as Schlesinger and Revitch (1997) point out: "Not all sex murders and assaults ... are of the type where sexual motives are overt and obvious. In many cases, the sexual dynamics are covert, not recognized by the authorities, and frequently rationalized and denied by the offender as well" (p. 203). Contrary to popular belief, erection, ejaculation, and intercourse may not accompany the violent act or murder; instead, the brutal and murderous assaults may serve as substitutes for the sexual act (Revitch, 1965).

The ambiguity of the definition of serial homicide, along with problems in detecting covert sexual dynamics in some cases, complicates efforts to determine the actual incidence of the behavior. National crime statistics on the number of sexual or serial homicides are not kept. Even homicides with distinctly overt signs of sexual motivation are not grouped separately but are included under the general category of homicide. As a result, estimates about the number of serial murderers and their victims vary widely. Holmes and DeBurger (1985) state that there are about 35 serial murderers in the U.S. at any given time, whereas Wilson (1988) believes that the number is closer to 100. Hickey (1997) estimates that as many as 4000 to 5000 Americans are the victims of serial killers each year. In contrast, Egger (1990) concludes that at least some of the current estimates are excessive and attributes the inflated figures to an attempt to call attention to this topic.

One approach used to estimate the magnitude of — and likely increase in — serial homicide in recent years is to examine murders with unknown motives, as many, but definitely not all, victims of serial murderers are strangers to the offenders. Ressler et al. (1988) reported a dramatic rise in the number of stranger homicides, committed for unknown motives, during the late 1970s and the 1980s, and the numbers have continued to increase in the 1990s. In 1976, 8.5% of all murders would fall under the "unknown motive" category, while in 1997 the figure rose to 38%, despite increased technological sophistication in solving crimes (*FBI Uniform Crime Reports*, 1997). But, even if the incidence of serial murder has increased tenfold in the last 20 years, as suggested by Hickey (1997), it remains a rare and poorly understood event. Murder, in general, is the least frequently committed type of violent crime (*FBI Uniform Crime Reports*, 1997), accounting for only .1% of total crimes. Of those who murder once, only a small fraction murders again (Busch and Cavanaugh, 1986).

This chapter examines serial homicide within a historical framework and focuses on the three common components of sexual homicide: sadism, fantasy, and a compulsion to kill. The chapter also discusses commonly associated paraphilias, occasional postmortem behavior, and general personality characteristics of such offenders.

SERIAL HOMICIDE IN HISTORICAL PERSPECTIVE

Serial homicide is by no means a modern — or, for that matter, an American — phenomenon. Perhaps the earliest examples of sexual sadism associated with murder can be found among the emperors of ancient Rome. With their absolute power, some of these emperors were able to indulge their sadistic propensities, including multiple murders, without much hindrance. Caligula, for example, enjoyed keeping his subordinates in abject fear. He would kill them, torture them, or humiliate them, all to enhance his sense of power and domination. For instance, he would have a subject's tongue cut out for no discernible reason. Or, during a banquet, he would order the wife of a patrician to follow him to his room, where he would rape her; he would then humiliate the couple by discussing her sexual techniques in front of the other guests (Barrett, 1998).

French nobleman Gilles de Rais, in the 1400s, with the help of underlings, tortured and killed several hundred children by decapitating or dismembering them or by breaking their necks. He allegedly derived more pleasure from witnessing these tortures than from having sex with the children. In court, he admitted his guilt, and in a speech he admonished parents not to allow their children to become idle or lazy or excessive in their habits, because such behavior could have evil consequences (Benedetti, 1972).

In 16th-century Europe, cases of apparent serial murder have become mixed up with tales of werewolves and vampires, so that the true nature of the crime in premodern times is unknown. Periodically, women's bodies were found so brutally mutilated that people attributed the attacks to the workings of a supernatural force — a werewolf or wolf-man who often appeared during a full moon. In 1573, Gilles Garnier was arrested in France for a series of savage attacks and murders of children. One of his victims was a 10-year-old girl whom he cannibalized after killing. Later, he strangled a 10-year-old boy and also ate part of him. He gave a full account of his offenses, claiming that he was a werewolf — a statement taken seriously by the courts at that time (Revitch and Schlesinger, 1989). In fact, lycanthropy (the transformation of people into wolves) was then regarded as a valid medical phenomenon (Hickey, 1997). Another 16th-century "werewolf," Peter Stubbe (Hickey, 1997), raped, sexually tortured, murdered, and also cannibalized at least 15 victims, including his own son.

Any history of serial murder would be incomplete without including the seminal work of Richard von Krafft-Ebing (1840–1902). Krafft-Ebing wrote the first comprehensive paper on sexual homicide, including serial homicide, which is contained in his classic text *Psychopathia Sexualis* ("Sexual Psychopathology"), first published in 1886. A careful reading of the chapter reveals that much of what we now know about the characteristics and behavior of serial murderers was carefully described by Krafft-Ebing over 100 years ago.

Table 1 lists some common characteristics of contemporary serial murderers, described previously by Krafft-Ebing. For example, he noted the tendency to lie and manipulate, take souvenirs from the crime scene, use ligatures, prolong torture for increased sexual arousal and pleasure, engage in animal cruelty early in life, target prostitutes, revisit the crime scene, engage in an escalation of sadistic behavior, use pornography, humiliate and degrade their victims, and carefully plan their murders to avoid detection. He noted also that these offenders often displayed no overt signs of abnormality. Finally, he described "signature" aspects of the crime, where the offender engages in idiosyncratic behavior that has little to do with the commission of the murder but is an outgrowth of the offender's own fantasies.

Krafft-Ebing cited several cases that clearly show the connection between murder and sexual arousal. The cases of Louis Menesclou and a clerk named Alton are illustrative: "The forearm of the child was found in his pocket ... the genitals could not be found ... the circumstances, as well as an obscene poem found on his person, left no doubt that he had violated the child and then murdered her. Menesclou expressed no remorse, asserting that his deed was an accident" (p. 63). Alton killed and dismembered a child whom he lured into the bushes. Following the murder, he wrote an entry in his notebook: "Killed today, a young girl; it was fine and hot" (p. 63).

Another serial murderer described by Krafft-Ebing was Vincenz Verzeni, who initially was accused of strangling, but not killing, three women. He eventually killed a 14-year-old girl and a 28-year-old woman. The genitals of the 14-year-old were torn from the body, and her mouth was filled with dirt. He used a ligature on the

TABLE 1
Characteristics of Contemporary Serial
Murderers as Noted by Krafft-Ebing (1886)

Serial murder is a male phenomenon.	"Such monstrous acts … are much more frequent [in men] than [in] women" (p. 59).
Lying and manipulation are common.	"M. expressed no remorse, asserting that his deed was an accident" (p. 63). "Arrested, at first he lied" (p. 64).
Murderer often takes trophies and souvenirs.	"A number of heads of particularly beautiful children were preserved as memorials" (p. 58). "I took the clothing … because of the pleasure it gave me to smell and touch them" (p. 67).
Ligatures are used.	"Her corpse [had] the mark of a thong around her neck" (p. 65). "His satisfaction in this garroting was greater than in masturbation" (p. 66).
Victims are tortured, often for prolonged periods.	"He then allowed his victims to live. …[The] sexual satisfaction was delayed, and then he continued to choke them until they died" (p. 60).
Offenders frequently do not harm wives or girlfriends.	"Two sweethearts that he had … it was very strange to him that he had no inclination to strangle them" (p. 66).
Sexual satisfaction is greater with murder than in nonaggressive sexual relations.	"But he had not had the same pleasure with [his girlfriends] as with his victims" (p. 66).
Offenders have a history of animal cruelty.	"When he was 12 years old, he expressed a peculiar feeling of pleasure while wringing the necks of chickens" (p. 67). "He killed animals himself" (p. 85).
Prostitutes are common victims.	"They were almost all public prostitutes" (p. 67).
Offenders sometimes revisit the crime scene.	"[He] fished her out again [for] renewed violation" (p. 68).
Disturbed relationship with mother is common.	"But on the way, he hid [the body] under a straw sack, for fear his mother would suspect him"
Crimes and sadistic acts tend to escalate.	"He obtained animals … These bodies no longer satisfied him. …He felt the desire to make use of human bodies" (p. 70).
Offenders make frequent use of pornography.	"Among his effects were found objects of art and obscene pictures painted by himself" (p. 73).
There is a need to humiliate and degrade victims.	"…Because its effect on her is humiliating, mortifying" (p. 66). "[He took] pleasure … in humiliating her" (p. 77). "Defilement of women … and put contempt and humiliation upon them … with disgusting, at least, foul things" (p. 79).
Crimes may have signature aspects — behavior idiosyncratic to a particular offender.	"It also gave me great pleasure to pull the hairpins out of the hair of my victims" (p. 67). "The mouth was filled with earth" (p. 65). "He pressed her hands together for some time" (p. 65).
Offenders often show no overt signs of abnormality.	"His external appearance was rather pleasing. He lived in very good circumstances" (p. 74). "23 years old, powerfully built, neat in dress, and decent in manner" (p. 79).
Some murders are highly planned and organized.	"He set about his horrible deeds with such care that he remained undetectable for ten years" (p. 67).

second victim and also slit open her abdomen with a knife so that her intestines were hanging out when the body was found. The third victim was his cousin, whom he released without killing after he assaulted her, "pressed her hands together for some time" (p. 65), and enjoyed pulling out her hairpins. When caught, Verzeni first tried to blame others, but eventually he gave an insightful confession, explaining the sexual arousal he felt while killing, especially during prolonged torture with a ligature. He described the sexual satisfaction of this garroting as "greater than in masturbation" (p. 66). Verzeni also took souvenirs of clothing and intestines because he enjoyed touching and smelling them, most likely to relive the crime in his fantasies. As a child, Verzeni engaged in animal cruelty, lying, and manipulation. He had no desire to hurt his girlfriends; interestingly, however, he said that his activity with his victims was much more pleasurable than sexual relations with his partners.

Krafft-Ebing reported several other interesting cases. The "Girl Stabber of Bozen" had an ejaculation as soon as he stabbed a woman; "the wounding of girls was an equivalent for coitus" (p. 73). The "Girl Cutter of Augsburg" had a growing compulsion that he was able to keep under control from ages 19 through 36. No longer able to contain the compulsion, however, he was finally arrested after cutting more than 50 women. Krafft-Ebing completed his chapter by citing several cases of men who, because of their fear of the consequences of criminal acts against humans, satisfied their sexually sadistic compulsion with the torture of animals. One of these men was a poet who "became powerfully excited sexually whenever he saw cows slaughtered." Another "committed sodomy with geese, and cut their necks off, *tempore ejaculationis!*" (p. 85).

In the late 1800s, Victorian England was terrorized by Jack the Ripper (Begg et al., 1991), who sadistically murdered five London prostitutes and possibly two other women whose mutilated bodies were found in the river. He earned his name, although his true identity was never ascertained, by letters he sent to the press, threatening to continue his murders: "I am down on whores and shan't quit ripping them." All victims were stabbed with a knife and disemboweled, their throats cut, vaginas mutilated, and internal organs removed and sometimes carried away. The last victim's head was nearly severed from her body; her breasts and nose were cut off; her forehead and legs were stripped of flesh, with the skin placed on a table; and one of her hands was put into her stomach.

The notorious Albert Fish (Schechter, 1990) — serial murderer, sadist, masochist, pedophile, and cannibal — operated during the early 1900s in New York but was not apprehended until 1934. Fish, who looked like a genteel grandfather, killed a man in 1910, tortured and killed a boy in 1919, and apparently was responsible for the murder of at least one other boy at that time. In 1927, he sexually violated and killed a 4-year-old boy. In 1928, he cleverly abducted a 12-year-old girl, telling her parents that he was taking her to a children's birthday party organized by his sister. He took the child to an empty house, strangled her, cut up her body, and literally made a stew (with potatoes and vegetables), eating her over a period of several days. Fish was not apprehended for 6 years. He then wrote a letter to the child's mother, explaining how he had killed and then eaten her daughter. Fish was arrested shortly afterward when the letter was traced to his home. Fish's life was replete with religious preoccupation and acts of sadomasochism. For example, he ate his own excrement, shoved rose stems up his penis, and inserted 29 sewing needles into his groin, clearly visible on X-ray years later.

During World War II, many sexual murder cases were reported but were not extensively publicized, probably because of the war effort. Jenkins (1988, 1989) researched newspaper clippings during this time period and located numerous cases that, at least from a distance, seemed to represent multiple murders that were sexually motivated. For example, in 1942, a little-known U.S. Army private, Edward Leonski, strangled three older women within a two-week period while stationed in Australia (Scott, 1998). Also during World War II, Marcel Petiot confessed to killing 63 men and women. Petiot, a physician with a history of criminal behavior, lured wealthy Jewish victims to his home with the promise to help them flee occupied France. He "inoculated" the victims with strychnine and "observed their death agonies through a peephole" (Schechter and Everitt, 1996, p. 221). It is clear that financial gain was a strong motive for Dr. Petiot, but the sadistic element here raises the strong probability of a covert sexual dynamic as well.

One of the most notorious serial murderers, William Heirens, terrorized Chicago during the mid-1940s (Freeman, 1956). He became known for writing with lipstick, on the bathroom mirror of one of his victims, "For Heaven's sakes, catch me before I kill more; I cannot control myself." Heirens murdered three women and dismembered a child, depositing her body parts in sewers and drains in the area. He developed a fetish for female underwear as a young child and began burglarizing homes in order to obtain the fetishistic objects. He was eventually arrested for burglary and linked to the murders.

Two interesting serial murderers, very different in their victim-abduction technique, were active in the 1950s. Harvey M. Glatman (Nash, 1973), a very intelligent, yet lonely and socially introverted, television repairman and part-time photographer, placed ads in newspapers for female models. Within a year, he raped and strangled three women whom he lured to his "studio." The models allowed Glatman to tie and gag them, as he told them they would be on the covers of some popular detective magazines that often featured women bound and gagged. Glatman's fourth victim overpowered him, and he was arrested.

Unlike Glatman, Edward Gein (Schechter, 1989) did not rely on verbal skills or high intelligence in the commission of his murders. Gein had had a disturbed relationship with a domineering and tyrannical mother, who often told him about the sinful nature of women. After his mother died, he preserved a room in his house as a shrine for her and began digging up corpses from local cemeteries. Later, he killed and disemboweled two women at his home. He upholstered furniture with the victims' skin, made soup bowls from their skulls, collected female genitals in a box, and mounted some human heads like trophies. Gein stated that he enjoyed dressing up in a vest made of human skin.

Albert DeSalvo, commonly known as the Boston Strangler (Rae, 1967), began his criminal career first as a voyeur, then became a burglar, later a rapist, and finally a serial murderer. He initially gained entry to the homes of women by posing as a scout for a modeling agency and later as a repairman. He killed 13 women during an 18-month period in the early 1960s. The victims were strangled and stabbed, and broomsticks were shoved in their vaginas; he frequently placed a bow (often made from the victims' stockings) around their necks. DeSalvo was arrested after being apprehended for burglary. He was subsequently charged with rape and confessed to the murders to another inmate.

Since the late 1970s, the media and the public have become increasing interested in serial murder. Contemporary offenders, however, are really not much different in behavior and technique from the men described by Krafft-Ebing at the end of the 19th century (see Table 1). Prostitutes, for example, are still common targets of serial murderers, and there have been recent cases of vampirism and cannibalism, as well. Many contemporary offenders are highly intelligent and outwardly charming, with histories of firesetting and animal cruelty; some still send taunting letters to the press. Interestingly, many contemporary serial murderers, just like their predecessors, have been married or have had girlfriends; their partners consistently claim that they knew nothing of their mate's behavior and have not become victims themselves.

COMPONENTS OF SERIAL HOMICIDE

Serial murderers employ different methods, target different types of victims, behave differently at the crime scene, and have different types of sadistic fantasies that direct much of their behavior and conduct. But, despite the diverse clinical pictures, serial homicide consists of three fundamental components: (1) sexual sadism, (2) intense fantasy, and (3) a compulsion to act out the fantasy. These elements are not separate and distinct, as fantasy and sexual sadism, for example, are clearly linked. However, without the compulsion to act, a crime would not be committed, and the individual's fantasies, no matter how violent and sadistic, would remain a private matter. Krafft-Ebing (1886) clearly identified these elements of sexual homicide in his presentation of various cases (see Table 2).

In serial murder, all three factors are present, but often one or another plays a dominant role, and each element can span a spectrum of intensity from mild to severe. Thus, sometimes sadism seems most pronounced, as in the case of Richard Cottingham, who prolonged his victim's lives so that they could "suffer through his torture [until] 'the master,' as he referred to himself, ... would be sexually satisfied" (Keppel, 1997, p. 74).

Fantasy is paramount in some cases and may go on for many years before any acting out occurs. For example, Revitch (1965) reported the case of a man who attacked a woman with a blackjack; for 31 years, this man had had fantasies of tying female legs, which was the purpose of the attack. The notorious Edmund Kemper — who, as an adult, killed, beheaded, and cannibalized several women — had more lethal adolescent fantasies (Ressler and Schachtman, 1992). "Twelve year old Edmund Kemper played 'gas-chamber' with his sister, a game in which the sister was required to tie him in a chair and click an imaginary switch that released the gas, so he could lean over the chair and die; a joyless hostile repetitive game that mingled sexual and death themes" (p. 96).

TABLE 2
Three Components of Sexual Homicide Noted by Krafft-Ebing (1886)

1. Sadism (and desire for complete control over victims)	"I performed the act ... that she might feel the power I had over her) (p. 76). " She should feel that she is completely in his power" (p. 76). "The object of desire is seen to be capable of absolute subjugation" (p. 68).
2. Fantasy	"He would imagine that he carried out the sexual act with them, and then killed them" (p. 69). "Bloody thoughts were constantly present, and induced lustful excitement" (p. 72). "He was compelled to fancy a scene" (p. 72). "Simple imagining representations of blood and scenes of blood. ...Without the assistance of this idea, no erection was possible" (p. 72).
3. Overpowering compulsion	"Then this impulse, with headaches and palpitations of the heart, became so powerful..." (p. 70). "The impulse became constantly more powerful" (p. 74). "He could not resist his impulses" (p. 66). "Often he could scarcely overcome the impulse" (p. 71). "Amidst the greatest dangers and difficulties, he satisfied his impulse some fifteen times" (p. 70).

An overpowering compulsion to act out is graphically illustrated by the case of William Heirens, who would develop headaches and sweat profusely when he tried to resist. Heirens described his experience as follows: "I resisted for about two hours. I tore sheets out of place and went into a sweat. I would take out plans and draw how to get into certain places. I would burn up the plans, sometimes this helped" (Kennedy et al., 1947, p. 118). A similar compulsion is evidenced by the serial murderer who prayed at bedtime that he would not wake up in the morning so that he would not have to commit his crimes the next day (Revitch and Schlesinger, 1978).

SADISM

Sadism — sexual arousal from physical suffering, humiliation, and control of the victim — is at the core of serial homicide. Krafft-Ebing (1886), in fact, suggested that the essential feature of sadism is the need for "mastery and possessing an absolutely defenseless human object ... the desire for ... complete subjugation of the woman" (p. 68). A 25-year-old male who committed 12 rapes, with increasing amounts of aggression, as well as two murders by strangulation and drowning, stated, "I want to be in control; having me in control is the thing; control is the main motivation; killing is the ultimate control." MacCulloch et al. (1983) also have emphasized the desire to control as the primary motivating force in sadism.

Bartholomew et al. (1975) described a 23-year-old male who killed a 12-year-old girl by cutting her throat and slitting her abdomen. Prior to the murder, however, he gained sadistic pleasure by exercising complete control over her through severe humiliation. For example, he made her eat biscuits soaked in urine, smeared feces on her face, undressed her, fondled her genitals, gagged her, and tied her up. Extreme torture and cruelty, as well as total control of victims, also was displayed by Gary Heidnik, who abducted and kept captive a total of six women. He killed at least two of his captives by electrocution, after prolonged torture; another woman died after hanging from her wrists for a week in his basement, which he had converted into a torture chamber. He drove screwdrivers into the ears of victims, forced them to watch each other being raped and tortured by him, and also made some of them eat the ground-up body of another victim (Englade, 1988).

FANTASY

Fantasy has been defined as "a group of symbols synthesized into a unified story. ... [It] may be a substitute for action, or it may prepare the way for later action" (Beres, 1960, p. 328). For a considerable period of time, fantasy may serve as a substitute for behavior, but once the fantasy builds to a point where inner tension is unbearable the way for action is prepared (Schlesinger and Revitch, 1980). Serial murderers frequently begin having intense morbid fantasies as children or early adolescents and as adults remain deeply immersed in their inner lives. Their fantasies usually involve themes of domination, control, revenge, and sexual aggression.

Ressler et al. (1988) strongly emphasize the role of fantasy in the development of the sexual murderer. In their FBI-sponsored study of 36 sexual murderers, these authors found that early sexualized and aggressive fantasy was a key ingredient in understanding their subjects' later violent behavior. MacCulloch and his associates (1983) concluded from their study of sadistic men that repetitive sadistic masturbatory fantasy often leads to behavioral "try-outs." Brittain (1970), in his classic profile of the sadistic murderer, noted that "he is typically a day-dreamer with a very rich, active fantasy life. He imagines sadistic scenes and these he acts out in his killings. ... [His] fantasy life is, in many ways, more important to him than is his ordinary life, and in a sense more real" (p. 200). Douglas and Olshaker (1997) describe some child abductors so driven by their fantasies that often they cannot carry out an abduction successfully; they cannot deviate from the fantasy, even if it increases their risk of apprehension. Similarly, Hazelwood and Douglas (1980) report cases of sex murders that seemed to occur impulsively but were really "premeditated in the obsessive fantasies of the perpetrator" (p. 2).

Prentky et al. (1989) found that fantasies often drive the serial sexual murderer. In an earlier study on the same subject, Burgess et al. (1986) proposed a theoretical model based, in large part, on the role of fantasy in motivating serial homicides. Using this model, these investigators found evidence of disturbed fantasy and compulsive masturbation in over 80% of their sexual murder subjects.

Sexual murderers frequently engage in repetitive ritualistic behavior at the crime scene. This behavior, referred to as "personation or signature" (Douglas et al., 1992) or as the offender's "calling card" (Keppel, 1997), has nothing to do with the perpetration of the crime itself but is an outgrowth of the offender's fantasies. "The offender often invests intimate meaning into the scene in the form of body-positioning, mutilation, items left, or other symbolic gestures involving the crime scene" (Douglas et al., 1992, p. 354). This "unique signature ... remains the same whether it is the first offense or one committed ten years later. The ritual may evolve, but the theme persists" (Keppel, 1995, p. 674). The "signature" or "calling card," which remains fairly constant and stems from the offender's fantasies, is different from the *modus operandi* (MO), which can change as the offender learns and perfects his method of abducting and killing.

COMPULSION TO KILL

Sexual sadism and fantasy, while fundamental and necessary in understanding the serial murderer, are not sufficient to explain the offender's drive to act out the fantasy. Because normal men also have sadistic fantasies, which they do not act out, one cannot postulate a cause-and-effect relationship between fantasy and murder. Crepault and Couture (1980), for example, studied erotic fantasy in 94 normal men and found that a large majority of their subjects frequently engaged in fantasy involving power and sexual aggression (including rape). This finding is supported by Templeman and Stinnett's (1991) similar study. Schlesinger and Revitch (1997) observed numerous individuals who had elaborate sadistic fantasies but never felt the desire to act them out; some even drew graphic sadistic pictures for their own entertainment. MacCulloch et al. (1983), after studying sadistic fantasy and its relationship to offending, concluded that the question of "why some people develop these fantasies and act on them and others do not" is fundamental but difficult to answer (p. 28).

Revitch and Schlesinger (1981, 1989) have concluded that those individuals who act out their sadistic fantasies do so because of a compulsion to act out. The word "compulsion" is derived from the Latin *compellere*, meaning "to compel, force, urge, and drive on." The acting out of a sadistic fantasy is not a casual matter — quite the opposite. The need to commit the act is powerful. For example, a 25-year-old serial murderer spoke of "a feeling that comes into my head; a sharp pain in the back of my head, an angry overwhelming feeling to kill." In some cases, the urge is so strong that an attempt to resist it will bring on anxiety with somatic manifestations. Krafft-Ebing (1886) reported the case of a 21-year-old man who attacked and stabbed girls in the genitals in broad daylight: "For a while he succeeded in mastering his morbid craving, but this produced feelings of anxiety and a copious perspiration would break out from his entire body" (p 74). Vincenz Verzeni, described previously, recognized the strength of his compulsion to kill: "Verzeni said, himself, that it would be a good thing if he were to be kept in prison, because with freedom he could not resist his impulses" (Krafft-Ebing, 1886, p. 66).

A compulsion is more abstract and nebulous, and more difficult for an offender to explain, than sadistic fantasies, which are simply a reporting of the offender's thoughts. For this reason, examiners sometimes overlook the compulsive aspect of the crime when they evaluate serial offenders. Many such offenders describe a state of tension created by the fantasy, a state that is not (to our knowledge) experienced by men who have sadistic fantasies and do not act out. In serial murderers, the acting out is a means of liberation from unbearable inner tension (see Figure 1). Once the fantasy is carried out, the tension is released, and the offender feels a certain sense of relief and satisfaction, at least for a period of time. As one offender stated, "After I kill, I am out of the zone and back to myself."

Sadism → Fantasy → Tension State → Compulsion → Action

FIGURE 1. Fantasy grows out of sexual sadism, creating a state of tension that leads to a compulsion to act out the fantasy and thereby gain relief.

Although the compulsion is strong and, in many cases, powerful, it does not constitute an "irresistible impulse" in the legal sense (e.g., *United States v. Currens*, 1961). Moreover, various descriptions by the offender of "another personality taking over" are not indications of multiple personality disorder or dissociation. The serial offender knows exactly what he is doing; he can control his actions to a large extent, but he chooses not to because he seeks relief from the state of tension he is in. The tension state of the compulsive offender is also different clinically and dynamically from the tension state found in individuals who commit catathymic homicides (Schlesinger, 1996). The catathymic offender is driven to kill not because of a fantasy and compulsion but because of a change in thinking associated with a deep (often psychotic) depression (Schlesinger, 1999, 2000). Catathymic homicides are rarely repeated, whereas the compulsive offender has a strong potential for repetition.

Although the serial murderer harbors a compulsion to act out his sadistic fantasies, he is not an obsessive-compulsive neurotic (nor does he necessarily have a rigid, inflexible compulsive personality). In many cases, the compulsive offenses have an overtly ritualistic appearance, as does some behavior of obsessive-compulsive neurotics. An urge to kill a loved one, or perhaps a newborn child, has been reported by some obsessional neurotics as what Rado (1959) referred to as "fits of horrific temptations." In such a state, "the patient, suddenly beset by the urge or idea to kill someone, … shrinks back in horror from a temptation so alien to his entire being" (p. 325). The obsessive-compulsive neurotic is concerned with inconsequential detail and orderliness; however, the clinical picture of the compulsive offender is much different. The offender knows that he has a dangerous urge, whereas the neurotic knows that he will not act out his "horrific temptations," although he fears that he might do so and thus seeks reassurance. In both the obsessive-compulsive neurotic and the compulsive offender, there is an urge for some type of action, but the clinical features of the acting out and the underlying dynamics have absolutely nothing in common.

THE SIGNIFICANCE OF VOYEURISM AND FETISHISM

Brittain (1970) found a history of voyeurism (the act of looking as a way of achieving sexual excitement) and fetishism (sexual arousal involving the use of nonliving objects) in his sadistic murder cases, although he did not link these paraphilias to the aggressive acts. A close examination of many cases, however, shows that a clear relationship does exist. For example, Ressler et al. (1988) found that, as children, 71% of their group of 36 sexual murderers engaged in voyeurism, and 72% engaged in fetishism of some sort. Only pornography (81%) and compulsive masturbation (79%) were engaged in more frequently. Prentky and his associates (1989) found that 75% of serial murderers engaged in fetishism and 71% in voyeurism; among their single-victim sexual murderers, 43% were voyeurs and 33% fetishists. Schlesinger and Revitch (1999) also found a strong association among voyeurism, fetishism, burglary, and sexual homicide. Although not all voyeurs or fetishists will go on to commit an act of sexual violence, the frequent occurrence of these paraphilias in the history of serial murderers is much too important to ignore.

Krafft-Ebing (1886) said little about voyeurism, but he did note the relationship between fetishism and aggression: "The impulse to destroy the fetish ... seems to occur quite frequently" (p. 170). One man described by Krafft-Ebing had "the impulse to injure the fetish, which ... represents an element of sadism towards the woman wearing the fetish" (p. 183). Another man was a fetishist who subsequently murdered a woman. A case of fetishism associated with serial murder is that of Jerome Brudos (Rule, 1983). At age 5, Brudos developed a foot and shoe fetish. As an early teen, he was stealing female underwear from clotheslines; he also stole a pair of shoes from his teacher and stalked women who were wearing high-heeled shoes. Several years later, he began breaking into homes. Brudos eventually murdered four women. William Heirens, previously mentioned in this chapter, developed a fetish for women's underwear before age 13. Richard Trenton Chase, a psychotic who murdered ten people and engaged in vampirism, also was a fetishist (Ressler and Schachtman, 1992) and committed fetish burglaries.

Yalom (1960) studied a group of voyeurs and noted an element of sadism in the act itself; he also found that many of these voyeurs went on to rape, assault, burglarize, and commit arson — all crimes that often have an underlying sexual basis. Gebhard et al. (1965) studied a more heterogeneous group of voyeurs and noted their extensive criminal records. Smith and Braun (1978) reported the case of a man who strangled over 20 women, murdered at least one, engaged in necrophilia, and had a history of voyeurism. The notorious Ted Bundy (Rule, 1988) and Albert DeSalvo (Rae, 1967) were voyeurs who had engaged in extensive peeping as adolescents, although this aspect of their cases is rarely emphasized. Finally, both Richard Ramirez, the "Night Stalker" who murdered 13 women and men (Lindecker, 1991), and Danny Rolling, the "Gainesville Ripper" who murdered five women, three men, and one child (Ryzuk, 1994), had engaged in voyeurism since childhood.

POSTMORTEM PARAPHILIAS: CANNIBALISM, VAMPIRISM, AND NECROPHILIA

Following death, serial murderers occasionally engage in primitive acts of cannibalism (eating human flesh), vampirism (drinking blood), and necrophilia (intercourse with the corpse). For example, in the 1920s, Fritz Haarmann killed and ate 50 young boys, George Grossmann ate and sold human flesh in the form of sausages, and Karl Denke killed and ate 30 people who stayed at his inn (Schechter and Everitt, 1996). In addition, Albert Fish, previously discussed, cannibalized a 12-year-old girl in 1928; Russian serial killer Andre Chikatilo (Fox and Levin, 1994), during the 1980s, consumed the genitals of some of his 53 victims; and Jeffrey Dahmer murdered 17 men (from 1978 through 1993) and cannibalized some of his victims. Dahmer found the experience sexually arousing: "Eating him was making him part of me ... it was just another step ... trying something new to get satisfied" (Ressler and Schachtman, 1997, p. 139).

Vampirism may take place in connection with cannibalism, as in several cases reported by Krafft-Ebing, or it may occur by itself, as in the case of Peter Kürten, known as the "Vampire of Düsseldorf" during the late 1920s (Wilson and Pitman, 1962). Kürten grew up in a pathological family. As a child, he tortured animals; from ages 13 through 15, he had sex with animals and stabbed them to death during intercourse with them. He engaged in vampirism with many of his victims. Once he cut off the head of a swan, drank its blood as it spurted from the neck, and then ejaculated. Kürten's preoccupation with blood was so intense that he reported becoming sexually excited watching the sunset, because the red sky reminded him of blood. Kürten hoped to be able to taste his own blood during his execution by decapitation.

In the classic type of necrophilia, the offender derives sexual excitement from having sex with disinterred bodies. The strange case of Sergeant Bertrand, which has been cited in many books and papers on the topic (e.g., Hirschfeld, 1944; Klaf and Brown, 1958; Krafft-Ebing, 1886), illustrates not only necrophilia but also the escalation of behavior and the overpowering compulsion to act. Bertrand fantasized having sex with and then killing women and subsequently defiling the corpses. He began with animals, but when they no longer satisfied him he progressed to human bodies. He explained that, rather than killing living women, he chose victims who were already dead: "All that one could enjoy with a living woman is nothing in comparison with the pleasure I experienced" (Krafft-Ebing, 1886, p. 70). Bertrand would disinter dead women, violate their bodies, and then mutilate the corpses. The controlling aspect of his behavior is evident in his statement that "I wanted to annihilate them completely."

A number of offenders have killed a victim specifically to have intercourse with an inert body. Bartholomew (1978) reports the case of a 22-year-old man who shot another man, engaged in various sexual activities with the body, and then threw it down a mine shaft. He said that he could not control his urge. Kennedy (1961) described a 55-year-old male who raped and then strangled several women after they had been anesthetized by gas. In another case, reported by Revitch and Schlesinger (1989), a 36-year-old male killed four women and two men and had sex with at least two of the women following their deaths. The murders were motivated, in part, by a strong necrophilic drive.

PERSONALITY CHARACTERISTICS OF SERIAL MURDERERS

In an attempt to draw an investigative profile of unidentified offenders, Hazelwood and Douglas (1980) and Douglas et al. (1986) divided sexual murderers into two groups — organized and disorganized — based on crime scene characteristics (see Table 3). The organized offender engages in a great deal of planning in the commission of the crime. Specifically, instead of randomly and spontaneously abducting his victims, he chooses a victim who presents a low risk for his being apprehended. Additionally, he displays control at the crime scene and clever manipulation before and after the crime. He often moves the body, engages in torture before death, and brings restraints and other "murder kit" devices to the scene with him to ensure that the murder goes according to his plan and his fantasy. He typically leaves little inculpatory evidence at the scene. He may stage the crime scene in an attempt to redirect the investigation, or he may inject himself into the investigation, in some manner, to check on the progress of the authorities.

TABLE 3
Characteristics of Organized and Disorganized Offenders

Organized Offenders	Disorganized Offenders
A. Crime Scene Characteristics	
Great deal of planning	No planning
Choose low-risk abduction	Choose high-risk abduction
Display control at crime scene	Behave haphazardly during crime
Clever manipulation of victim	Little manipulation of victim
Transport body	Leave body where killed
Bring restraint devices	Do not bring restraint devices
Torture before death	Mutilation after death
Crime scene staged	No staging
Often inject themselves in investigation	Rarely inject selves in investigation
Geographically mobile	Geographically stable
B. Personality Characteristics	
Psychopathic, antisocial, narcissistic personalities	Borderline, schizoid, schizophrenic
Pleasant-looking and physically attractive	Strange-looking, often odd, unkempt and dishevelled
Have wives, girlfriends, and experience with females	Little experience with females
Live with a woman	Live by themselves or with family members
Good verbal skills	Poor verbal skills
History of behavior problems and conflicts with authority	History of psychiatric treatment and suicide attempts

---

The disorganized offender, on the other hand, while driven to kill by the same dynamics, approaches the murder in an unplanned, impulsive way and behaves haphazardly during the crime. He abducts a victim spontaneously, placing himself at great risk for identification and apprehension. He often leaves incriminating evidence such as blood, hair, fibers, or fingerprints at the scene. He does not bring along a murder weapon or restraints, because he had not planned on committing a murder at that particular time. Usually, he does not move the body or torture the victim before death. There is typically no staging and little effective manipulation of the victim or the police.

Thus, organized and disorganized offenders display markedly different approaches to murder. They also have markedly different personality traits and characteristics. The organized offender is usually manipulative, methodical, and cunning, with an amiable facade typical of the psychopathic, sociopathic, or antisocial personality (Cleckley, 1976; Hare, 1993; Schlesinger, 1980). He is typically narcissistic (Schlesinger, 1998), concerned only for himself. He can be charming and verbally fluent, appears neat and physically attractive, and is easily able to put a woman at ease. He usually has a wife or girlfriend and often comes from a relatively stable family. Following the crime, his demeanor does not change.

The disorganized offender, in contrast, is much more unstable mentally, either schizoid, borderline, or sometimes schizophrenic. He may be physically unattractive, unkempt, disheveled, and strange in appearance, quite off-putting to a woman. Typically a loner, he has had limited experience with females; he also has a poor self-image and poor verbal skills and is, in general, the type of individual hardly remembered by former schoolmates. Typically, he lives by himself or with family members, comes from an unstable family with a history of psychiatric problems and substance abuse, has had prior psychiatric treatment, and perhaps has made suicide attempts.

The personality type — whether antisocial, narcissistic, or some form of a more serious condition such as borderline, schizoid, or even perhaps schizophrenic — is not the cause of serial homicide. Sexual murder is fueled by sadism, fantasy, and a compulsion to kill, not by a personality disorder or mental illness. The murder itself, however, is carried out differently, depending on the offender's personality makeup and level of personality integration. The serial murderer (with many victims) is more frequently an organized offender, because the planning involved makes apprehension much more difficult; therefore, the offender is able to continue his exploits for a longer period of time. The disorganized offender is likely to get caught after the first or second murder, because the crime was not well planned and the victims were grabbed impulsively and often close to home, making identification and apprehension quicker.

DISCUSSION

There have been many popularized accounts of serial murder, but, unfortunately, relatively little in the way of serious scientific study. Dietz (1986) has suggested that the dearth of scientific papers on serial homicide is attributable, in part, to its extreme rarity, which does not permit ordinary research methods to be easily employed. Comparatively few cases are available to most mental health researchers, as the subjects are incarcerated, often in different institutions. Forensic clinicians who do have access to cases are often chiefly concerned with legal issues, such as competency, sanity, and mitigation in capital cases, as opposed to research and study of the clinical disorder. In fact, for a complete understanding of serial homicide, biological, psychological, and social factors all must be taken into account, because the disorder is complex and multifaceted.

In spite of the absence of exhaustive research on the subject, a number of provocative — if incomplete — theories have been developed. Krafft-Ebing, for instance, offered a theory to explain why sexual murderers are largely male. "In the intercourse of the sexes, the active or aggressive role belongs to man. ...It affords the man great pleasure to win a woman, to conquer her. ...This aggressive character, however, under pathological conditions, may likewise be excessively developed, and express itself in an impulse to subdue absolutely the object of desire, even to destroy or kill it" (Krafft-Ebing, 1886, p. 60). Such "outbreaks of sadism," Krafft-

Ebing added, are partly atavistic, because in earlier times men commonly used aggression to "obtain females." There have been a few reported cases of supposed female serial murderers, but it remains questionable whether these were, in fact, sexually motivated murders or whether, instead, these women murdered their victims out of anger or for profit. Thus, Krafft-Ebing's observations call our attention to biological differences that may partially account for the phenomenon. More recently, MacLean (1962), in a study of psychosexual functions of the brain, found that the limbic structures governing feeding and aggression (amygdala) are interconnected with the structures governing sexual functions (septum, hippocampus). Additionally, he noted the display of genitals in male squirrel monkeys during a fight. These observations point to a possible anatomical substrate of the connection between sex and aggression and perhaps sex and cannibalism in some cases. Money (1990) contends that a variety of biological problems — stemming from heredity, hormones, or brain injury — may be associated with serial sexual aggression. Some investigators have even studied the role of individual hormones and neurotransmitters (Lidberg et al., 1985; Zeiss, 1984). In fact, a complex interaction of several biological components is likely.

There have also been a number of psychological explanations of serial homicide. For example, Revitch and Schlesinger (1981, 1989) found that an unhealthy emotional involvement with the mother is a key component in many cases of sexual murder. The mother may be rejecting, punitive, and hated, or she may be overprotective, infantilizing, or seductive. In some cases, the mother's promiscuity results in overt sexual stimulation of the child. Repressed incestuous feelings often seem to be a main stimulus in some forms of gynocide. This type of sexual murder is, in essence, a displaced matricide — a displacement of affect from the mother to other women. Liebert (1985) also has recognized the importance of the mother-son relationship. He theorizes that the serial murderer may have internalized the aggressive aspects of the early mother-son relationship and then projects them onto a female victim. "It is the fusion of destructive impulses from disorganized sexual impulses evolving out of the pre-oedipal matrix of these individuals ... that provides a motivational model for comprehension of the serial lust murderer" (p. 194).

Other studies have offered insights on sadism, fetishism, or voyeurism — three paraphilias that appear frequently in the histories of serial murderers, with sexual sadism being present in all cases. These paraphilias have in common an underlying dynamic of castration anxiety, at least from a psychodynamic perspective. From this point of view, as enunciated by Fenichel (1945), sadistic behavior is essentially a reassurance against anxiety connected with fear of castration. Accordingly, sadism develops in stages. First, the individual derives a feeling of power from acts of cruelty, then he derives sexual satisfaction from torturing others. Finally, the feelings of power and satisfaction lead to a sense of security, as the individual can inflict on others what he would not like inflicted on himself.

The psychodynamic view of fetishism, as summarized by Wulff (1946), is that the fetishistic object is a substitute for the mother's missing penis and a token of triumph over the threat of castration. In addition, Romm (1949) has noted the elements of aggression and sadism in fetishism. The psychoanalytic theory of voyeurism, like the psychodynamic view of fetishism, is that the voyeur is trying to reassure himself that the fantasized penis of the female exists (Obendorf, 1939). Thus, in sadism, fetishism, and voyeurism, there is a common theme of acting out in order to compensate for castration anxiety. Although this theory has not been documented empirically, it is well worth considering further, as in many instances the facts supporting it are obvious.

Social factors probably do not play a dominant role in the genesis of the serial murderer, but the environment does exert an influence, as no behavior occurs in a vacuum. Pathological individuals with a need for violence may be influenced by the social climate, which may release, give meaning to, and direct the violent act. Rapes, murders, and sadistic acts during times of war, or whenever social order is lacking, have occurred since antiquity. History and common observation of numerous contemporary events provide examples of multiple rapes and murders during times when society cannot impose restraints and discipline.

Although relatively few in number, serial murderers have a major negative impact on society. Not only are the direct victims affected, but so are their immediate and distant families, the community, and even the entire country in highly publicized cases. Considerable financial resources are allotted to the apprehension, incarceration, trial, and legal appeals of offenders. For example, the investigation of the "Green River Killer" in Washington State has cost well over $20 million, while Ted Bundy's trial and subsequent appeals totaled about $9 million (Hickey, 1997). Yet, despite these enormous expenditures, little is allocated for the scientific study of the problem. What is needed now is a reconceptualization of serial homicide as a clinical disorder, with a biopsychosocial etiology, as opposed to simply a criminal problem. Such a recognition will stimulate further scientific interest, research, and thinking on this most perplexing phenomenon.

REFERENCES

Barrett, A. (1998). *Caligula: The Corruption of Power.* New Haven: Yale University Press.

Bartholomew, A.A. (1978). Homosexual necrophilia. *Medicine, Science, and Law,* 18:29–35.

Bartholomew, A.A., Milte, K.L., and Galballi, F. (1975). Sexual murder: psychopathology and psychiatric jurisprudential considerations. *New Zealand Journal of Criminology,* 8:143–153.

Begg, P., Fido, M., and Skinner, K. (1991). *Jack the Ripper A–Z.* London: Headline.

Benedetti, J. (1972). *Gilles de Rais.* New York: Stein and Day.

Beres, D. (1960). Perception, imagination, and reality. *International Journal of Psychoanalysis,* 41:327–334.

Brittain, R.P. (1970). The sadistic murderer. *Medicine, Science, and Law,* 10:198–207.

Burgess, A.W., Hartman, C.R., Ressler, R.K., Douglas, J.E., and McCormack, A. (1986). Sexual homicide: a motivational model. *Journal of Interpersonal Violence,* 1:151–272.

Busch, K.A. and Cavanaugh, J.L. (1986). The study of multiple murder: preliminary examination of the interface between epistemology and methodology. *Journal of Interpersonal Violence,* 1:5–23.

Cleckley, H. (1976). *The Mask of Sanity,* 5th ed. St. Louis, MO: Mosby.

Crepault, C. and Couture, M. (1980). Men's erotic fantasies. *Archives of Sexual Behavior,* 9:565–581.

Dietz, P.E. (1986). Mass, serial, and sensational homicides. *Bulletin of the New York Academy of Medicine*, 62:477–491.

Douglas, J. and Olshaker, M. (1997). *Journey into Darkness*. New York: Pocket Books.

Douglas, J.E., Ressler, K.E., Burgess, A.W., and Hartman, C.R. (1986). Criminal profiling from crime scene analysis. *Behavioral Sciences and the Law*, 4:401–421.

Douglas, J.E., Burgess, A.W., Burgess, A.G., and Ressler, R.K. (1992). *Crime Classification Manual*. San Francisco, CA: Jossey-Bass.

Egger, S.A. (1990). Serial murder. In Egger, S.A. (Ed.), *Serial Murder*. New York: Praeger.

Englade, K. (1988). *Cellar of Horror*. New York: St. Martin's Press.

FBI (1997). *Uniform Crime Reports for the United States*. Washington, D.C.: U.S. Department of Justice.

Fenichel, O. (1945). *The Psychoanalytic Theory of Neurosis*. New York: Norton.

Fox, J.A., and Levin, J. (1994). *Overkill*. New York: Dell.

Freeman, L. (1956). *Catch Me Before I Kill More*. New York: Pocket Books.

Geberth, V. J. and Turco, R.N. (1997). Antisocial personality disorder, sexual sadism, malignant narcissism, and serial murder. *Journal of Forensic Sciences*, 42:49–60.

Gebhard, P.H., Gagnon, J.H., Pomeroy, W.B., and Christenson, C.V. (1965). *Sex Offenders*. New York: Harper & Row.

Grubin, D. (1994). Sexual murder. *British Journal of Psychiatry*, 165:624–629.

Hare, R.D. (1993). *Without Conscience: The Disturbing World of the Psychopaths Among Us*. New York: Pocket Books.

Hazelwood, R.R. and Douglas, J.E. (1980). The lust murderer. *FBI Law Enforcement Bulletin*, April, 1–5.

Hickey, E.W. (1997). *Serial Murderers and Their Victims*, 2nd ed. Belmont, CA: Wadsworth.

Hirschfeld, M. (1944). *Sexual Anomalies*. London: Francis Aldor.

Holmes, R.M. and DeBurger, J.E. (1985). Profiles in terror: the serial murderer. *Federal Probation*, 49:29–34.

Jenkins, P. (1988). Serial murder in England, 1940–1985. *Journal of Criminal Justice*, 16:1–15.

Jenkins, P. (1989). Serial murder in the United States, 1900–1940. *Journal of Criminal Justice*, 17:377–397.

Keeney, B.T. and Heide, K.N. (1995). Serial murder: a more accurate and inclusive definition. *International Journal of Offender Therapy and Comparative Criminology*, 39:299–306.

Kennedy, F., Hoffman, H., and Haines, W.A. (1947). A study of William Heirens. *American Journal of Psychiatry*, 104:113–121.

Kennedy, L. (1961). *The Rilington Place*. New York: Simon & Schuster.

Keppel, R.D. (1995). Signature murderers: a report of several related cases. *Journal of Forensic Sciences*, 40:670–674.

Keppel, R.D. (1997). *Signature Killers: Interpreting the Calling Cards of Serial Murderers*. New York: Pocket Books.

Klaf, F.S. and Brown, W. (1958). Necrophilia: brief review and case report. *Psychiatric Quarterly*, 32:645–652.

Krafft-Ebing, R. von (1886). *Psychopathia Sexualis*. Philadelphia, PA: F.A. Davis.

Lidberg, L., Tuck, J.R., Asberg, M., Scalia-Tomba, B.P., and Bertilsson, L. (1985). Homicide, suicide, and CSF 5-HIAA. *Acta Psychiatrica Scandinavica*, 71:230–236.

Liebert, J.A. (1985). Contributions of psychiatric consultation in the investigation of serial murder. *International Journal of Offender Therapy and Comparative Criminology*, 28:187–200.

Lindecker, L.L. (1991). *Night Stalker*. New York: St. Martin's Press.

Lunde, D.T. (1976). *Murder and Madness*. San Francisco, CA: San Francisco Book Co.

MacCulloch, M.J., Snowden, P.J., Wood, P., and Mill, H. (1983). Sadistic fantasy, sadistic behavior, and offending. *British Journal of Psychiatry*, 143:20–29.

MacLean, P.D. (1962). New findings relevant to the evolution of psycho-sexual functions of the brain. *Journal of Nervous and Mental Disease*, 135:289–301.

McKenzie, C. (1995). A study of serial murder. *International Journal of Offender Therapy and Comparative Criminology*, 39:3–10.

Money, J. (1990). Forensic sexology. Paraphiliac serial rape (biastophilia) and lust murder (erotophonophilia). *American Journal of Psychotherapy*, 44:26–36.

Myers, W. C., Reccoppa, L., Burton, K., and McElroy, R. (1993). Malignant sex and aggression: an overview of serial sexua homicide. *Bulletin of the American Academy of Psychiatry and Law*, 21:435–451.

Nash, J.R. (1973). Blood letters and bad men. In *A Narrative Encyclopedia of American Criminals*. New York: Evans & Co.

Obendorf, C.P. (1939). Voyeurism as a crime. *Journal of Criminal Psychopathology*, 1:103–111.

Prentky, R.A., Burgess, A.W., Rokous, R., Lee, A., Hartman, C., Ressler, R.K., and Douglas, J. (1989). The presumptive role of fantasy in serial sexual homicide. *American Journal of Psychiatry*, 146:887–891.

Rado, S. (1959). Obsessive compulsive behavior: so-called obsessive neurosis. In Arietti, S. (Ed.), *American Textbook of Psychiatry*, Vol. 1. New York: Basic Books.

Rae, G.W. (1967). *Confessions of the Boston Strangler*. New York: Pyramid Books.

Ressler, R.K. and Shachtman, T. (1992). *Whoever Fights Monsters*. New York: St. Martin's Press.

Ressler, R.K., and Shachtman, T. (1997). *I Have Lived in the Monster*. New York: St. Martin's Press.

Ressler, R.K., Burgess, A., and Douglas, J. (1988). *Sexual Homicide: Patterns and Motives*. New York: Free Press.

Revitch, E. (1965). Sex murder and the potential sex murderer. *Diseases of the Nervous System*, 26:640–648.

Revitch, E. and Schlesinger, L.B. (1978). Murder: evaluation, classification, and prediction. In Kutash., I.L., Kutash, S.B., and Schlesinger, L.B. (Eds.), *Violence: Perspectives on Murder and Aggression*. San Francisco, CA: Jossey-Bass.

Revitch, E. and Schlesinger, L.B. (1981). *Psychopathology of Homicide*. Springfield, IL: Charles C Thomas.

Revitch, E. and Schlesinger, L.B. (1989). *Sex Murder and Sex Aggression*. Springfield, IL: Charles C Thomas.

Romm, M.E. (1949). Some dynamics in fetishism. *Psychoanalytic Quarterly*, 18:137–153.

Rule, A. (1983). *Lust Killer*. New York: Signet.

Rule, A. (1988). *The Stranger Beside Me*. New York: Signet.

Ryzuk, M. (1994). *The Gainesville Ripper*. New York: St. Martin's Press.

Schechter, H. (1989). *Deviant*. New York: Pocket Books.

Schechter, H. (1990). *Deranged*. New York: Pocket Books.

Schechter, H. and Everitt, D. (1996). *The A to Z Encyclopedia of Serial Killers*. New York: Pocket Books.

Schlesinger, L.B. (1980). Distinction between psychopathic, sociopathic, and antisocial personality disorders. *Psychological Reports*, 147:15–21.

Schlesinger, L.B. (1996). The catathymic crisis (1912–present): a review and clinical study. *Violent and Aggressive Behavior*, 1:307–316.

Schlesinger, L.B. (1998). Pathological narcissism and serial homicide: review and case report. *Current Psychology*, 17:212–221.

Schlesinger, L.B. (1999). Adolescent sexual matricide following repetitive mother-son incest. *Journal of Forensic Sciences*, 44:746–749.

Schlesinger, L.B. (2000). Familicide, depression, and catathymic process. *Journal of Forensic Sciences*, 45:200–203.

Schlesinger, L.B. and Revitch, E. (1980). Stress, violence, and crime. In Kutash, I.L. and Schlesinger, L.B. (Eds.), *Handbook on Stress and Anxiety*. San Francisco, CA: Jossey-Bass.

Schlesinger, L.B. and Revitch, E. (1997). Sexual dynamics in homicide and assault. In Schlesinger, L.B. and Revitch, E. (Eds.), *Sexual Dynamics of Antisocial Behavior*, 2nd ed. Springfield, IL: Charles C Thomas.

Schlesinger, L.B. and Revitch, E. (1999). Sexual burglaries and sexual homicide: clinical, forensic, and investigative considerations. *Journal of the American Academy of Psychiatry and Law*, 27:227–238.

Scott, G.G. (1998). *Homicide: One Hundred Years of Homicide in America*. Los Angeles: Lowell House.

Smith, S. and Braun, C. (1978). Necrophilia and lust murder: report of a rare occurrence. *Bulletin of the American Academy of Psychiatry and Law*, 6:259–268.

Templeman, T.L. and Stinnett, R.D. (1991). Patterns of sexual arousal and history in a "normal" sample of young men. *Archives of Sexual Behavior*, 20:137–150.

Warren, J.I., Hazelwood, R.R., and Dietz, P.E. (1996). The sexually sadistic serial killer. *Journal of Forensic Sciences*, 41:970–974.

Wilson, C. and Pitman, P. (1962). *Encyclopedia of Murder*. New York: Putnam.

Wilson, P.R. (1988). "Stranger" child murder: issues relating to causes and controls. *Forensic Science International*, 36:267–277.

Wulff, M. (1946). Fetishism and object choice in early childhood. *Psychiatric Quarterly*, 15:450–471.

Yalom, I.D. (1960). Aggression and forbiddenness in voyeurism. *Archives of General Psychiatry*, 3:305–319.

Zeiss, C.A. (1984). Hypothesis on sexual violence "not convincing." *American Journal of Psychiatry*, 141:1133–1138.

2 Child Sexual Abusers: A Review and Update

Sharon K. Araji

CONTENTS

It is time to expand our thinking about child sexual abusers. They are not all old, male, or mentally ill. They come in all shades, shapes, sizes, ages, and sexes. They are found in all occupations, around the world, and on the Internet. Most have multiple victims.

INTRODUCTION

Adults' sexual involvement with children, frequently called *pedophilia,* has occurred throughout history (Ames and Houston, 1990; Masson, 1984; Peters, 1976; Rush, 1980; Travin et al., 1985). Pedophiles are often called child molesters;[1] both terms conger up images of strangers who are senile old men on the fringes of society.

0-8493-2236-7/00/$0.00+$.50
© 2000 by CRC Press LLC

Some aspects of this stereotype have been refuted. It is now recognized that most abusers are family members or acquaintances (Berlin, 1983; Conte and Berliner, 1981; Finkelhor and Associates, 1986; Wyatt, 1985). Further, they usually are not elderly, at least not at the onset of abusive sexual behaviors. It is also recognized that regardless of the label we attach to them, almost all are serial offenders. We know of very few who have only one victim.

Some research has begun to focus on adult female (Howitt, 1995), adolescent (Becker, 1994; Ryan and Lane, 1991), and preadolescent sexual offenders (Araji, 1997), as well as sex rings (Burgess et al., 1984). The public is less aware of these hidden groups.

Advances in technology have also created a new group of abusers. They are "electronic pedophiles" who work alone or as members of rings and use the Internet to recruit victims (Mauney, 1999). A classic example of such abuse and its tragic outcomes can be found in the Samuel Menzie case. In September, 1997, Samuel Menzie was charged with murder, felony murder, robbery, and aggravated assault for the rape and strangulation of Edward Werner, 11 years of age. Werner had gone to Menzie's home to sell holiday items for a school fundraiser.

In 1999, Menzie was sentenced to 70 years in prison. New Jersey Superior Court Judge Peter J. Giovine called Menzie a homicidal predator who was impulsive, unable to control his anger, and a programmed child molester who presented a great risk of re-offending. Under a recent New Jersey law, Menzie must serve 85% of his sentence; he will be nearly 77 years of age before he is eligible for release. He is thought to be the youngest person sentenced under the new law.

Menzie's attorney pleaded for leniency, as did Menzie's mother. She told the court that Sam was her only son and that three days before the murder she and her husband had attempted to get New Jersey's Family Court to put Sam in long-term psychiatric treatment. Their pleas had been rejected. At the time of the murder, Sam was being treated as an outpatient and was receiving medication.

Samuel Menzie himself was the victim of a twice-convicted pedophile, Phillip Simmons, 43. The two had met in a chat room on the Internet when Menzie was 14. This meeting led to personal encounters during the summer of 1996, during which time Simmons began having sex with Menzie at his (Simmons') home and in motels. The relationship also involved Simmons taking pictures of Menzie engaging in prohibitive sexual acts. The relationship ended when Sam's father discovered it and reported it to the police. Simmons had a problematic past and a long history of preying on children. The record extended back to at least 1984, and the police and the FBI were aware of this. Simmons was arrested and charged with sodomy in the case of Samuel Menzie (Crittenden et al., 1997; Hanley, 1999).

Extensive media attention to cases such as Samuel Menzie's has led to increased awareness and concern for people who recruit and sexually abuse children, whether the contact is personal or through mediums such as the Internet.

CHAPTER PURPOSE

This chapter focuses on individuals who are sexually involved with children. Herein, they are called *child sexual abusers* because this concept characterizes their actions as described in the literature. There is no commonly agreed upon definition of child sexual abuse (Finkelhor et al., 1986; Peters et al., 1986),[2] so a broad definition guides the literature review. For our purposes here, child sexual abuse is defined as any sexual contact between an offender and a child victim (primarily 12 years of age and younger) who, due to age and/or immaturity, is incapable of giving consent. The acts may range from viewing, exhibitionism, touching, fondling, and oral sex to all types of intercourse. The offending process includes use of pressure, coercion, and/or deception.

The specific purposes of this chapter are to: (1) review empirical studies that contribute to our knowledge of the demographic and other social and personal characteristics of child sexual abusers; (2) present explanations for abusers' thinking, emotional, and behavioral patterns; and, (3) describe societal responses to the abusers. Reviews are selective due to space limitations, but an attempt has been made to be representative. Critical evaluations and directions for future thinking and research are offered where possible.

CHILD SEXUAL ABUSERS: WHO ARE THEY?

In examining the demographic, psychological, behavioral, and situational characteristics associated with known child sexual abusers, the literature on adult male offenders is a logical entrance. This is the most widely researched area and adult males represent the largest percentage of known offenders.

ADULT MALE SEXUAL ABUSERS

About 90% of all reported child sexual abusers are male (Finkelhor, 1984; Russell, 1983) and have been married (DeYoung, 1982), although the marital percentages appear to vary by offenders' sexual orientations (e.g., see Langevin et al., 1985; Mohr et al., 1964). While the age of offenders varies widely (DeYoung, 1982), the American Association for Protecting Children (AAPC) reports a mean age of 32-1/2 years. Abusers cut across all socioeconomic, racial, ethnic, religious, and geographic groups, and the majority of offenders are related to or acquainted with victims.

The age range of victims is usually 8 to 12 years (Finkelhor and Baron, 1986), and most abusers have multiple victims. Based on data from 232 child sexual offenders where victims were 14 years of age and younger, Abel et al. (1985) concluded that the average number per offender was 75.8.

Types of sexual acts vary widely, including kissing, touching parts of the victim's clothed or unclothed body, having the victim touch the offender, oral sex, and all types of attempted or completed intercourse (Gomez-Swartz et al., 1990; Russell, 1983). Offenders target victims who are vulnerable, such as appearing needy, passive, trusting, lonely, or lacking in supervision (Conte et al., 1989; Elliot et al., 1995), and/or those who can be desensitized through the grooming process (Berliner and Conte, 1990; Howitt, 1995, chap. 3). Once the abusive relationship is established, the offender uses many techniques to maintain it. These may include giving gifts and the appeal of keeping secrets, as well as bribery, threats, and physical aggression.

Child sexual abusers, particularly when referred to as pedophiles, frequently are characterized as nonviolent, to the extent that the victim may be blamed for the offender's actions (Amir, 1972; Revitch and Weiss, 1962). Other studies suggest that abusers employ threats of harming the child, a significant other, or a pet (Becker, 1994; Budin and Johnson, 1989; Stermeck et al., 1989). At the other extreme are those abusers who sexually abuse their victims and kill them, such as Charles Jaynes and Salvatore Sicari.

Charles Jaynes, 22, and Salvatore (Salvi) Sicari, 21, were charged with kidnapping, rape, and the murder of 10-year-old Jeffrey Curley. Police contended that Salvatore, who had a history of violent offenses, and Charles Jaynes smothered Curley with a gasoline-soaked rag, raped his lifeless body in a New Hampshire apartment, and dumped the body in a Maine river.

Sicari confessed to his role in the murder and was sentenced to life but insisted that Jaynes was the killer. The Middlesex Assistant District Attorney, David Yannetti, indicated that literature from the North American Man-Boy Love Association (NAMBLA) was found in Jaynes apartment. He also presented a note found in Jaynes' desk that described his attraction to the Curley boy. Further, Jaynes had told a friend that he had a boy in Cambridge that he was going to have sex with, and if the boy refused, Sicari would take care of him. Jaynes was charged with accessory to murder (Weber, 1998).

When offenders sexually abuse and kill multiple victims, they are referred to as serial sex killers. In the U.S., two high media profile examples are John Gacy and Jeffrey Dahmer, although most of their victims were adolescents or young adults. Some notorious international child serial sex killers are Marc Dutroux of Belgium and Jean Gerald Dionne of Canada.

There continues to be a debate among professionals and researchers (Ivey and Simpson, 1998; Panton, 1978) concerning whether child sexual offenders are manipulative, aggressive, and violent or shy, passive, and lacking in social skills. Currently, there is no psychological or behavioral profile that fits all adult sexual abusers (Conte, 1985; Okami and Goldberg, 1992). However, there is general agreement that reported adult sexual offenders are a very heterogeneous group, with the exception that most are men.

FEMALE SEXUAL ABUSERS

Although it is known that females sexually abuse children (Erickson et al., 1988), few researchers, authors, or clinicians address this. In a review of child sexual abuse literature, Finkelhor and Associates (1986) found so few studies (three) on female abusers (p. 172) that Finkelhor concluded that males had a monopoly (p. 126). Some professionals challenge the male-monopoly assumption (e.g., Plummer, 1981; Sgroi, 1982), and a few studies have begun including discussions about female offenders. Tingle et al. (1986), in their sample of male abusers, found that about 13% of the men had been sexually abused by females only, and another 17% had been abused by both males and females. Carlson (1991) found that about one third of the males in a long-term sex offender program had experienced abuse by females in the form of oral sex, masturbation, fondling, or intercourse. Similar findings were reported by Risin and Koss (1987) and Urquiza (1988).

Howitt (1995, pp. 35–36), citing Finkelhor and Williams' (1988) research, indicates that one area where sexual abuse by females is well documented is daycare centers. In the Finkelhor and Williams (1988) study, it was reported that about 20% of both boys and girls had been abused by female caretakers acting alone or together. When demographics for male and female abusers were compared, females were less likely to be single, socially isolated from peers, or have histories of school problems, alcohol problems, drug problems, psychiatric problems, or prior arrests. However, the differences were not statistically significant.

Other characteristics associated with women as compared to men abusers were (1) a tendency to choose younger and more victims; (2) an increased likelihood of abusing as a group; (3) a greater likelihood of threatening to harm the child's family, (4) a greater tendency to employ kissing, digital-anal penetration, insertion of objects into the vagina or anus; and, (5) an increased use of forced child-to-child activity or ritualistic abuse. Howitt (1995) concluded from his review that there were contextual differences in the abuse patterns of male and female sexual offenders.

Some support for Howitt's conclusion is found in a typology developed by Mathews et al. (1990) to determine whether women act alone or with others. These researchers placed women who acted alone in a category labeled "self-initiated offenses" and proposed three different types of abusers. The first type was called "intergenerationally predisposed" and was viewed as the most common group. These women were likely to select female victims (generally their children) and to reenact their own sexually and physically abusive childhood histories. The second type of abuser was labeled the "experimenter-exploiter." These women, normally adolescents, abuse boys six or under while babysitting; fear of sexuality is given as an explanation for their interest in young children. The third type of female sexual abuser who acts alone is called the "teacher-lover." This woman views her involvement as a "love affair" with a boy 11 to 16 years of age. An example of this type of abuser can be seen in the Mary Kay LeTourneau case described below.

Mary Kay LeTourneau was a 34-year-old sixth grade teacher in Burien, WA, who was married with four children. She also had a lengthy sexual relationship with Villi, one of her 13-year-old male students. She says she was in love with Villi; he says he loved her. The first of two children to come from this relationship was born in May of 1997. In August of that year, Mary Kay LeTourneau pled guilty to two counts of child rape. A psychiatrist diagnosed her with bipolar disorder.

LeTourneau was sentenced to 7-1/2 years in prison in November, 1997, which was suspended on the condition that she enter a treatment program. In January, she was released on the stipulation that she have no contact with Villi. On February 3, 1998, she was arrested after the two were found together in a car. On February 6, LeTourneau was sentenced to the remainder of her original 7-1/2-year sentence. On March 14, 1998, her attorney announced that she was pregnant with the second child fathered by Villi.

Mary Kay is in prison; Villi and his mother are raising the two children. LeTourneau's husband, with their four children, moved to Alaska.

There is no recorded abuse found in Mary Kay's background. One interesting parallel, however, is that Mary Kay's father, John Schmitz, a former U.S. Congressman from California and a college instructor, had a 9-year sexual affair with one of his college students. This affair also produced two out-of-wedlock children (adapted from Edwards and Willwerth, 1998; Fielder, 1998; Kaye, 1998; "Leeza Exclusive," September 21, 1999).

Mathews et al. (1990) call the second category of female offenders "accompanied offenses" and include two types: "male coerced" and "psychologically disturbed." The former are conceptualized as women who are frequently in a multiple family incest situation, and are forced to abuse (usually their own children) by a male partner or older brother(s). The "psychologically disturbed" women are described as those with strong dependency needs who may indirectly abuse their children by setting up situations in which abuse can happen. Other studies of female sexual abusers (e.g., Faller, 1995; Kalders et al., 1997) are using typologies similar to Mathews et al. (1990). While this research is interesting, currently there is no empirical evidence to validate the typologies.

The typology method of identifying and classifying female sexual offenders should proceed with caution. This was one of the initial methods used in the development of literature on male sexual offenders. Groth (1979) and his colleagues (Groth et al., 1982) differentiated child sex offenders who met the American Psychology Association's (APA) definition of pedophilia by labeling them "fixated" offenders, and those who did not were labeled "regressed" offenders. Others differentiated abusers on the basis of "incestuous" or "non-incestuous" (Glasser, 1988), "heterosexual" or "homosexual" (Marshall et al., 1988), and "aggressive" or "non-aggressive" (Avery-Clark and Laws, 1984; Quinsey and Chaplin, 1988). Over time, the validity of these typologies has been questioned. Conte (1990), in a review paper on child sexual abuse, comments on Groth's popular "fixated-regressed" typology. He notes that it was developed on sex offender populations which may psychologically vary from men outside prisons who are engaged in similar behaviors. Further, he noted that this typology has not been empirically validated.

Conte (1990) also cites Abel et al. (1988), who found that the largest group of offenders in their study demonstrated characteristics of both fixated and regressed types. Findings by the Abel et al. (1988) group similarly challenged the incestuous-non-incestuous typology.

Others have also been critical of the psychological-typology method of researching child sexual abusers (Abel and Osborn, 1992; Becker, 1994; Howitt, 1995; Scott, 1994).[3] Hence, at the present time, the safest conclusions about adult female abusers may be that they are more prevalent than past literature indicates and that they share some similar patterns of abuse with their male counterparts.

ADOLESCENT SEXUAL ABUSERS

Professionals and researchers working with adult sex offenders found many began their abusive behaviors prior to the age of 18 (Abel, 1986; Becker, 1994; Breer, 1987; Freeman-Longo, 1982). Rogers and Trieman (1984) suggested that juveniles may represent as many as 30 to 50% of sexually abusive acts perpetrated against children.

Ryan (1991a) indicates that juvenile sexual offenders are proportionately represented across all racial, ethnic, religious, and geographic groups. While there is not a profile that can be applied to every adolescent offender, Ryan cites findings from six studies from which she paints a modal or composite picture. These characteristics are depicted in Table 1. As can be seen in the left-hand column, the typical juvenile sexual offender is male (91–93%), 14 years old, and likely to be white and living with both parents at the time of the offense. When first arrested, it is unlikely that he has a previous conviction for sexual assault, but he has had other victims. Prior convictions for nonsexual delinquent behavior are likely. The offender may also be a victim of sexual abuse.

The most likely victim-scenario involves a female, 7 or 8 years of age, who is not related to the offender by blood or marriage but is known by the offender (over 95% of cases). The assault is unwanted, involves genital touching, involves penetration over 60% of the time, and is accompanied by force.

In addition to the "modal" juvenile sexual offender profile, Ryan sketches a broader picture to demonstrate the range of characteristics, offense scenes, and behaviors exhibited by this group. These are shown in the right-hand column of Table 1. It can be seen that most are attending school and receiving average grades, they are found in all school social groups, and few are suffering from mental illnesses. Most have multiple victims (average number is seven). The offenses may include both "hands on" and "hands off" behaviors. Offenses occur in a variety of places, and acts such as stalking may precede the sexually abusive acts.

The incidence of female adolescent perpetrators is unknown. Lane (1991a, pp. 324–329) reviewed programs and concluded that female offenders are very similar to their male counterparts. As a whole, it appears that adolescent offenders largely resemble adult abusers, except for age.[4]

PREADOLESCENT SEXUAL ABUSERS

As professionals, researchers, and the public reluctantly acknowledged that adolescents were engaged in sexually abusive behaviors, several researchers and/or practitioners (Gil, 1987; Gil and Johnson, 1993; Hindman, 1994; Issac, 1987; Johnson, 1993) provided evidence that preadolescents (12 years of age and younger) were also sexual offenders. Araji (1997, chap. 1) reviewed this body of knowledge and reported that clinicians and researchers use a developmental continuum that ranges from "sexually normal" to "sexually abusive" (many terms are applied to the latter) behaviors to determine where preadolescents fit. From a review of the classifications and studies of 11 clinicians and/or researchers, Araji (1997) provided a summary of characteristics that are being used to identify sexually abusive children. The summary demonstrates that preadolescent offenders, with the exception of age, are remarkably similar to their adolescent and adult counterparts. Like adults and adolescents, preadolescents present a wide variety of demographic and social characteristics. They are similar in the range and types of sexual behaviors as well as sexual and nonsexual motives (e.g., release of feelings of anger, fear, and loneliness and the need for power and control). Preadolescents' actions may be opportunistic or calculated and predatory; hence, victims are selected because they are available and/or

TABLE 1

Modal Profile and Range of Other Characteristics Associated with Adolescent Sexual Offenders

Modal Profile of Adolescent Sexual Offenders

Range of Characteristics Not Included in Modal Profile

Demographics

Male (91–93%); 14 years of age; likely to be white; living with both parents.

History of Offender's Sexual Abuse

May or may not have been victim of sexual abuse.

Arrest History

Upon first arrest for sexual abuse, unlikely prior sexual abuse arrest is found; prior convictions for nonsexual delinquent behaviors likely.

Victim-Offender Scenario

Victim is female, 7 to 8 years old; unrelated to offender by blood or marriage but is known to offender (95% of cases); assault is unwanted, involves genital touching, often penetration (over 60%); is accompanied by coercion or force to overcome victim's resistance.

Mental Conditions

Fewer than 5% identified as suffering from mental illness or psychosis; may be over-represented in areas of emotional-behavioral disorders and/or affective or attention disorders; only about 30% involved in nonsexual delinquent behaviors that support diagnosis of conduct disorder or antisocial personality; remaining offenders demonstrate no other observable personality or behavioral characteristics that differentiate them from peer groups.

School-Related Characteristics

Most attending school and achieving at least average grades, although significant number have learning problems, have special education needs, are involved in truancy or behavioral problems; found represented in every social group, including the delinquent hood, undersocialized youth, social outcasts, popular students, athletes, and honor students.

Victims and Behaviors

Sexual assaults may be aimed at peers, those younger (see modal profile), or older persons; victims may be one victim on multiple occasions over a period of months or even years or multiple victims (average is 7, but some offenders reported as many as 30); most victims are known by the offender (95%); types of assaults vary widely and may include "hands-off" behaviors such as peeping, flashing, or obscene communication, as well as "hands-on" behaviors such as rape and those described in left-hand column.

Scenes of Offenses

Frequently happens in offender's or victim's home; also happens outdoors in neighborhoods or in the context of acquaintance rapes; assaults on older persons frequently happen in context of robberies or burglaries.

Source: Material adapted from Ryan (1991a).

vulnerable. The sexual behaviors are frequently associated with other antisocial behaviors, such as conduct and oppositional disorders.

The victims may be family members, relatives, friends, or acquaintances. Siblings appear to be common targets, especially among younger preadolescents and female offenders. Most abusers have multiple victims, but this varies by age and opportunities. These preadolescents employ the techniques of keeping secrets, bribes, threats, coercion, and force, as well as grooming activities when initiating and maintaining abusive relationships.

Preadolescent abusers may or may not be victims of sexual abuse, but all have been abused in some way: emotionally, physically, or sexually. Many have been neglected. Most come from families with multiple problems, such as lack of sexual boundaries, frequent exposure to pornography, substance abuse, and abusive and conflictive family interactions.

The modal age range of initial perpetration by preadolescent abusers appears to be 6 to 9. Unlike the adult and adolescent groups, a sizable number of abusers are female. Araji (1997, pp. 72–79), using statistics from ongoing studies by Gray and Pithers (n = 72 in treatment group) and Bonner et al. (n = 155 in treatment group), reported that the proportion of girls ranged from 32% (ages 10 to 12) to 36% (ages 6 to 9) in the Gray and Pithers study. The Bonner et al. study reported percentages for each age group. Overall, their findings showed that boys and girls were about evenly represented in the 6- and 9-year-old groups, but there were substantially more boys in the 7-, 8-, 10-, and 11-year-old categories.

Four case studies are presented below to demonstrate the degree to which preadolescent abusers mirror their adolescent and adult counterparts. Cases 1, 2, and 3 reveal how aggressive or violent these youthful offenders can be and that they may be predatory and offend as groups. Case 4, a 9-year-old male offender, shows that preadolescents use bribes, threats, select vulnerable victims, experience pleasure from sexual contact, and express little empathy for victims. This case also shows that preadolescents have multiple victims — this young boy had even more than those described.

Case 1

In Vermont, a fourth-grade girl was sexually assaulted in a country-school bathroom by several classmates. The perpetrators were two 10-year-old boys who initiated the attempted rape. Three other boys watched or helped hold the struggling victim while her attackers tried to penetrate her. One of the boys was 8 years old and the other two were 6 (Johnson, 1993a).

Case 2

An Alaskan newspaper reported that three boys ages 11, 12, and 13 years were apprehended by police and charged with first-degree sexual assault. The charge related to the boys forcibly raping a 5-year-old girl numerous times. Police indicated that objects were involved. The three boys apparently chased the young girl, caught her, held her on the ground, took off her pants, and took turns raping her. The crime took place in a wooded area near the victim's home and came to light in a therapy session (Kizzia, 1993).

Case 3

In St. Paul, MN, a 9-year-old boy instigated the gang rape of his 8-year-old sister. According to an Associated Press article reprinted in the *Anchorage Daily News,* the boy persuaded his sister to enter an abandoned house. There, seven boys, ages 6 to 13, are suspected by the police of participating in the sexual attack. Four of the boys, including the girl's brother, raped the young girl. No arrests had been made when the article was written (Associated Press, Sept. 23, 1999).

Case 4

This was a 9-year-old-male offender at time of recorded information.

About Victim 1

"This time I put my penis in an adoptive sister's vagina. One time I put it one-half way. I stopped because she was crying and I didn't want to get caught. She was 4 years old."

About Victim 2

"I molested my 4- or 5-year-old cousin in my bedroom. He was my fourth victim. I said, 'If you don't pull your draws I will tell your mother.' He pulled his pants and underwear down. I was on his back and I was thinking about what I did to my sister and what my sister looked like when she was naked. I forced his mouth on my penis. I told him not to bite me or I would kill him. It felt good so I didn't want to stop."

About Victim 3

"[The victim] was 6-1/2 years old. I picked him because he stuttered. I used to stutter so I know it is hard to understand kids like that. I know that adults sometimes don't even bother listening because it takes so long to talk. I molested him one time, at the frog pond. I threatened to put a snake in his bed if he didn't pull down his pants."

About Victim 4

"I am responsible for molesting a 7-year-old male. We lived at a group home together. We were at a beach. I picked him because he wasn't swimming and he trusted me. I pulled down his pants. He asked me what I was doing. I said, 'I'm doing something you don't want to know.' He did what I asked because I threatened him. I felt like I didn't care if he cried because we were in the woods and far from others so they couldn't hear him and I wouldn't get caught. I felt a little sad, but I didn't stop because it felt good" (Araji, 1997, pp. 82–83).

Overall, as previously noted, it can be seen that preadolescent abusers are very much like their adolescent and adult counterparts. Further, the above findings support researchers who believe that many child sexual offenders' abusive behaviors begin in childhood (Ryan, 1991a; West, 1981) and that females are involved in child sexual abuse (Sgroi, 1982).

OTHER HIDDEN AND EMERGING SEXUALLY ABUSIVE GROUPS

Other social groups, in addition to females, adolescents, and preadolescents, have generally remained hidden from public view; however, newspapers, magazines, radio, and television are exposing clergy members, scout leaders, teachers, coaches, and other upstanding community leaders who have been accused, arrested, or convicted of child sexual abuse. O'Brien (1988) described several cases. These included a 70-year-old Roman Catholic priest who was arrested for molesting a 12-year-old mentally-retarded boy who could not speak; a 49-year-old Methodist minister who was convicted for crimes of rape, sodomy, and sexual abuse of four boys and one girl, ages 3 and 4; and a 41-year-old priest who was a Boy Scout leader and confessed to abusing 37 children.

In a special report in *Sports Illustrated,* Nack and Yaeger (1999) exposed child molestation in youth sports. Most cases involved coaches who were trusted and respected and who had built winning teams. They also had molested many boys over many years.

At the global level, Dennis Ward, a 66-year-old British Scout leader was sentenced to 4 years for his part in the abuse of a 13-year-old boy. Ward was a member of a pedophile ring that, it was believed, had abused up to 300 children over the course of 30 years. Uncovering the pedophile ring led international police to a large library of child pornography (BBC News, 1998). Groups or "rings" of abusers are not confined to adults. In York Haven, PA, a child sex ring was discovered that was thought to involve 17 children, some as young as 7 (Associated Press, July 6, 1999).

Currently, increased global concern is being focused on "electronic pedophiles." These are child sexual abusers who act alone or as pedophile or pornography rings and recruit children through the Internet (Mauney, 1999). Many of these offenders have been involved in child sexual abuse prior to using the Internet; others appear to be newcomers.

EXPLAINING CHILD SEXUAL ABUSE

ADULTS' SEXUAL INVOLVEMENT WITH CHILDREN

Most explanations for the sexual involvement of adults (primarily males) with children have been associated with the field of psychology. As such, these explanations focus on the individual. Psychoanalytic theory was particularly influential in the development of early explanations, while behavioral and cognitive frameworks predominate today. Influenced by these theories, most psychological explanations for child sexual abuse fall into several categories: (1) psychological pathologies and personality characteristics, (2) deviant sexual arousal, (3) childhood sexual victimization,[5] (4) social inadequacies, and (5) dysfunctional families.

As sociologists and feminists became concerned with the child sexual abuse issue, explanations then included: (1) social attitudes, primarily those associated with a patriarchal social system; (2) sex role socialization; and (3) child pornography. Empirical support for single-factor explanations varies, as noted by Araji and Finkelhor (1986) and Barnett et al. (1997).

Following a review of empirical studies associated with the above explanations, Araji and Finkelhor (1986) proposed a four-factor model under which single-factor explanations were subsumed. The four factors were (1) Emotional Congruence, (2) Sexual Arousal, (3) Blockage, and (4) Disinhibition.

Emotional Congruence captured explanations for why an adult would feel emotionally comfortable associating with or relating to a child, perhaps as a substitute for an adult. Explanations included children lacking dominance, offender's low self-esteem, mastery over offender's own sexual abuse history through repeating acts with children, male socialization to dominance, immaturity, and psychoanalytic explanations such as narcissism, arrested development, and identification with the aggressor.

Under the second factor, Sexual Arousal, were factors that might explain why abusers were sexually aroused by children, or believed they were. Explanations included in this category were heightened arousal to children or misattribution of arousal, early childhood conditioning, modeling from childhood experiences, hormonal or chromosomal abnormalities, and socialization through child pornography.

Blockage, the third factor, included psychological or physical attributes that might prevent the abuser from interacting with a desired peer and as a substitute turn to a child. Factors in this category included difficulty relating to females, inadequate social skills, sexual anxiety, repressive norms about sexual behavior, disturbances in romantic or adult relationships, and unresolved Oedipal issues. With respect to the latter explanation, Araji and Finkelhor noted that studies did demonstrate the presence of family problems, but not necessarily the ones the Oedipal theory would predict (i.e., castration anxiety and Oedipal conflicts).

Within the final factor, Disinhibition, were explanations for why adults would not be deterred by societal restraints and inhibitions against sexual involvement with children. Examples included substance abuse, use of child pornography, senility, impulse disorder, mental retardation, failure of the incest taboo to operate, cultural toleration, patriarchal norms, and situational stress.

While empirical support for the various single-factor explanations listed in the four categories has varied widely, the four-factor model remains a viable framework for exploring sexual involvement with children. One area, however, that should receive more visibility within the model is cognitive factors (Hartley, 1998; Horley, 1988). Stermac and Segal (1989), using adult sex offenders and non-offender comparison groups, found that men who had sexual contact with children differed from others in the types of cognitions and beliefs they had about sexual interactions with children. The child sexual abusers were more likely to view children as benefiting from the sexual interactions and playing a more active role in these interactions. These cognitions could certainly be included under the Disinhibition category, as they would act to reduce normal inhibitors against sexual involvement with children.

Another factor implicit in the model, but one that should receive increased visibility, is the role of fantasies in the sexual abuse process (Langevin et al., 1998; Marshall, 1973; 1988). Depending on the content of fantasies, they could create beliefs that the adult and child are similar (Emotional Congruence), sexually arouse the adult when the object of fantasy is a child, and/or cognitively break down social controls that would prevent sexual involvement with children (Disinhibition).

While the single-factor explanations that make up the integrative four-factor model were used primarily to explain adult males' attraction to children, the model itself should be applicable to female offenders. However, like most of the single-factor theories from which the four-factor model was developed, the model has not been empirically validated.

ADOLESCENTS' SEXUAL INVOLVEMENT WITH CHILDREN

It should not be surprising, given that adolescent offenders have many of the individual and social characteristics of adult offenders, that explanations for involvement with children are similar to those offered for adults. Ryan (1991b) provided a group of theories, which included "psychosis theory" (the notion of mental pathologies), "physiological theory" (neurological and hormonal problems), "intrapsychic theory" (a focus on Freudian intrapsychic conflicts and personality abnormalities), "learning theory" (the idea that sexually deviant behavior, like all other behavior, is learned through conditioning and reinforcement), "developmental theories" (emphasis on factors that may prevent normal cognitive, psycho-social, or personality development), "cognitive theory" (emphasis on cognitively distorted thinking patterns in interpreting sexual attraction to or involvement with children, as well as similar problems in other areas of life), "addictive theory" (the notion that sexual behaviors become unmanageable or out of control), and "family systems theory" (dysfunction in the family is viewed as an explanation for offenders' deviant sexual behaviors). Ryan's "integrative theories" category is similar to Araji and Finkelhor's (1986) four-factor model, as it provides a multiple-factor explanation.

PREADOLESCENTS' SEXUAL INVOLVEMENT WITH CHILDREN

Araji (1997, chap. 1) reviewed theories that have been offered as explanations for preadolescents' sexually abusive behaviors. She indicated that the explanations could, similar to the above discussions, be grouped into three categories: psychological/biological (focus on the individual), social psychological (focus on social and symbolic interaction), and sociological (focus on culture and social structures). In comparison to explanations offered for adolescent and adult sex offenders, there was much less emphasis on individual pathologies and personality characteristics, perhaps due to the young ages of these abusers. The greatest emphasis was on social psychological explanations, particularly traumatic interactions that could interfere with normal sexual, cognitive, emotional, and social development. Most of the theorists reviewed by Araji (1997) offered a number of outcomes that resulted from traumas generally, but not exclusively, associated with being sexually victimized. For example, Finkelhor and Browne (1985, 1986) presented a Traumagenic Dynamics model, which focuses on the consequences of sexual victimization, including: (1) traumatic sexualization, which can result in sexual identity problems and an aversion to sexual intimacy; (2) feelings of betrayal, which can lead to a lack of trust, fear of intimacy, anger, and hostility; (3) a sense of powerlessness, which can cause children to dissociate, view themselves as victims in other areas of their lives, and have problems with power and control issues; and (4) stigmatization, which might cause children to withdraw and develop feelings of guilt, shame, depression, and lowered self-esteem.

Friedrich discusses problems children may have with coping skills. Isaac and Lane (1990) view all of the aforementioned problems as contributing to the development of a sexual abuse cycle, once sexually abusive thoughts or behaviors begin. If children become involved in sexual behaviors that offer positive reinforcements, Cunningham and MacFarlane (1996) indicate they can become addicted. For children whose sexually abusive acts include an aggressive component, Friedrich (1990) suggests that physical abuse in the history of the preadolescent offender may represent a key factor in explaining aggressiveness or violence.

Closely associated with trauma theories of preadolescents' sexually abusive behavior is the "multiple problem" family explanation. These types of families are characterized by a lack of sexual boundaries, neglect, covert and overt abuse, conflictive patterns of interactions, substance abuse, and exposure to pornography.

As an integrative explanation, Rasmussen et al. (1992) adapted Araji and Finkehor's (1986) four-factor model, previously discussed, and delineated five factors that they believed were necessary for preadolescents to sexually abuse others. These included prior traumatization, social inadequacy, lack of empathy, impulsiveness, and lack of accountability. They referred to this as the Trauma Outcome Process Approach. Araji (1997, pp. 155–157) proposed a systems theory approach, arguing that it is the only one that includes all the levels and types of factors needed to explain preadolescents' sexually reactive and/or sexually offending behaviors.

Similar to the explanations offered for adult and adolescent offenders, those offered for preadolescents have not been empirically verified.

EXPLANATION SIMILARITIES

Explanations offered for adults', adolescents', and preadolescents' sexual abuse against children and others viewed as vulnerable demonstrate many similarities. As such, it is logical to conclude that the best time to intervene is at the preadolescent stage, before the contributing factors have an opportunity to produce cumulative negative effects on an offender's cognitive, emotional, and sexual behavior development.

SOCIETAL RESPONSES TO CHILD SEXUAL ABUSERS

There are three primary social systems that respond to child sexual abusers: mental health agencies, the criminal justice system, and the socio-political system. The first focuses on treatment, the second on punishment, and the third on policy and legislation. Many responses associated with these systems have resulted from public advocacy.

OFFENDER TREATMENT: THE ISSUE OF RECIDIVISM

The primary treatment objective is to reduce the probability of recidivism or repetition of sexual offenses. With respect to adult offenders, primarily males, there is disagreement about the extent to which this goal is met. Furby et al. (1989) reviewed sex offender recidivism studies and concluded that there was no evidence that treatment either reduced sex offender recidivism or that its effectiveness varied by offender groups. Becker (1994), in a review article, provided evidence from a variety of practitioners/researchers who offered more optimistic assessments of the effectiveness of treatment. Dr. Martin Atrops has worked with sex offenders for many years in several states and estimates a 50% success rate; however, he and his colleagues believe that this is very dependent on follow-up treatment and/or supervision after release (personal interview, 1999). At the present time, the degree to which treatment reduces recidivism remains open to debate.

In addition to treatment, several practitioners/researchers (Grubin, 1999; McGrath, 1991; Quinsey et al., 1995) indicate that there are factors other than treatment that must be considered in assessing recidivism probabilities. These include type of sex offense(s), prior criminal record, sexual arousal patterns, empathy development, and social and emotional isolation, among others.

Any evaluation of the connection between treatment and recidivism must be viewed in the context that many incarcerated and non-incarcerated offenders never receive treatment (Becker, 1994). Some studies report little difference between offenders who were assigned to "probation only" as compared to "treatment and probation" (Becker, 1994).

Minimal reliable information of the treatment-recidivism connection exists for female or adolescent sexual offenders. This is true to an even greater extent in countries such as Great Britain (Fisher and Beech, 1999). Likewise, we know little about preadolescents' recidivism because they infrequently come in contact with the criminal justice system.

TREATMENT PROGRAMS

Treatment programs parallel explanations for sexual offenders' actions and can be grouped into five categories that apply to adult as well as adolescent and preadolescent offenders, taking into consideration developmental differences. These treatment types include biological, psychoanalysis and psychodynamics, behavioral, family systems, and relapse prevention. A program overview is shown in Table 2.

Most programs use a combination cognitive-behavioral and relapse prevention approach (Becker, 1994; Laws, 1999). In almost all cases, a multidimensional treatment program is the norm, given the heterogeneous offender population (Marshall and Pithers, 1994). Further, commenting primarily on relapse prevention, Marshall (1999) indicates that treatment programs must be in a continuous state of development. He advocates for more communication among treatment providers as to what works, what does not work, and what needs to be improved.

The chosen treatment approach dictates to some degree whether the form of therapy is individual, group, or family. Adult offenders' programs may include individual therapies, but the emphasis is on group treatment. In the case of incest offenders, a community-based family component may be added. Adolescent treatment, similar to adult programs, may include individual therapy, but again the emphasis is on group treatment. Involvement of the family is stressed (Thomas, 1991). In the case of preadolescents, individual and group therapies are utilized but participation by the family is considered a critical treatment component (Sirles et al., 1997).

TABLE 2

Overview of Common Treatments Used with Child Sexual Abusers and Treatment

Treatment Types/Descriptions	Evaluations

Biological Therapies

Include such treatments as (1) castration (once rare in U.S. but increasingly being considered — see Table 3), and (2) anti-androgenic medications.

Castration: Based on European studies; does lower recidivism rates, but no scientific or ethical basis for using castration in treatment of sex offenders. Only known cases refer to adult offenders.

Anti-androgenic blockers: Do appear to affect direction of sexual drives, but decreases sexual drives in general and produces side effects such as weight gain, lethargy, and hypertension. No expectation that these medical treatments alone will stop sexual offending behavior, but may aid in relapse prevention.

Psychoanalysis/Psychodynamic Therapies

Focus on identifying and resolving early life conflicts and traumas.

Emphasis on individual counseling, while most other programs prefer group therapy. Effectiveness of treatment very difficult to assess.

Cognitive Behavior Therapies (C-B)

Goal of C-B treatments is to teach offenders how to change their behaviors.

Treatments usually multi-component; use a variety of behavioral techniques, especially those aimed at correcting thinking errors, learning to control inappropriate fantasies and behaviors, building social skills and victim empathy.

Play therapy may be used with preadolescents.

Most widely available and most widely used forms of therapy. Low recidivism rates have been reported; however, currently no overall scientific agreement as to how effective treatments are.

Relapse Prevention

Treatment focuses on therapists helping offenders identify cognitive and behavioral patterns that act as precursors to offending behavior.

Model enhances self-management through cognitive-behavioral techniques, which are combined with community-based supervision that may include probation or parole officers, family, and/or designated community residents.

In adolescent and preadolescent program, the sexual abuse cycle treatment model is similar.

Model gaining in popularity and in continuous stage of development.

Does not work with preadolescent abusers who have not reached cognitive development necessary for self-management.

TABLE 2 (cont.)

Treatment Types/Descriptions	Evaluations
Family Therapy	
Model combines individual, group, and family therapy in self-help groups.	For adult sex offenders, criminal justice system participation is essential.
For adolescents and particularly preadolescents, involvement of family therapy is viewed as critical.	For adolescents, but particularly preadolescents, assessments only in early stages.
Multidimensional Treatment	
Combines aspects of various types of treatments noted above.	Most preferred method of treatment and viewed as most effective.

Source: Some material adapted from Becker, 1994; Araji, 1997.

There are additional issues that must be addressed when treating preadolescent abusers. One of these is that they may be simultaneously a victim and perpetrator. Thus, therapists are confronted with the need to address some children as both "victim" and "offender." If providers define sexual acts solely as "reactions" to abuse, including those acts that are premeditated, the young offender may not get adequate treatment for the offending behaviors. This practice appears to be more common among those who refer to themselves as "victim therapists" in comparison to those who view themselves as "offender therapists." On the other hand, if the "victim" issues are not addressed, treatment will not be effective (Araji, 1997, p. xxxvi).

Perhaps the greatest issue surrounding treatment of preadolescents is the lack of awareness that these abusers exist and/or that many states and communities have no appropriate programs or qualified staff to offer treatment (Araji, 1997, chap. 6).[6] One state that has made substantial progress in this area is Utah, through their Utah Task Force of the Utah Network on Juveniles Offending Sexually (1996).

As a section summary, there is some consensus among researchers and practitioners that the value of the cognitive-behavioral model has been demonstrated, at least with adult offenders (Marshall and Pithers, 1994). Most (Barbaree et al., 1993; Becker, 1994; Sirles et al., 1997) would also agree, however, that methodological issues (e.g., reliance on self-report data, lack of appropriate control groups, and absence of scientific studies) associated with measuring the effectiveness of treatment programs prevent any definitive conclusions at this time.

CRIMINAL JUSTICE/LEGISLATIVE RESPONSES

The criminal justice system focuses on the punishment of sex offenders as well as an assessment of the probability of their rehabilitation. Like other crimes, the system has a range of choices that include plea bargains, prison sentences, and probation.

Some evidence suggests that child sexual abuse cases are prosecuted much like other crimes (Barnett et al., 1997, pp. 101–102).

The criminal justice system also responds to legislation. Forty states have some type of laws that require sex offenders to register with local law enforcement agencies after release from prison and following geographic moves. At the national level, President Clinton signed a 1993 National Protection Act requiring states to report child sexual abuse arrests and convictions to the Federal Bureau of Investigation (FBI). Currently, debate continues around the constitutional and ethical issues of releasing this information to the public (Barnett et al., 1997, p. 102; Bass, 1999).

The criminal justice system has encountered a number of problems as a result of increased reporting and prosecution of sex offenders. One is prison overcrowding; particularly in states which have population demographics and social characteristics conducive to sexual offending. A second problem is lack of appropriate treatment programs and facilities, especially for female, adolescent, and preadolescent offenders. In a 1999 review of juvenile sex offenders in Idaho, for example, Jensen and Sipe found that sex offender placement costs made up 70% of the annual budget for the Department of Juvenile Corrections. Most offenders had to be sent out of state for treatment, because not enough existed in Idaho. As most offenders averaged 2 years in custody, the average cost per youth, excluding transportation, ranged from $71,000 to $175,000.

With respect to preadolescents, there is debate as to whether they should even have contact with the justice system (Araji, 1997, chap. 6).

SOCIETAL ADVOCACY

As previously noted, there has been recent legislation passed to protect society against primarily adult males who sexually abuse children. Much legislation results from citizen advocacy, even sexual offenders themselves. With the advent of increased pornography and pedophile activity on the Internet, groups have emerged as social controls to prevent children from exposure to these individuals/groups. Hidden offenders are being exposed by adults who were victimized as youth, and institutional changes are occurring (e.g., religious and educational organizations, Boy Scouts, sports). These responses are happening at the local, state, national, and international levels. Examples of individual and institutional responses to child sexual offenders are shown in Table 3.

CONCLUSION

This chapter has reviewed and updated information about the demographic, psychological, and social characteristics of child sexual abusers; explanations for their abusive behaviors; and societal responses to these actions. The information demonstrates that we have significantly increased our knowledge about child sexual offenders in a relatively short span of time. In the process, we have also discovered how much remains unknown and empirically untested.

TABLE 3
Individual and Institutional Responses to Child Sexual Offenders

Castration

Texas is the first state to put a castration law into effect; Michigan and South Carolina had similar laws struck down. Scandinavian countries and Germany offer chemical castration. In Texas, offenders must volunteer for castration. To prevent state coercion, an independent third party monitors the process. Much of the impetus for the Texan bill came from Larry Don McQuay, a convicted child molester from San Antonio. He publicly begged authorities to castrate him. He claims to have assaulted over 200 children and says if he is not castrated he will add to that number as soon as he is released (*Economist,* May 17, 1997).

Prison or Death Is the Only Control

Norman Watson, a Little League coach, has spent most of his 54 years sexually preying on children — a couple of hundred and mostly young boys. After many years of counseling and therapy, Watson says he should die in the California prison because he is sexually aroused by young boys and can't be where he has access to them (Nack and Yaeger, 1999). LeRoy Hendricks, a child molester sitting in a Kansas prison, has openly expressed similar sentiments.

Megan's Laws

In July, 1994, 7-year old Megan Kanka from New Jersey had been invited by Jesse Timmendequas, a 33-year-old landscaper who lived next door, to come into his house and pet his new puppy. She did. He strangled her unconscious with his belt, raped her, and smothered her with a plastic bag. He put her in a tool box, drove to a soccer field several miles away, and dumped her body. Megan's death led to outrage around the state which was further fueled when it became known that Timmendequas, who confessed to the killing, had previously served 6 years in prison for aggravated assault and attempted sexual assault of a child. It was learned his two housemates had also done time for sex crimes. Megan's parents led a large grassroots movement for tougher legislation against sex offenders. It was particularly aimed at the right of communities to know where sex offenders are living. They were successful in gaining the support of New Jersey's Governor, Christine Todd Whitman, and the bill, known as Megan's Law, was passed. New Jersey's sentiments are widely shared by other states. Washington, in 1990, adopted the first Community Protection Act. At least 40 states now have bills that require released sex offenders to register with local police and, in some states, that police then inform the community residents; the latter was ruled as unconstitutional in New Jersey (*The New York Times,* May 12, 1997).

Anti-pedophile Groups Attempt To Protect
Children from Electronic Pedophiles

A large number of anti-pedophile groups have appeared on the Internet to combat pedophiles and pedophile/child pornographers who lure children into their chat rooms or web sites. The anti-pedophile groups are found in many countries. Some of these include the Movement Against Pedophiles on the Internet (Belgium), Save the Children Norway's (Norway), and Pedowatch, Ethical Hackers Against Pedophilia, and Cyber Angels in the U.S. (Mauney, 1999), as well as Safeguarding Our Children—United Mothers, also in the U.S.

International Conferences

Queen Silvia of Sweden hosted an international conference on child sex trade held in Stockholm, September 1996. The event was prompted by her exposure to pornographic films involving children after which she made a rare television appearance criticizing liberal Swedish laws that deal with sex offenses (*Christian Science Monitor,* August 23, 1996).

NOTES

1. It is unfortunate that once the scientific community began generating research and literature on adults who were sexually involved with children, they borrowed popular words, created new concepts, and began mixing scientific and popular terms. "Pedophile" (the Americanized version of *paedophile*) is consistently used interchangeably with terms such as child molester, child sexual abuser, child sexual offender, and child rapist. This mixing may occur because paedophile historically meant "love or fondness for children." To demonstrate that sexual involvement with young children is not valued, the use of pedophile may be consciously or unconsciously paired with concepts that denote societal disapproval. Whatever the reason, researchers (e.g., Araji and Finkelhor, 1986; Becker and Hunter, 1992) and professionals (Bradford, 1994; Lanning, 1986) have called attention to legal, research, and treatment problems that arise when concepts that are conceptually different are equated.

2. It is recognized that not everyone views the involvement of children in sexual activities as harmful or abusive. Groups who object to this characterization are the Rene Guyon Society, the North American Man-Boy Love Association (NAM-BLA) and the Childhood Sensuality Circle (Holmes, 1991, pp. 39–40).

3. As those involved in expert witnessing have learned, these typologies are sometimes looked upon with skepticism by the court system (Murphy and Peters, 1992).

4. For more information on juvenile offenders, see *The Juvenile Sex Offender,* a book edited by Barbaree et al. (1993); National Adolescent Perpetrator (1988) Preliminary Report from the National Task Force on Juvenile Sexual Offending; and Grant and McDonald (1996).

5. Freund et al. (1990) have claimed that many pedophiles falsely claim they have been victims of sexual abuse which casts doubt on the "molestation theory of sexual abuse." Some support for this contention is found in a study by Hindman (1988) who interviewed two groups of paroled adult male sex offenders. One group was interviewed between 1980 and 1982; the other between 1982 and 1988. Both groups were asked about childhood victimization. The 1982–1988 group, however, was informed they would be subjected to a lie-detector test to evaluate the truthfulness of their self-reports. In the 1980–1982 group, no such condition was included. In the "no lie detector condition," 67% of the offenders reported victimization histories, while 29% reported in the negative. In the "lie-detector test" condition, Hindman found the results reversed — 67% reported no victimization histories, while 29% reported abuse.

6. The present author is becoming concerned about the use of medication in the treatment of preadolescents who are either sexually reactive and/or sexually offending. Observations suggest that if there is no appropriate treatment program or knowledgeable staff for these young victims and/or offenders, they may be over-medicated and/or diagnosed with a problem or disorder other than reactions to sexual victimization and/or sexually offending behaviors. These approaches will not address the problem and may make matters worse.

REFERENCES

Abel, G.G., Mittelman M.S., and Becker, J.V. (1985). Sexual offenders: results of assessment and recommendations for treatment. In Ben-Aron, M.H., Hucker, S.J., and Webster, D.D. (Eds), *Clinical Criminology: The Assessment and Treatment of Criminal Behavior* (pp. 191–207). Toronto: M & M Graphics, Ltd.

Abel, G., Becker, J., Cunningham-Rathner, J. et. al. (1988). Multiple paraphilic diagnoses among sex offenders. *Bulletin of the American Academy of Psychiatry and the Law,* 16(2):153–168.

Abel G., Becker J.V., Murphy, W.E., and Flanagan B. (1981). Identifying dangerous child molesters. In Stuart, R. (Ed.), *Violent Behavior — Social Learning Approaches to Prediction, Management and Treatment.* New York: Brunner/Mazel.

Abel, G. and Osborn, C. (1992). The paraphilias: the extent and nature of sexually deviant and criminal behavior. In Bradford, J. (Ed.), *Psychiatric Clinics of North America* (pp. 675–687). Philadelphia: W.B. Saunders.

American Association for Protecting Children (1988). *Highlights of Official Child Neglect and Abuse Reporting, 1986.* Denver, CO: American Humane Association.

American Association for Protecting Children (1989). *Highlights of Official Child Neglect and Abuse Reporting, 1987.* Denver, CO: American Humane Association.

Ames, M.A. and Houston, D.A. (1990). Legal, social and biological definitions of pedophilia. *Archives of Sexual Behiavior,* 19(4):333–342.

Amir, M. (1972). The role of the victim in sex offenses. In Resnik, H.L.P. and Wolfgang, M.E. (Eds.), *Sexual Behaviors: Social, Clinical and Legal Aspects.* Boston: Little Brown & Company.

Araji, S. and Finkelhor, D. (1986). Abusers: a review of the research. In Finkelhor, D. et al. (Eds.), *A Sourcebook on Child Sexual Abuse* (pp. 89–118). Newbury Park, CA: Sage.

Araji, S.K. (1997). *Sexually Aggressive Children: Coming To Understand Them.* Thousand Oaks, CA: Sage.

Associated Press. (July 6, 1999). Police uncover child sex ring. *Anchorage Daily News*, p. A4.

Associated Press (Sept. 23, 1999). Boy, 9, led gang rape of sister, 8, police say. *Anchorage Daily News*, p. A5.

Atrops, M. (July 12, 1999). Personal interview. Eagle River, AK: Hiland Correctional Facility.

Avery-Clark, C.A. and Laws, D.R. (1984). Differential erection response patterns of child sexual abusers to stimuli describing activities with children. *Behavior Therapy,* 15:71–83.

Awad, G., Saunders, E., and Levene, J. (1979). A clinical study of male adolescent sex offenders. *International Journal of Offender Therapy and Comparative Criminology,* 28(2):105–116.

Barbaree, H.E., Bogaert, A.F., and Seto, M.C. (1995). Sexual reorientation therapy for pedo-
philes: practices and controversies. In Diamant, L. and McAnulty, R.D. (Eds.), *The
Psychology of Sexual Orientation, Behavior, and Identity* (pp. 357–383). Westport, CT:
Greenwood Press.

Barbaree, H., Marshall, W., and Hudson, S. (1993). *The Juvenile Sex Offender.* New York:
Guilford.

Barnett, W.W., Miller-Perrin, C.L., and Perrin, R.D. (1997). *Family Violence Across the
Lifespan* (pp. 69–103). Thousand Oaks, CA: Sage.

Bass, A. (1999). Sex offender registry stirs fear, legal fights. *Anchorage Daily News* (from
The Boston Globe), Sept. 22, pp. A1, A12.

Becker, J.V. (1994). Offenders: characteristics and treatment. *Future of Children*, 4:176–197.

Becker, J.V. and Hunter, J.A., Jr. (1992). Evaluation of treatment outcome for adult perpetrators of child sexual abuse. *Criminal Justice and Behavior*, 18(1):74–92.

Berlin, F. and Krout, E. (1986). Pedophilia: diagnostic concepts, treatment, and ethical considerations. *American Journal of Forensic Psychiatry*, 7(1):13–30.

Berlin, F. (1983). Sex offenders: a biomedical perspective and a status report on biomedical
treatment. *The Sexual Aggressor, Current Perspectives on Treatment*, 83:86–87.

Berliner, L. and Conte, J.R. (1990). The process of victimization: the victims' perspective.
Child Abuse and Neglect, 14:29–40.

Bradford, J.M.W. (1994). Can pedophilia be treated? *The Harvard Mental Health Letter*,
10(9):8–15.

Breer, W. (1987). *The Adolescent Molester.* Springfield, IL: Charles C Thomas.

BBC (October 2, 1998). *UK Paedophile Scout Leader Jailed.* British Broadcasting Corpora-
tion Online Network.

Browne, A. and Finkelhor, D. (1986). Impact of child sexual abuse: a review of the research.
Psychological Bulletin, 99:66–77.

Budin, L.E. and Johnson, C.F. (1989). Sex abuse prevention programs: offenders' attitudes
about their efficacy. *Child Abuse and Neglect*, 13:77–87.

Burgess, A.W., Hartman C.R., McCausland M.P., and Powers P. (1984). Response patterns
in children and adolescents exploited through sex rings and pornography. *American
Journal of Psychiatry*, May, 141:656.

Carlson, S. (1991). The victim/perpetrator. In Hunger, M. (Ed.), *The Sexually Abused Male:
Prevalence, Impact, and Treatment*, Vol. 2. (pp. 249–266). Lexington, MA: Lexington
Books.

Christian Science Monitor (1996). Child abductions highlight world issue. *Christian Science
Monitor*, August 23, 88(189):7.

Congressional Quarterly (1998). Bill may curb internet use by pedophiles. *Congressional
Quarterly*, May 9, 56(19):1227.

Conte, J.R. (1990). *Overview of Child Sexual Abuse* (mimeographed paper).

Conte, J.R. (1985). Clinical dimensions of adult sexual abuse of children. *Behavioral Sciences
and the Law*, 3(4):341–344.

Conte, J.R. (1993). Sexual abuse of children. In Hampton, R.L. et al. (Eds.), *Family Violence:
Prevention and Treatment* (pp. 56–85). Newbury Park, CA: Sage.

Conte, J.R., Wolf, S., and Smith, T. (1989). What sexual offenders tell us about prevention
strategies. *Child Abuse and Neglect*, 13:293–301.

Conte, J.R. and Berliner, L. (1981). Sexual abuse of children: implications for practice. *Social
Casework*, 62:601-606.

Crittenden, J., Gelastopoulas, E., and Mueller, M. (1997). Cry of pain; killed kid's dad vows
to fight for death penalty. *The Boston Globe*, October 5, News Section, p. 1.

Cunningham, C. and MacFarlane, L. (1996). *When Children Abuse*. Brandon, VT: Safer Society Press.

DeFrancis, V. (1969). *Protecting the Child Victim of Sex Crimes Committed by Adults*. Denver, CO: American Humane Association.

deYoung, M. (1982). *Sexual Victimization of Children*. Jefferson, NC: McFarland.

Economist (May 17, 1997). Manhood for the chop. *Economist*, 343(8017):30.

Economist (Aug. 30, 1997). Wages of sin. *Economist*, 344(8032):18.

Edwards, T. and Willwerth, J. (1998). Mad about the boy. *Time Canada*, 151(6):69.

Elliott, M., Browne, K., and Kilcoyne, J. (1995). Child sexual abuse prevention: what offenders tell us. *Child Abuse and Neglect*, 19:579–594.

Erickson, W.D., Walbek, N.H., and Seely, R.K. (1988). Behavior patterns of child molesters. *Archives of Sexual Behavior*, 17(1):77–86.

Faller, K.C. (1995). A clinical sample of women who have sexually abused children. *Journal of Child Sexual Abuse* 4(3):13–30.

Fielder, J. (1998). Lovesick. *Mirabella*, 89:168–175.

Finkelhor, D. (1984). *Child Sexual Abuse: New Theory and Research*. New York: Free Press.

Finkelhor, D. and Baron, L. (1986). High risk children. In Finkelhor, D. (Ed.), *A Sourcebook on Child Sexual Abuse* (pp. 60–88). Beverly Hills, CA: Sage.

Finkelhor, D. and Browne, A. (1985). The traumatic impact of child sexual abuse: a conceptualization. *American Journal of Orthopsychiatry*, 55(4):530–541.

Finkelhor, D. and Browne, A. (1986). Initial and long-term effects: a conceptual framework. In Finkelhor, D. (Ed.), *A Sourcebook on Child Sexual Abuse*. Beverly Hills, CA: Sage.

Finkelhor, D. and Williams, L.M. (1988). *Nursery Crimes: Sexual Abuse in Day Care*. Beverly Hills, CA: Sage.

Finkelhor, D., Hotaling, G., Lewis, I.A., and Smith, C. (1990). Sexual abuse in a national survey of adult men and women: prevalence, characteristics, and risk factors. *Child Abuse and Neglect*, 14:19–28.

Fisher, D. and Beech, A.R. (1999). Current practice in Britain with sexual offenders. *Journal of Interpersonal Violence*, 14(3):240–256.

Freeman-Longo, R.E. (1982). Sexual learning and experience among adolescent sexual offenders. *International Journal of Offender Therapy and Comparative Criminology*, 26(2):235–241.

Freund, K., Watson, R., and Dickey, R. (1990). Does sexual abuse in childhood cause pedophilia? An exploratory study. *Archives of Sexual Behavior*, 19(6):557–568.

Friedrich, W.N. (1990). *Psychotherapy of Sexually Abused Children and their Families*. New York: Norton.

Friedrich, W.N. (1991). *Casebook of Sexual Abuse Treatment*. New York: Norton.

Furby, L., Weinrott, M., and Blackshaw, L. (1989). Sex offender recidivism: a review. *Psychological Bulletin*, 105(1):3–30.

Gil, E. (1987). *Children Who Molest: A Guide for Parents of Young Sex Offenders*. Walnut Creek, CA: Launch Press.

Gil, E. and Johnson, T.C. (1993). *Sexualized Children: Assessment and Treatment of Sexualized Children Who Molest Children*. Rockville, MD: Launch Press.

Glasser, M. (1988). Psychodynamic aspects of paedophilia. *Psychoanalytic Psychotherapy*, 3(2):121–135.

Gomes-Schwartz, B., Horowitz, J.M., and Cardarelli, A.P. (1990). *Child Sexual Abuse: The Initial Effects*. Beverly Hills, CA: Sage.

Grant, C. and McDonald, M. (1996). Adolescent sex offenders. *Journal of Child and Youth Care*, 11(1):15–25.

Groth, A.N. (1979). Sexual trauma in the lives of rapists and child molesters. *Victimology*, 4: 10–16.

Groth, A.N., Birnbaum, H.J., and Gary, T.S. (1982). The child molester: clinical observations. In Conte, J.R. and Shorte, D.A. (Eds.), *Social Work and Child Abuse* (pp. 129–144). New York: Haworth.

Grubin, D. (1999). Actuarial and clinical assessment of risk in sex offenders. *Journal of Interpersonal Violence,* 14(3):331–343.

Hanley, R. (1999). Teenager is given 70-year sentence in boy's murder. *The New York Times,* April 15, p. B5.

Hartley, C.C. (1998). How incest offenders overcome internal inhibitions through the use of cognitions and cognitive distortions. *Journal of Interpersonal Violence*, 13(1):25–39.

Hayashino, D.S., Wurtele, S.K., and Klebe, K.J. (1995). Child molesters: an examination of cognitive factors. *Journal of Interpersonal Violence,* 10:106–116.

Hindman, J. (1988). Research disputes assumptions about child molesters. *NDAA Bulletin,* 7:1–3.

Hindman, J. (1994). *JCA: Juvenile Culpability Assessment,* 2nd rev. ed. Ontario, OR: Alexandria.

Holmes, R.M. (1991). *Sex Crimes.* Beverly Hills, CA: Sage.

Horley, J. (1988). Cognitions of child sexual abusers. *The Journal of Sex Research*, 25(4):542–545.

Howitt, D. (1995). *Paedophilies and Sexual Offences Against Children.* Chichester: John Wiley & Sons.

Isaac, C. (1987). Identification and Interruption of Sexually Offending Behaviors in Prepubescent Children, paper presented at the Proc. of the Sixteenth Annual Child Abuse and Neglect Symposium, Keystone, CO, May 1987.

Isaac, C. and Lane, S. (1990). *The Sexual Abuse Cycle in the Treatment of Adolescent Sexual Abusers.* Shorham, VT: Safer Society Program and Press.

Ivey, G. and Simpson, P. (1998). The psychological life of paedophiles: a phenomenological study. *South African Journal of Psychology,* 25(1):15–20.

Jensen, E. and Sipe, R. (1999). Juveniles Committed to State Custody for Sexual Offenses in Idaho, report presented to the Office of Juvenile Justice and Delinquency Prevention, State of Idaho, January.

Johnson, T.C. (1993). Assessment of sexual behavior problems in preschool-aged and latency aged children. *Child and Adolescent Psychiatric Clinics of North America,* 2(3):431–449.

Kalders, A., Inkster, H., and Britt, E. (1997). Females who offend sexually against children in New Zealand. *Journal of Sexual Aggression,* 3(1):15–29.

Kaye, E. (1998). It's a family affair. *George,* 73(8):90–99.

Kizza, T. (1993). Homer police want charges of rape against three boys. *Anchorage Daily News,* October 1, pp. A1, A10.

Knight, R., Carter, D., and Prentky, R. (1989). A system for classification of child molesters. *Journal of Interpersonal Violence,* 4(1):3–23.

Langevin, R., Handy, L., Hook, H., Day, D., and Russon, A. (1985). Are incestuous fathers pedophilic and aggressive? In Langevin, R. (Ed.), *Erotic Preference Gender Identity and Aggression.* New York: Erlbaum.

Langevin, R., Lang, R.A., Wright, P., and Hardy, L. (1988). Pornography and sexual offenses. *Annals of Sex Research,* 1(3):355–362.

Lanning, K.V. (1986). Child molesters: a behavioral analysis for law-enforcement officers investigating cases of child sexual exploitation (p. 2). Washington, D.C.: National Center for Missing and Exploited Children.

Laws, D.R. (1999). Relapse prevention: the state of the art. *Journal of Interpersonal Violence,* 14(3):285–302.

"Leeza" (1999). Mary Kay LeTourneau: two years later. KYES 5-TV/UPN network programming, September 21.

Marshall, W.L. (1973). The modification of sexual fantasies: a combined treatment approach to the reduction of deviant sexual behavior. *Behavioral Research and Therapy,* 11:557–564.

Marshall, W.L. (1988). The use of sexually explicit stimuli by rapists, child molesters and non-offenders. *Journal of Sex Research,* 25(2):267–288.

Marshall, W.L. (1999). Current status of North American assessment and treatment programs for sexual offenders. 14(3):221–239.

Marshall, W.L., Barbaree, H.E., and Christophe, D. (1986). Sexual offenders against female children: sexual preferences for age of victims and type of behavior. *Canadian Journal of Behavioural Science,* 18:424–439.

Marshall, W.L. and Hall, G.C.N. (1995). The value of the MMPI in deciding forensic issues in accused sexual offenders. *Sexual Abuse: A Journal of Research and Treatment,* 7:205–219.

Marshall, W. and Pithers, W. (1994). A reconsideration of treatment outcome with sex offenders. *Criminal Justice and Behavior,* 21:10–27.

Masson J.M. (1984). *The Assault on Truth: Freud's Suppression of the Seduction Theory.* New York: Farrar, Straus and Giroux.

Mathews, R., Mathews, J., and Speltz, K. (1990). Female sexual offenders. In Hunger, M. (Ed.), *The Sexually Abused Male: Prevalance, Impact, and Treatment,* Vol. 1. (pp. 175–293). Lexington, MA: Lexington Books.

Mauney, T. (1999). Controlling Cybersex: The Case of Pedophilia, paper presented at 70th Annual Pacific Sociological Association Conference, Portland, OR, April, 1999.

McGrath, R. (1991). Sex-offender risk assessment and disposition planning: a review of empirical and clinical findings. *International Journal of Offender Therapy and Comparative Criminology,* 34:328–350.

Mohr, I.W., Turner, R.E., and Jerry, M.B. (1964). *Pedophilia and Exhibitionism.* Toronto: University of Toronto Press.

Murphy, K. (1997). Teacher who had baby by sixth-grader is sentenced. *Los Angeles Times,* Nov. 15, pp. A1+.

Murphy, W.D. and Peters, J.M. (1992). Profiling child sexual abusers: psychological considerations. *Criminal Justice and Behavior,* 19(1):24–37.

Nack, W. and Yaeger, D. (1999). Every parent's nightmare. *Sports Illustrated,* Sept. 13, 91(10):40–53.

National Adolescent Perpetrator Network (1988). Preliminary report from the national task force on juvenile sexual offending. *Juvenile and Family Court Journal,* 39(2):41–43.

National Center for Prosecution of Child Abuse (1993). *Legislation Requiring Sex Offenders To Register with a Government Agency.* Alexandria, VA: Author.

New York Times (1997). In Megan case, a passive suspect with a violent past. *The New York Times,* May 12, pp. B1, B6.

O'Brien, R.C. (1988). Pedophilia: the legal predicament of clergy. *Journal of Contemporary Health, Law and Policy,* 4:91–154.

Okami, P. and Goldberg, S. (1992). Personality correlates of pedophilia. *Journal of Sex Research,* 29(3):297–328.

Panton, J.H. (1978). Personality differences appearing between rapists of adults, rapists of children and nonviolent sexual molesters of female children. *Research Communications in Psychology, Psychiatry and Behavior,* 3(4):385–393.

People (1995). Little Megan Kanka was brutally murdered. Now her family wants other parents to know when a sex offender moves in next door. *People,* March 20, 43(11):46–51.

Peters, J.J. (1976). Children who are victims of sexual assault and the psychology of offenders. *American Journal of Psychotherapy,* 30(3):398–421.

Peters, S.D., Wyatt, G.E., and Finkelhor, D. (1986). Prevalence. In Finkelhor, D. (Ed.), *A Sourcebook on Child Sexual Abuse* (pp. 15–39). Beverly Hills, CA: Sage.

Plummer, K. (1981). Pedophilia: constructing a sociological baseline. In Cook, M. and Howells, K. (Eds.), *Adult Sexual Interest in Children.* New York: Academic Press.

Quinsey, V.L. and Chapling, T.C. (1988). Preventing faking in phallometric assessments of sexual preference. *Annals of the New York Academy of Sciences,* 528:49–58.

Quinsey, V.L., Rice, M.E., and Harris, G.T. (1995). Actuarial prediction of sexual recidivism. *Journal of Interpersonal Violence,* 10:85–103.

Rasmussen, L.A., Burton, J.E., and Christopherson, B.J. (1992). Precursors to offending and the trauma outcome process in sexually reactive children. *Journal of Child Sexual Abuse,* 1(1):33–48.

Revitch E. and Weiss, R.G. (1984). The pedophiliac offender. *Dis Nervous System,* 23:73–78.

Risin, L.I. and Koss, M.P. (1987). The sexual abuse of boys: prevalence and descriptive characteristics of childhood victimisations. *Journal of Interpersonal Violence,* 2: 309–323.

Rogers, C. and Tremain, T. (1962). Clinical interventions with boy victims of sexual abuse. In Stuart, I. and Greer, J. (Eds.), *Victims of Sexual Aggression* (pp. 91–104). New York: Van Nostrand Reinhold.

Rush, F. (1980). *The Best Kept Secret: Sexual Abuse of Children.* New York: McGraw-Hill.

Russell, D.E.H. (1983). The incidence and prevalence of intrafamilial and extrafamilial sexual abuse of female children. *Child Abuse and Neglect,* 7:133–146.

Ryan, G. (1991a). Juvenile sex offenders: defining the population. In Ryan, G.D. and Lane, S.L. (Eds.), *Juvenile Sexual Offending* (pp. 3–8). Lexington: Lexington Books.

Ryan, G. (1991b). Theories of etiology. In Ryan, G.D. and Lane, S.L. (Eds.), *Juvenile Sex Offending: Causes, Consequences and Correction* (pp. 41–55). Lexington, MA: Lexington Books.

Ryan, G.D. and Lane, S.L. (1991). *Juvenile Sex Offending: Causes, Consequences, and Correction.* Lexington, MA: Lexington Books.

Scott, L. (1994). Sex offenders: prevalence, trends, model programs, and costs. In Roberts, A. (Ed.), *Critical Issues in Crime and Justice.* Thousand Oaks, CA: Sage.

Sgroi, S. (1982). *Handbook of Clinical Intervention in Child Sexual Abuse.* Lexington, MA: Lexington Books.

Sirles, B., Araji, S.K., and Bosek, R.C. (1997). Redirecting children's sexually abusive and sexually aggressive behaviors: programs and practices. In Araji, S.K. (Ed.), *Sexually Aggressive Children: Coming To Understand Them* (pp. 161–192). Thousand Oaks, CA: Sage.

Stermac, L., Hall, K., and Henskens, M. (1989). Violence among child molesters. *Journal of Sex Research,* 26:450–459.

Stermac, L.E. and Segal, W.V. (1989). Adult sexual contact with children: an examination of cognitive factors. *Behavior Therapy,* 20:573–584.

Thomas, J. (1991). The adolescent sex offender's family in treatment. In Ryan, G.D. and Lane, S.L. (Eds.), *Juvenile Sex Offending: Causes, Consequences, and Correction* (pp. 333–390). Lexington, MA: Lexington Books.

Tingle, D., Barnard, G.W., Robbins, L., Newman, G., and Hutchinson, D. (1986). Childhood and adolescent characteristics of pedophiles and rapists. *International Journal of Law and Psychiatry,* 9:103–116.

Travin, S., Bluestone, H., Coleman, E., Cullen, K., and Melella, J. (1984). Pedophilia: an update on theory and practice. *Psychiatric Quarterly,* 57(2):89–103.

Urquiza, A.J. (1988). The Effects of Childhood Sexual Abuse in an Adult Male Population, unpublished doctoral dissertation, University of Washington, Seattle.

Utah Task Force of the Utah Network on Juveniles Offending Sexually (1996). *The Utah Report on Juvenile Sex Offenders.* Salt Lake City: Author.

Weber, D. (1998). Prosecutor: Jaynes was sinister seducer. *The Boston Herald,* Dec. 3, News, p. 004.

West, D.J. (1981). Adult sexual interest in children: implications for social control. *Sexual Interest in Children, Personality and Psychopathy,* 252.

Williams, L.M. and Finkelhor, D. (1990). The characteristics of incestuous fathers: a review of recent studies. In Marshall, W.L. et al. (Eds.), *Handbook of Sexual Assault: Issues, Theories, and Treatment of the Offender* (pp. 231–255). New York: Plenum.

Wyatt, G.E. (1985). The sexual abuse of Afro-American and white American women in childhood. *Child Abuse and Neglect,* 9:507–519.

3 Serial Rape: An Evolutionary Perspective

Craig T. Palmer and Randy Thornhill

CONTENTS

WHY TAKE AN EVOLUTIONARY PERSPECTIVE?

Some men use force and the threat of force to obtain sex, and often these men do so repeatedly. Examining the causes of such criminal behavior from an evolutionary perspective may seem unusual to many readers and objectionable to others. This is because evolutionary theory has been either ignored or misunderstood by most social scientists studying criminal behavior. However, given that nearly all social scientists accept that humans are the product of evolution, there is no valid reason for not taking an evolutionary perspective on criminal behavior. Indeed, "Darwinian selection is the only known source of the functional complexity of living things, and biologists have no reason to suspect that there are any others" (Wilson et al., 1997, p. 433). Hence, what is needed is a clear understanding of what evolutionary theory says, and doesn't say, about the causes of criminal behaviors such as serial rape.

0-8493-2236-7/00/$0.00+$.50

MISUNDERSTANDINGS OF EVOLUTIONARY THEORY

Perhaps no other theoretical approach in the history of the social sciences has been as consistently and fundamentally misunderstood as evolutionary theory. Further, these misunderstandings have led to more passionate acrimony when applied to the subject of rape than to any other subject. Hence, the first step in examining what an evolutionary perspective might contribute to the understanding and prevention of serial rape is to clarify these misunderstandings.

MISUNDERSTANDING ONE: THE NATURALISTIC FALLACY

Perhaps the most common misunderstanding of evolutionary theory, and the one most destructive to knowledge, is the naturalistic fallacy: the view that what ought to be is defined by what is, and especially by what is natural (Moore, 1903). The flaw in this view has been explained many times by evolutionists (e.g., Alexander, 1979, 1987; Symons, 1979; Wright, 1994) and seems obvious when one considers natural phenomena such as diseases, floods, and tornadoes. Nonetheless, many scholars have called for the rejection of evolutionary explanations of human behavior on the insupportable grounds that evolutionary explanations of undesirable behaviors, such as crimes, excuse the perpetrators because they were only doing what was natural (Gould and Lewontin, 1979; Sahlins, 1976). The naturalistic fallacy was particularly pervasive in the criticisms of early evolutionary analyses of rape: Shields and Shields (1983), Thornhill (1980), Thornhill and Thornhill (1983), and Thiessen (1983/1986); see especially Baron (1985), Dusek (1984), Fausto-Sterling (1985), Kitcher (1985), Sunday and Tobach (1985). The false reasoning of the naturalistic fallacy was used to argue that any claim that rape was natural in the sense of occurring in other "natural" species, that it was favored by "natural" selection, or that it was the result of the "natural" desire for sex was equivalent to claiming that rape was justifiable. For example, Baron stated that the "claim that rape occurs widely among plants and animals ... is likely to trivialize the meaning of rape and give it a veneer of justifiability" (Baron, 1985, p. 273; see also Blackman, 1985; Dusek, 1984; Schwendinger and Schwendinger, 1985; Sunday, 1985). The fact is that rape or, if one prefers, "forced copulations" are well documented in a large number of species (for references, see Thornhill and Palmer, 2000); rape is likely to be an adaptation in some of these species and probably cannot occur without some sexual arousal on behalf of the rapist, but none of these things excuses or justifies rape in any way.

MISUNDERSTANDING TWO: GENETIC DETERMINISM

The naturalistic fallacy is often intertwined with the equally erroneous view that evolutionary explanations are based on the assumption that behavior is genetically determined — meaning rigidly fixed by genes alone and hence not alterable except by changing those genes. Although the myth of genetic determinism has also been debunked countless times by evolutionists, the psychologist Russell Gray only recently stated that, typically, "evolutionary explanations are [still] taken to imply that our behavior is, in some way, programmed by our genes, and thus the behavior is natural and immutable" (1997, p. 385). Pointing out the absurdity of this situation, the eminent evolutionary biologist John Maynard Smith called genetic determinism "an incorrect idea that is largely irrelevant, because it is not held by anyone, or at least not by any competent evolutionary biologist" (1997, p. 524). "The phrase 'genetic determinism,'" Maynard Smith continued, "is one that is usually met in the writings of those who criticize sociobiology, or behavioral ecology."

The reason the meaningless concept of genetic determinism remains so popular is that most people inaccurately equate "biological" with "genetic." In reality, every aspect of every living thing is, by definition, biological, but everything biological is a result of interaction between genes and environmental factors. Even an individual cell — the most fundamental building block of any larger organism — is a product of genes and certain aspects of the environment (e.g., various chemicals). As an organism continues to develop, genes will create new cells only when they interact with certain additional environmental triggers, and differences in the developmental environment will produce a variety of cells (muscle cells, nerve cells, and so on). This constant intertwining of genetic and environmental factors continues throughout the life of the organism. Hence, this interaction of genes and environment in development is too intimate to be separated into genes and environment. Instead of forcing us to accept unalterable behaviors, an understanding of how organisms develop, with equal causal input from genes and from environment, makes it more likely that traits and behaviors can be altered by changing one or more of their developmental causes.

MISUNDERSTANDING THREE: PROXIMATE VS. ULTIMATE CAUSATION

The first reaction of many people to the claim that rape is the result of evolution is to dismiss it as nonsense because rapists are rarely, if ever, motivated by a conscious desire to reproduce. This argument, however, confuses two separate levels of causation: proximate and ultimate.

Proximate causes of behavior are those that operate over the short term — immediate causes of behavior. These are the types of causes with which most people, including most social scientists studying crime, are exclusively concerned. Proximate causes include genes, hormones, physiological structures (including brain mechanisms), conscious motivations, and environmental stimuli (including environmental experiences that affect learning). Proximate explanations have to do with how such developmental or physiological mechanisms cause something to happen; ultimate explanations have to do with why particular proximate mechanisms exist in the first place. That is, they ask why those particular gene/environment interactions were favored by natural selection during our evolutionary history.

Proximate and ultimate levels of explanation are complements, not alternatives. For example, the claim that millions of years of selection caused the human eye to have its current form (an ultimate explanation) is in no way contradictory to the claim that a series of rods and cones enable the eye to relay visual information to the brain (a proximate explanation). Similarly, the claim that learning affects men's rape behavior (i.e., that it is a proximate cause) does not contradict the view that the behavior has evolved. Identifying ultimate causes, however, is important because certain proximate explanations may be incompatible with certain ultimate explanations. This is because certain ultimate explanations specify the existence of certain types of proximate mechanisms. For example, the ultimate explanation that the human eye evolved by natural selection because it increased our ancestors' ability to detect light requires the existence of proximate light-detection mechanisms in the eye. This is a crucial point because, as will be discussed below, certain widely held proximate explanations of rape are incompatible with certain well-established evolutionary principles.

The relationship between proximate and ultimate explanations has often been misunderstood by critics of evolutionary explanations of rape. For example, the argument that rape has not evolved because rapists are not motivated by the conscious desire to reproduce clearly confuses the proximate level of immediate motivation with the ultimate level of reproductive consequences during our evolutionary history.

WHAT AN EVOLUTIONARY PERSPECTIVE CAN CONTRIBUTE

If the common misunderstandings of evolutionary theory are avoided, its contribution to our understanding of serial rape can be evaluated. All aspects of human behavior are in some way the product of our evolutionary history. In the case of serial rape, our evolutionary history is directly relevant to the following questions:

1. Why are males the rapists and females (usually) the victims?
2. Why is rape a horrendous experience for the victim?
3. Why does the mental trauma of rape vary with the victim's age and marital status?
4. Why does the mental trauma of rape vary with the type of sex acts that occur?
5. Why does the mental trauma of rape vary with the degree of visible physical injuries to the victim, but in a direction one might not expect?
6. Why do young males rape more often than older males?
7. Why are young women more often the victims of rape than older women or girls (i.e., pre-pubertal females)?
8. Why is rape more frequent in some situations, such as war, than in others?
9. Why does rape occur in all known cultures?
10. Why are some instances of rape punished in all known cultures?
11. Why are people (especially husbands) often suspicious of an individual's claim to have been raped?
12. Why is rape often treated as a crime against the victim's husband?
13. Why have attempts to reform rape laws met with only limited success?
14. Why does rape exist in many, but not all, other species?
15. Why does rape still occur among humans?
16. How can rape be prevented?

EVOLUTIONARY THEORY

The first step in understanding that evolutionary theory can help answer these questions is understanding how natural selection produces adaptations. The next step is to understand why natural selection has produced different adaptations in males and females, and why some of these lead to the occurrence of rape.

THE EVOLUTIONARY CONCEPT OF ADAPTATION

The key to understanding the power of evolutionary theory is the recognition of natural selection's ability to produce adaptations. Adaptations are phenotypic features (morphological structures, physiological mechanisms, and behaviors) that are present in individual organisms because they were favored by natural selection in the past. Unlike the other evolutionary agents — mutation, drift, and gene flow, which only produce random changes in the gene frequencies pertaining to better adaptation to the environment — selection can act in a directional, cumulative manner over long periods of time, creating complex phenotypic (bodily) designs out of the random genetic variation generated by the other evolutionary agents. An adaptation, then, is a phenotypic solution to a past environmental problem that persistently affected individuals for long periods of evolutionary time and thereby caused cumulative, directional selection. Evolution by selection is not a purposive process; however, it produces, by means of gradual and persistent effects, traits that serve certain functions — that is, adaptations.

The idea of psychological (brain) adaptations should be compelling to anyone who accepts that the rest of the human body has evolved by Darwinian selection. Indeed, the notion that the rest of the body could have been designed by selection without selection simultaneously acting on the brain and the nervous system that control the body is absurd. To those who accept the notion of evolution, it is clear that the human brain must contain evolved structures that process environmental information in a manner that guides feelings and behavior toward ends that were adaptive in past human environments.

ADAPTATIONS ARE DOMAIN SPECIFIC

There are several reasons why the human brain is likely composed of many specialized, domain-specific adaptations. First, the environmental problems our evolutionary ancestors faced were quite specific. Because adaptations are solutions to these specific environmental problems that impinged on ancestors during evolutionary history, they should be equally specific. Second, the fact that much of successful human behavior depends on environmental circumstances that are variable requires that human psychology consist of many specialized mechanisms in order to produce the necessary behavioral plasticity (Symons, 1987). Third, our knowledge of the functional design of non-psychological adaptations indicates that these are special purpose. The human body, for example, is not a single general-purpose adaptation; it is a bundle of innumerable specific adaptations designed to solve specific challenges to reproduction in past environments. Finally, cognitive neuroscientists continue to find evidence that similar specialized adaptations exist in the brain (Gazzaniga, 1989).

It is important to realize that adaptations, whether psychological or non-psychological, do not necessarily increase reproductive success in current environments if those environments differ significantly from past environments. The difference between current and evolutionary historical environments is especially important to keep in mind when one is considering human behavioral adaptations. Today most humans live in environments that have evolutionary novel components. Modern contraception is an example and one that obviously influences the reproductive success of individuals in an evolutionarily novel way.

By-Products

It is also important to realize that not all aspects of living organisms are adaptations. Indeed, the evolutionary biologist George Williams emphasized that, "Adaptation is a special and onerous concept that should be used only where it is really necessary" (1966, pp. 4–5). In addition to adaptations — traits formed directly by selective pressures — living things also consist of by-products — traits formed indirectly by selective pressures. An example of a by-product is the red color of human arterial blood (Symons, 1987). This trait did not arise because of selection in the context of blood-color variation among individuals. That is, redness of arterial blood did not cause individuals with arterial blood of that color to become more frequent in succeeding generations. Instead, selection acting in other contexts gave rise to the trait as an epiphenomenon of adaptations. Human arterial blood is red for two proximate reasons: the chemistry of oxygen and hemoglobin in blood, and human color vision. Hence, the ultimate causation of the color of blood lies in the selective pressures that produced the chemical composition of human blood and human color vision. As will be discussed below, the key legitimate scientific debate about the evolutionary cause of human rape concerns whether rape is a result of rape-specific adaptation or a by-product of other adaptations. That is, does rape result from men's special-purpose psychology designed by selection for rape, or is rape a by-product of special-purpose adaptation to circumstances other than rape?

Male and Female Reproductive Strategies

If female ancestors faced different environmental obstacles to reproduction than those faced by male ancestors in human evolutionary history, natural selection and sexual selection will have formed different adaptations in females and males. The different evolved physical adaptations in men and women means there can be no question that different obstacles were faced by our male and female ancestors. The evolution of these traits could not have occurred without the simultaneous evolution of certain movements (behaviors) and psychological adaptations, both cognitive and emotional, to guide those behaviors. Acknowledging the evolution of physical (non-brain) sex differences while denying the evolution of the accompanying behavioral and psychological sex differences is not scientifically tenable.

Robert Trivers (1972) provided the basic theory of what governs the sexual selection that produces sexual dimorphism in physiology, psychology, and behavior. The key concept is parental effort: the time, energy, and risk that an individual invests in one offspring. Because a population is a collection of interbreeding individuals, the parental effort of all the individuals of one sex is potentially accessible to each member of the opposite sex. Thus, parental effort will be the object of all competition among members of one sex for the opposite sex. Males will compete with other males to gain access to the parental effort of females, and females will compete with other females to gain access to the parental effort of males. The competition, and resulting selection pressure for traits successful in the competition, will be more intense in the sex with less parental investment because they are playing for higher stakes (i.e., the greater parental effort of members of the opposite sex).

From an evolutionary perspective, parental effort is the essential resource, because it determines how many offspring there will be and their likelihood of surviving. The usual way of obtaining this resource from another individual is through sexual copulation, in which one individual's parental investment is, in a sense, "taken" by another and used by that individual to produce its offspring. This is why, if the amount of parental investment is unequal between the sexes, the sex that makes the greater parental investment becomes a limited resource for the other sex. Individuals of the desired sex are then in a position to choose mates, while individuals of the other sex must compete to get chosen.

In humans, the differences in typical parental effort between the sexes are small relative to most mammals, thanks to the large amount of parental effort often exhibited by human males. But in our species, as in most others, males may successfully reproduce by expending only a very small amount of time and energy. In contrast, the minimum effort required for a woman to reproduce successfully includes vastly greater amounts of time, energy, and risk. This meant that our male ancestors had a much greater variation in reproductive success than our female ancestors, and males were selected to compete in various ways to be polygynous (i.e., to obtain multiple mates).

The human evolutionary history of polygyny presented males and females with very different environmental challenges to reproduction. Hence, present-day men and women, as descendants of the members of ancestral populations who responded to those challenges most successfully, have very different psychological adaptations. Men exhibit a greater desire for sex-partner variety than women (Buss, 1994; Symons, 1979; Townsend, 1998), a greater eagerness to copulate, a greater interest in and satisfaction with casual sex, and a greater willingness to expend resources simply in order to copulate. Age is important in the attractiveness of both sexes, but especially in that of women, and the most attractive age in women is much younger than that in men, peaking in the teens or early twenties (Jones, 1996; Quinsey et al., 1993; Quinsey and Lalumière, 1995; Symons, 1979). The large parental investment, compared to males in other species, by human males has also led to the selection for sexual jealousy in human males. The male brain is designed, in part, to increase the probability that a man will direct parental benefits toward his genetic offspring rather than toward another man's. Thus, human anti-cuckoldry mechanisms include the emotions and behaviors associated with sexual jealousy, related forms of mate guarding, and a strong preference for fidelity in mates.

Evolutionary theory also predicts a greater level of mate discrimination by human females than by human males, with the expectation that female choice will often revolve around the male's resources and status, as well as quality of genes. According to Margo Wilson et al. (1997, p. 443), "Perhaps the most important priority for many female animals in their heterosexual interactions is the maintenance of [mate] choice." According to Donald Symons (1979, p. 92), this is because "throughout evolutionary history, perhaps nothing was more critical to a female's reproductive success than the circumstances surrounding copulation and conception. A woman's reproductive success is jeopardized by anything that interferes with her ability: to conceive no children that cannot be raised; to choose the best available father for her children; to induce males to aid her and her children; to maximize the return on sexual favors she bestows and to minimize the risk of violence or withdrawal of support by her husband and kinsmen."

In summary, the males of most species — including humans — are usually more eager to mate than the females, and this enables females to choose among males who are competing with one another for access to them. But getting chosen is not the only way to gain sexual access to females. In rape, the male is circumventing the female's choice.

EVOLUTIONARY EXPLANATIONS OF RAPE

There are currently only two likely candidates for ultimate causes of human rape (for a discussion of the problems with other alternative explanations, see Thornhill and Palmer, 2000):

1. Rape may be an adaptation that was directly favored by selection because it increased male reproductive success by way of increasing mate number. That is, there may be psychological mechanisms designed specifically to influence males to rape in ways that would have produced a net repro-ductive benefit in the past through the fertilization of females.

2. Rape may be only a by-product of other psychological adaptations, especially those involved in the human male's greater visual sexual arousal, greater autonomous sex drive, reduced ability to abstain from sexual activity, much greater desire for sexual variety *per se*, greater willingness to engage in impersonal sex, and less discriminating criteria for sexual partners (Symons, 1979, pp. 264–267; see also Palmer, 1991). As a result of these sexually selected adaptations (designed to increase men's mating success by increasing the number of sexual partners that men acquire), "The typical male is at least slightly sexually attracted to most females, whereas the typical female is not sexually attracted to most males" (Symons, 1979, p. 267). In this view, rape is a by-product, or side effect, of the adaptations producing this situation — that is, rape is not itself an adaptation, because none of the evolved mechanisms involved in rape were selected specifically for rape. Instead, the mechanisms exist

because of their promotion of male reproductive success in contexts other than rape.

PROXIMATE CAUSATION

While the question of "whether there exist psychological adaptations specifically for sexual coercion [or rape], adaptations that entail something more than the simultaneous arousal of sexual and coercive inclinations, has yet to be elucidated" (Wilson et al., 1997, p. 453), an evolutionary approach does challenge much of the accepted wisdom about the proximate causes of rape. On the other hand, such an approach does not imply some of the proximate causes ascribed to it by its critics.

The greatest challenge an evolutionary perspective makes to the standard social science explanations of rape is its claim that rape is the result of evolved differences in sexual desires, emotions, and behaviors. Since the 1970s it has been assumed that Brownmiller's book (*Against Our Will,* 1975) established decisively that rape is a crime of violence rather than passion (Buchwald et al., 1993, p. 1). Although fatal flaws in the arguments used to support this view have been repeatedly exposed (see Ellis, 1989; Hagen, 1979; Palmer, 1988; Symons, 1979; Thornhill and Palmer, 2000), it is still "generally accepted by criminologists, psychologists, and other professionals working with rapists and rape victims that rape is not primarily a sex crime; it is a crime of violence" (Warner, 1980, p. 94; see also Palmer et al., 1999).

While an evolutionary approach does stand in direct contrast to accepted social science wisdom in asserting that sexual motivation is crucial to the behavior of rapists, evolutionists agree with social scientists on another issue. "Evolutionary psychologists, contrary to common expectation, subscribe to a cardinal doctrine of twentieth-century psychology and psychiatry, the potency of early social environment in shaping the adult mind" (Wright, 1994, p. 8). Of course, some individual differences in levels of sexual restraint and willingness to use violence to obtain desired goals may be due to genetic differences (Ellis, 1989). For example, the evolutionary psychologist Linda Mealey (1995) has proposed that men with psychopathy (and thus sociopathy) are a genetically distinct morph, or form, and that normal men do not have the same adaptation (see also Lalumière and Seto, 1998). However, even if this is true, and males with psychopathy are more prone to rape, this is not an argument based on genetic determinism. Receiving genes for psychopathy from parents does not inevitably lead to psychopathy. Psychopathy, like every behavioral trait of the individual, is the result of gene-environment interactions during development, and thus it requires external cues for its manifestation (Lykken, 1995). In any case, in regard to the proximate causes of rape, "a larger role is played by genetic commonalities: by a generic species-wide developmental program that absorbs information from the social environment and adjusts the maturing mind accordingly" (Wright, 1994, p. 8).

The evolutionary model views the human brain as a bundle of numerous specialized adaptations created by specific, evolved gene-environment interactions during their ontogeny. After their ontogenetic construction, these adaptations interact with specific aspects of the environment to produce rape. Essentially all men have sexual psychological adaptations designed for obtaining a large number of mates.

However, heritable adjustments in the details of certain sexual adaptations in response to environmental cues processed during development probably create some individual differences in ease of activation of these adaptations. The mechanisms that make such adjustments are facultative — that is, dependent on specific environmental variables. Even if there are significant genetic differences among individual men in some or all of the psychological adaptations that underlie rape, fully understanding and reducing rape require determination of how environmental differences affect the propensity to rape. This is also the case if the psychological adaptations that generate rape reflect multiple sexual adaptations that exist in a mix in the population of men as a result of frequency-dependent selection (as may be true of psychopathic vs. non-psychopathic phenotypes, for example).

It is important to realize that, "This emphasis on psychological development doesn't leave us back where social scientists were twenty-five years ago, attributing everything they saw to often unspecified 'environmental forces'" (Wright, 1994, p. 82). Instead, an understanding of the ultimate evolutionary reasons why humans have facultative adaptations that respond to variables in the social environment greatly enhances our ability to specify what social variables influence development in what ways. The first step in understanding how the "social environment" (that is, the behavior of other people) influences the ontogeny of male sexuality is to remember the crucial finding from the evidence on non-human species: male pursuit of unwilling females commonly emerges from ontogenies that lack any sexual socialization. That is, rape occurs even when males are not encouraged to rape. Hence, more effective ways of deterring males from raping must be sought, and an evolutionary approach can contribute to such efforts.

PRACTICAL IMPLICATIONS FOR PREVENTING RAPE

Like current approaches to rape, an evolutionary approach suggests that educational programs for young men and women, and other people in society, may help prevent rape. Unlike most current approaches, an evolutionary approach suggests that these programs must focus on evolved male sexual desires and how they differ from the evolved sexual desires of females. The goal of many current educational programs (e.g., Fonow et al., 1992; Parrot, 1991; Syzmanski et al., 1993; Ward, 1995) is to persuade people that sex is not a motivating factor in rape. In essence, such "education" tells boys that, as long as their acts are motivated by sexual desire, they cannot be committing rape. In contrast, an evolutionarily informed education program might start by getting young men to acknowledge the extent and nature of their sexual impulses and then explaining why human males have evolved to be that way. Then, the fallacy of the naturalistic fallacy should be strenuously emphasized — that a young man's evolved sexual desires offer him no excuse whatsoever for raping a woman. A detailed description of severe punishments for rape might then be presented.

In addition to instruction in self-defense, a program of anti-rape education for females should begin with the same explanation of male sexual adaptations that are used in the program for males. This should be followed by a skeptical discussion of the popular notion that females share the exact same desires. Once the differences in evolved male and female sexuality have been established, the factors influencing a woman's chances of being raped should be discussed. This means challenging the popular notion that a woman's sexual attractiveness is irrelevant to her chances of being raped. A chart showing the close parallel between the age distribution of rape victims and ages of peak female attractiveness (Thornhill and Thornhill, 1983) might help make this point. However, it should be emphasized that while a female's appearance is likely to influence her chances of being raped, this does not imply that the rapist's punishment for the crime should be lessened.

The evolutionary perspective also holds great potential for improving the treatment of the post-rape mental pain of rape victims and of their significant others. By acknowledging the sexual aspect of rape, and considering the evolutionary consequences of various sex acts for females of different ages, an evolutionary approach has been able to successfully predict variations in the type and degree of mental pain experienced by victims of different forms of sexual assaults (see Thornhhill and Palmer, 2000). This knowledge, in conjunction with an understanding of the evolutionary significance of pain, could help lead to more efficient recovery programs for victims.

An evolutionary approach can also lead to changes in rape laws by helping to explain disturbing aspects of traditional rape laws. Foremost among social scientists' concerns about the laws regarding rape is the fact that rape has traditionally been defined and punished not from the victim's perspective but from a male perspective, and particularly from the perspective of the victim's mate. Also, there has been an exaggerated degree of skepticism exhibited toward the claims of rape victims, accompanied by the view that a victim's past sexual behavior is somehow relevant to her claim of being raped. We suggest that the reason the rape-law-reform movement has met with only limited success in changing these features of rape law is that the reformers are trying to change attitudes toward rape in the absence of an understanding of the evolved psychological mechanisms that produce those attitudes.

Rape has been perceived as a crime against the victim's mate because, throughout evolutionary history, rape threatened the mate's reproductive success by potentially lowering his paternity certainty. Hence, selection favored males who responded to the possible rape of their wives in certain ways. One of those responses was to be suspicious that the copulation was actually a rape. If the male perceived from his mate's actions that she had mated with other males under any number of circumstances, and that she was likely to continue to do so, his best evolutionary option was probably to abandon her, hence the interest of mates of rape victims in evidence of prior sexual promiscuity, physical injury indicating resistance, and collaborating testimony.

Far from being a moral prescription about male behavior, this evolutionary analysis of why males and the rape laws they have formulated are so uncharitable toward victims' claims of rape may be of help to those seeking changes in the rape laws. Indeed, this help may already be starting to manifest itself. The legal scholars Owen Jones and Jack Beckstrom, who have been introducing lawyers and law professors to the evolutionary reasons for rape in their writings and at law conferences, have argued that a better understanding of the evolved psychological mechanisms influencing patterns of rape may make law more effective in deterring rape

(Beckstrom, 1993; Jones, 1999). To the extent that knowledge about the causes of things becomes a part of the environment and increases our ability to change things, men who are made aware of the evolutionary reasons for their suspicions about their wives' or girlfriends' claims of rape should be in a better position to change their reactions to such claims.

The idea that punishment can influence the frequency of rape is far from unique to the evolutionary approach, as is evident from the fact that rape is punished in all known societies (Palmer, 1989). However, only the evolutionary approach asks why, and to what degree, certain environmental stimuli constitute punishment (Wright, 1994). Because psychological adaptations change in sex-specific ways over the course of an individual's life in correspondence to the environmental challenges our ancestors faced in their various life stages (Geary, 1998), an individual is expected to perceive as punishments environmental conditions that were particularly severe obstacles to the reproductive success of our ancestors of the same age and same sex as that individual. Because the majority of rapes are committed by males in their teens or their twenties, the punishments most effective in deterring rape may correspond to the obstacles faced by our male ancestors at those ages. It is during the teens and the twenties that competition for status and for sexual access to females is most intense and most crucial to a male's reproductive success; therefore, punishments that impair such competition may be the most effective deterrents to further rape.

It is important to find punishments that not only deter potential first-time rapists but also potential repeat rapists because data on recidivism among convicted rapists indicate that rape is likely to be a serial crime. Lalumière and Quinsey (1999) report from follow-up studies of criminal offenders that rapists are more likely to commit a new sex offense than offenders who have never committed a sex offense. Using an evolutionarily informed approach, these researchers have also been able to identify factors characterizing sex offenders in general, and the ones most likely to be repeat sex offenders. Among the variables they have identified are that the rapist did not live with both biological parents to age 16, the rapist either never married or never lived common law, and the rapist had deviant (statistically rare) results on phallometric tests (meaning arousal preference for nonconsensual sex) and diagnosis of personality disorder (psychopathy) (also see Malamuth and Heilmann, 1998). The deviant arousal is not surprising as a variable predicting males who are rapists, nor is psychopathy. The other two variables mentioned also are understandable in evolutionary terms. The absence of biological parents during upbringing is expected to trigger coercive sexual tactics because, in human evolutionary history, the reduction or absence of parental investment for boys would have been associated with reduced resources for obtaining consensual mates upon reaching adulthood. Resources allow men consensual sex, and in pre-industrial societies parents, including fathers, provided important resources. Selection, therefore, is expected to have shaped male sexual development such that the amount of parental investment during rearing is a cue that tracks males into consensual vs. nonconsensual sexual pursuits. The variable involving no long-term mating relationship is related. Rape-prone males have relatively few relationships with women that involve commitment (see also Malamuth and Heilmann, 1998), in part due to their limited ability to invest in women. The implication of these findings is that rape proneness could be reduced by increased parental investment (and possible surrogates of it) during boys' development.

Another topic illustrates the importance of adopting a view of human behavior informed by modern evolutionary theory and modern concepts of biology. A debate over anti-androgen drugs (so-called "chemical castration") in the treatment of rapists is now underway in several states. The popular claim that rape is caused by non-biological cultural forces and has nothing to do with sexual desire plays a central role in this debate (see Jones, 1999; Palmer et al., 1999). Once the true meaning of biology is grasped, the argument that anti-androgen drugs should not be used because they influence only the biological aspects of human behavior becomes absurd. Rape, like every other behavior of living things, is biological; hence, any attempt to change this behavior will, by definition, involve influencing human biology. In view of the pervasiveness of the view that rapists are not sexually motivated, it is also not surprising that "many experts say that castration will not work because rape is not a crime about sex, but rather a crime about power and violence" (Hicks, 1993, p. 647). Given the flaws in the view that rapists are not sexually motivated, this is also a questionable reason for rejecting chemical means of preventing recidivism among rapists. This does not mean that anti-androgen drugs should automatically be used in the treatment of sex offenders. There are numerous practical and ethical problems surrounding such use; however, any decision as to whether or not to use drugs should be based on how they actually affect behavior, not on mistaken views about the role of biology and sex in rape.

CONCLUSION

Although certain questions still remain about the ultimate causes of human rape, an evolutionary approach can help identify proximate causes of rape which in turn may lead to more efficient means of lowering the frequency of rape. Important here is the view that the ultimate causes of rape lie in the evolution of different proximate mechanisms governing sexual emotions and behaviors in males and females. This suggests the need for a profound reevaluation of the popular view that rapists are not motivated by sexual desires. Far from being a claim that rape is good and/or inevitable, such a view is the key to identifying the environmental factors that are a proximate cause of rape. This in turn can lead to ways of more effectively preventing the crime of rape and its repetition.

REFERENCES

Alexander, R. (1979). *Darwinism and Human Affairs.* Seattle: University of Washington Press.

Alexander, R. (1987). *The Biology of Moral Systems.* New York: Aldine de Gruyter.

Baron, L. (1985). Does rape contribute to reproductive success? Evaluations of sociobiological views of rape. *International Journal of Women's Studies,* 8:266–277.

Beckstrom, J. (1993). *Darwinism Applied: Evolutionary Paths to Social Goals.* New York: Praeger.

Blackman, J. (1985). The language of sexual violence: more than a matter of semantics. In Sunday, S. and Tobach, E. (Eds.), *Violence Against Women: A Critique of the Sociobiology of Rape* (pp. 115–128). New York: Gordian Press.

Brownmiller, S. (1975). *Against Our Will: Men, Women, and Rape.* New York: Simon and Schuster.

Buchwald, E., Fletcher, P., and Roth, M. (1993). Editor's preface. In Buchwald, E. et al. (Eds.), *Transforming a Rape Culture* (pp. 1–2). Minneapolis, MN: Milkweed.

Buss, D. (1994). *The Evolution of Desire: Strategies of Human Mating.* New York: Basic Books.

Dusek, V. (1984). Sociobiology and rape. *Science for the People,* 16:10–16.

Ellis, L. (1989). *Theories of Rape: Inquires into the Causes of Sexual Aggression.* New York: Hemisphere.

Fausto-Sterling, A. (1985). *Myths of Gender: Biological Theories about Women and Men.* New York: Basic Books.

Fonow, M., Richardson, L., and Wemmerus, V. (1992). Feminist rape education: does it work? *Gender and Society,* 6:108–121.

Gazzaniga, M. (1989). Organization of the human brain. *Science,* 245:947–952.

Geary, D. (1998). *Male, Female: The Evolution of Human Sex Differences.* Washington, D.C.: American Psychological Association.

Gould, S. and Lewontin, R. (1979). The spandrels of San Marco and the Panglossian paradigm: a critique of the adaptationist program. *Proceedings of the Royal Society of London B,* 205: 581–598.

Gray, R. (1997). "In the belly of the monster": feminism, developmental systems, and evolutionary explanations. In Gowaty, P. (Ed.) *Feminism and Evolutionary Biology* (pp. 385–414). New York: Chapman & Hall.

Hagen, R. (1979). *The Biosexual Factor.* New York: Doubleday.

Hicks, P. (1993). Comment: castration of sexual offenders, legal and ethical issues. *Journal of Legal Medicine,* 14: 641–644.

Jones, D. (1996). *Physical Attractiveness and the Theory of Sexual Selection: Results from Five Populations.* Ann Arbor: Museum of Anthropology, University of Michigan.

Jones, O. (1999). Sex, culture and the biology of rape. *California Law Review,* 87:827–942.

Kitcher, P. (1985). Vaulting ambition: sociobiology and the quest for human nature. Cambridge, MA: MIT Press.

Lalumière, M. and Quinsey, V. (1999) A Darwinian interpretation of individual differences in male propensity for sexual aggression. *Jurimetrics,* 39:201–216.

Lalumière, M. and Seto, M. (1998). What's wrong with psychopaths? Defining the causes and effects of psychopathy. *Psychiatry Rounds,* 2(6).

Lykken, D. (1995). *The Antisocial Personalities.* Hillsdale, NJ: Erlbaum.

Malamuth, N. and Heilmann, M. (1998). Evolutionary psychology and sexual aggression. In Crawford, C. and Krebs, D. (Eds.) *Handbook of Evolutionary Psychology* (pp. 515–542). New York: Erlbaum.

Maynard Smith, J. (1997). Commentary. In Gowaty, P. (Ed.) *Feminism and Evolutionary Biology: Boundaries, Intersections, and Frontiers* (pp. 522–526). New York: Chapman & Hall.

Mealey, L. (1995). The sociobiology of sociopathy: an integrated evolutionary model. *Behavioral and Brain Sciences,* 18:523–541.

Moore, G. (1903). *Principia Ethica.* Cambridge: Cambridge University Press.

Palmer, C. (1988). Twelve reasons why rape is not sexually motivated: a skeptical examination. *Journal of Sex Research,* 25(4):512–530.

Palmer, C. (1989). Is rape a cultural universal? A re-examination of the ethnographic evidence. *Ethnology,* 28:1–16.

Palmer, C. (1991). Human rape: adaptation or by-product? *Journal of Sex Research,* 28:365–386.

Palmer, C., DiBari, D., and Wright, S. (1999). Is it sex yet? Theoretical and practical implications of the debate over rapists' motives. *Jurimetrics,* 39:271–282.

Parrot, A. (1991). Vital childhood lessons: the role of parenting in preventing sexual coercion. In Grauerholz, E. and Koralewski, M. (Eds.), *Sexual Coercion* (pp. 123–132). Lexington, MA: Lexington.

Quinsey, V. and Lalumière, M. (1995). Evolutionary perspectives on sexual offending. *Sexual Abuse,* 7:301–315.

Quinsey, V., Rice, M., Harris, G., and Reid, K. (1993). The phylogenetic and ontogenetic development of sexual age preferences in males: conceptual and measurement issues. In Barbaree, H. et al. (Eds.), *The Juvenile Sex Offender* (pp. 143–163). New York: Guilford.

Sahlins, M. (1976). *The Use and Abuse of Biology: An Anthropological Critique of Sociobiology.* Ann Arbor: University of Michigan Press.

Schwendinger, J. and Schwendinger H. (1985). *Homo economicus* as rapist. In Sunday, S. and Tobach, E. (Eds.), *Violence against Women: A Critique of the Sociobiology of Rape* (pp. 85–114). New York: Gordian Press.

Shields, W. and Shields, L. (1983). Forcible rape: an evolutionary perspective. *Ethology and Sociobiology,* 4:115–136.

Sunday, S. (1985). Introduction. In Sunday, S. and Tobach, E. (Eds.), *Violence against Women: A Critique of the Sociobiology of Rape* (pp. 1–12). New York: Gordian Press.

Sunday, S. and Tobach, E. (Eds). (1985). *Violence against Women: A Critique of the Sociobiology of Rape.* New York: Gordian Press.

Symons, D. (1979). *The Evolution of Human Sexuality.* New York: Oxford University Press.

Symons, D. (1987). If we're all Darwinians, what's the fuss about? In Crawford, C., Smith, M., and Krebs, D. (Eds.), *Sociobiology and Psychology: Ideas, Issues and Applications* (pp. 121–146). Hillsdale, NJ: Erlbaum.

Syzmanski, L.A., Devlin, J., and Vyse, S. (1993). Gender role and attitudes toward rape in male and female college students. *Sex Roles,* 29:37–57.

Thiessen, D. (1983). The Unseen Roots of Rape: The Theoretical Untouchable. Paper presented at 1983 meetings of American Psychological Association, published in *Revue Europeenne des Sciences Sociales,* 24:9–40, 1986.

Thornhill, R. (1980). Rape in Panorpa scorpionflies and a general rape hypothesis. *Animal Behavior,* 28:52–59.

Thornhill, R. and Palmer, C. (2000). *A Natural History of Rape: The Biological Bases of Sexual Coercion.* Cambridge, MA: MIT Press.

Thornhill, R. and Thornhill, N. (1983). Human rape: an evolutionary analysis. *Ethology and Sociobiology,* 4:137–173.

Townsend, J. (1998). *What Women Want — What Men Want: Why the Sexes Still See Love and Commitment So Differently.* New York: Oxford University Press.

Trivers, R. (1972). Parental investment and sexual selection. In Campbell, B. (Ed.), *Sexual Selection and the Descent of Man, 1871–1971* (pp. 136–179). Chicago: Aldine.

Ward, C. (1995). *Attitudes Toward Rape: Feminist and Social Psychological Perspectives.* New York: Sage.

Warner, C. (1980). *Rape and Sexual Assault: Management and Intervention.* Germantown, MD: Aspen.

Williams, G. (1966). *Adaptation and Natural Selection.* Princeton, NJ: Princeton University Press.

Wilson, M., Daly, M., and Scheib, J. (1997). Femicide: an evolutionary psychological perspective. In Gowaty, P. (Ed.), *Feminism and Evolutionary Biology* (pp. 431–465). New York: Chapman & Hall.

Wright, R. (1994). *The Moral Animal.* New York: Vintage.

4 Serial Arson: Repetitive Firesetting and Pyromania

Mary Mavromatis

CONTENTS

0-8493-2236-7/00/$0.00+$.50
© 2000 by CRC Press LLC

INTRODUCTION

Fire is symbolic of life force and passion and is of universal fascination. In mythology, it was the prize that had to be stolen from the gods to benefit mankind. The mastery over fire represents civilization's mastery over natural forces. Fire is of intense interest, but this interest and pleasure are sublimated so that fire can be used for the good of the community. Only in a few does the desire to start fires and to use them destructively escape societal inhibitions.

Firesetting is a complex symptom, a behavior that is the end product of various motivations and factors. Much of the confusion surrounding the nature of firesetting behavior is derived from this complexity. Arson for profit is beyond the scope of our investigations, and there is no apparent connection between arson for profit and pathological firesetting. Unless the firesetter is a professional torch, the firesetting tends not to be repeated.

Some firesetters with singular motives, such as revenge or jealousy, and singular targets, such as girlfriends who betrayed them or bosses who fired them, set only a single fire; however, even among this class of "motivated" firesetters, firesetting is often repeated. The motives may be more complex and less rational than they might appear at first glance. A concrete motive may be offered as an explanation for that particular fire, but the pattern of repetitive firesetting indicates a more pathological process, and the motive is often illogical and/or trivial (see Case 3 in case-report section).

Steckel (1924) identifies the significant peculiarity of arson that often "… deed and motives fail to show any logical relationship" (p. 124). This makes arson an unusual crime. Most types of crimes are committed with rather clear motives (Table 1).

Firesetting begins as a common behavior in young children (especially boys). We all have experienced the pleasure of watching a campfire or bonfire. There is a universal attraction to fire, but there exists no other behavior that starts out as being so harmless (child's play) and becomes so destructive. What intrigues us most about arson, especially serial arson and/or pyromania, is that it is a crime least associated with violence and most associated with serious psychopathology. It is in its end result a violent, destructive act, oftentimes lethal, which may begin quietly, passively, and even playfully. Pyromaniacs tend not to be violent offenders who plan on causing bodily harm; in fact, they typically tend to dissociate themselves from the damage to human life that might result from their fires. As we shall see later on in the section on childhood firesetting, playful firesetting is a common activity of almost universal appeal among latency-age boys. When we compare firesetting to other crimes such as murder or rape, we observe that the violence and aggression are certainly less personal and less direct. This, of course, does not make it any less dangerous a crime, as many individuals have their lost their lives to arson and firesetting, but it does provide a contrast and contradiction to our usual understanding of the "criminal mind."

In this chapter, I hope to review the concepts and clinical presentations of pathological firesetting and pyromania. I will discuss the history, theories, controversy, clinical patterns, developmental progression, associated phenomena, profiles, recidivism, and treatments of pathological firesetters.

TABLE 1
Motives for Arson

Rational Motives

Direct economic gain (e.g., to collect on an insurance policy)
Indirect economic gain (e.g., setting fire to a competitor's business)
Terrorism (e.g., setting fire to abortion clinics)
Concealment (to hide a crime or destroy criminal evidence)

Pathological Firesetting

Revenge
Jealousy
Vanity (setting fire to be a hero by being the first one on the scene)
Fire buff (enjoys the fire trucks and fire paraphernalia)
Pyromania — no motive other than impulse or excitement of setting a fire
   "Transitional pyromania" — other motives inferred
   "True pyromania" (corresponds to DSM-IV diagnosis)
   Fire fetishist — sets the fire for the purpose of sexual gratification
Severe psychopathology such as psychosis
Sociopathy or conduct disorder (antisocial acts directed against authority)
Mental retardation
Alcohol intoxication
Communicative arson

ARSON

Arson is a law enforcement term used to describe a deliberate act of firesetting. Many law enforcement workers consider arson a neglected crime. Each year, the FBI compiles and issues a uniform crime report in which crimes are classified as "Part I" or "Part II." In these reports, arson is given a secondary classification along with drunken driving, forgery, and vagrancy. It is not included with the more "serious" crimes of murder, rape, and robbery. Arrests for arson are made in only a small percentage of fires, but arson is the major cause of deaths, injuries, and dollar loss involving commercial properties and the second leading cause of deaths in residential fires. Arson is a crime that is simple to commit, yet it is difficult to detect and prosecute arson and to obtain direct evidence. Most firesetters can easily set a fire without being seen.

SERIAL ARSON

Serial arson is a term used to describe repetitive acts of firesetting. Serial arson is not a diagnosis or a motive for firesetting. It is only a term used to describe a pattern of repetitive firesetting frequently encountered in revenge or terrorist arsons or in the case of pyromaniacs. Serial arson does not appear to strike fear into the public in the same manner that serial homicide (e.g., the Boston Strangler) or serial rape does, even though the damage and loss of life can be much greater. In fact, several serial murderers were serial arsonists before their killing sprees. Their firesetting typically went undetected (see the section on the correlation between serial murder and serial arson).

PYROMANIA

"Pyromania has appeared for a long time as an unsolved psychological riddle" (Steckel, p. 124). So begins Steckel's 1924 chapter on pyromania. It appears that this subject still remains for the most part an unsolved psychological riddle. In fact, there exists considerable debate as to whether pyromania represents a valid diagnosis.

Pyromania is a term that appears to be used differently by different sources. This confusion about definition has spawned considerable debate and controversy as to whether or not pyromania even exists. The *Diagnostics and Statistical Manual of Mental Disorders* (DSM-IV) classifies pyromania under the category of Impulse Control Disorders Not Otherwise Classified (see Table 2). According to the DSM-IV, "The essential feature of pyromania is the presence of multiple episodes of deliberate and purposeful firesetting" (pp. 614–615). Other essential characteristics are the experience of "tension or affective arousal before the act" and a "fascination with, interest in, curiosity about, or attraction to fire and its situational context." Additionally, there is "pleasure, gratification, or relief when setting fires or when witnessing or participating in their aftermath." There is no rational motive for firesetting, and "the firesetting is not better accounted for by conduct disorder, a manic episode, or antisocial personality disorder." In addition, the diagnosis of "pyromania should also not be given when firesetting results from impaired judgment associated with dementia, mental retardation, or substance intoxication." According to the DSM-IV, the prevalence of pyromania is described as being "apparently rare."

TABLE 2
DSM-IV Diagnostic Criteria for Pyromania

A. Deliberate and purposeful firesetting on more than one occasion
B. Tension or affective arousal before the act
C. Fascination with, interest in, curiosity about, or attraction to fire and its situational contexts (e.g., paraphernalia, uses, consequences)
D. Pleasure, gratification, or relief when setting fires, or when witnessing or participating in this aftermath
E. Firesetting not done for monetary gain, as an expression of sociopolitical ideology, to conceal criminal activity, to express anger or vengeance, to improve one's living circumstances, in response to a delusion or hallucination, or as a result of impaired judgment (e.g., in dementia, mental retardation, substance intoxication)
F. Firesetting not better accounted for by conduct disorder, a manic episode, or antisocial personality disorder

Source: From the *Diagnostic and Statistical Manual of Mental Disorders,* 4th ed., American Psychiatric Association, Washington, D.C., 1994. With permission.

Lewis and Yarnell (1951) present a very similar definition of pyromania. After eliminating cases involving children, female firesetters, and firesetters for which there was incomplete information or followup, Lewis and Yarnell (1951) came up with a series of 1145 adult males over the age of 15 years who engaged in what they termed "pathological firesetting" (see Table 3). *Pathological firesetting* is firesetting other than that performed for profit or material advantage. Although there may exist a stated motive, the behavior and the reasoning are often very pathological. The reason they included the entire gamut of pathological firesetters in their study is because they felt that many of these cases represented what they termed "transitional cases of pyromania." They also felt that all the representative types of firesetting that were for other than profit motives shared many similar characteristics. These individuals were driven by stated motives which included revenge, vanity, jealousy, etc., but their motives also included excitement about setting the fire. The cases that Lewis and Yarnell (1951) identified as "pyromaniacs" were those individuals who could offer no motive for the act except for "irresistible impulse." Even among those firesetters who offered no motive, Lewis and Yarnell (1951) eliminated from that category those firesetters who appeared to have some implied motive, such as revenge if the fire, for example, was set at the property of a relative or family member whom they were angry with. Among their 1145 adult male cases, a relatively large number of 688 provided no apparent motive. Of those, though, 241 appeared to have some motive such as to help the firemen (the "would-be heroes") or the enjoyment of the destruction of property (conduct disorder), while 447 could say only that something within them "forced them to set fires" and offered no motive whatsoever. They represented approximately 40% of the sample and were loosely referred to as pyromaniacs. However, of these 447, Lewis and Yarnell (1951) felt that only 50 (or approximately 4% of the entire sample) fit the strict criteria for "pyromania" — no other motive, no alcoholism or alcohol use, no possibility that the fire was motivated by revenge or jealousy, no organicity, no mental retardation, and no other serious psychiatric illnesses such as psychoses or schizophrenia. "The reasons for the fires are unknown; the act is so little their own that they feel no responsibility for the crime. ...These offenders are able to give a classical description of the irresistible impulse. They describe the mounting tension, the restlessness, the urge for motion, the conversion symptoms such as headaches, palpitations, ringing in the ears, and the gradual merging of their identity into a state of unreality; then the fires are set" (p. 87). This description of "true pyromania" is a narrow description and fits very closely with what is described in the DSM-IV criteria (see Table 2); however, the DSM-IV criteria are somewhat broader in that they may include those who derive direct sexual satisfaction from watching the fires. In the Lewis and Yarnell study, 40 men were in this group. What is interesting is that Lewis and Yarnell separated out these cases as not being "true pyromania."

The DSM-IV criteria, current psychiatric literature, and law enforcement literature group together the "true pyromaniacs" with the firesetters who become sexually aroused. However, some authors consider pyromaniacs to be only those who derive sexual satisfaction from watching a fire they have set — in other words, someone for whom the fire or the act of setting a fire is a fetish. On the other hand, Lewis and Yarnell (1951) observed that the "true pyromaniac" is conscious of no sexual

TABLE 3
Summary of Lewis and Yarnell's Study

Total in series: 1145 adult males (over age 15)

Motives
Tramps: 74
Psychosis: 154
Revenge: 266
    Against employers or institutions: 174
    Against women who spurned them or their rivals: 92
Would-be heros: 69
Volunteer firemen or fire buffs: 98
Pyromaniacs: 447 (no motives given other than excitement or impulse)
    "True pyromaniacs": 50
    Fire fetishists: 40

Intelligence
Mental retardation: 48%
Borderline retardation: 22%
Dull normal to low average: 13%
Average to superior: 17%

Age
Predominantly between age of 16 and 28
Peak incidence at 17

Sex
Predominantly male

Race
Predominantly white

Physical defects
Frequent

Enuresis
Present in some

Mental disorders
"Psychopathy" (sociopathic personality), psychosis

Alcoholism
Alcohol use common

Suicidality
In some cases, fires set as a means of suicide or accompanying a suicide
  attempt

Social history
Social, marital, and sexual adjustments tend to be poor; typically
  isolated young men, often from broken homes

feelings during the firesetting act. The firesetting act is not a substitute for sexual gratification, and masturbation and orgasm are not a part of the ritual for the "true pyromaniac."

In this chapter, I will refer to pyromania as the concept used by DSM-IV, which includes the "true pyromaniacs" of Lewis and Yarnell as well as the fire fetishists whom, I believe, share in common the essential features of a buildup in tension and a release once the fires are set.

Arson investigators label anyone who sets a fire with no apparent rational motive a "pyro" and utilize the concept of irresistible impulse (more about the derivation of this term later). Many authors across various fields and across history point out that this has been a difficult concept to define. At what point does the impulse to satisfy an urge become "irresistible?" Arson investigators have a similar familiarity with what they term "sex pyros" — individuals who obtain sexual gratification including masturbation and orgasms from setting fires. Arson investigators correctly describe the "sex pyro" as a fetishist. The fetish is the object of sexual desire and the means to gratification (in this case, fire). Because arson investigators include in their definition of pyromaniacs (those who set fires without rational motive) individuals with mental retardation, the psychotic, and individuals who set vanity fires or recognition fires, they are using the broader definition of pyromania described by Lewis and Yarnell as "pathological firesetting."

A HISTORY OF THE CONCEPT OF PYROMANIA

During the 19th century, a huge literature focused on pyromania. This interest (even to this day) appears not to have been proportional to the incidence or the significance of the condition, but rather was a function of conflicting psychological theories as well as conflicting medical and legal opinions.

Pinel, a product of the humanitarian movement arising from the French Revolution, advocated humane treatment of the insane. He described a kind of insanity in which judgment was affected while intellectual capabilities remained intact. He termed this *manie sans delire* (insanity without delirium). Esquirol used the same concept but coined the term *monomanie,* an insanity of circumscribed nature. This term was then expanded to the concept of *instinctive monomanie*, which he described as an involuntary, irresistible impulse. This concept persists into our present day understanding and definition of pyromania. M. Marc was the first to classify firesetters under the heading of monomanie as *monomanie incendiarie* or pyromania. A parallel development took place in the German literature.

Throughout the 1800s the debate raged as to whether or not monomania or pyromania qualified as legal insanity — thus removing the criminal responsibility for the act from the firesetter. Was the person legally responsible if motivated by an irresistible impulse to burn and an absence of any other motive? How irresistible did an impulse have to be? Different countries as well as different historical contexts produced various opinions.

Under English law, as commented on by Baker in 1892, the question of responsibility was rarely considered. In America, especially in the latter part of the 1800s, pyromania was not acknowledged; firesetting was either a criminal act or a product of a diseased brain, as opposed to a monomania in which intellectual facilities remained intact. The French appeared to have been the only ones to accept the concept of pyromania on an ongoing basis. The German writers throughout the 1800s appeared to focus on firesetters as predominantly young women of deficient intellect, typically at the age of puberty.

In 1872 and 1883, Krafft-Ebing published a series of case reports on firesetters who were abused servant girls and nursemaids and who were depressed and fearful. Jasper, in 1909, reported that these girls were homesick and unhappy and set fires in the hope of destroying their source of employment (the children and home they cared for) so that they could be allowed to return home. A modern-day version of this motive for firesetting may be present in what was dubbed by the press as the Swiss "nanny" case. A young woman named Olivia Riner, who was actually an *au pair* (close to the profile of the adolescent servant girl far from home as opposed to the professional nanny), was accused of setting fire to a baby under her care. Although she was acquitted, there was strong evidence that she did set the fire, and she was acquitted largely because the prosecution could find no convincing apparent motive. A reporter who covered the story, Joyce Egington, saw the *au pair* system as creating isolation in young women far from home and drew the parallel to the Central European nursemaids described by Jasper.

Schmid (1914) was the first psychoanalyst to review the literature and present case reports. He personally studied 52 cases in which revenge was seen as a common motive. In his cases, he noted that the fires were set when individuals were faced with significant psychological challenges to which they could not adapt or find a solution. He saw the firesetting as a displacement of suicidal urges brought about by having to face a painful decision. Schmid was also the first to report the case of a firesetter who masturbated with "sexual orgasms" while watching a fire. This was the first of many descriptions of individuals who are fire fetishists.

Steckle (1924) felt that firesetting and pyromania had a "sexual root." He noted that fire dreams occurred previous to the firesetting, some on the night before the fire was set, and that many firesetters were compulsive masturbators. He also observed that many authors considered menstruation to be a predisposing factor to firesetting (particularly the 19th-century German literature).

Cobbin, in a 1934 study, elaborated on the role of alcohol intoxication in firesetting. He noted that intoxication lowers normal inhibitions and so allows for usually latent and repressed impulses to manifest themselves, for example, in firesetting. Although the primary motive may be revenge, jealousy, or vanity, alcohol intoxication can be a crucial factor. Lewis and Yarnell (1951) came to a similar conclusion in many of their cases. Particularly after the age of 20, alcoholism was found to accompany firesetting with increasing frequency.

In 1951, Lewis and Yarnell published their comprehensive study of pathological firesetting. The sheer number of cases studied and presented in this book is remarkable and has yet to be duplicated. Approximately 2000 cases were examined, out of which, as mentioned previously, 1145 adult male cases were reported on. Additionally, cases of childhood firesetters and female setters are included in the book. This monograph is written in the tradition of descriptive psychiatry; general comments and conclusions relate specifically to the clinical material without theoretical bias.

Contemporary authors have, as in the past, disagreed as to the validity or usefulness of pyromania as a clinical diagnosis (see "Does Pyromania Exist?" section). Some authors argue that pyromania is so rare that it is more useful to view firesetting as a complex symptom found across a spectrum of psychiatric disorders and that it is "best understood through a social skills deficit-social learning model" (Geller, 1987, p. 505).

Another contemporary version of Jasper's servant girls burning their place of employment so that they can return home is the phenomenon of psychiatric patients setting fires to change the location of psychiatric services. Geller (1983) believes this to be a result of deinstitutionalization, with patients trying to communicate their unhappiness with their current care (i.e., trying to get back into the hospital). He refers to his type of firesetting as "communicative arson" (see Table 1).

PATHOLOGICAL FIRESETTING

Although it was written half a century ago, Lewis and Yarnell's monograph on pyromania and pathological firesetting provides the most comprehensive, descriptive, understandable, and bias-free descriptions of these conditions, thus it would be most constructive for the reader to review their work. It might be expected that profiles and statistics regarding firesetters would be significantly different now from what they were half a century previously, given that American culture is now so different; however, this may not be the case. For example, a recent study in 1992 by Leong described a high incidence of psychoses in individuals who are homeless and mentally disordered (and substance abusing) in their study sample (29 patients) of firesetters. He even described a "new" phenomenon of the homeless who set fires to stay warm. Interestingly, Lewis and Yarnell also described a large number of patients with serious pathology and psychoses and also described a class of firesetter they called "vagrant."

Lewis and Yarnell (1951) began their study by reviewing approximately 2000 cases they had obtained from the national board of fire underwriters (see Table 3). Out of these cases, they obtained sufficient information, including some followup, on 1145 adult males 15 and over (they also have data on 201 female adults). Of this group, 154 men were severely psychotic at the time the fire was set and 266 committed arson out of a specific revenge motive; of the latter, 174 set the fire to get back at an employer, an institution, or someone who had insulted them and 92 set the fire to get back at someone who had spurned them. Sixty-nine of the firesetters were would-be heroes (more about that later), and 98 were volunteer firemen or fire "buffs." There was also, as mentioned previously, a group referred to as vagrants. Then there were the pyromaniacs — those loosely classified as having no clear motives and impelled to make the fires because of an "irresistible impulse." The pyromaniacs, according to Lewis and Yarnell, characteristically make their fires impulsively. No significant thought is given to people who may be trapped by the fire. Afterwards, usually no particular concern is demonstrated for those who may have died in the fire. The motivation is not to destroy property (as opposed to those who set revenge fires), but to light the fire simply for the purpose of watching the fire, although Lewis and Yarnell noted that with repeated acts of firesetting, the "desire for destruction" becomes greater than the desire to set the fire.

Investigation into the family background of the firesetters revealed that the adolescents, the vagrants, the heroes, and those who set fire for revenge tended to come from broken homes, many from orphanages or foster care. Lewis and Yarnell also noted a relatively high incidence of deformities and debilitating physical illness. The authors postulated that this factor pushes many of the firesetters to "distinguish" themselves or perhaps to wreak vengeance against the world (see also the section on psychoanalytic theory and in particular the discussion of Mishima).

In Lewis and Yarnell's study, as well as in many subsequent studies (and previous literature from the 1800s), the role of intelligence in firesetting is a significant factor; 48% of the sample had mental retardation, and only 17% of the sample demonstrated average to superior intelligence. In general, poor school performance and poor occupational adjustment were found among all the groups. There was a low incidence of married men compared to the general population.

After the age of 20, alcoholism was found to accompany firesetting with increasing frequency. Only one half of the sample had been in trouble with the law for other antisocial activities that ranged from petty theft to manslaughter. Although all firesetters are potential murderers, given the act (particularly the vengeful type), few firesetters actually commit murder intentionally; however, some firesetters have been known to transition into serial murder (discussed later). The loss of life associated with the fires does not cause conscious guilt or anxiety, according to Lewis and Yarnell (1951); it is in most cases "incidental," which corresponds to the literature on juvenile firesetting with juvenile firesetters demonstrating little ability for empathy.

Although Lewis and Yarnell do not include in their sample arson for direct or indirect economic gain, they do consider arson where the motives include revenge, jealousy, and vanity as falling within the realm of what they call "pathological firesetting." Although firesetters with definite motives are considered by the criminal justice system as criminals and legally responsible, Lewis and Yarnell include these examples of "motivated" firesetting within the category of pathological firesetting, because they feel that there is no clear demarcation in many of these cases between the motivated firesetter (other than for economic gain) and the pyromaniac. Rather, they consider there to be a spectrum, with a gradual transition from those with motives to those individuals who set fire without motives.

In those cases motivated by jealousy, the goal is to effect immediate retribution. This tends to be an older group with a median age of 39. Lewis and Yarnell found that there was a greater incidence of blacks and foreign-born, relative to the other classes of firesetters, and that exposure to violence and alcohol were prominent factors. These individuals tended to be chronic offenders. They had no real interest in fires or fire ritual. Recidivism was not the rule in this group. One fire would suffice for the purpose. Some of the cases, however, although motivated predominantly by jealousy and revenge, also included the impulse to set a fire, which existed for a period of time before the fire was set, as well as the impulse to set fire for other motives in the future. These cases were transitional, falling somewhere between the pure jealousy type and the true pyromaniac. In some of the cases sparked by jealousy, the fire was directed against the male rival.

Another class of firesetters described by Lewis and Yarnell (1951) was the suicidal firesetter. More recently, modern investigators, such as Repo and Virkkunen (1997a), have also found a high incidence of suicidal tendencies in firesetters. Also, a certain number of fires studied by Lewis and Yarnell were centered against the mother. These were uncommon, however, and these individuals appeared to have been deeply disturbed.

Among those firesetters motivated by revenge, there was often a deep-seated grievance. The classic illustration provided by Lewis and Yarnell was the underpaid farmhand who sets fire to the farmer's barn. In some cases, anger and desire for revenge were sparked by a seemingly trivial incident. In other cases, the perception of having been insulted appears to have been almost delusional. In this group, Lewis and Yarnell again found transitional cases where the arson was often repeated with revenge as the apparent motive for some of the fires, but other fires were set because the individual liked to see the flames. This group in general tended to be unhappy and discouraged. Many tended to see themselves as victims — of family, society, institutions, and authority — and thus entitled to revenge. They tended to be physically or mentally inadequate and resentful of their inferior position in life. They tended to attack property belonging to a paternal figure.

Volunteer firemen who set fires are a very interesting phenomenon. Lewis and Yarnell devote an entire chapter to these individuals. In no other crime do we see this type of phenomenon; for example, policemen and security guards do not steal property for the purpose of being the heroes who solve the crime. Volunteer firemen are community heroes; there exists a camaraderie and a fraternity among them. Even to this day, most communities outside of large metropolitan areas are served by volunteer firemen. The firemen participate in parades, participate in many activities and celebrations, and are frequently an important focus of suburban and small-town celebrations. Of course, the vast majority of volunteer firemen are selfless, community-minded citizens, but for those who may have feelings of inadequacy, setting a fire for the purpose of becoming the hero (like the "would-be hero") may provide a pathological gratification. Schmid (1914) and Steckel (1944) both noted the association between arson and firefighters. A possible psychoanalytic explanation for why a firefighter sets fires (see discussion below on the psychoanalytic theory of pyromania) is that a member of an all-male fraternal organization rushing to be the first to put out a fire with his "hose" may be enacting a homosexual act encompassing the issues of masculine potency, competition, and rivalry.

Is Lewis and Yarnell's description of the volunteer firemen who set fires still relevant? Contemporary reports by arson investigators describe in detail the profile of volunteer firemen as firesetters, and cases of volunteer firemen who set fires are reported in periodicals throughout the country. Even abroad, this appears to be regarded as a serious problem. Psychological testing is being used in Australia during recruitment to weed out potential arsonists. A recent notorious case involved not a volunteer fireman but a top arson investigator in California. This man was convicted on 20 counts of arson and four counts of murder. He was caught when someone noted a similarity between a novel he had written and a Pasedena arson case, where two people were killed in a deliberately set fire.

Excitement is a significant motivation among firefighters; it is widely acknowledged that young men volunteer to become firefighters because of the thrill and excitement of the fire. A young man interviewed by the author quoted a fellow volunteer fireman, who clearly expressed his sentiment as well, who described firefighting as being "the greatest thrill you can get with your pants on." Not only does this statement convey the degree of thrill and excitement experienced at a fire but it also suggests the sexual quality of the experience. When asked specifically what produced the thrill, this volunteer fireman cited the fire itself and the enormity and the intensity of the danger, with the element of being a hero mentioned last. When describing a "practice" fire he would be participating in the following day (the fire would be set in a trailer with the firemen inside so they could experience how quickly a fire ignites), the volunteer fireman showed and verbalized excitement and pleasurable anticipation. If we can see this type of excitement, thrill, anticipation, and pleasure in a normal healthy community-minded volunteer, it becomes even easier to imagine these same dynamics operating in a volunteer plagued with insecurity or inadequacies.

The "would-be hero" firesetters are motivated more by vanity and the need to compensate for inadequacies and feelings of inferiority than they are by excitement. They are interested less in extinguishing the fires than they are in being the "spotters." Like so many of the other classes of firesetters, they may have additional motives as well — revenge, jealousy, etc. Schmid (1914) reported a few cases of men who would set a fire after quarrels with their loved ones (a combination of revenge and would-be heroes) and then returned with the fire department to put out the fires. These men tended to be older than the group of firesetters in Lewis and Yarnell's (1951) series.

FEMALE FIRESETTERS

In Lewis and Yarnell's series, the incidence of female firesetters was 14.8% of the total number of adult firesetters. They noted that this was in contrast to the studies reported during the 19th century that concluded that firesetting was primarily a crime of the female adolescent. However, in studies since Lewis and Yarnell, this finding of male firesetters greatly outnumbering female firesetters has been replicated consistently.

According to Lewis and Yarnell (1951), women are often dangerous and certainly dramatic firesetters. When motives are reviewed, they are essentially the same as among the adult male firesetting population. One significant difference, however, is that they "do not seem to be instinctual firefighters. …They do not seem to make fires for the purpose of setting the firemen et al. in action" (p. 345). They also tend to set fires within their own "world" — in other words, they tend to set fire to their own or their family's property. Although many female firesetters subjectively experience the same buildup in tension and release after they set the fire, they tend to be more likely to tack on concrete motives than their male counterparts. Thus, they are less likely to be classified as pyromaniacs, as they are more likely to present a motive.

Only 21 of the cases in Lewis and Yarnell's series consisted of female servants setting fires, which represents a much lower incidence compared to the European

19th-century literature. However, most of the European literature was from the previous century, when servants were much more commonplace, particularly in Europe. Also, we can hypothesize that in America, from where Lewis and Yarnell's sample was drawn, there was much greater mobility and opportunity and a more democratic attitude. Servant girls probably felt less trapped and less likely to see burning their employer's house down as the only choice (although as noted in a previous section, the modern-day parallel may be the *au pair*). There is also a higher incidence of psychosis in female firesetters than in males in Lewis and Yarnell's sample. Of 200 female firesetters, 64 were considered psychotic, whereas only 154 of the 1145 adult male firesetters were classified as psychotic.

THE PSYCHOANALYTIC THEORY OF PYROMANIA

Schmid (1914) was the first psychoanalyst to review the literature on pyromania. His contribution to our understanding of pyromania was to describe the firesetting as a displacement of suicidal urges brought about by the individual having to face a painful decision. Stekel (1924) emphasized the "sexual root" of pyromania and found it easier to understand the symbolic meaning of firesetting by studying the play of children, because children are closer to "the symbolic realm" than are adults. That children like to play with fire and like to play a game of being firemen was interpreted by him as a sublimation of infantile sexuality. The fireman puts out the fire with his stream of urine or, in a more sublimated form, a bucket of water or a fire hose.

The psychoanalytic description of the sexual symbolism and the sexual nature of man's relationship with fire was further elaborated in Freud's *Civilization and Its Discontents* (1930). When discussing the basic purpose of civilization ("to protect men against nature and to adjust their mutual relations," p. 36), Freud described the first stages of civilization as "the use of tools, the gaining of control over fire, and the construction of dwellings" (p. 37). Among these, the control of fire stands out as a quite extraordinary and unexampled achievement. His conjecture regarding the taming of fire is that early man must have had the habit of putting out fire with a stream of urine. Because tongues of flame can be seen as phallic, putting out fire by micturating can be interpreted as a sexual act with a male, a homosexual competition, and an enjoyment of potency. Freud (1930) hypothesized further that the first man to refrain from this libidinously gratifying activity could then use the power of the fire for survival. "By damping down the fire of his own sexual excitation, he attained the natural force of fire. This great cultural conquest was thus the reward for his renunciation of instinct" (p. 37). Freud then went on further to describe the role of the female as the keeper of the flame in the hearth, because she lacked the anatomy to gratify her instincts in the same manner.

Freud amplified his footnote in *Civilization and its Discontents* in his paper "The Acquisition of Power Over Fire" (1932). He begins with the myth of Prometheus, who brings fire to mankind. Prometheus steals fire from the gods and carries it in a phallic fennel stalk. The gods are tricked and angered and seek to punish Prometheus. Freud equates the id with the gods who are defrauded and who, according to Freud, must renounce the gratification connected to extinguishing the fire in order to allow civilization (or the ego) to survive and flourish. The punishment of Prometheus (whose liver, the seat of emotions, is daily torn and eaten) also represents, according to Freud, "the resentment which the hero of civilization inevitably aroused in instinct ridden humanity" (p. 407). Freud described the pleasure involved in extinguishing the fire as "a pleasurable struggle with another phallus" (p. 408). The daily rejuvenation of the liver symbolized the "imperishable nature of these desires and the ability of the flaccid penis to again and again become potent" (p. 408).

In this paper, Freud also related the myth of the Phoenix, which arose from the flames, to the acquisition of fire. This myth provides some reassurance that renunciation of instinct is not irreparable and permanent, but that instinct (and the phallus) can rise again. The last myth that Freud described in this article was the myth of Herakles vanquishing the Hydra (water snake) with fire. Freud suggests reversing the manifest content of this myth so it becomes Herakles extinguishing the Hydra (fire) with water, in order to understand its significance in the acquisition of power over fire. Freud (1932) further suggests that this myth represents a later development of civilization (and perhaps ego development): "The second myth seems to correspond to the reaction of a later epoch of civilization to the circumstances in which power over fire was acquired" (p. 409). In the first myth, Prometheus seized fire and protected it from the instinctual urge to extinguish it. In the myth of the Hydra, the notion of using water to put out fire (an expression of instinctual urges) was allowed greater expression. By referring to this second myth (the Hydra) as well as to the dual function of the phallus, Freud attempts to relate water (and micturition) to firesetting, a connection that continues to be made by investigators in understanding firesetters who are volunteer firemen and firefighting buffs. Relating micturition to firesetting also helps explain the often cited (although controversial) increased incidence of enuresis among firesetters.

The psychodynamics of the firesetter, according to Freud, would suggest a fixation at the phallic urethral stage of development, a relatively late stage of psychosexual development following the oral and anal stages. Fixation at this stage (phallic) is traditionally associated with hysterical neuroses (terminology deriving from Freud) rather than the impulse-ridden character pathology which is usually associated with fixation at the oral stage.

In a much later paper by Kaufman et al. (1961), "A Re-evaluation of the Psychodynamics of Firesetting," 30 boys referred for firesetting were found to demonstrate significant psychopathology, including diagnoses of conduct disorder, borderline psychoses (a previous term for borderline personality disorder), and psychoses. These authors noted that almost half of the children were enuretic, but rather than this finding lending support for the association between micturition and firesetting as a "phallic urethral" fixation, they suggested it would be better understood as "enuresis of impulsivity," or more representative of "oral" stage pathology. The children in this sample appeared to be very disturbed and quite primitive. When followed, many of these children who were initially given the diagnosis of conduct disorder were later diagnosed with childhood schizophrenia. These children were not followed up long term, so it is unclear as to whether these children became the so-called "true pyromaniacs" of the Lewis and Yarnell series or those firesetters who set fires as a function of severe psychopathology.

By the time Fenichel (1945) published his text *The Psychoanalytic Theory of Neuroses*, the psychoanalytic interpretation of pyromania and firesetting was widely accepted. Fenichel included a section on pyromania in his chapter, "Perversions and Impulse Neuroses," classifying pyromania as both a perversion (the act of firesetting being necessary for sexual gratification) and an impulse neuroses (a pathological impulse experienced as egosyntonic and "irresistible"). According to Fenichel, firesetting represents an obvious expression of a sadistic drive meant to destroy the object, coupled with "a cutaneous pleasure in the warmth of the fire" (p. 371). Fenichel agreed with Freud's assessment of firesetting as an expression of urethral eroticism but described a sadistic component as well.

Fenichel did not necessarily divide pyromaniacs into two distinct categories of pervert and "true pyromaniac" as did Lewis and Yarnell, but he did imply a gradation and relationship between pyromania as a perversion (when the impulse to discharge tension results in an orgasmic release or a sexual act) and as an impulse neurosis or "irresistible impulse" (when the impulse leads to a discharge of tension that is not directly sexual).

Fenichel provided an excellent clinical description of "irresistible impulse" removed from the concept of legal responsibility (pp. 367–368): "Irresistibility means that the patients in question are intolerant of tensions. Whatever they need, they must attain immediately … their actions are not directed (or are less directed) towards the positive aim of achieving a goal but rather toward the negative aim of getting rid of tension."

In Grinstein's paper "Stages in the Development of Control Over Fire" (1952), Freud's paper was used as a point of departure. Grinstein raised the possibility (specifically discarded by Freud) that the gods who were defrauded by Prometheus represented the superego or a "parent figure." He suggested that the force responsible for the renunciation of the (homosexually derived) impulse to urinate on the fire is the parental authority. Grinstein reviewed mythology and folklore across many different cultures as they were described by Frazer (1930) in *Myth of the Origin of Fire*. His interesting conclusion is that because so many myths indicate that primitives believed women originally possessed fire it was the mother who originally demanded instinctual renunciation from her children. This theory is also consistent with Freud's description in *Civilization and Its Discontents* (1930, p. 37): "Further, it is as though women had been appointed guardian of the fire, which was held captive on the domestic hearths, because her anatomy made it impossible for her to yield to the temptation of this desire."

Grinstein (1952) suggested that early on in the child's development and early on in the development of civilization the maternal figure demands renunciation of instinctual urges. Also at that stage in the development of civilization, a fire is kept rather than kindled anew. Later on, during the Oedipal stage and during the development of more advanced patriarchal societies, the primitive and potentially castrating power of the father figure now demands renunciation of instinctual urges (of a more phallic nature). Grinstein's hypothesis is that the control of fire in man represents a highly complex array of instinctual control in response to multi-stage drives and derivatives. Conversely, the inability to control any of these drives can result in firesetting. In addition to Freud's interpretation of firesetting as an expression of urethral eroticism, Grinstein (1952) interprets (as did Fenichel) the aggressive component of firesetting as being an expression of anal sadistic urges. He also gives examples such as blowing (on a fire or blowing a fire out) and spitting, which he feels are expressions of oral aggression. Finally, Grinstein credits the ability to sublimate phallic impulses to "man's learning the secret of starting a fire." Only then could he "act out with primitive tools an expression of his incompletely gratified sexual longing and could thus learn to kindle fire" (p. 420).

Both Freud (1930) and Grinstein (1952) utilized mythology to explain humans' relationship with fire historically as well as developmentally. Perhaps this is because the relationship with fire is so primal and reaches back to our early history, as does mythology, an early attempt to understand nature.

Simmel (1949), in his presentation of a case of firesetting, postulated that, as an escape from the threat of incestuous feelings and subsequent castration anxiety during the Oedipal stage, a child would use masturbation to relieve tension and avoid incestuous contact. If the masturbation were prohibited, then there might be regression to the urethral phallic phase of development. Firesetting then becomes a substitute for masturbation. The firesetting and the subsequent urinating on the fire would provide substitutive gratification for both the aggressive drive and urethral eroticism.

Pyromania continues to be of interest to the psychoanalytic community. In a 1975 paper by Arlow, "Pryomania and the Primal Scene: A Psychoanalytic Comment on the Work of Yukio Mishima," the author analyzed the act of firesetting as described by Mishima in his novel, *The Temple of the Golden Pavilion*, as a substitutive act of vengeance deriving from the primal scene experience. "The sense of shock and betrayal from witnessing a loved one having sexual relations becomes the basic motivation of the characters around whom the plots revolve" (p. 34).

Arlow (1975) also found the recurrent themes of primal scenes, vengeance, and fire in several other works by Mishima. In *Forbidden Colors*, the main characters include a novelist who has been betrayed and humiliated by women (including, of course, his own mother) and his alter-ego, a beautiful young man who seduces and then betrays and humiliates all the women who had ever humiliated the novelist (vengeance). The element of fire recurs throughout the book. Whenever Yuichi feels a surge of sexual excitement, he thinks of fire and sometimes hears the sound of fire sirens. In another novel, *The Sailor Who Fell From Grace with the Sea*, not only are the themes of the primal scene, fire, and vengeance repeated, but there is also a scene of cruelty to animals. The gang of teenagers dissect a cat in a kind of initiation ceremony which confers potency on them and which is later repeated in the murder and dissection of the man (the sailor) who was the rival for the mother's affection. This novel includes the fantasy of the mother and son trapped and engulfed by flames (as in sexual passion). This is a compelling association in fiction between firesetting and cruelty to animals (part of the "triad" of firesetting, enuresis, and cruelty to animals).

Arlow (1975, pp. 40–41) concluded that the repetitive themes in Mishima's writing (and one would conclude in his fantasy life) were the following: "Three responses to the primal scene seem to be prominent — first, the primal scene is experienced as a humiliating defeat leading to a wish to retaliate in kind; second, one observes the evocation of tremendous destructive rage against one or both parents; and, third, the primal scene is symbolically represented by the element of fire or screened off by memories of fire. ...Because of its great power to destroy, fire lends itself readily as a vehicle to gratify sadistic impulses used to redress grievances from whatever source. The literature on firesetting is full of case reports of fire set for the purpose of revenge."

Two very significant facts about Mishimo may relate to significant trends seen in firesetters. First, as described in repeated cases by Lewis and Yarnell (1951), pathologic firesetters (especially "true pyromaniacs") very often have a history of physical inadequacy, weakness, or deformity. Mishimo was raised in the sickroom of his "irascible, domineering, neurotic grandmother" until he was 12 years old. "To make matters worse, he was a puny, sickly, unattractive child. ...In addition, he suffered from anemia and attacks of respiratory illness" (Arlow, 1975, p. 44). The main character in *Temple of the Golden Pavilion* considered himself extremely ugly and was described as being a lifelong stutterer. Clearly, this character was a stand-in for Mishima. A second element revealed in the connection between Mishima, his works, and firesetting is the self-destructive, suicidal urge described by Schmid (1914) and later elaborated by Lewis and Yarnell (1951) and others. In *Temple of the Golden Pavilion*, the main character fled from the burning building and attempted suicide. Mishima ended his own life, in a dramatic exhibitionistic disembowelment at the headquarters of the commanding general of the eastern army, following an attempt on his part to convince the soldiers to rise up in revolt to restore the imperial power of Japan. Mishima's suicide, although not by fire, had the quality of a spectacular, grand effect.

FIRESETTING IN CHILDREN

Firesetting in children is a common occurrence. Play with matches is considered typical and developmentally appropriate in young boys. Kafry (1978) conducted a survey of normal, young boys and found that interest in fire is almost universal; 40% of these children engaged in fire play. Although curiosity-driven fire play is normal, it nevertheless can result in great danger. What makes some of these children go on to continue to engage in fire play and to engage in more pathological and destructive firesetting is an area of great interest and concern. Kafry (1978) characterized the children who engage in fire play as more likely to test limits. Firesetting in children is cause for alarm, however, as even accidental fire play is capable of turning into tragedy with great loss of property and at times even human life.

The early literature of childhood firesetting is exemplified by Yarnell's 1939 paper, "Firesetting in Children." She summarized earlier clinical and theoretical work and presented her own very extensive study of 60 children admitted to Bellevue Hospital for firesetting from 1937 to 1938, out of a total of 1755 admissions. Of these children, 60% were between 6 and 8 years of age, and 35% were between 11 and 15 years of age. As has been found in both prior and subsequent studies, there was a very small percentage of girls (only 2 out of 60). The adolescent boys tended to plan the fires, set them away from home, watched the fires, and enjoyed the noise and excitement. It was noted by Yarnell that many of these boys set fires in pairs, suggesting a homosexual association.

The younger children tend to start by playing with matches, usually in streets or vacant lots, but then proceed to eventually making a fire in the home. They have no interest in the out-of-control aspect of the fire and are usually frightened rather than excited by the fire engines and attempts to put out the fire. The cases reported by Yarnell (1939) demonstrated significant psychopathology and especially aggressive fantasies. These children also had a high incidence of learning disabilities. In most of the cases discussed, the children had experienced losses and deprivation and were frequently abused. Aggressive fantasies were very prominent in these children, and fire represented power. The children typically set fires when under stress. Yarnell postulated that deprivation in the family life (death of a parent, inadequate parenting, step-parents, foster homes, etc.) make it difficult for the child to successfully negotiate the Oedipal phase and that the child "carries over his sadistic impulses with their accompanying anxiety" (p. 283). The child has not had the benefit of an intact family with a loving mother and father — the mother providing love and security and the father providing an effective role model. These children tend to direct their aggressive fantasies against the person refusing them love or their perceived rival (a step-parent or a sibling). Yarnell noted that the etiological factors and aggressive impulses to kill are similar to those seen in children who do kill.

Yarnell's conclusions are that "in every case the child has been deprived of love and security in his home life. ...Some were children from boarding homes who had not succeeded in finding any person whom they loved and with whom they could identify. In the children coming from their own homes, there has always been some serious, traumatic factor..." (p. 283). What is so interesting about this paper is that the case studies include the children's fantasy material, which was noted to be "a mixture of aggression, destructiveness, anxiety, and self-punishment" (p. 283). The aim of the aggression seemed to be to hurt the person refusing them love or to destroy their rival for love.

Yarnell postulated that the reason fire was used as a means of aggression for these particular children was that they had vivid imaginations and an "unusual ability to build a fantasy life" (p. 284). Many of these children expressed a similar fantasy — that fire would destroy what was bad in the loved one and then restore them (or purify them) so that they would then be good. The fire is destructive yet confers a magical power to the user to purify and restore. Modern studies of child and adolescent firesetters present less psychoanalytic clinical material but appear to demonstrate a similar profile of a high incidence of deprivation, trauma, and abuse.

An extensive review of the literature on childhood firesetters by Heath et al. (1976) examined the validity of three presumed associations to firesetting: (1) a higher prevalence of enuresis, (2) decreased intellectual functioning, and (3) sexual problems or motives. These authors found all three associations to be unproven. Numerous studies have been done with juvenile firesetters to try to assess the characteristics that differentiate them from the psychiatric population at large. The obvious flaw in earlier papers and studies, which attempted to formulate a hypothesis about a symptom or syndrome from case reports or even from a series without comparisons to a control group, is that one cannot be sure that features of the larger population are not being described. For example, as Heath et al. (1976) pointed out, the incidence of enuresis in firesetters is very high, but it is also very high in juvenile psychiatric populations, especially in populations with a high incidence of family disorganization and in populations with a high percentage of males (both of which are characteristics of juvenile firesetters).

Recently, a number of studies have provided a matched control group to use as a basis for comparison. A study of juvenile firesetters in residential treatment by Sakheim et al. (1985) compared firesetters with non-firesetters in the same population and matched for age, sex, and IQ. Some interesting differences became apparent. The non-firesetters displayed a greater ability to express anger directly, especially in response to being made to feel inadequate. The firesetters were less capable of becoming overtly enraged. This perhaps correlates with the typical presentation of the adult firesetter as someone plagued with inadequacies and rage but unable to express them overtly — firesetting provides the firesetter with great power to destroy but in a passive, covert way.

Other significant differences between the two populations were that the firesetters had less super-ego control, exhibited poor judgment and planning, were more reactive, were less obsessive, and were less able to tolerate tension and anxiety of any kind. They were also less empathetic, tended to form fewer attachments, and were more likely to be diagnosed as conduct disorder. They also tended to utilize less internalization and to demonstrate less capacity for reflection. This profile again correlates well with the picture of the adult firesetter and is consistent with the lack of guilt and concern for human life typically described among firesetters, both juvenile and adults. A further interesting finding in these children, at odds with several recent authors, was that the firesetters had "significantly more direct as well as symbolic means of sexual activity and excitement … they were often highly aroused children who entertained strong erotic fantasies" (p. 466). They seemed to obtain some sort of sexual thrill or satisfaction from setting or watching fires. These children also experienced deep feelings of maternal and at times paternal rejection. In fact, the combination of maternal rejection and high levels of sexual arousal was the combination most predictive of firesetting in these children. Sackheim et al. (1985) hypothesized that the firesetting symbolizes a sexualized relationship with the parent of the opposite sex, but a relationship which also includes unexpressed destructive rage regarding abandonment. A more recent study by Sakheim and Osborn (1999) identifies many of these same factors as further differentiating between severe and non-severe firesetters.

Showers and Pickerel (1987) studied a large number of juvenile firesetters and matched controls in a number of different facilities, including inpatient units, community mental health centers, and a children's medical hospital. The majority of the firesetters, as in other samples, were male. Boys were more likely to set multiple fires and to be motivated by excitement (the adult pyromaniac profile). Revenge as a motivation was more common among the 9- to 12-year-olds than among the younger or older children. Boys who set fires were more likely to come from physically abusive households and to have a step-parent or other non-parental adult in the home. The firesetting boys were also likely to have a mother who abused drugs or alcohol. Although there was a high incidence of abuse and neglect among the firesetters, the non-firesetters were more likely to have received intervention for physical abuse. This may be consistent with Sakheim's findings that children who are capable of verbally expressing their anger and/or who have been protected against abuse are more empowered and less likely to resort to firesetting. Other commonly cited correlations such as enuresis, low intelligence, and a diagnosis of psychosis were not corroborated in this study. The association with conduct disorder and multiple anti-social behaviors was supported.

A third study by Ritvo and Shanok (1983) found that the only significant differences between firesetters and non-firesetters were that the firesetters were less likely to have their biological mother in the home and that a number of them had a history of being severely burned in an accident or burned as a punishment. Using fire or burning as a punishment is an obvious way of teaching a child that fire can be used for retaliation. The other commonly cited correlations such as psychosis, neurological impairments, mental retardation, learning disabilities, and abuse (other than being burned) were unsupported.

A fourth control study by Heath et al. (1985) examined an inpatient population. The only significant difference that they found was that firesetters had a much higher likelihood of having a diagnosis of conduct disorder. Two of their sample of 32 fit the criteria for pyromania.

A more recent study by Moore et al. (1996) used the Minnesota Multiphasic Personality Inventory (MMPI)-A (designed for use with adolescents) to try to get a better handle on the features that differentiate firesetters. Using the MMPI-A, they determined that the firesetting group was much more severely disturbed than what would be expected with the diagnosis of conduct disorder. Specifically, the firesetters scored high on scales of schizophrenia, mania, depression, alienation, bizarre mentation, anger, conduct problems, family problems, school problems, and negative treatment indicators.

The composite picture of juvenile firesetting that emerges is one of impulse-ridden children with poor boundaries who have an inability to tolerate tension and anxiety and an inability to directly express their anger. The family background is typically chaotic, and higher rates of alcohol and drug use are found among the mothers. The DSM-IV diagnosis is most often conduct disorder, but these children are often much more disturbed than this single diagnosis would suggest.

It is not a stretch to imagine these children growing up to be the impulse-ridden, acting-out, pathological repetitive firesetters studied in adult samples and case reports. Unfortunately, there are no prospective studies to determine which and how many of the juvenile firesetters become adult pathological firesetters, but we do know from clinical material that many pyromaniacs and repetitive firesetters began firesetting as children.

Pyromania and Repetitive Arson in Children

Pyromania as a diagnostic concept has fallen out of favor in the investigation of children as well as adults. DSM-III excluded the diagnosis of pyromania if a diagnosis of conduct disorder was met. In DSM-IV, the diagnosis of pyromania can be made (along with the other criteria) if "the firesetting is not better accounted for by conduct disorder." Because the diagnosis of conduct disorder is so commonly made in these children, the rarity of the diagnosis of pyromania may in part be an artifact of this criterion. The diagnosis of pyromania tends to be reserved for those children who have severe firesetting behavior. By definition, the firesetting must be impulsive, without motives, and repetitive.

Many children engage in repeated firesetting. This is particularly the case among adolescents, with many setting multiple fires (Lewis and Yarnell 1951). In contrast, most younger children set only a single fire, usually in the home, and then often are referred for treatment. Because many of the younger children who have been studied have been referred for their first firesetting behavior, this may result in a major methodological flaw in the study of juvenile firesetters, particularly our understanding of recidivism.

MOTIVES IN CHILDHOOD FIRESETTING

Children act out of many of the same motives that adults do. The children who are described as pyromaniacs display the characteristic excitement and repetitive need to set fires that the adult pyromaniacs do. A frequent motive in juvenile firesetters, again similar to adults, is the motive of revenge and retaliation. A small number of juvenile firesetters are similar to the adult fire "buffs" (Lewis and Yarnell 1951), who set fires at least in part because of their interest in the firetrucks and the firefighting paraphernalia.

TREATMENT OF JUVENILE FIRESETTERS

The literature regarding the treatment of juvenile firesetters is much more extensive than the treatment of adult firesetters, probably because children are more often seen in treatment facilities, whereas adult firesetters are for the most part identified and evaluated (and only sometimes treated) within the confines of the criminal justice system.

Various treatments have been applied to juvenile firesetters. Behavioral approaches are common, including positive reinforcement (Holland, 1969), threat of punishment (Holland, 1969), stimulus fixation (Walsh, 1971), and learning alternative behaviors (McGrath et al., 1979). Menuchin (1974) utilized structural family therapy in a crisis-oriented model of treatment. Bumpus et al. (1983) used a "graphing" technique to help children correlate external stress, behavior, and feelings in order to help these children more directly express their emotions in response to a given stress. Koles and Jenson (1985) used a combination of behavioral techniques and social skills training. Unfortunately, many of these reports on treatment provide only single case reports, and even when more than one child is treated there is no control group for comparison.

ENURESIS, FIRESETTING, AND CRUELTY TO ANIMALS — ARE THEY PREDICTIVE OF ADULT CRIME?

Much has been written about the triad of persistent enuresis, firesetting, and cruelty to animals and its value in predicting adult crime. There has been considerable debate concerning the association of enuresis and firesetting. It has been noted by some authors and rejected by others. Both behaviors have been associated independently with parental rejection and with aggressive and violent behavior. As has been discussed in the previous section on the psychoanalytic theory of firesetting, some postulate that firesetting and the desire to put out the fire with a stream of urine represent a urethral, sadistic drive.

The third element of the triad, cruelty to animals, is the most direct expression of aggression and sadism. It is certainly not difficult to imagine that this factor would be predictive of more violent acts in adulthood.

A retrospective study by Helman and Blackman (1964) of 84 inpatients remanded for evaluation by the court system clearly demonstrated the validity of the triad as being predictive of aggressive behaviors. Of the 31 individuals charged with aggressive crimes, 3/4 of them demonstrated the triad of enuresis, firesetting, and cruelty to animals, whereas only 15 out of 53 charged with non-aggressive crime demonstrated either the triad or a partial triad (2 out of 3). The following case example from this study is illustrative (Helman and Blackman, 1964, p. 1434):

> "Clarence was a 39-year-old, married male charged with first-degree robbery. His parents and siblings continually made fun of him. He was enuretic until age 14. As a boy, he would pour gasoline on dogs and cats and set them on fire. He deliberately set a barn on fire and burned various other property. He served three prison terms for assault, intent to kill, and two armed robberies. Intellectual functioning is in the borderline defective range."

A second study by Wax and Haddox (1974) also clearly demonstrated the predictive value of the triad. Furthermore, the cases in which the triad was demonstrated ranked among the most overtly dangerous assaultive youth in the sample study.

A recent study by Sakheim and Osborn (1999) demonstrates evidence that severe firesetters (as opposed to non-severe firesetters) are more likely to be cruel and sadistic to other children and to animals. Further support for at least the partial triad of firesetting and cruelty to animals can be found in the case history of serial murderers such as David Berkowitz (see section on a correlation between serial murder and serial arson).

RECIDIVISM

Pyromania is by definition a repetitive act. One of the essential criteria for pyromania in DSM-IV is "a deliberate and purposeful firesetting on more than one occasion." However, many other types of pathological firesetting tend to be repetitive, as well, which is why I have chosen to discuss these other forms of firesetting as well as pyromania in this text on serial offenders.

Lewis and Yarnell (1951) have cited the recidivism rate for all pathological firesetters as 28%; however, a lower recidivism rate of 4.5% has been reported in a small population of convicted arsonists (Soothill and Pope, 1973). This difference in reported recidivism may reflect a difference in the sample. The Lewis and Yarnell samples were all pathological firesetters (of one type or another), who tend to be repetitive firesetters, whereas a sample of convicted arsonists may have included some "motivated" arsonists (i.e., arson for profit or as a specific motivated act), who tend to set single fires. Consistent with Lewis and Yarnell's study, arsonists referred for pretrial psychiatric evaluations, presumably having demonstrated some type of psychopathology to warrant a referral, had recidivism rates of 20% (Leong, 1992) and 38% (Koson and Dvoskin, 1992). Even in the pyromaniac, the impulse to set fires is episodic and in many cases self-limited, appearing only during a developmental or situational crisis. Often an arrest will end a firesetting spree even after the firesetter is released from custody (Lewis and Yarnell, 1951).

In a long-term (up to 15 years) followup study of Finnish firesetters (Repo and Virkkunen, 1997a), the recidivist firesetters demonstrated severe psychopathology and poor socialization. The recidivist firesetters received the least treatment and social services, while at the same time expressing disappointment that more help was not available. (Apparently this group is less motivated to take advantage of treatment.) Very few of them had been treated with medication. The incidence of alcoholism and suicide was much higher among the recidivist firesetters.

In another study of recidivism and arsonists (Barnett et al., 1996), mentally disordered firesetters were found to have a much higher rate of recidivism than firesetters who were not mentally disordered and were more likely to commit fewer criminal offenses other than firesetting. In other words, the recidivist firesetters tended to be mentally ill, whereas the single-episode firesetters were more likely to be simple criminals.

A CORRELATION BETWEEN SERIAL MURDER AND SERIAL ARSON

Both destructive and sexual motives play a part in pyromania and serial murder. It should be no surprise, then, that several serial killers have also been serial arsonists. Arson is a crime that frequently precedes more violent and direct personal crimes such as murder and may in some cases represent a phase in which the aggression is more passive and more remote (supported by the literature regarding juvenile firesetters, who have more anger, but are less able to express it directly).

Back in the late 1800s, Thomas Piper, "The Boston Belfry Murderer," confessed that in between outbursts of murder and rape he would set fires. Other serial killers also engaged in serial arson through history, such as Jane Toppan, the turn-of-the-century killer nurse, and Peter Kürten, the "Düsseldorf Monster." Kürten was born into a family characterized by violence, alcoholism, brutality, and incest. Kürten frequently watched as his drunk father repeatedly raped his mother. In childhood, he was fascinated with watching a sadistic dogcatcher torture dogs. From the age of 13 on throughout adolescence, he had sexual relations with animals, at times stabbing sheep or having sex with them for additional excitement. During one period of his life before embarking on his final killing spree, he set frequent fires to barns and other buildings and experienced sexual excitement while watching the fires. He dreamed of demolishing the city of Düsseldorf with dynamite.

More recently, David Berkowitz, the "Son of Sam" murderer, was reported to have set 1488 fires in New York by his own account and also to have pulled several hundred false alarms (Ressler and Shachtman, 1992). He had a desire to be a fireman but never took the test. In addition to his interest in firefighting, a number of other factors fit the profile of a pathological firesetter or serial arsonist — he was given up for adoption by his biological mother, he had problems with his adoptive family, and his adoptive mother died when he was 14. In addition, he had limited social and relationship skills and very limited heterosexual experience. His sole sexual experience was with a prostitute, from whom he contracted venereal disease. Berkowitz also displayed cruelty to animals. At an early age, he recalled pouring ammonia into his mother's fish tank to kill her fish and then piercing them with a pin. He also killed her pet bird with rat poison. With these acts, he may have been expressing his sadistic urges and his enraged vengefulness and hatred toward his mother as well as his wish to be in control. He also described fantasies of causing fiery air crashes (similar to Peter Kürten's dreams of fiery destruction). Although he never caused a plane crash (he was inadequate and ineffectual at most things he tried to do), his numerous fires must have been an extension of that fantasy — "Berkowitz loved to watch bodies being carried out of burning buildings" (Ressler and Shachtman, 1992, p. 80). The extension of his fantasy was that he would go out in a blaze of glory, a grand exhibitionist shootout where he and many others would be killed.

PROFILING

Information gathered from studying large numbers of arsonists and arson crimes yields valuable profiling information, which can steer the investigator in the right direction. For example, whether the arson crime is highly organized or disorganized is an important piece of information. A highly organized act suggests arson for profit, perhaps a professional torch. Evidence of a highly organized arson would be elaborate incendiary devices, a relative lack of physical evidence, and a methodical, premeditated approach. The arsonist most likely would be working alone, be an adult, and be fairly intelligent. A disorganized crime scene, as indicated by the use of whatever material was on hand and the presence of a good deal of physical evidence (e.g., footprints, handwriting, fingerprints), would suggest an act of vandalism or pathological firesetting. Typically, pathological firesetters may set dozens or even hundreds of fires before being apprehended.

The profiler recognizes that most serial offenders have a characteristic *modus operandi* (Douglas et al., 1995). An arsonist's *modus operandi* includes targeting certain types of structures or using a certain type of incendiary device. An arsonist may also have a certain "signature" such as defecating or urinating or stealing from the premises (see Case 2 below). An advantage to the arson investigator is that when firesetters are caught, many readily confess guilt, although they typically express no remorse or regret. Profilers such as Holmes and Holmes (1996) have also relied heavily on material gathered by investigators such as Lewis and Yarnell (1951) to construct a clinical profile of the pathological firesetter (see Table 3).

CASE REPORTS

Nothing else conveys the clinical presentation of a disorder the way a case report does. Statistics describing samples of a heterogeneous group engaging in a single behavior (in this case, the act of firesetting) cannot effectively describe the small subset of this population that presents in a characteristic, syndromal manner. The following case reports are reproduced from several sources, some relatively recent.

CASE 1

This case, described by Lande (1980), is typical of pyromania — a young man who began to set fires in childhood for excitement and then progressed to setting fires for sexual arousal. This type of pyromaniac would be considered a fire fetishist (p. 292):

"The patient was a 20-year-old white male referred to the Behavior Therapy Unit by the court. He had been imprisoned for two incidents of firesetting which resulted in extensive damage to the house in which he and his family resided. During both incidents, the patient lit a small fire in the attic, masturbated to orgasm, and left the house. Several firesetting incidents associated with masturbation were reported by prison guards.

"The patient's earliest recollections of the effects of fire stimuli on his behaviors were of non-sexual excitement and arousal at the sight of a fire on television and of an actual fire in his neighborhood. At about age 11, he recalled masturbating to fantasies of burning houses and cars. He also recalled that at about 13, he began masturbating to orgasm about one or two times per week in the presence of controlled fires which he set in trash cans or on the ground. The fires would be put out after he achieved orgasms. More recently, the patient reported five or more fantasies of fire each day, some of which were associated with masturbation. Lighters and lit matches had also been frequent and effective sources of sexual arousal.

"The patient reported that during his childhood he had been teased frequently regarding the leg brace and ragged clothes he wore in his mid-teens. Attempts to approach girls were often met with ridicule and rejection. Realizing the oddity of his behavior, he unsuccessfully attempted masturbation to pictures of nude females and made no further overtures. At about age 17, the patient developed his only reported relationship with a female, lasting six or seven months. His first attempt at intercourse with her was without success. He then lit a fire in a fireplace and was able to achieve orgasm during intercourse by watching the fire. No further attempts at intercourse were reported."

CASE 2

This next case report is that of a young man quoted by DeRivers (1958) in his chapter on sexual incendiarism. This young man also would be considered a fire fetishist. Interestingly, in this case, burglary is the first choice for sexual arousal. Also of note is the evacuation of his bowels as part of his pattern (pp. 247–248):

"This is a case of a white male, age 22, high school graduate. He was arrested on suspicion of arson and confessed to starting some 20 to 30 fires in various neighborhoods. His sexual history revealed that he had had sexual intercourse at the age of 18 but had masturbated ever since he was 11 or 12 years of age. He stated that he has an urge to start a fire practically every evening. He wanders about the neighborhood and looks for a place where the occupants of the house may be out for the evening so that he can go about undetected. He stated that he first tries to get into the house, becoming highly excited while doing so. After getting indoors, he ransacks the house, going through the dresser drawers looking for pictures mostly of females and when he finds them he becomes greatly excited. He then strews things about the house in a most disorderly fashion and suddenly has an orgasm and ejaculates. Then he experiences a great amount of relaxation and usually picks a spot in the center of the carpet and has a very loose evacuation of the bowels. He stated that if he does not rob the house, he will take some fire and matches and set fire to the house or to the garage. When he sees the first sign of fire or smoke, he has a seminal emission and feels greatly at ease. Then he chooses a spot on a nearby lawn where he can be free of detection and has an evacuation of the bowels. As the house burns up, he feels sorry that he started the fire."

Case 3

The following excerpt from Lewis and Yarnell (1951) is an example of a "motivated" arson, where the motive is illogical and is a good example of what Lewis and Yarnell referred to as "transitional" pyromania (p. 65):

"Bert (age 18; single) [set fire to his] employer's barn in which 20 cows and 3 horses were killed because he said the wife gave him 'leftover food from the table.' He had run away from home because his father beat him. He was sent to the reformatory, but we have not been able to locate him since 1933."

Case 4

The following, also from Lewis and Yarnell (1951), is an example of repeated motivated arson, again with some "transitional" features, and is typical of how sprees of firesetting can be terminated by incarceration or hospitalization (p. 77):

"Fritz (age 40; married; alcoholic; average intelligence) burned the 'pound' when a new administration no longer allowed him to be volunteer executioner for the condemned animals (interesting sublimation of the pathological impulse to torture animals). He had used fire all his life, beginning by burning his parents' barn at 12. He burned grain elevators, farms, and garages whenever he had a grudge against someone. He had been arrested for larceny, assault, sodomy, and abuse of animals. When drunk, he delighted in stripping his wife and knocking her down. This man was sent to the criminal insane ward in 1938, and the hospital now informs that he was paroled one year ago and is working in a garage and is in no trouble."

Case 5

This case is an excellent example of repetitive firesetting, again from Lewis and Yarnell's series, with no stated motive but an implied motive (against his employer). Lewis and Yarnell (1951) would refer to this as pyromania, but not "true pyromania" (p. 76):

"Jules (age 28; married; 3 children; alcoholic; low average intelligence) burned down his employer's dairy barn five times over a five-year period because he 'liked to see the flames.' He was slightly crippled from infantile paralysis. He said the employer's wife made sexual advances to him. He was not conscious of any direct desire to avenge himself on his employer. He is now in a reformatory and has a good record."

CASE 6

The following, also from Lewis and Yarnell (1951), is an example of a volunteer fireman who set fires. Because he was retired, he may have missed the excitement of watching fires (p. 211):

"J. (age 70; retired fire chief) had been a member of the fire department since he was 18 years of age. For seven years, a great number of fires occurred in the town, generally small fires set in the early morning around warehouses. Jay always arose at four and was known to prowl, but he was a respected citizen and worked regularly as a blacksmith. He was not immediately associated with the fires. One morning, a watchman saw him go into an entrance of some railroad property and as he left, a fire was seen burning. They shadowed him and found that, in these prowlings, he would go into either hallways or alleys, urinate, and then set a fire. He was arrested, but no charges were pressed. Now, two years later he is still prowling in the morning hours but is not setting fires, and there have been practically no fires in the town since that time."

TREATMENT

Motivated arson is criminal behavior that obviously would not be a focus of treatment. As we have seen, however, there are many "transitional" cases which represent both motivated and pathological firesetting. To the extent that many recidivist firesetters suffer from severe psychopathology, any treatment that addresses the psychopathology (e.g., depression, suicidality, alcoholism, psychosis) may help treat the firesetting behavior. Typically, however, the recidivist firesetter with mental pathology makes least use of treatment and mental health facilities (Repo and Virkkunen, 1997a). Also, it should be noted that the typical features of these individuals — impulsive, low degrees of empathy, poor insight, poor judgment, social isolation — make them unlikely candidates for any type of psychotherapeutic intervention. Furthermore, few researchers have shown any interest in treatment of firesetting or pyromania in adults. Treatment of juvenile firesetters has been more extensive; however, no large-scale or controlled studies have been conducted. Behavioral therapy, which has been extensively reported in children, has been reported in only one adult case (Lande, 1980). As far as psychopharmacology is concerned, this area also has not been explored. However, some of the work done regarding the biological correlates of firesetting would suggest that treatment aimed at increasing brain seratonin levels and treating reactive hypoglycemia might be of benefit with a certain subgroup of firesetters (see the following section).

BIOLOGICAL CORRELATES OF FIRESETTING

Firesetting was one of the behaviors measured in a study of enzyme activity and behavior in hyperactive children grown up (Kuperman et al., 1987). Monamine oxidase (MAO) levels were found to be inversely associated with measures of firesetting (as well as drug use, nicotine use, and sensation seeking). The correlation between MAO levels and impulsive aggression had been documented previously. Although this study was preliminary and very limited in scope, it is tempting to speculate that the use of medication which has helped hyperactive children with impulsiveness and aggression and which alters levels of monoamine neurotransmitters may help diminish firesetting behavior. To my knowledge, no study has been reported utilizing these medications to target firesetting behaviors in either hyperactive children who set fires or adult firesetters.

In another study Virkkunen et al. (1989b) found that arsonists had significantly lower levels of the serotonin metabolite 5-HIAA and lower levels of the norepinephrine metabolite MHPG (lower levels of a neurotransmitter metabolite implies lower levels of that neurotransmitter). Virkkunen's group postulated that low brain serotonin results in violence secondary to poor impulse control.

In another paper by Stein et al. (1993), the essential features of impulse disorder were correlated to serotonergic transmission. Stein et al., like Virkkunen et al. (1989b), postulated that a decrease in seratonergic transmission leads to the inability to maintain a waiting attitude or inhibition. There also may be a connection between diminished seratonin and suicidal feelings often seen in pyromaniacs. Postmortem studies have shown diminished seratonin in the brains of suicide victims. Virkkunen et al. (1989b) have demonstrated lower levels of 5-HIAA and MHPG in suicidal arsonists, and Stein et al. (1993) described a number of studies correlating some of the impulse disorders with evidence of diminished seratonergic transmission and in some studies diminished noradrenergic transmission.

Another study by Roy et al. (1986) suggests that violent offenders, including firesetters, suffer from significant reactive hypoglycemia as measured by the glucose tolerance test. Reactive hypoglycemia was specifically a factor in those arsonists who tended to become aggressive and confused with alcohol ingestion. This study suggests that there may be a subset of firesetters who have reactive hypoglycemia and who become impulsive, violent, and confused following alcohol ingestion. This certainly correlates with the reported high incidence of alcohol use preceding firesetting. Virkkunen et al. (1989b) have also demonstrated that recidivist arsonists, when compared to non-recidivist arsonists, have lower 5-HIAA levels and lower blood glucose levels following glucose challenge, suggesting that recidivist arsonists have lower brain serotonin levels and a higher incidence of reactive hypoglycemia.

THE SEXUAL NATURE OF FIRESETTING

Many authors have described the obvious associations between fire and sexuality. Examples abound in literature and common speech — "flames of love," "fires of passion," feeling as if one were "set on fire" by passion, etc. Authors from the 1800s described firesetting in women during or just prior to menstruation. As described previously in this chapter, Steckel (1924) described pyromania as having "a sexual root." The early descriptions in the literature place a great emphasis on the phenomena of a buildup of tension, the impulse to set a fire, and the subsequent decrease in tension. This tension is equated with sexual energy or libido, and sexual motivations are considered "implicit" or "explicit" (as a perversion).

Recent literature, however, questions the assumption that pyromania has as its basis a direct or indirect, implicit or explicit, sexual derivation (Rice and Harris, 1991). In a paper by Quinsey et al. (1989), the authors attempted to disprove the theory that "a sizable proportion of arsonists were sexually motivated to start fires." The study measured the penile responses of 26 firesetters and 15 non-firesetters to audiotaped descriptions depicting a variety of motivations for firesetting. The small sample size was a significant problem given the fact that sexual arousal to firesetting is an uncommon event. In the Lewis and Yarnell (1951) sample, only 3% were classified as setting fires for sexual arousal. Obviously, 3% of a sample size of 26 would not be expected to yield a statistically significant result. Also, the major authors of this century who have written about firesetting describe the *many* different types of firesetting and the various multiple motivations involved. Those motivated only or even predominantly by sexual arousal are the minority in all the major works on firesetting and pyromania, but that does not mean that the correlation does not exist for a small group of firesetters. In addition, the authors of this study appear to have confused the concept of "sexual roots" (Steckel) or unconscious sexual motives, with firesetting as a fetish or act of perversion. It is no surprise that no significant difference was found between the firesetters and non-firesetters in a measure of *direct* sexual response.

Raines and Foy (1994), in a comprehensive review article on juvenile firesetters, stated that none of the researchers found evidence of sexual motives. They suggest that the DSM-III-R criteria are an extension of the myth that sexual motives are an essential component of pyromania. They argue that DSM-III-R "describes three of the five diagnostic criteria in terms of sexual drive" (p. 596) and that the DSM-III Case Book "does not describe a case that matches these criteria but rather focuses on a six-year-old firesetter who has no sexual problems." There appears to be a common misinterpretation of the concepts of "tension or affective arousal" and "irresistible impulse" (which may indirectly be related to sexual drive) as a directly motivated sexual behavior or a sexual problem (both in the child and the adult literature).

In addition, to expect to apply criteria developed for the description of an adult disorder to children, especially when attempting to disprove the application of "sexual" criteria, is illogical. Children have not passed through the necessary stages of psychosexual development, nor have they passed through the necessary biological stages (puberty) which would even allow them to display the same "sexual" behavior as adults. As described in the section on juvenile firesetting, several authors including Yarnell (1939) and Sakheim et al. (1985) have found significant evidence of sexual conflict in children who are firesetters (except that it is not typically displayed in a directly sexual manner).

A more understandable approach to explaining the discrepancy between the literature on childhood firesetting and adult firesetting is taken by Fras (1997). He reviewed the literature on childhood firesetting together with his own clinical experience and concluded that the juvenile firesetter can be in general characterized as "an immature, developmentally delayed, often organically impaired person with primitive cognitive processes and poor impulse control" (p. 192). He suggests that the frequent choice of firesetting as a breaking through of impulse in these children with such immature egos is determined by the "primeval human attraction" to fire

(p. 192). "There is no indication that firesetting is a substitution for sexuality in these children" (p. 193). In fact, many of them lack sexual interest as a manifestation of their maturational delay.

Fras believed that adult firesetters represented "a heterogeneous group in terms of motivation and psychodynamics" and that "sexual excitement is sometimes described but not necessarily so" (p. 195). Fras concluded by stating (p. 195):

> "Before late adolescence, there is homogeneity within the group: the combination of characteristic developmental inferiority and environmental disorganization and absence of specific sexual pathology. The late adolescent and adult firesetters, on the other hand, are a heterogeneous group of which the sexually motivated firesetters are but one subgroup. Sexual psychopathology is linked to the archetypal human attraction to fire. The sexually motivated firesetters' goals are to achieve both instinctual gratification of the sexual need and the magic resolution of the intrapsychic conflict — all of this in an individual who has started out with feelings of sexually inferiority and recently suffered social setback."

In a recent study on juvenile firesetters by Sakheim and Osborn (1999), "sexual excitement" or "pleasurable arousal" while watching or setting fires was one of the important predictive variables in differentiating severe from non-severe firesetters. Unfortunately, there are no studies of juvenile firesetters into adulthood. There is no question that, as noted from actual case histories presented (DeRiver, 1958; Lande, 1980; Lewis and Yarnell, 1951), there is a subgroup of individuals who fit the DSM-IV criteria for pyromania. They begin setting fires in childhood, but without any overt sexual behaviors. These individuals may set many fires in their lifetime, but the motivation and the behaviors may change with development.

An interesting case history described by DeRiver (1958) in a chapter on "sexual incendierism" may suggest a possible relationship between the juvenile firesetter and the adult firesetter. In this case report, a middle-aged man is questioned by DeRiver about his many, many years of firesetting activity. The man describes having started fires as a child for the thrill of it but denied any sexual component to the firesetting until the age of 30, at which time he began to ejaculate in response to firesetting activities. He frequented prostitutes on a regular basis, and it was only when he was unable to visit a prostitute that he set a fire for the purpose of sexual gratification. Interestingly, this individual as well as several other individuals reported by DeRiver would frequently urinate in response to the firesetting as well as ejaculate. This, of course, provides an interesting clinical correlation between firesetting and urethral eroticism. If there exists any doubt in the reader's mind as to the sexual nature of firesetting in at least one subgroup of serial firesetters, then please review the case-report section of this chapter.

DOES PYROMANIA EXIST?

Pyromania has a peculiar history of being a psychiatric diagnosis derived and developed in the context of medical-legal definitions and the insanity plea. Geller et al. (1986) have written an extremely interesting and scholarly discussion of pyromania placed in the historical context of shifting attitudes and beliefs, particularly as they apply to the insanity plea. His thesis is that "pyromania is an example of psychiatry's attempt to come to terms with individual responsibility for one's acts and with the concept of moral blameworthiness" (p. 202).

Prichard, a British physician who published his papers on his theories of insanity from 1822 to 1842, indicated that firesetting can be one form that moral insanity can take. Ray (1838), the first American to address the issue of pathological firesetting, described it as a "partial moral mania" in which "a morbid propensity to incendiarism, where the mind, though otherwise sound, is born on by an invisible power to the commission of this crime, has been so frequently observed that it is now generally recognized as a distinct form of insanity" (p. 195). These authors and others believed and advocated for the disease concept of pyromania which held that the individual is not legally responsible for the acts. Treatment rather than punishment was indicated.

Geller et al. (1986) chronicled the authors of the first half of the 1800s who described pyromania as a disease characterized by an instinctive, uncontrollable impulse to set fires. The concept of "irresistible impulse" emerged at this time. Around 1850, a counter-argument was presented which deemed firesetting to be a criminal act and not one of insanity. The issue was hotly contested and appears to have been predominantly a medical-legal issue of the time, a matter of opinion rather than a well-studied clinical issue.

The debate as to whether pyromania (or the concept of moral insanity in general) was a valid psychiatric diagnosis raged throughout the 1800s. The assassination of Garfield in 1881 resulted in a strong reaction against the insanity defense. For the remainder of the 19th century, medical opinion for the most part was against pyromania as a mental disorder.

As described by Geller et al. (1986), this confusion about the diagnosis or even existence of pyromania continued into the 20th century. The DSM-I classified pyromania as an obsessive-compulsive reaction, DSM-II contained no description whatsoever of pyromania, and DSM-III and DSM-IV described pyromania as a recurrent failure to resist impulses to set fires.

The above highlights the fact that the diagnosis of pyromania rests on the concept of an "irresistible impulse." The question then becomes, "What is an irresistible impulse?" How does it relate to the medical-legal system? Geller et al. (1986) hinted that even Lewis and Yarnell questioned the validity of the phenomenon of irresistible impulse. In a footnote at the beginning of their chapter on pyromaniacs, they stated that "caution in accepting this reason [irresistible impulse] should be exercised … frequently the term is not their own but has been suggested to them" (p. 86). However, a careful reading of Lewis and Yarnell (1951) makes clear that they had many cases of patients with no conscious motives, who had only the motivation of the irresistible impulse. They only made the point that it was necessary to carefully examine all other possible motivations, including attempts to claim a psychiatric disorder in order to escape criminal prosecution. By carefully eliminating all other motives, all other factors, and what they termed the transitional cases, they in fact were better able to validate the concept of "true pyromania" which they described as firesetting driven by irresistible impulse and no other motives. The DSM-IV diagnosis of pyromania and Lewis and Yarnell's description of "true pyromania" may be uncommon diagnoses, but certainly ones that retain validity and usefulness.

CONCLUSION

It is hoped that this chapter has made it clear that repetitive firesetting is a complex behavior that in some instances may be a symptom of severe psychopathology; in some instances, (at least in part) a motivated act; in some instances, a function of a primitive, disorganized ego (i.e., as a function of alcohol intoxication or a diminished cognitive ability); and, in some instances, a characteristic pattern of behavior we have described as pyromania.

REFERENCES

APA (1968) *Diagnostic and Statistical Manual of Mental Disorders,* 2nd ed., Washington, D.C.: American Psychiatric Association.

APA (1987) *Diagnostic and Statistical Manual of Mental Disorders,* 3rd ed. (rev.), Washington, D.C.: American Psychiatric Association.

APA (1994) *Diagnostic and Statistical Manual of Mental Disorders,* 4th ed., Washington, D.C.: American Psychiatric Association.

Arlow, J. (1978). Pyromania and the primal scene: a psychoanalytic comment on the work of Yukio Mishima. *Psychoanalytic Quarterly,* 47(1):24–51.

Barnett, W., Richter, P., Sigmund, D., and Spitzer, M. (1997). Recidivism and concomitant criminality in pathological firesetters. *Journal of Forensic Sciences,* 42(5):879–883.

Battle, B.P. and Weston, P.B. (1978). *Arson Detection and Investigation.* New York: Arco Publishing.

Brandford, J. and Dimock, J. (1986). A comparative study of adolescents and adults who willfully set fires. *Psychiatric Journal of the University of Ottawa,* 11(4):228–234.

Bumpass, E.R., Fagelman, F.D., and Brix, R.J. (1983). Intervention with children who set fires. *American Journal of Psychotherapy,* 37(3):328–343.

DeRiver, J.P. (1958). *Crime and the Sexual Psychopath* (pp. 246–268). Springfield, IL: Charles C Thomas.

Douglas, J.E., Burgess, A.W., Burgess, A.G., and Ressler, R.K. (1995). *Crime Classification Manual* (pp. 186–189, 263–264). San Francisco: Jossey-Bass Publishers.

Egginton, J. (1994). *Circle of Fire.* New York: William Morrow and Co.

Fenichel, O. (1945). *The Psychoanalytic Theory of Neuroses* (pp. 371–372). New York, W. W. Norton.

Fras, I. (1997). Firesetting (pyromania) and its relationship to sexuality. In Shlesinger, L.B. and Revitch, E. (Eds.), *Sexual Dynamics of Anti-Social Behavior,* 2nd ed. (pp. 188–196). Springfield, IL: Charles C Thomas.

Frazer, J.G. (1930). *Myths of the Origin of Fire.* London: Macmillan.

Freud, S. (1930). *Civilization and its Discontents* (pp. 50–51). London: Hogarth Press.

Freud, S. (1932). The acquisition of power over fire. *International Journal of Psychoanalysis,* 13:405–410.

Gabbard, G.O. (1995). *Treatments of Psychiatric Disorders,* Vol. 2, 2nd ed. (pp. 2458–2467). Washington, D.C.: American Psychiatric Press.

Geller, J.L. (1984). Arson: an unforeseen sequela of deinstitutionalization. *American Journal of Psychiatry,* 141(4):504–508

Geller, J.L. (1987). Firesetting in the adult psychiatric population. *Hospital & Community Psychiatry,* 38(5):501–506.

Geller, L., Erlen, J., and Pinkus, L. (1986). A historical appraisal of America's experience with "pyromania": a diagnosis in search of a disorder. *International Journal of Law & Psychiatry*, 9(2):201–229.

Geller, L., McDermeit, M., and Brown, J.L. (1997). Pyromania? What does it mean? *Journal of Forensic Sciences*, 42(6):1052–1057.

Grinstein, A. (1952): Stages in the development of control over fire. *International Journal of Psychoanalysis*, XXXIII:416–420.

Gruber, A.R., Heck, E.T, and Mintzer, E. (1981). Children who set fires: some background and behavioral characteristics. *American Journal of Orthopsychiatry*, 51(3):484–488.

Heath, G.A., Gayton, W.F., and Hardesty, V.A. (1976). Childhood firesetting. *Canadian Psychiatric Associates Journal*, 21:229–237.

Heath, G., Hardesty, A., Goldfine, E., and Walker, M. (1985). Diagnosis and childhood firesetting. *Journal of Clinical Psychology*, 41(4):571–575.

Hellman, D.S. and Blackman, N. (1966). Enuresis, firesetting and cruelty to animals: a triad predictive of adult crime. *American Journal of Psychiatry*, 122:1431–1435.

Holmes, R.M. and Holmes, S.T. (1996). *Profiling Violent Crimes* (pp. 92–112). Thousand Oaks, CA: Sage.

Jackson, F., Glass, C., and Hope, S. (1987). A functional analysis of recidivistic arson. *British Journal of Clinical Psychology*, 26(3):175–185.

Justice, B., Justice, R., and Kraft, I. (1974). Early-warning signs of violence: is a triad enough? *American Journal of Psychiatry*, 131:457–459.

Kafry, D. (1978). *Fire Survival Skills: Who Plays with Matches?* Technical report for Pacific Southwest Fires and Range Services, Experimental Station. U.S. Department of Agriculture.

Karpman, B. (1954). A case of fulminating pyromania. *Journal of Nervous and Mental Diseases*, CXIX:205–232.

Kaufman, I., Heims, L.W., and Reiser, D.E. (1961). A re-evaluation of the psychodynamics of firesetting. *American Journal of Orthopsychiatry*, 22:63–72.

Koles, R. and Jenson, R. (1985). Comprehensive treatment of chronic firesetting in a severely disordered boy. *Journal of Behavior Therapy & Experimental Psychiatry*, 16(1):81–85.

Kolko, J. (1989). Firesetting and pyromania. In Last, G. and Hersen, M. (Eds.), *Handbook of Child Psychiatric Diagnosis* (Wiley Series on Personality Processes). New York: John Wiley & Sons.

Koson, F. and Dvoskin, J. (1982). Arson: a diagnostic survey. *Bulletin of the American Academy of Psychiatry and the Law*, 10(1):39–49.

Krzeszowski, F.E. (1993). *What Sets Off an Arsonist*. Arlington, VA: Security Management.

Kuperman, S., Kramer, J., and Loney, J. (1988) Enzyme activity and behavior in hyperactive children growing up. *Biological Psychiatry*, 24(4):375–383.

Lande, S. (1980). A combination of orgasmic reconditioning and covert sensitization in the treatment of a fire fetish. *Journal of Behavior Therapy & Experimental Psychiatry*, 11(4):291–296.

Leong, B. (1992). A psychiatric study of persons charged with arson. *Journal of Forensic Sciences*, 37(5):1319–1326.

Lewis, N.D.C. and Yarnell, H. (1951). Pathological firesetting (pyromania), *Nervous and Mental Disease Monographs*, Monograph No. 82, New York: Coolidge Foundation.

Lowenstein, L.F. (1981). The diagnosis of child arsonists. *Acta Paedopsychiatrica*, 47(3):151–154.

Lowenstein, L.F. (1989). The etiology, diagnosis, and treatment of the firesetting behavior of children. *Child Psychiatry & Human Development*, 19(3):186–194.

Mavromatis, M. and Lion, J.R. (1977). A primer on pyromania. *Diseases of the Nervous System*, 38(11):954–955.

McElroy, S.L., Hudson, J.I., Pope, H.G., Keck, P.E., and Aizley, H.G. (1992). The DSM-III-R impulse control disorders not elsewhere classified: clinical characteristics and relationship to other psychiatric disorders. *American Journal of Psychiatry*,149(3):318–327.

McGrath, P., Marshall, P.G., and Prvor, K. (1979). A comprehensive treatment program for a firesetting child. *Journal of Behavior Therapy & Experimental Psychiatry*, 10:69–72.

Moore, K., Jr., Thompson-Pope, K., and Whited, M. (1996). MMPI-A profiles of adolescent boys with a history of firesetting. *Journal of Personality Assessment*, 67(1):116–126.

New Zealand Press Association (1999). Testing urged to beat arson by firefighters. *Waikato Times* (Hamilton), March 3.

Quinsey, V.L., Chaplin, T. C., and Upfold, D. (1989). Arsonists and sexual arousal to firesetting: correlation unsupported. *Journal of Behavior Therapy & Experimental Psychiatry*, 20(3):203–209.

Raines, J.C. and Foy, C.W. (1994). Extinguishing the fires within: treating juvenile firesetters. *Families in Society: The Journal of Contemporary Human Services*, 75(10):595–607.

Räsäne, P., Hakko, H., and Väisänen, E. (1995). The mental state of arsonists as determined by forensic psychiatric examinations. *Bulletin of the American Academy of Psychiatry Law*, 23(4):547–553.

Ray, I (1838). *A Treatise on the Medical Jurisprudence of Insanity.* Boston: Charles C Thomas/James Brown.

Reed, C. (1998). Top fireman was "serial arsonist". *The Guardian* (Manchester), April 28.

Repo, E. and Virkkunen, M. (1997a). Outcomes in a sample of Finnish firesetters. *Journal of Forensic Psychiatry*, 8(1):127–137.

Repo, E. and Virkkunen, M. (1997b). Young arsonists: history of conduct disorder, psychiatric diagnoses, and criminal recidivism. *The Journal of Forensic Psychiatry*, 8(2):311–320.

Repo, E. and Virkkunen, M. (1997c). Criminal recidivism and family histories of schizophrenic and nonschizophrenic firesetters: comorbid alcohol dependence in schizophrenic firesetters. *Bulletin of the American Academy of Psychiatry and the Law*, 25(2):207–215.

Ressler, R.K. and Schachtman, T. (1982). *Whoever Fights Monsters* (pp. 76–81). New York: St. Martin's.

Rice, M.E. and Harris, G.T. (1991). Firesetters admitted to a maximum security psychiatric institution. *Journal of Interpersonal Violence*, 6(4):461–475.

Ritvo, E. and Shanok, S.S. (1983). Firesetting and non-firesetting delinquents — a comparison of neuropsychiatric, psychoeducational, experiential, and behavioral characteristics. *Child Psychiatry and Human Development*, 13(4):259–267.

Robbins, E. and Robbins, L. (1967). Arson with special reference to pyromania. *New York State Journal of Medicine*, 67:795–798.

Roy, A., Virkkunen, M. Gurthrie, S., and Linnoila, M. (1986). Indices of serotonin and glucose metabolism in violent offenders, arsonists, and alcoholics. *Annals of the New York Academy of Science*, 489:202–220.

Sakheim, G.A. and Osborn, E. (1999). Severe vs. nonsevere firesetters revisited. *Child Welfare*, LXXVIII(4):411–433.

Sakheim, G.A., Vigdor, M.G., Gordon, M., and Helprun, L.M. (1985). A psychological profile of juvenile firesetters in residential treatment. *Child Welfare*, LXIV(5):453–476.

Showers, J. and Pickrell, E. (1987). Child firesetters: a study of three populations. *Hospital and Community Psychiatry*, 38(5):495–500.

Simmel, E. (1949) Incendiarism. In Eissler, K.R. (Ed.), *Searchlights on Delinquency* (pp. 90–101). New York, International University Press.

Soltys, S.M. (1992). Pyromania and firesetting behaviors. *Psychiatric Annals*, 22(2):79–83.

Soothill, K.D. and Pope, P.J. (1973). Arson: twenty-year cohort study. *Medicine, Science, and Law,* 13:127–138.

Stein, J., Hollander, E., and Liebowitz, R. (1993). Neurobiology of impulsivity and the impulse control disorders. *Journal of Neuropsychiatry & Clinical Neurosciences,* 5(1):9–17.

Stekel, W. (1924). *Peculiarities of Behavior,* Vol. 2 (pp. 124–181). New York: Boni and Liveright.

Virkkunen, M., DeJong, J., Bartko, J., and Linnoila, M. (1989a) Psychological concomitants of history of suicide attempts among violent offenders and impulsive firesetters. *Archives of General Psychiatry,* 46:604–606.

Virkkunen, M., DeJong, J., Bartko, J., Goodwin, F.K., and Linnoila, M. (1989b). Relationship of psychobiological variables to recidivism in violent offenders and impulsive firesetters. *Archives of General Psychiatry,* 46:600–603.

Wax, E. and Haddox, G. (1974). Enuresis, firesetting, and animal cruelty: a useful danger signal in predicting vulnerability of adolescent males to assaultive behavior. *Child Psychiatry & Human Development,* 4(3):151–156.

Wolff, R. (1984). Satiation in the treatment of inappropriate firesetting. *Journal of Behavior Therapy & Experimental Psychiatry,* 15(4):337–340.

Yarnell, H. (1939). Firesetting in children. *American Journal of Orthopsychiatry,* 10:262–286.

5 The Nonviolent Serial Offender: Exhibitionism, Frotteurism, and Telephone Scatologia

Richard B. Krueger and Meg S. Kaplan

CONTENTS

Sexual violence is a serious and widespread problem in our society and has been recognized as such by the public, the criminal justice system, and, more recently, the psychiatric community. Within the class of psychiatric disorders called *paraphilias* are the "hands-off" offenses, which include exhibitionism, frotteurism, and telephone scatologia. Because of the attention to and consequences of the more severe paraphilias, which include child victimization, for instance, these "nuisance" paraphilias have generally not been the focus of much attention or study and usually do not result in the severity of sentences that other sexual crimes do. Nevertheless, they are usually repetitive crimes with compulsive overtones, they can cause considerable trauma to innocent victims, and they can result in significant punishments if offenders continue their repetitive behavior.

This chapter examines the above-mentioned disorders of exhibitionism, frotteurism, and telephone scatologia and includes a discussion of the epidemiology, etiology, and current empirical findings (which are quite limited) regarding the treatment of these disorders. Information about these specific disorders is oftentimes generalized from what is known about the assessment and treatment of other paraphilias, as they, too, involve a deviation of sexual interest and repetitive behavior, and many of them coexist in the same individual, often becoming an additional focus of treatment.

The *Oxford English Dictionary* (Burchfield, 1972; Murray, 1969) defines exhibitionism as the "indecent exposure of the sexual organs, esp. as a manifestation of sexual perversion" and indicates that it is based on the Latin stems *ex-* ("out") and *habere* (to hold); thus, to "hold out." The *Diagnostic and Statistical Manual of Mental Disorders* (4th edition, American Psychiatric Association, p. 526; or DSM-IV) lists the diagnostic criteria for exhibitionism as being

A. Over a period of at least 6 months, recurrent, intense sexually arousing fantasies, sexual urges, or behaviors involving the exposure of one's genitals to an unsuspecting stranger.
B. The fantasies, sexual urges, or behaviors cause clinically significant distress or impairment in social, occupational, or other important areas of functioning.

Frotteurism, or frottage, derives from the French word *frottage* meaning "rubbing" or "friction." The *Oxford English Dictionary* notes that, "The special perversion of frottage … consists in a desire to bring the clothed body, and usually though not exclusively the genital region, into close contact with the clothed body of a woman." The DSM-IV lists the following diagnostic criteria (p. 527):

A. Over a period of at least 6 months, recurrent, intense sexually arousing fantasies, sexual urges, or behaviors involving touching and rubbing against a non-consenting person.
B. The fantasies, sexual urges, or behaviors cause clinically significant distress or impairment in social, occupational, or other important areas of functioning.

Telephone scatologia derives from a Greek stem meaning "dung." It is not listed as a separate paraphilia in the DSM-IV; however, it is mentioned in the DSM-IV (p. 532) as falling within a category entitled "paraphilia not otherwise specified" and is identified as meaning "obscene phone calls." Coding for this category does not require any specific duration nor does it specify clinically significant distress or impairment in social, occupational, or other important areas of functioning, although, presumably, one of these aspects would be present in order for someone to seek out a therapist.

Douglas et al. (1992) authored the *Crime Classification Manual,* which presents a standardized system for the investigation and classification of violent crimes. The main classifications of violent crimes are homicide, arson, and rape and sexual assault, with many categories of rape and sexual assault. All of the disorders to which our chapter is devoted would presumably fall within the category of "311, Nuisance Offenses" in the *Crime Classification Manual* (pp. 203–204). These are offenses that occur for purposes of sexual gratification. While the text in the *Crime Classification Manual* suggests that there is no physical contact between the victim and the offender, there is the notation that these offenses also relate to the paraphilias. Exhibitionism is mentioned specifically in the text, but frotteurism, which does involve physical contact through clothing, and telephone scatologia (which is referred to in an example, but not specifically labeled as such) are not, but it would seem appropriate to place both within this classification, as they are considered nuisance paraphilias.

The category of nuisance offenses noted above is divided into the following categories:

1. 311.01 Isolated/Opportunistic Offense — consists of incidents in which individuals take an opportunity to engage in deviant sexual activity when one is presented, such as dialing the wrong number and blurting out an obscenity or, while intoxicated and urinating in a public place, exposing themselves to a woman who might walk by.
2. 311.02 Preferential Offense — consists of the paraphilias.
3. 311.03 Transition Offense — an individual is experimenting with his behavior, and arousal patterns and his interest might not be fixed.
4. 311.04 Preliminary Offense — a non-contact offense might be a prelude to other serious sex offenses, such as when a rapist might be engaged in voyeuristic activity prior to raping an individual.

The manual notes that there is often a pattern of long-term compulsive behavior, with oftentimes rigid and ritualistic patterns of behavior, such as an offender exposing himself in a certain way, returning again and again to the same location, or an offender repeatedly making obscene phone calls. This is certainly true in our clinical experience.

Although these crimes often have a highly distinctive pattern of behavior, and with appropriate resources are potentially quite solvable, the authors note that contact sex offenses frequently assume a higher priority and command more resources than do these lesser, non-contact offenses (Douglas et al., 1992, p. 204). The authors also express concern that investigators and interviewers establish whether or not there is a pattern of escalation and whether or not any such nuisance offense is a "preliminary offense" and thus could possibly lead to more serious offenses. Thus, these paraphilias, although not considered to be as dangerous as other paraphilias, should be taken seriously because of their high frequency and because of the concern that they may be precursors to other, more serious offenses.

EPIDEMIOLOGY

Limited epidemiological data are available on the paraphilias. To our knowledge, no items or questions regarding such behavior have been included in any of the national surveys of sexual behavior in the U.S. (Hite, 1976; Kinsey et al., 1953a,b; Laumann et al., 1994) or in the national surveys of mental disorder conducted by the National Institute of Mental Health (Robins and Regier, 1991). Barriers to such surveys include: (1) the illegality of such behavior and possible consequences in the criminal justice system, (2) a lack of knowledge or interest regarding such behaviors on the part of researchers, and (3) the reluctance and embarrassment of individuals to discuss their sexuality and sexual practices.

In perhaps the most complete and detailed survey of incarcerated sex offenders available, using interviewing techniques developed and tested with the Kinsey reports, Gebhard et al. (1965) interviewed 1356 white males convicted of one or more sex offenses and subsequently incarcerated. They compared this group with 888 white males who had never been convicted for a sex offense and with 477 white males never convicted of anything beyond traffic violations. Of the males convicted of sex offenses, 135, or 10%, were exhibitionists. Only six individuals acknowledged making obscene telephone calls, while 16 others were convicted on the basis of obscene notes, pictures, gestures, or speech but not phone calls.

Limited data are available from smaller studies. Crepault and Couture (1980) interviewed 94 men, ages 20 to 45 years, regarding sexual fantasies they had during intercourse. These subjects were volunteers recruited through posters in public places and through advertising in a major French-language newspaper and so were a highly selected sample, but they still were not as selected as individuals who had been arrested and referred for an evaluation or had been incarcerated and interviewed in prison. Of these men, 61.7% reported fantasies of sexually initiating a young girl; 33.0% reported fantasies of raping adult women; 11.7% had fantasies of being humiliated; 5.3% had fantasies of sexual activity with an animal; 5.3% had fantasies of being beaten up; and 3.2% had fantasies of sexually initiating a young boy. It is important to note that this study involved interviews of males who had not been arrested or accused of sexual crimes and who simply reported on only their fantasies, not their behavior. Also, it is not clear what exactly the advertisement in the newspaper specified.

Templemann and Stinnett (1991) studied 60 undergraduate men who volunteered for college credit to participate in a study of their sexual arousal patterns. The Clarke Sexual History Questionnaire (Paitich et al., 1977) was used to identify anomalous sexual interest patterns. Overall, 65% reported having actually engaged in some form of sexual misconduct; 42% reported having engaged in voyeurism, 8% in obscene phone calls, 35% in frottage, and 2% in exhibitionism. Subjects were asked if they had ever been arrested for sexual offenses, and two of the 60 men studied reported that they had; two others reported that they had been in trouble with parents, school, or an employer for their sexual behavior.

Abel et al. (1988) reported on 561 non-incarcerated individuals who identified themselves as sex offenders and who were recruited via newspaper advertisements and interviewed under the protection of a certificate of confidentiality, which offered the assurance that information obtained from such individuals could not be subpoenaed by legal authorities. Additional protection was afforded by keeping a key that matched offenders' names with their record numbers outside of the U.S. Of these 561 men, 62 (12%) engaged in frottage, 142 (25%) engaged in exhibitionism, and 19 (3%) engaged in obscene phone calling.

In another report, Abel et al. (1987) described an aggregate analysis of 291,000 paraphilic acts committed against more than 195,000 victims. Of all the victims, 37.3% were victims of exhibitionism; 28.6%, frottage; and 1%, obscene telephone calls.

The American Psychiatric Association's Task Force Report, *Dangerous Sexual Offenders* (APA, 1999), included data (in the form of a personal communication) regarding the sexual behavior of 2129 sex offenders who were evaluated by Abel. Of these offenders, 13.8% reported exhibitionism, 11.2% frottage, and 6.3% obscene phone calls.

Bradford et al. (1992), assessing 443 adult males who had been consecutively admitted to the Sexual Behaviours Clinic at the Royal Ottawa Hospital for a forensic psychiatric assessment reported that, of the 274 individuals retained in the final analysis, 37 (14%) admitted to scatologia, 58 (21%) admitted to frotteurism, and 60 (22%) admitted to exhibitionism.

In a more recent study, Kafka and Hennen (1999) reported on a sample of 206 males, consecutively evaluated, who were seeking help for what they referred to as sexual impulsivity disorders consisting of either paraphilia-related disorders (such as compulsive masturbation, protracted heterosexual or homosexual promiscuity, or telephone sex dependence) or paraphilias. They found that 24% of this total sample complained of telephone-sex dependence. Kafka and Prentky (1992) distinguished the entity "telephone sex dependence" from paraphilic behavior because of its requirement for mutual consent rather than involving coercive victimization, a characteristic of the paraphilias. In a study by Kafka and Hennan (1999) among the group who had paraphilias (n = 143), the prevalence of specific paraphilias, in descending order, was exhibitionism, 37%; voyeurism, 24%; pedophilia, 22%; fetishistic transvestitism, 17%; sexual masochism, 17%; telephone scatologia, 14%; fetishism, 12%; sexual sadism, 9%; frotteurism, 8%; rape, 7.5%; and paraphilia not otherwise specified, 9%. Telephone sex dependence was statistically significantly more common in the paraphilia-related disorder group than in the paraphilia group.

From the above studies of normals and sex offenders, it would appear that exhibitionism, frotteurism, and telephone scatologia are all relatively prevalent fantasies and/or paraphilias.

ETIOLOGY

Little is known of the etiology of paraphilias. Theories of etiology have been hypothesized based on learning theory, psychoanalytic theory, biological observations, or other explanations. Numerous researchers have cited social learning theory and conditioning experiences as contributory causes of paraphilias. McGuire et al. (1965) wrote that the theoretical basis for behavior therapy is that the symptom or behavior to be treated had been learned at some point in the past and that it could be changed by learning new patterns of behavior.

The data in the study by Gebhard et al. (1965) cited above, which found that about one third of exhibitionists with a compulsive and repetitive pattern of behavior had problems with impotence (p. 397), lends some support to the analytic theory that genital inadequacy is characteristic of the exhibitionist (Apfelberg et al., 1944). Psychoanalysts have postulated that paraphilias are due to unresolved problems of childhood development and intrapsychic conflict. Stoller (1986) suggested that perversion is the erotic form of hatred: "The hostility … takes form in a fantasy of revenge hidden in the actions that make up the perversion and serves to convert childhood trauma to adult triumph" (p. 4). Stoller (1976) also posited that perversion arises as a way of coping with threats to one's sense of masculinity or gender identity, and that it contains elements of risk, revenge, and triumph. "In the case of the exhibitionist, the risk is that the woman will find one unmanly. ...The fact that one may be arrested becomes proof that one really has a penis that detonates other's fear" (p. 907).

Pearson (1990) suggested that paraphilias may be related to obsessive-compulsive disorder, not only because of the compulsive and repetitive nature of these disorders, but also because of the occurrence of concurrent diagnoses of paraphilias in individuals with obsessive-compulsive disorder and because of the importance of serotonin in impulse control. Additionally, serotonin is involved in sexual responsiveness, and there is a substantial occurrence of sexual side-effects related to the selective serotonin reuptake inhibitors (Rothschild, 1995), again suggesting that serotonin is important in these disorders.

Freund et al. (1983) have suggested that voyeurism, exhibitionism, toucherism, frotteurism, and obscene telephone calling are all based on the same disturbance, which is a distortion of a hypothesized normal sequence of human sexual interactions. Freund and Kolarsky (1965) set forth such a four-phase sequence:

1. *Finding phase,* consisting of locating and appraising a potential partner
2. *Affiliative phase,* characterized by nonverbal and verbal overtures, such as looking, smiling, and talking to a potential partner
3. *Tactile phase,* in which physical contact is made
4. *Copulatory phase,* in which sexual intercourse occurs

Freund and Kolarsky (1965) suggest that a paraphilia involves the omission or distortion of one of these phases and that a particular paraphilia would reflect the preference of the patient for a virtually instant conversion of sexual arousal into orgasm during this phase. Thus, exhibitionism and telephone scatologia would constitute an exacerbation of the affiliative phase, and frotteurism an exacerbation of the tactile phase. Much remains to be clarified, however, about the origin and development of the paraphilias.

MULTIPLE PARAPHILIC DIAGNOSES AMONG SEX OFFENDERS

Several researchers have reported that multiple paraphilic diagnoses frequently exist in the same offender. Abel et al. (1988), in the sample previously described, reported that many of the subjects had more than one paraphilic diagnosis. Of those subjects who were diagnosed as exhibitionists, only 7% had this as a sole paraphilic diagnosis; the remaining exhibitionists had an average number of paraphilias of 4.2. Of frotteurs, 21% had frotteurism as a sole diagnosis, while the other frotteurs had an average of 3.8 paraphilic diagnoses. Only 5.5% of those individuals who made obscene phone calls had this as a sole diagnosis; the remaining obscene phone callers had an average of 5.1 paraphilias.

In another report, Abel et al. (1987) reported high means (or average numbers of acts) and high medians (or that number of acts that divides the group into equal halves) for the paraphiles that they studied; 142 exhibitionists had a mean number of 504.9 acts per subject and a median of 50.5; 62 frotteurs had a mean number of 849.5 acts and a median of 19.5; and 19 subjects who made obscene phone calls had a mean of 135.7 acts and a median of 30.0, suggesting that these are high-frequency behaviors. Individuals engaging in these paraphilias also had a high number of victims. In the above described sample, exhibitionists had a mean or average number of 513.9 victims; frotteurs, an average of 901.4 victims; and obscene phone callers, an average of 102.9 victims. In their sample, this would compare, for instance, with a mean of 7.0 victims per rapist; for female targets of incest pedophilia, 1.8; or for male targets of incest pedophilia, 1.7.

Bradford et al. (1992), in their analysis of 274 male sex offenders who were evaluated, reported quite substantially lower incidents and mean number of incidents for subjects engaging in these behaviors. Sixty individuals admitting exhibitionism reported 1055 total incidents, with a mean of 17.58 incidents per offender; for frotteurism, 58 subjects reported 173 incidents with a mean of 2.08 incidents per frotteur; and for scatologia, 37 individuals reported 681 incidents, with a mean of 18.41 incidents per subject. The difference in the results of these two studies may be due to the different populations (outpatient and not compelled for referral vs. inpatient), the degree of confidentiality afforded those in Abel's study vs. Bradford's, or the difference in interviewing questionnaires, with Abel et al. relying on DSM-III criteria and Bradford et al. utilizing an instrument called the Male Sexual History questionnaire (Paitich et al., 1977).

Abel et al. (1988) reported that, for the three categories of exhibitionism, frotteurism, and telephone scatologia, there was a co-occurrence of additional paraphilias in many of these individuals. For the exhibitionists studied, 46% had also engaged in female nonincestuous pedophilia; 22%, in male nonincestuous pedophilia; 22%, in female incestuous pedophilia; 5%, in male incestuous pedophilia; 25%, in rape; 28%, in voyeurism; 16%, in frottage; and 9%, in obscene phone calling. Of frotteurs, 39% engaged in female nonincestuous pedophilia; 19%, in male nonincestuous pedophilia; 16%, in female incestuous pedophilia; 7%, in male incestuous pedophilia; 23%, in rape; 37%, in exhibitionism; 23%, in voyeurism; and 7%, in obscene phone calls. For obscene phone callers, 42% engaged in female nonincestuous pedophilia; 16%, in male nonincestuous pedophilia; 26%, in female incestuous pedophilia; 0%, in male incestuous pedophilia; 37%, in rape; 63%, in exhibitionism; and 47%, in frottage. At least 5% of paraphiliacs reported six or more paraphilias, some as many as ten.

Bradford et al. (1992) obtained similar data in their research. They computed a proportional index of multiple deviation, which was obtained by tabulating the frequency of each admitted sexually deviant behavior, adding all positive responses for each paraphilic category, and calculating the proportion of subjects within each of these divisions who also responded affirmatively to questions diagnosing other paraphilias. Thus, of those diagnosed with frotteurism, 24% met criteria for heterosexual pedophilia; 35%, for heterosexual hebephilia; 21%, for homosexual pedophilia; 66%, for voyeurism; 29%, for scatologia; 31%, for attempted rape; 16%, for rape; and 31%, for exhibitionism. For those involved with scatologia, 27% met criteria for heterosexual pedophilia; 24%, for heterosexual hebephilia; 24%, for homosexual pedophilia; 8%, for homosexual hebephilia; 62%, for voyeurism; 46%, for frotteurism; 24%, for attempted rape; 14%, for rape; and 35%, for exhibitionism. For exhibitionism, 20% engaged in heterosexual pedophilia; 20%, in heterosexual hebephilia; 10%, in homosexual pedophilia; 8%, in homosexual hebephilia; 52%, in voyeurism; 22%, in scatologia; 30%, in frotteurism; 13%, in attempted rape; and 7%, in rape.

ADOLESCENT ISSUES

Some data and studies on adolescents and the occurrence of deviant sexual interest and behavior in adolescence are available. Data from a research project by Abel et al. (1985) indicated that, of 411 adult sex offenders who presented for evaluation voluntarily at an outpatient clinic, 58.4% reported that the onset of their deviant sexual arousal occurred before they were 18. Longo and Groth (1983), interviewing 231 institutionalized sexual offenders, found that for a "significant number" of offenders their sexually inappropriate behaviors manifested themselves from early adolescence on.

Becker et al. (1986) reported on 67 male adolescent sexual offenders (ages 13 to 19) who had been accused or convicted of committing a sexual crime and who were referred for treatment. Although the majority (89.2%) had been arrested for a sexual crime only once or not at all, they had committed many more sex offenses and many had begun to cross paraphilias. For example, one adolescent referred to as an incest offender self-reported that he had previously engaged in six acts of frottage against six victims; another adolescent incest offender had made 78 obscene phone calls to 39 victims (Becker and Kaplan, 1992).

Fehrenbach et al. (1986), reporting on 305 juveniles treated at an adolescent clinic between 1976 and 1981, found that the most frequently occurring referral offense for male offenders was "indecent liberties" (59%), followed by rape (23%), exposure (11%), and other hands-off offenses, including peeping, stealing women's underwear, making obscene calls, or sending obscene letters (7%).

Saunders et al. (1986) studied 63 adolescent sexual offenders who were divided up according to (1) those who had engaged in exhibitionism, toucherism (referring to the brief touching of a woman's breasts or genitalia), and making obscene phone calls; (2) those who had engaged in sexual assaults; and (3) those convicted of pedophilia. Initial findings revealed that the first group, when compared with the other two groups, came from a less disorganized family background, were better adjusted in school and in the community, and were seen by clinicians as being less seriously disturbed than members of the other two groups. However, upon further examination of the 19 members of this group, it was found that the majority were maladjusted, had committed numerous sexual offenses, and came from multi-problem families.

OFFENDER AND VICTIM CHARACTERISTICS

Gittleson et al. (1978), in an early British study, examined victims of indecent exposure and reported on 100 female nurses who worked at a psychiatric hospital who were interviewed to obtain information regarding the overall frequency of indecent exposure and to ascertain how it was experienced by the victim. Of these nurses, 45 had been the subjects of indecent exposure; one third of them had been a victim on two or more occasions. Histories of 67 separate exposures obtained from members of this group disclosed that 51% of them occurred to these females before their 15th birthday.

The majority of victims (58%) were alone at the time of being exposed to; the rest were in the company of children or other females. Of the exposures, 39% occurred in a park or woodland, 45% occurred in the street, and 16% occurred in other places such as public buildings or vehicles; 34% occurred after dark. The exhibitionist's age was estimated by the victims as being under 40 in 42% of the incidents, between 40 and 60 in 49%, and over 60 in 6%. Three percent of the victims could not remember the age of the offender or reported that they did not know. The victims knew the offender in 15% of cases. The study reported that the exposer stood still in 66% of the incidents, walked toward the victim in 21%, walked behind the victim in 4%, sprang out in 7%, and opened a car door in 1% of the incidents.

In the study by Gebhard et al. (1965, pp. 380–399), cited above, the average exhibitionist was nearly 30 at the time of his first conviction for exhibition. A large number (31%) of exhibitionists were married at the time of the offense, 40% had never married, and 29% were separated, divorced, or widowed. Having a sexual partner did not seriously lessen their tendency to expose themselves; 92% chose strangers as objects, 5% acquaintances, 2% girlfriends, and 1% relatives. They also found that about one quarter of all exhibitionists had suffered from impotence, chiefly erectile impotence, and slightly more than a third of those with an extensive pattern of this behavior also had this sexual dysfunction. They found that half of the exhibitionists were "patterned" exhibitionists who repeated this behavior again and again in a compulsive fashion; one eighth of these began exposing themselves when they were 10 or younger, nearly one fifth began between the ages of 16 and 20, and another fifth between 21 and 25. The authors found that one fifth of exhibitionists had problems with alcohol, that the great majority of exhibitionists had or achieved an erection while exposing their genitalia, and that a small percentage reached orgasm through self-masturbation while exposing themselves.

Gebhard et al. (pp. 406–409) also found that five of the six individuals who made obscene phone calls had quite adequate heterosexual coital activity, and that their overall sexual outlet was well above average, with three of the six for some years in their lives averaging more than an orgasm a day. In addition, three of the six had no convictions other than for obscene communication; the other three had numerous other criminal histories and histories of sex offenses.

Forgac et al. (1984) reported on a study using the Minnesota Multiphasic Personality Inventory (MMPI) to assess the degree of psychopathology in male exhibitionists. An increase in psychopathology as measured by the MMPI was not found to be associated with an increase in chronicity of exhibitionist activity.

Marshall et al. (1991b) studied the sexual preferences of exhibitionists and matched non-offenders using audiotapes and plethysmography. They found that only a small proportion of exhibitionists displayed deviant arousal and suggested that this indicated that a sexual motivation was not a primary one in exhibitionistic behavior.

Smukler and Schiebel (1975) evaluated, retrospectively, the charts of all patients admitted with a major presenting problem of exhibitionism as part of a 5-year ongoing research and treatment project of exhibitionists and voyeurs; 41 were examined clinically and 34 psychometrically with the MMPI and the Comrey Personality Scale. They found no data to support any definitive character type or evidence of severe psychopathology.

Kafka and Prentky (1994) surveyed 60 consecutively evaluated outpatient males, 21 to 53 years old, who were seeking treatment for paraphilias (n = 34) and/or paraphilia-related disorders (n = 26). Those individuals with paraphilias included 13 exhibitionists, three frotteurs, and three with scatologia. Both groups of males were diagnosed with an elevated lifetime prevalence of mood disorders (76.7%), especially early onset dysthymia (53.3%); psychoactive substance abuse (46.7%), including especially alcohol abuse (40.0%); and anxiety disorders (46.7%), including especially social phobia (31.6%).

In another study (Kafka & Prentky, 1998) reported on a group of 42 males with a paraphilia and 18 with a paraphilia-related disorder; the sample with paraphilias included six individuals with frotteurism, six with telephone scatologia, and 15 with exhibitionism. While both samples had mood disorders (71.7%), anxiety disorders (43.3%), and psychoactive substance abuse disorders (45.0%), the only diagnosis which had statistical significance in separating these two groups was childhood attention-deficit hyperactivity disorder, which was identified in 50.0% of individuals with paraphilic disorders and only 16.7% of individuals with paraphilia-related disorders.

POSSIBLE PROGRESSION OF PARAPHILIC INTEREST AND ACTIONS AND ASSOCIATION OF HAND'S OFF DISORDERS WITH VIOLENCE

Is there any evidence to suggest that lesser paraphilias progress to more serious ones? In his book on sex crimes, Holmes (1991, p. 9) noted that Ted Bundy, a serial killer and rapist, reported that he began his sex crimes as a voyeur at the age of 9. Abel et al. (1988) suggested that when multiple paraphilias existed in the same individual one paraphilia initially takes dominance, then a second paraphilia develops and overtakes the first in dominance. The second paraphilia continues for a number of years, while the first continues at a greatly reduced intensity. In an unstructured series of case histories, Johnson and Becker (1997) reported on nine male teenagers who had fantasies of committing serial killings. None had actually done so, and most were referred for a forensic evaluation after having committed a legal offense; three of these at some point had frotteuristic fantasies or behavior, and one of these three additionally had had exhibitionistic fantasies.

Rooth (1973) reported on a study by Grassberger (1964), who examined criminal records for 220 exposers in Austria convicted over a 25-year period. Of these individuals, 12% were subsequently convicted of serious sexual offenses, particularly sexual assaults. Twenty-five percent of them were convicted of nonsexual offenses involving violence. Rooth (1973) reported on information from 30 exhibitionists.

He noted the several hundred sexual offenses for which these men were convicted, but only five consisted of indecent assault. Interestingly, of this series, 12 individuals described at least one episode of frottage and eight had had extensive experience with this paraphilia.

Gebhard et al. (1965, pp. 393, 399) noted that one in ten of the convicted exposers in his study had attempted or seriously contemplated rape, while about one fifth had engaged in sexual offenses involving the use of force on unwilling females.

Longo and Groth (1983) reported on a sample of 231 sexual offenders drawn from a maximum security prison and a forensic state hospital. Of this sample, 24% had sexually exposed themselves repetitively as juveniles.

Dietz et al. (1990) reported on 30 sexually sadistic male criminals, all of whom tortured their victims in order to arouse themselves. Of this sample, 20% had a history of peeping, obscene telephone calls, or indecent exposure.

Firestone et al. (1998) compared 17 extrafamilial homicidal child molesters with 35 extrafamilial child molesters who had not murdered or attempted to murder their victims — 11.8% of the homicidal child molesters and 2.9% of the nonhomicidal child molesters had had a diagnosis of fetishism, voyeurism, exhibitionism, frotteurism, and/or transvestic fetishism; however, this was not a statistically significant difference between these two groups.

In summary, while there is some occurrence of the lesser paraphilias in the histories of more aggressive sexual criminals, there is no clear evidence that minor paraphilias lead to more aggressive ones, or that they, in fact, are even associated with sexual aggression or other violent crimes. The problem with studying the relationship of the hands-off paraphilias with more aggressive paraphilias or with sexual or other violence is that, while a substantial proportion of individuals convicted of more violent crimes may have engaged in lesser paraphilias, the proportion of individuals involved in lesser paraphilias who progress to violent crimes is not known. Further research is required to examine this issue as well as other variables that may affect the development and progression of paraphilias.

TREATMENT

There is a paucity of literature regarding the treatment of these three paraphilias specifically. Most descriptions of such treatment are included within aggregate analyses of groups of individuals who have a large variety of paraphilias, including pedophilia and other paraphilias.

Freeman-Longo et al. (1994) surveyed 1784 treatment programs and treatment providers for juvenile and adult sex offenders in the U.S. and found that the treatment modalities of victim empathy, anger/aggression management, social skills, sex education, communication, personal victimization/trauma, cognitive distortions, assertiveness training, and frustration tolerance/impulse control comprised the top 10 categories of the 55 categories listed in their questionnaire (p. 14). Regarding medication treatment, fluoxetine was used by 25.8% of the entities queried; lithium, by 19.5 %; Anafranil®, by 15.3%; BuSpar®, by 15.3%; and Depo-Provera® (hormonal), by 11.3% (p. 14).

Blair and Lanyon (1981) reviewed the literature regarding the etiology and treatment of exhibitionism and concluded that all of the methodologically adequate treatment studies that had been published involved behavioral treatments. These studies showed that the behavioral technique of covert sensitization reduced the frequency of overt exhibiting acts and that treatment effects persisted at followup for 3 to 12 months.

Marshall et al. (1991a,b) described two studies comparing treatment of exhibitionists which aimed at either modifying deviant sexual preferences or changing cognitions, enhancing relationships and interpersonal skills, and improving awareness with relapse prevention. The first study was comprised of 44 men; the second, 17. The results suggested that a focus on changing cognitions, enhancing relationships and interpersonal skills, and relapse prevention was more effective than behavioral techniques aimed at modifying deviant sexual preferences.

Moergen et al. (1990) described a case study in which covert sensitization and social skills training were used successfully to treat an obscene telephone caller on a behaviorally oriented inpatient psychiatric unit. This treatment included assessment with penile tumescence. A rapid decrease in deviant arousal was associated with the above treatments and maintained at one-year followup.

Alford et al. (1980) reported on the use of covert aversion therapy to treat obscene phone calling and exhibitionism in the same individual; using plethysmographic assessment, they found that treatment of one deviancy resulted in lowering of arousal to both deviancies and that treatment gains were sustained over a 10-month followup period.

Goldberg and Wise (1985) described the successful psychodynamic psychotherapy of a male who had the paraphilia of telephone scatologia. Myers (1991) also described the use of such therapy to successfully treat a man who made obscene telephone calls and who practiced frotteurism.

Gijs and Gooren (1996) reviewed the hormonal and psychopharmacological treatment of the paraphilias; both antiandrogens and antidepressants have been found to be useful, although there is a paucity of well-controlled and well-designed studies.

Kafka and Prentky (1992) reported on 20 men: 10 with non-paraphilic sexual addictions, and 10 with paraphilias. Of the 20 men, 19 met DSM-III-R criteria for dysthymia, and 11 met criteria for current major depression. This group included two individuals with the diagnosis of exhibitionism, one with frotteurism, and two with telephone scatologia. Sixteen individuals completed an open trial of fluoxetine pharmacotherapy. Significant effects were found in both groups over time for all variables related to depression and for both paraphilic and non-paraphilic sexual behaviors as measured by self-report; a response was evident by week four and conventional sexual behavior was not affected adversely by pharmacotherapy.

In a later study, Kafka (1994) reported on the treatment of 24 men with paraphilias and paraphilia-related disorders, including three individuals with a diagnosis of exhibitionism and two with telephone scatologia. Sertraline was used initially, with a mean dose of 100 mg per day; the mean duration of sertraline treatment was 17.4 weeks (±18.6 weeks). Sertraline resulted in a significant reduction in the unconventional total sexual outlet score and in the average time per day spent in unconventional sexual activity. Significant improvement was found in approximately one half of those men who received at least 4 weeks of sertraline therapy. Nine men who failed to respond to sertraline were then given fluoxetine, which produced a clinically significant effect in six additional men.

Zohar et al. (1994) described a single-case study in which an exhibitionist was treated under partial single-blind conditions with fluvoxamine, desipramine, and a placebo that looked like fluvoxamine. They found that fluvoxamine eliminated the undesired impulse and behavior without affecting sexual desire, but desipramine and single-blind fluvoxamine-placebo treatment were both associated with relapses.

Krueger and Kaplan (1997, 1999) reviewed the existing literature relevant to the treatment of frotteurism and suggested a number of stepwise treatment strategies from less to more restrictive, depending on the responsiveness of the individual to any particular treatment.

CONCLUSIONS

Overall, it may be said that exhibitionism, frotteurism, and telephone scatologia are well-described disorders, and they constitute a significant number of the paraphilias that one is apt to encounter in both outpatient and inpatient populations. These paraphilias are often associated with each other in the same individual and with other paraphilias in the same individuals. Oftentimes, these paraphilias begin in adolescence. Alcohol abuse, affective disorder (including dysthymia and depression), and anxiety disorders (including primarily social phobias) are also coexistent in this population. Many individuals who engage in this paraphilic behavior are in satisfactory sexual relationships, while many are not. There is concern that individuals with these disorders may go on to more violent sexual crimes, and some studies of individuals who have committed violent crimes do show a greater association of these paraphilias, but this has not been demonstrated to be statistically significant. The importance of a thorough evaluation must be stressed in order to make correct diagnoses. Effective treatment exists, according to case reports of dynamic therapy, cognitive-behavioral therapy, and pharmacotherapy, with more extensive behavioral and pharmacological studies showing efficacy for these therapies used to treat this population. There is a lack, however, of solid epidemiological studies and of well-designed and controlled pharmacological studies with this population. While auditing a recent lecture given to second-year medical students at Columbia University, College of Physicians and Surgeons, one author learned that in the past 15 years over 17 double-blind placebo controlled studies have been published studying the treatment of what is now called bulimia-nervosa, yet we have been unable to find even one such study that has targeted the three disorders discussed in this chapter. This would certainly seem to be an area which is in need of further exploration and research.

REFERENCES

Abel, G.G., Mittelman, M., and Becker, J.V. (1985). Sex offenders: results of assessment and recommendations for treatment. In Ben-Aron, H., Hucker, S., and Webster, C. (Eds.), *Clinical Criminology: Current Concepts*. Toronto: M & M Graphics.

Abel, G.G., Becker, J.B., Mittelman, M., Cunningham-Rathner J., Rouleau, J.L., and Murphy W.D. (1987). Self-reported sex crimes of nonincarcerated paraphiliacs. *Journal of Interpersonal Violence,* 2(1):3–25.

Abel, G.G., Becker, J.V., Cunningham-Rathner, J., Mittelman, M., and Rouleau, J.L. (1988). Multiple paraphilic diagnoses among sex offenders. *Bulletin of the American Academy of Psychiatry and the Law,* 2:153–168.

Alford, G.S., Webster, J.S., and Sanders, S.H. (1980). Covert aversion of two interrelated deviant sexual practices: obscene phone calling and exhibitionism. A single case analysis. *Behavior Therapy,* 11:15–25.

APA (1994). *Diagnostic and Statistical Manual of Mental Disorders,* 4th ed., Washington, D.C.: American Psychiatric Association.

APA (1999). *Dangerous Sex Offenders.* Task Force Report of the American Psychiatric Association. Washington, D.C.: American Psychiatric Association.

Apfelberg, B., Sugar, C., and Pfeffer, A.Z. (1944). A psychiatric study of 250 sex offenders. *American Journal of Psychiatry,* 100:762–770.

Becker, J.V. and Kaplan, M.S. (1992). Research on adolescent sex offenders. In Burgess, A. (Ed.), *Child Trauma I: Issues and Research* (pp. 383–405). New York: Garland Publishing.

Becker, J.V., Cunningham-Rathner, J., and Kaplan, M.S. (1987). Adolescent sexual offenders: demographics, criminal and sexual histories, and recommendations for reducing future offenses. *Journal of Interpersonal Violence,* 1:431–445.

Blair, C.D. and Lanyon, R.I. (1981). Exhibitionism: etiology and treatment. *Psychological Bulletin,* 89:439–463.

Bradford, J.M., Boulet, J., and Pawlak, A. (1992). The paraphilias: a multiplicity of deviant behaviors. *Canadian Journal of Psychiatry,* 37(2):104–108.

Burchfield, R.W., Ed. (1972). *A Supplement to the Oxford English Dictionary.* Oxford: Oxford University Press.

Crepault, C. and Coulture, M. (1980). Men's erotic fantasies. *Archives of Sexual Behavior,* 9:565–580.

Dietz, P.E., Hazelwood, R.R., and Warren, J. (1990). The sexually sadistic criminal and his offenses. *Bulletin of the American Academy of Psychiatry and the Law,* 18:163–178.

Douglas, J.E., Burgess, A.W., Burgess, A.G., and Ressler, R.K. (1992). *Crime Classification Manual.* New York: Lexington Books.

Fehrenbach, P.A., Smith, W., Monastersky, C., and Deisher, R.W. (1986). Adolescent sexual offenders: offender and offense characteristics. *American Journal of Orthopsychiatry,* 56:225–233.

Firestone, P., Bradford, J.M., Greenberg, D.M., Larose, M.R., and Curry, S. (1998). Homicidal and nonhomicidal child molesters: psychological, phallametric and criminal features. *Sexual Abuse: A Journal of Research and Treatment,* 10:305–323.

Forgac, G.B., Cassel, C.A., and Michaels, E.J. (1984). Chronicity of criminal behavior and psychopathology in male exhibitionists. *Journal of Clinical Psychology,* 40:827–832.

Freeman-Longo, R.E., Bird, S., Stevenson, W.F., and Fiske, J.A. (1994). *1994 Nationwide Survey of Treatment Programs and Models.* Brandon, VT: The Safer Society Press.

Freund, K. and Kolarsky, A. (1965). A simple reference system for the analysis of sexual dysfunctions. *Psychiatrie, Neurologie, Und Medizinische Psychologie,* 17:221–225.

Freund, K., Scher, H., and Hucker, S. (1983). The courtship disorders. *Archives of Sexual Behavior,* 12:369–379.

Gebhard, P.H., Gagnon, J.H., Pomeroy, W.B., and Christenson, C.V. (1965). *Sex Offenders.* New York: Harper & Row.

Gijs, L. and Gooren, L. (1996). Hormonal and psychopharmacological interventions in the treatment of paraphilias: an update. *The Journal of Sex Research,* 33:273–290.

Gittleson, N.L., Eacott, S.E., and Mehta, B.M. (1978). Victims of indecent exposure. *British Journal of Psychiatry,* 132:61–66.

Goldberg, R.L. and Wise, T.N. (1985). Psychodynamic treatment for telephone scatologia. *The American Journal of Psychoanalysis,* 45:291–297.

Grassberger, R. (1964). Der Exhibitionismus. *Kriminalistick,* 18:557–562.

Hite, S. (1976). *The Hite Report.* New York: Macmillan.

Holmes, R.M. (1991). *Sex Crimes.* Newbury Park, CA: Sage.

Johnson, B.R. and Becker, J.V. (1997). Natural born killers? The development of the sexually sadistic serial killer. *Journal of the American Academy of Psychiatry and the Law,* 25:335–348.

Kafka, M.P. (1994). Sertraline pharmacotherapy for paraphilias and paraphilia-related disorders: an open trial. *Annals of Clinical Psychiatry,* 6:189–195.

Kafka, M.P. and Hennen, J. (1999). The paraphilia-related disorders: an empirical investigation of nonparaphilic hypersexuality disorders in outpatient males. *Journal of Sex and Marital Therapy,* 25:305–319.

Kafka, M.P. and Prentky, R.A. (1992a). A comparative study of nonparaphilic sexual addictions and paraphilias in men. *Journal of Clinical Psychiatry,* 53:345–350.

Kafka, M.P. and Prentky, R.A. (1992b). Fluoxetine treatment of nonparaphilic sexual addictions and paraphilias in men. *Journal of Clinical Psychiatry,* 52:351–358.

Kafka, M.P. and Prentky, R.A. (1994). Preliminary observations of DSM III R axis I comorbidity in men with paraphilias and paraphilia-related disorders. *Journal of Clinical Psychiatry,* 55(11):481–487.

Kafka, M.P. and Prentky, R.A. (1998). Attention-deficit/hyperactivity disorder in males with paraphilias and paraphilia-related disorders: a comorbidity study. *Journal of Clinical Psychiatry,* 59:388–396.

Kinsey, A.C., Pomery, W.B., Martin, C.E., and Gebhard, P.H. (1953a). *Sexual Behavior in The Human Female.* Philadelphia, PA: W.B. Saunders.

Kinsey, A.C., Pomery, W.B., Martin, C.E., and Gebhard, P.H. (1953b). *Sexual Behavior in the Human Male.* Philadelphia, PA: W.B. Saunders.

Krueger, R.B. and Kaplan, M.S. (1997). Frotteurism: assessment and treatment. In Laws, R.D. and O'Donohue, W. (Eds.), *Sexual Deviance* (pp. 131–151). New York: Guilford Press.

Krueger, R.B. and Kaplan, M.S. (1999) Evaluation and treatment of sexual disorders: frottage. In Vande Creek, L. (Ed.), *Innovations in Clinical Practice: A Source Book,* Vol. 18. Sarasota, FL: Professional Resource Press.

Laumann, E.O., Gagnon, J.H., Michael, R.T., and Michaels, S. (1994). *The Social Organization of Sexuality. Sexual Practices in the United States.* Chicago, IL: The University of Chicago Press.

Longo, R.E. and Groth, A. (1983). Juvenile sexual offenses in the histories of adult rapists and child molesters. *International Journal of Offender Therapy and Comparative Criminology,* 27:150–155.

Marshall, W.L., Eccles, A., and Barbaree, H.E. (1991a). The treatment of exhibitionists: a focus on sexual deviance versus cognitive and relationship features. *Behavioral Research and Therapy,* 29:129–135.

Marshall, W.L., Payne, K., Barbaree, H.E., and Eccles, A. (1991b). Exhibitionists: sexual preferences for exposing. *Behavior Research and Therapy,* 29:37–40.

McGuire, R., Carlisle, J., and Young, B. (1965). Sexual deviations as conditioned behavior: a hypothesis. *Behavior Research and Therapy,* 2:185–190.

Moergen, S.A., Merkel, W.T., and Brown, S. (1990). The use of covert sensitization and social skills training in the treatment of an obscene telephone caller. *Journal of Behavior Therapy and Experimental Psychiatry,* 21:269–275.

Murray, Sir J.A.H.I. (1969). *The Oxford English Dictionary,* Vol. IX, S–Soldo. Oxford: Oxford University Press.

Myers, W.A. (1991). A case history of a man who made obscene telephone calls and practiced frotteurism. In Fogel, G. and Myers, W. (Eds.), *Perversions and Near Perversions in Clinical Practice* (pp. 109–123). New Haven, CT: Yale University Press.

Paitich, D., Langevin, R., Freeman, R., Mann, K., and Handy, L. (1977). The Clarke SHQ: a clinical sex history questionnaire for males. *Archives of Sexual Behavior,* 6:421–436.

Pearson, H.J. (1990). Paraphilias, impulse control, and serotonin. *Journal of Clinical Psychopharmacology,* 10:233.

Robins, L.N. and Regier, D.A., Eds. (1991). *Psychiatric Disorders in America. The Epidemiologic Catchment Area Study.* New York: The Free Press.

Rooth, G. (1973). Exhibitionism, sexual violence and paedophilia. *British Journal of Psychiatry,* 122:705–710.

Rothschild, A.J. (1995). Selective serotonin reuptake inhibitor-induced sexual dysfunction: efficacy of a drug holiday. *American Journal of Psychiatry,* 152:1514–1516.

Saunders, E.B. and Awad, G.A. (1991). Male adolescent sexual offenders: exhibitionism and obscene phone calls. *Child Psychiatry and Human Development,* 21:169–178.

Saunders, E., Awad, G.A., and White, G. (1986). Male adolescent sexual offenders: the offender and the offense. *Canadian Journal of Psychiatry,* 31:542–549.

Smukler, A.J. and Schiebel, D. (1975). Personality characteristics of exhibitionists. *Diseases of the Nervous System,* 36:600–603.

Stoller, R.J. (1976). Sexual excitement. *Archives of General Psychiatry,* 33:899–909.

Stoller, R.J. (1986) *Perversion: The Erotic Fear of Hatred.* London: Karnac Books.

Templeman, T.L. and Stinnett, R.D. (1991). Patterns of sexual arousal and history in a "normal" sample of young men. *Archives of Sexual Behavior,* 20(2):137–150.

Zohar, J., Kaplan, Z., and Benjamin, J. (1994). Compulsive exhibitionism successfully treated with fluvoxamine: a controlled case study. *Journal of Clinical Psychiatry,* 55:86–88.

Part II

Introduction

For many years, law enforcement officers have used criminal investigative profiling techniques in an attempt to narrow the field of unidentified offenders. In Chapter 6, Robert D. Keppel reviews one aspect of investigative profiling by explaining how different cases can be linked through an understanding of the concepts of *modus operandi* (MO) and signature. *Modus operandi* — an individual's method of carrying out crimes — can change as the offender gains experience and learns new criminal techniques. On the other hand, signature — behavior at the crime scene that is an outgrowth of the offender's personality — usually does not change. Dr. Keppel discusses signature and MO within an historical perspective and illustrates the differences in these concepts by describing several interesting cases that he has investigated. The chapter concludes with a discussion of how signature and MO are used in the apprehension of the serial offender.

In Chapter 7, Laurence Miller explains the interaction of neurological, neuro-psychological, and psychodynamic factors in serial offending, specifically serial homicide. He argues that neuropsychodynamic mechanisms in serial murder are similar to the adaptive brain mechanisms of stalking and predation that characterize many "normal" social activities of human, primate, mammalian, and vertebrate life. This chapter reviews not only the neuropsychological aspects of impulsive and pred-atory aggression, but also the neurochemistry and psychophysiology of violence. The author discusses the possible effects of brain injury on various aspects of aggression and concludes that a neurophylogenetic model of serial sexual homicide is necessary for a full understanding of this offense. The predatory serial murderer, Dr. Miller argues, is a "limbically kindled engine of destruction" who believes he is entitled to kill. The sexual/aggressive element found in serial homicide is a greatly exaggerated fusion of the sex and aggression that occur commonly in many forms of sexual activity. The connection of sex and aggression may have become permanently magnified, perhaps by an abusive hypersexualized upbringing.

Stalking has been described as the quintessential crime of the 1990s. In Chapter 8, Robert Lloyd-Goldstein discusses serial stalkers, a subject that has not been studied or reported previously. He begins with a typology of stalkers, including the erotomaniac stalker, celebrity stalkers, former intimate stalkers, casual acquaintance stalkers, predatory/sociopathic stalkers, and a miscellaneous group including those who are socially inept or intellectually limited. Dr. Lloyd-Goldstein then reviews stalkers' demographics, psychiatric status, psychodynamics, and management and provides an illustrative case that exemplifies many of the characteristics of serial stalkers. He also discusses fruitful avenues for future research, particularly cyberstalking, an area that is sure to be of increased concern in years to come.

Serial burglary is covered in Chapter 9 by Louis B. Schlesinger. The author discusses various types of repetitive burglary: offenses that are a result of a primary disorder, such as psychosis or substance abuse; burglaries that result from social or environmental factors, such as burglaries committed by youth gangs and by professional burglars; burglary as a result of situational factors; burglaries committed by impulsive offenders; and sexually motivated burglaries. Fetishism and voyeurism, which contribute to many sexually motivated burglaries and often escalate into acts of sexual aggression or even sexual homicide, are also discussed. Dr. Schlesinger explains various levels of motivation in the various types of burglary and argues that burglaries committed solo and under bizarre circumstances, where material gain is minimal or rationalized, often have a strong underlying sexual basis. An understanding of the different types of serial burglary and their differing behavioral characteristics, motives, and dynamics will assist practitioners in the proper assessment of such cases.

The final chapter in Part II, by John B. Pryor and Adena B. Meyers, is on a topic that is usually overlooked when serial offenders are discussed — namely, men who sexually harass women and do so in a repetitive manner. Professors Pryor and Meyers present a typology of the sexual harasser, including perspectives from social science and law. They then discuss personality and situational variables as predictors of various types of sexual harassment, such as gender harassment, unwanted sexual attention, and sexual coercion. Finally, they show how Pryor's "Likelihood to Sexually Harass" scale is used to assess an individual's proclivity toward sexual harassment. Because sexual harassment often represents a pattern of behavior over time, individual differences in conduct could be facilitated or inhibited by various situational factors, such as social pressures experienced by the offender. Thus, awareness of both personality characteristics and situational events is necessary if we are to understand this conduct fully and to develop methods for its prevention.

6 Investigation of the Serial Offender: Linking Cases Through *Modus Operandi* and Signature

Robert D. Keppel

CONTENTS

INTRODUCTION TO CRIME SCENE ASSESSMENT

The methodology for determining the signature and *modus operandi* (MO) of a killer is similar to that for "profiling" a case. The major differences lie in the type of information used and the results. In order to perform signature analysis and profiling, one must thoroughly examine the police case file.

Throughout history, police investigators, psychologists, and forensic psychiatrists have analyzed cases to determine the "profile" of an unknown offender. This process has been referred to as applied criminology, psychological profiling, crime scene assessment, criminal personality profiling, crime scene profiling, and investigative psychology, among others. For purposes of this chapter, the process will be called "crime scene assessment." Several outcomes are possible from crime scene assessment (Keppel and Walter, 1999): (1) determining the physical, behavioral, and demographic characteristics of the unknown offender; (2) developing post-offense behavior of the offender and strategies for apprehension; (3) developing interviewing strategies once the offender is apprehended; (4) determining the signature of the offender; and (5) determining where evidence may be located.

For any of the above outcomes, the type of information used for analysis may differ. Typically, the information comes from the police investigative file, which includes officer's reports, statements, crime laboratory reports, crime scene diagrams, photographs, videotapes of crime scenes, and autopsy reports. This chapter, however, will focus only on the methodology for determining the signature of the offender. In order to accomplish this, it is important to understand how the offender's signature differs from his *modus operandi* from case to case.

What really confirms that two or more crimes can be linked to the same offender has not been through *modus operandi* analysis *per se*, but through signature analysis. It is the purpose of this chapter to explain the differences between *modus operandi* and signature and demonstrate the uses of both in linking murders to the same offender.

HISTORICAL PERSPECTIVE

The concept of *modus operandi* has been subjected to extensive analysis through the criminal appeals of serial offenders, and its definition has remained stable. Generally, the terms *modus operandi*, method of operation, or MO are used interchangeably to describe a certain criminal's way of operating (*State v. Pennell*, 1989; *State v. Prince*, 1992; *State v. Code*, 1994; *State v. Russell*, 1994).

Police investigators and prosecutors need to have cases linked for their own purposes. From an investigative standpoint, the linking of crimes enables investigators to pursue one suspect instead of operating without the knowledge that particular cases are linked. Prosecutors want similar cases linked so the defendant can be tried on multiple charges in the same trial. Of course, it is the defendant's prerogative to request that each charge be heard separately by a different jury.

The threshold for using MO and signature as evidence at trial that cases are linked differs from state to state. For example, the Supreme Court of Virginia held that, "Evidence of other crimes, to qualify for admission as proof of *modus operandi*, need not bear such an exact resemblance to the crime on trial as to constitute a 'signature,' but it is sufficient if the other crimes bear a singular strong resemblance to the pattern of the offense charged and the incidents are 'sufficiently idiosyncratic to permit an inference of pattern for purposes of proof,' thus tending to establish the probability of a common perpetrator" (*Timothy Wilson Spencer v. Commonwealth of Virginia*, 1990).

The phrase "*modus operandi*" first appeared in literature in 1654 in a piece called *Zootomia:* "Because their causes, or their *modus operandi* (which is but the Application of Cause and Effect) doth not fall under Demonstration." The term appears to have become popular in the 1800s, with citations in the *Edinburgh Review* in 1835, Mill's *Logic III* in 1843, and in Kenneth Grahame's short story "Justifiable Homicide" in the *Pagan Papers* in 1898 (Grahame, 1904; *Oxford English Dictionary*, 1933).

The earliest mention of *modus operandi* in the U.S. is not associated with criminal law or police investigations but is traced to the law of patents dealing with inventions of machines (Robinson, 1890). In the case of *Whittenmore v. Cutter*

(1813), the Massachusetts Circuit Court declared, "By the principles of a machine (as these words are used in the statute) is not meant the original elementary principles of motion, which philosophy and science have discovered, but the *Modus operandi*, the peculiar device or manner of producing any given effect. The expansive powers of steam, and the mechanical powers of wheels, have been understood for many ages; yet a machine may well employ either one or the other, and yet be so entirely new, in its mode of applying these elements, as to entitle the party to a patent for his whole combination."

The first pioneer in the use of *modus operandi* in police operations was Major L.W. Atcherley, Chief Constable of the West Riding Yorkshire Constabulary in England. His efforts superseded the establishment of *modus operandi* files in Scotland Yard in 1896 by 17 years. Major Atcherley devised workable clearinghouses for information on various criminal's methods so they could be tracked from district to district. He constructed ten categories relating to an offender's *modus operandi:*

1. Classword: Kind of property attacked (whether dwelling house, lodging house, hotel, etc.)
2. Entry: The actual point of entry (front window, back window, etc.)
3. Means: Whether with implements or tools (such as a ladder, jimmy, etc.)
4. Object: Kind of property taken
5. Time: Not only the time of day or night, but also whether at church time, on market day, during meal hours, etc.
6. Style: Whether the criminal describes himself as a mechanic, canvasser, agent, etc. to obtain entrance
7. Tale: Any disclosure as to his alleged business or errand that the criminal may make
8. Pals: Whether the crime was committed with confederates
9. Transport: Whether bicycle or other vehicle was used in connection with the crime
10. Trademark: Whether the criminal committed any unusual act in connection with the crime (such as poisoning the dog, changing clothes, leaving a note for the owner, etc.)

These ten categories related specifically to a criminal's *modus operandi*; however, Major Atcherley recognized that special individual things or unusual acts occurred at the scene of a crime, and he called these the criminal's "trademark" (Fosdick, 1916). This recognition of a criminal's trademark was the precursor for what would become known as the offender's signature today. By the late 1930s, *modus operandi* identification techniques and procedures became a standard part of criminal investigation literature (Soderman and O'Connell, 1936). Edwin Sutherland (1947) defined *modus operandi* as the "principle that a criminal is likely to use the same technique repeatedly, and that any analysis and record of the technique used in every serious crime will provide a means of identification in a particular crime."

The investigative use of *modus operandi* began to change in the late 1980s. It became apparent that the MO of an offender would change slightly from crime to crime. For example, a burglar who normally used a pipe wrench on the front door knob to gain entry might change his MO after discovering that the front door was unlocked. Thus, the burglar would enter through an unlocked front door without using the pipe wrench and his MO changed to fit the circumstances. Also, it became apparent that a murderer or rapist would have to do the same thing from crime to crime (Douglas and Munn, 1992; Douglas et al., 1992; Geberth, 1996; Hazelwood and Michaud, 1999; Keppel, 1995; Keppel, 2000; Keppel and Birnes, 1997; Keppel and Weis, 1999).

WHAT IS A KILLER'S SIGNATURE?

A killer's signature, sometimes referred to as his psychological "calling card," is left at each crime scene across a spectrum of several murders. Homicide detectives are trained to look for the unusual — for those characteristics that distinguish one murder from all others. Thus, when one sees something rare in one murder and recognizes the same element a week later, one sees the personification of a lone killer in those unusual acts. For example, when the killer in one murder intentionally leaves the victim in an open and displayed position, posed physically in a spread-eagle position as if for a bizarre photographic portrait, and when he savagely beats the victim to a point of overkill and violently rapes her with an iron rod, you have to consider such behavior as fundamentally unusual. When a second murder is committed in which the killer has done the same things as in the first, even though he may slightly modify one or two of the features, there is little doubt the two murders are related. The crime analyst reacts to the killer's signature in this instance (Keppel, 1997).

Some people confuse MO, or *modus operandi*, with signature as if the two were the same thing. They're not. An MO is simply the way a particular criminal operates. If a criminal commits breaking-and-entry burglaries by using a glass cutter to get through a door and suctions the glass away so it does not fall to the ground and make noise, that's his MO. If the criminal uses flypaper instead of a suction cup to hold the glass fragments together so they do not make noise, that is a different MO. When police find flypaper traces at a crime scene, they go back to their files and look for breaking-and-entry burglars who have used flypaper and utilize this knowledge to form a list of suspects. For the crime of murder, MO includes only those factors necessary to commit the murder and can change over time as the killer discovers that some things he or she does are more effective (Douglas et al., 1992; Keppel, 1995).

Basically, an MO accounts for the type of crime and property attacked, including the person, the time and place the crime was committed, the tools or implements used, and the way the criminal gained entry or how he got his victim, which includes disguises or uniforms, ways he represented himself to a victim, or props such as a bike or crutches.

The problem is that MO investigations can be too much of a good thing. Police detectives rely so much on MO that if it even slightly changes, from crime to crime, they begin looking for a different criminal despite other striking similarities from crime to crime. For example, the race of the victim changes in a series of killings in which there are three white female victims and one black woman. Even though the crimes may be similar — all on or near university campuses, all committed in isolated areas within 10 to 15 miles of one another, all cases of rape murder — the fact that one young victim was black while the others were white usually sends police off on a hunt for two suspects. That is what happened in Rochester, NY, in the Arthur Shawcross cases. When the killer attacked both black and white prostitutes and other women who crossed his path who were not prostitutes, investigators searched for different killers (Keppel et al., 1997).

SIGNATURE VS. MO

There are crime scene indicators that relate murders even when the MO changes. Many sexually sadistic repetitive killers, for example, go beyond the actions necessary to commit a murder. As discussed previously, the MO of a killer can and does change over time as the killer finds that some things he does are more effective. The FBI's John Douglas and others (1992) of the Behavioral Sciences Unit in Quantico, VA, said that the *modus operandi* of a killer is only those actions that are necessary to commit the murder.

Beyond the MO, there are many, many killers who are not satisfied with just committing the murder; they have a compulsion to express themselves (or do something that reflects their unique personality). The killer's personal expression is his signature, an imprint he leaves at the scene, an imprint he feels psychologically compelled to leave in order to satisfy himself sexually. The core of a killer's signature will never change. Unlike the characteristics of an offender's MO, the core remains constant. However, a signature may evolve over time, such as in some cases where a necrophilic killer performs more and more postmortem mutilation from one murder to the next. The FBI's Behavioral Sciences Unit defends the premise of a constant signature by saying that the elements of the original personal expression only become more fully developed (Douglas et al., 1992).

Douglas and others (1992) once described the nature of the signature as the person's violent fantasies, which progress in nature and contribute to thoughts of committing extremely violent behavior. As a person fantasizes over time, he develops a need to express those violent fantasies. Most serial killers have been living with their fantasies for years before they finally bubble to the surface and are translated into behavior. When the killer finally acts out, some characteristic of the murder will reflect a unique aspect played over and over in his fantasies. Likewise, retired NYPD homicide detective Vernon Geberth (1996) wrote that it is not enough simply to consummate the murder; the killer must act out his fantasies in some manner over and beyond inflicting death-producing injuries. This "acting out" is the signature of the killer.

Detectives who investigate a series of murder scenes look for the same type of extraordinary violence and a bizarre set of similarities, and their gut instincts will tell them there is more here that is alike than different. Another homicide investigator, however, might point out that the killer used a pipe wrench as a blunt instrument here, a hammer there, and in a third crime no one can even figure out what weapon was used. Maybe one time the killer draped a pair of underpants on the victim's left leg, then, at the next crime scene, the underpants were on the victim's right leg or maybe still on the bed. In each case, though, the victim was obviously beaten well beyond the point of death by an assailant whose violence seemed to increase in frenzy while he was attacking her. Also, the killer seemed preoccupied with the victim's clothing and took some time to arrange the crime scene even though there might have been people living just upstairs. These are the psychological calling cards the killer actually needs to leave at each scene. Other examples of signatures are mutilation, overkill, carving on the body, leaving messages, rearranging or positioning the body, engaging in postmortem activity, or making the victim respond verbally in a specified manner. These constitute a signature. What is important about a killer's signature, then, is that killers learn to treat victims the way they do in their fantasies, always attempting to satisfy their fantasies as they move from one victim to the next.

THE SHORELINE MURDERS

The Shoreline district lies north of the city limits of Seattle in unincorporated King County, WA. The area includes a shopping mall to the north, near the King/Snohomish County line, made up of small to mid-size businesses, convenience shops, and stores. The immediate area of the murders consists of multi-family dwellings, apartments, and some single-family homes. An apartment complex is located on a cul-de-sac in the 19700 block of 22nd Avenue Northeast in an area called "Ballinger Terrace." The Ballinger Terrace area does not have many murders within a year's time; in the previous year, the neighborhood experienced the average variety of crimes and one murder of a male victim. But, within 30 days, the locale experienced two separate, atypical murders within the same apartment complex.

Robert Lee Parker was convicted of two counts of aggravated first-degree murder. Before trial, members of the King County Prosecutor's Office, Seattle, WA, requested that a signature analysis be completed on the two murders. Their main question was, "Were both murders committed by the same person?" The analysis did not include any information about Parker or evidence about why he was connected to either case.

RENEE POWELL

Renee Powell relocated from St. Louis to Seattle. As a registered nurse, she was employed by several hospital facilities in the area. Powell was described as a 43-year-old white female; 5 feet, 4-1/2 inches tall; small build; and weighing 100 pounds. She had no criminal record and had not been a crime victim in the past.

Powell was last seen alive at approximately 7:30 p.m. on February 24, 1995. Previously, she had driven to a nearby Albertson's Supermarket to purchase some cigarettes, a newspaper, and some ice. Police investigation revealed that upon returning to her apartment at 2228 NE 197th Place, Apartment B, she had sufficient time to make a jar of iced tea. Also, it was discovered that Renee was doing laundry in the building's laundry room, which was adjacent to her lower apartment unit. The apartment structure was a two-story residence containing four units. No one would see Powell again until firemen discovered her charred remains inside her apartment shortly after midnight on February 25.

At about 11:50 p.m., neighbors reported a fire in Powell's apartment. By 12:40 a.m., the firemen had put out the fire and discovered Powell's body. They discovered that she was bound, gagged, and constrained by a ligature. Homicide detectives from the King County Police were called. Investigation revealed that Powell probably heard a noise at the front door of her apartment because the killer had broken her door open. She probably had no time to respond. Powell was discovered face down on the floor of her bedroom with a bookshelf pulled down and lying on top of her body. The killer appeared to have stripped her naked from the waist down and then tore her shirt from her body. Her bra remained fairly intact, pushed up, exposing her breasts. Her left arm was bound with an electrical cord cut from a study lamp later found in her bedroom.

Arson investigators determined that separate and distinct fires had been started around the residence. They did not communicate with each other. The first fire was started in the master bedroom near the victim's body. The second began in the living room next to the fireplace.

The autopsy examination discovered that Powell suffered two stab wounds. One was in the right abdomen and stomach; the other, in her left back in the parasacral muscle. The gag in her mouth was an elastic bra, tied tightly and fastened in the back with a double overhand knot. The medical examiner removed a segment of electrical cord from around the victim's left forearm and outside of the shirt. The loops were tied with a complicated set of overhand knots. The plug end of the cord was present and the other end appeared cut.

The presence of conjunctival petechiae indicated that there was probable asphyxia. The victim's body was more badly burned in the front than in the back. There was no soot found in the throat; therefore, death occurred prior to the fires. Powell had been vaginally raped and semen was preserved as evidence.

Further investigation revealed that the killer had stolen items from the apartment, including an overcoat, a dress, a videocassette recorder, several bottles of wine, a duffel bag, and some frozen meat.

Barbara Walsh

Barbara Walsh was a 54-year-old white female who lived alone. She had been widowed over 20 years ago and never remarried. In the weeks prior to her death, she had not developed any significant relationships. Like Renee Powell, Walsh lived in a lower unit of the same apartment complex. Walsh worked as a receptionist at Group Health Hospital.

Thirty days after the murder of Renee Powell, at about 10:30 p.m., a neighbor saw Barbara Walsh returning from the laundry room of their four-plex. Walsh lived at 2202 NE 197th Place, Apartment B, which was about 100 yards northwest of Powell's apartment (see Figure 1). Unlike Powell's one-door apartment, Walsh's had a front door and a back sliding door that opened to a common patio and a wooded area. Her sliding door could not be unlocked from the outside, so police investigators surmised that during one of Barbara's trips down to the laundry room, the killer slipped inside.

FIGURE 1. Aerial view of Powell and Walsh's apartments in proximity to Parker's residence.

At about 1:06 a.m. the following morning, neighbors reported smelling smoke and discovered a fire in progress in Walsh's apartment unit. Fire personnel extinguished the fire and discovered the body of Barbara Walsh. They could see that she was face down, bound, and gagged with a ligature. She was found on the floor of her bedroom with her head next to the foot of her bed. She was nude except for her shirt, which was shoved up nearly to her neck. Multiple fires had been set within the apartment. In the bathroom, between the sink cabinetry and a throw rug, a Trojan condom wrapper was located. Having found a knife in Walsh's kitchen, electrical cords from her lamps, and tights from her drawers and in her laundry, the killer was prepared for his night's work.

The autopsy report stated that Walsh was gagged with three pairs of tights, tan (innermost), white (overlain over the tan), and green (overlain over the white). The tan and white tights circled circumferentially around the back of the head once. The green tight circled once through the mouth and once around the anterior aspect of the neck at approximately the level of the thyroid prominence. All of the crotch regions of the tights were located anteriorly. The white tight was knotted once in the midline posterior region and once around the green tight, slightly left of midline. Approximately 11 inches away was another knot in the green tights through which was threaded a yellow electrical cord. The pathologist found several strands of blue yarn located next to the male adapter of the cord.

FIGURE 2. Knife used in the Walsh murder; found on the couch where one of the fires was started.

Police discovered that similar blue yarn was also tied to the bedstead, as if the victim had been tied to the bed at one point. Of note was a knife found in the kitchen that police believe the killer used on the victim. The knife had a 7-inch blade attached to a 4-inch handle (Figure 2). All items and materials used by the killer belonged to the victim. Several items were taken from the victim's residence. Those items included a television set, videocassette player, compact disc player, wicker baskets, a box of silverware, Raggedy Anne and Andy figures, miniature red wire old-fashioned bicycles, a glass prism, and small polished stones.

On the victim's left wrist was a ligature that was extensively burned and consisted of multiple types of wires. There was a 9-1/2-inch length of black insulated wire, incompletely burned through and attached by a few strands to a portion of yellow-tan insulated wire. The yellow-tan wire, from a lamp in the residence, was wrapped and knotted circumferentially around her wrist. The knot was located on the lateral aspect. One portion of the wire completely encircled the thumb.

Walsh suffered three stab wounds clustered on the right side of her abdomen. The stab wounds were gaping and extensively charred around the edges. Near this cluster of wounds was a solitary stab wound. All of the stab wounds proceeded from right to left without appreciable upward or front-to-back deviation.

In summary, the pathologist stated that Walsh died as a result of ligature strangulation by the stocking, which also served as a gag. Additionally, a ligature was present on her left wrist and multiple abdominal stab wounds were identified, which produced injuries insufficient to account for her death. The thermal injuries were incurred after death and no soot was present in her throat.

SIGNATURE ANALYSIS

In these sexually perverted murders, the killer's approach to the victims and his selection of the location were preparatory, enabling the killer to carry out his highly personalized fantasies. Thus, evidence left as a direct result of carrying out his fantasy was far more revealing of the killer's nature than his MO.

In testimony at a hearing regarding separation of the two charges of first-degree murder, the following characteristics were described as being features of the killer's signature in the Shoreline murders. First, the act of binding was present in both murders. The killer used binding materials found at the scenes. Binding materials were not brought to each scene by the killer. The use of electrical cord and the ligatures exceeded the necessary violence to control the victims for rape-murder. The electrical cord binding and loops around both victims were the specific and necessary control devices that the killer had to use at each crime scene. Typically, these types of arm bindings are used by killers who prance the victim around (much like a dog on a leash) and poke them with a knife, thus evoking terror and satisfying his anger.

Second, the number of stabbing strokes was necessary for this killer and increased from the first murder to the second murder. The killer stabbed Powell, the first victim, twice and inflicted four stab wounds on Walsh, the second victim. Third, the disposition of both victims' bodies reflected this killer's personal feelings. The killer had to leave the victims in a sexually degrading and submissive position. Both were essentially nude from the neck down and intentionally placed face down. The killer purposefully left the victims so they would be found.

Fourth, the taking of souvenirs enabled this killer to relive the event at some future time. Such thievery was crucial to this killer's needs. Psychologically, the killer regarded these victims as "bitches," which, in his mind, justified his thefts. Finally, the presence of arson was evidence of another form of violence inflicted by the killer. The arson fires were a product of refinement and learning. There were more fires set at the second murder scene. Setting fires at the crotch of both victims was totally unnecessary but was an act this killer felt compelled to do.

In summary, as this killer proceeded from one victim to the next, his true signature evolved. More stab wounds, more percussive activity with the body, and additional fires allowed this killer to feel more attached to his victims and vent his anger. These factors led to the conclusion that the two victims were killed by the same person.

HITS STATISTICAL ANALYSIS

The Homicide Investigation and Tracking System (HITS) in the Washington State Attorney General's Office is a central repository of murder and sexual assault information in the state of Washington. The HITS program is a database with 227 query capabilities (Keppel and Weis, 1993). Prior to a hearing on the separation of charges a statistical analysis was performed to determine the relative frequency of the signature characteristics in the Powell and Walsh murders.

At the beginning of the analysis, there were 5788 murder cases in the HITS program. The first search revealed that there were 1164 cases in which the body recovery site was the victim's home. Of those cases, there were 90 victims that were discovered bound in some way. From those 90 victims, 49 cases were found in which trophies or significant items were removed by the killer(s). Of those 49 cases, there were 16 victims who received stabbing or cutting wounds. When those 16 victims were checked, only two victims, Powell and Walsh, were found burned. The rarity of these characteristics was significant to the prosecution.

CATCHING THE KILLER

Detective followup work and crime laboratory analyses further corroborated the opinion that these two murders were committed by the same person. Robert Parker lived across the street from the woods that overlooked the apartment complex where Renee Powell and Barbara Walsh lived. Police detectives contacted Parker's residence during the initial canvas, but the residence was in the name of his girlfriend and Parker provided a false name. Parker's residence was only 130 feet from Walsh's home and 150 yards from the home of Powell. Parker was known to go out for long periods alone at night without explanation.

In late October 1996, detectives were contacted by a therapist. The therapist was treating a woman by the name of Princess Gray. The therapist told police that her client had information about murders that occurred in the Shoreline area. On November 1, 1996, detectives contacted Princess Gray in the King County Jail. Gray had been charged and booked for Assault and Reckless Endangerment and was awaiting trial. Gray told detectives that Parker told her two white guys were involved in the first lady's murder and Parker had stolen Powell's property from them.

She related that on the night of the murder, Parker brought home a videocassette recorder, eight or nine bottles of wine, and freezer food that included pork chops. He also had a container with $30 to $40 in change. Gray said that after the second murder, Parker came back with a television, another videocassette recorder, and a compact disc player. Parker also brought some spices. Gray was asked if Parker had also brought any trinkets. She said, "Yes, things you set on your table." Detectives subsequently recovered most items from Gray's residence. They also recovered Powell's duffel bag from Parker's residence at the time of his arrest for the murders. Inside the duffel bag's pocket were polished stones that Walsh was known to collect. Killers frequently remove items belonging to their victims as souvenirs or for monetary gain (Douglas et al., 1992). Parker's retention of stolen items found in the possession of Princess Gray and himself contributed to the evidence against him in these cases.

More specific evidence linking Parker to both murders was discovered. From semen found on Powell's vaginal swabs, investigators requested that DNA analysis be performed and compared to Parker's DNA. It was found to be a match.

In addition, hair was found on Walsh's bathroom counter. The hair was protected from the fire by a towel that lay on top of it (Figure 3). DNA analysis was performed on the hair and compared to Parker's DNA, and another match was discovered.

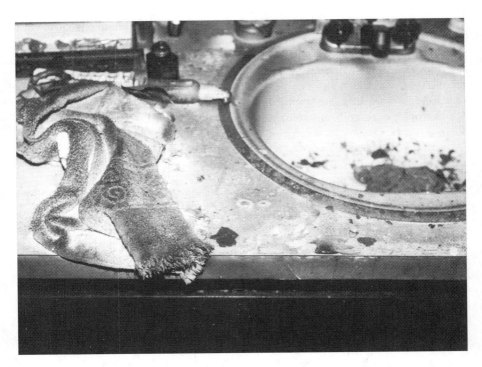

FIGURE 3. Location of the towel in Walsh's bathroom. Hair, linked by DNA profiling to Parker, was found under the towel.

For the experienced homicide detective, linking murder cases by distinguishing between a killer's MO and his or her signature should not be difficult. What is problematic is that the elements of the signature, at times, can be hidden due to decomposition of the remains and/or contamination of the crime scene. The two scenes in the Shoreline cases were contaminated by fire, but the early discovery of the fire prevented more destruction of evidence that would have possibly hidden the killer's signature elements.

SUMMARY

A killer's method of operation contains those actions that are necessary to commit the murders. They may change from one murder to the next as the killer gains experience and finds more beneficial methods of operation from murder to murder (Keppel, 1995). Whatever the killer does beyond the murder, such as some forms of binding, arson, unnecessary stabbing, and arranging the bodies, should be the major focus of investigators in determining if murders are committed by the same person. It is the signature that remains the same from the first offense through subsequent offenses. The ritual may evolve, but the theme persists (Douglas et al., 1992).

REFERENCES

Douglas, J.E. and Munn, C. (1992). Violent crime scene analysis, *Homicide Investigators Journal*, Spring, 63–69.

Douglas, J.E., Burgess, A.W., Burgess, A.G., and Ressler, R.K. (1992). *Crime Classification Manual*, New York: Lexington Books.

Fosdick, R.B. (1916). *European Police Systems*, New York: The Century Co.

Geberth, V.J. (1996). *Practical Homicide Investigation: Tactics, Procedures, and Forensic Techniques*, Boca Raton, FL: CRC Press.

Grahame, K. (1904). *Pagan Papers*, New York: John Lame: The Bodley Head.

Hanfland, K.J., Keppel, R.D., and Weis, J.P. (1997). *Case Management for Missing Children Homicides*, Seattle, WA: Washington State Attorney General's Office.

Hazelwood, R. and Michaud, S. G. (1999). *The Evil That Men Do*, New York: St. Martin's Press.

Keppel, R.D. (1995). Signature murders: a report of several related cases, *Journal of Forensic Sciences*, 40(4): 658–662.

Keppel, R.D. (2000). Signature murders: a report of the 1984 Cranbrook, British Columbia, cases, *Journal of Forensic Sciences*, 45(2):50–503.

Keppel, R.D. and Birnes, W.J. (1995). *The Riverman: Ted Bundy and I Hunt the Green River Killer*, New York: Pocket Books.

Keppel, R.D. and Birnes, W.J. (1997). *Signature Killers*, New York: Pocket Books.

Keppel, R.D. and Walter, R.A. (1999). Profiling killers: a revised classification model for understanding sexual murder, *Journal of Offender Therapy and Comparative Criminology*, 43(4):417–437.

Keppel, R.D. and Weis, J.P. (1993). HITS: catching criminals in the northwest, *Federal Bureau of Investigation Law Enforcement Bulletin*, April, 14–19.

Keppel, R.D. and Weis, J.P. (1994). Time and distance as solvability factors in murder cases, *Journal of Forensic Sciences*, 39(2):386-401.

Keppel, R.D. and Weis, J.P. (1999). *Murder: A Multidisciplinary Anthology of Readings*, Orlando, FL: Harcourt Brace Custom Publishing.

Oxford English Dictionary (1933). Oxford: The Clarendon Press.

Robinson, W.C. (1890). *The Law of Patents for Useful Inventions*. Boston: Little, Brown, & Co.

Soderman, H. and O'Connell, J. (1936). *Modern Criminal Investigation,* New York: Funk & Wagnalls.

State of California v. Cleophus Prince (1992) 9 CAL.APP.4th 1176, 10 CAL.RPTR.2D 855.

State of Delaware v. Steven B. Pennell (1989). Del.Super., 584 A.2d 513.

State of Louisiana v. Nathaniel Code (1994). 627 So.2d 1373.

State of Washington v. George W. Russell (1994). 125 Wash.2d 24, 882 P.2D 747.

Sutherland, E.H. (1947). *Principles of Criminology,* New York: J.B. Lippincott.

Timothy Wilson Spencer v. Commonwealth of Virginia (1990). 240 Va. 78, 393 S.E.2d.

Whittenmore v. Cutter (1813). 29 F.Cas. 1123, No. 17, 601, 1 Gall. 478.

7 The Predator's Brain: Neuropsychodynamics of Serial Killers

Laurence Miller

CONTENTS

INTRODUCTION

After tracking its prey for days, a pack of wolves surrounds a wounded deer and closes in for the kill. Each wolf seems to know exactly what to do, and their hunt is a coordinated team effort. Later, one of the wolves seems to continue the "hunt" upon other pack members. He persistently chases other members and bites them. In interactions with rival packs for mates and territory, he deviates from the ritualized form of group combat and aggressively pursues members of the other pack, thereby placing his own packmates in danger. Finally, he is driven out of the pack and becomes the proverbial "lone wolf," surviving by his canine wits but shunning (and shunned by) the company of his own kind.

A commanding officer of an ancient Roman legion, or World War II Wehrmacht regiment, or grunt platoon in Vietnam, or Rwandan or Serbian paramilitary unit is told to take a strategically located village and hold the position. After overcoming resistance by the town's defenders, the invading soldiers express the thrill of victory by engaging in a spree of murder, rape, and torture of civilians. Later investigations conclude that most of the actions were justifiable, or at least understandable, in terms of the "heat of battle." However, one soldier seems to have taken extraordinary delight and satisfaction in inflicting gratuitous cruelty on the townspeople; further-more, an investigation discovers that this cruelty represents a consistent pattern in his behavior. His troopmates may consider him a good warrior, but they don't really like him because he enjoys his work too much. Eventually, his atrocities catch up to him and he is court-marshaled or dishonorably discharged. He becomes a "lone wolf," satisfying his hunger for cruelty and domination in any form he can get away with. Eventually, he becomes very good at it.

In ordinary civilian life, most people do not kill, but we may enjoy watching others do it on television and at the movies or reading about it in books. We also like to "study" murder, which is one of the reasons why the contributors to this book have written these chapters and you are reading them. Perhaps some of us have fantasies that resemble those of the murderer, yet we retain control of our behavior and remain law-abiding. For actual murderers, however, such fantasies lose their vicarious, cathartic function and become a cognitive staging ground for the actual commission of their crimes (Hickey, 1997; Simon, 1996).

The serial killer watches the same spy movies and cop programs as we do, shows where detectives or glamorous international agents doggedly and cleverly pursue malfeasors (the lead character of one such popular television detective series was actually named "Hunter"), ostensibly for the good of society. The nascent killer absorbs society's fascination with media portrayals of criminals and others who don't play by the rules, and he feels the same tingle of exhilaration at the possibility of vicariously tracking down and destroying those who "have it coming."

While our involvement in such mayhem normally begins and ends at the level of fantasy, the killer goes further. For most of us, dramatized portrayals of violence are entertaining, perhaps even cathartic, as the ancient Greeks suggested. For the serial killer, however, such fantasies are simply the first step of a violent process. His fantasies build, along with a neuropsychodynamically driven hunger that only the orgiastic release of torturing and murdering another human being will provide. What for most human males constitutes a momentary journey into cruelty during the "heat of battle" becomes for the serial killer his life's guiding purpose and mission. That is why he is so relentless. That is why he will always continue to kill until he is dead or securely confined.

This chapter will argue that the neuropsychodynamic mechanisms of serial killing are similar in kind to the adaptive brain mechanisms of stalking and predation that characterize many of the "normal" social activities of human, primate, mammalian, and vertebrate life. A naturalistic conceptualization of serial murder no more means we must "accept" or decriminalize it than a naturalistic conceptualization of microbial biology and epidemiology means we cannot take measures to prevent and treat harmful infections. Indeed, a better understanding of the similarities and differences between "normal" and "criminal" behavior may lead to better means of apprehending these predators and protecting society from their actions. In this effort, brain research has recently made some important advances in illuminating the neuropsychodynamics of the "criminal mind," and this will be the focus of the present chapter.

CHARACTERISTICS OF SERIAL KILLERS

DEFINITIONS AND DESCRIPTIONS

In the U.S., homicide accounts for approximately 20,000 deaths annually. The term *serial murderer* was coined by FBI Special Agent Robert Ressler during the "Son of Sam" killings in New York in the 1970s. Up until that time, there were probably only about half a dozen such murderers in the U.S. In the 1980s, though, the FBI calculated that approximately 35 serial killers were active in the U.S., and in recent years that estimate has swelled to from 200 to 500, accounting for 2000 to 3500 murders a year, more than 10% of all murders in the U.S. In fact, with only 5% of the world's population, the U.S. may have up to 75% of the world's serial killers, perhaps due to the open, mobile nature of American society. The increase in the number of serial killers captured and recorded may be due to an actual surge in the rate of this crime or to better profiling and crime-solving techniques.

Serial killers are especially dangerous because they rarely stop killing unless they die or are apprehended (Hickey, 1997; Holmes and Holmes, 1994, 1996; Johnson and Becker, 1997; Simon, 1996; Volavka, 1999). By the FBI's operational definition, serial murderers are those who, either alone or with an accomplice, kill at least three people over a period of time, with "cooling-off" periods between the murders, indicating premeditation of each killing. When serial killers are identified, it is usually because, in acting out their fantasies, they leave their characteristic "signatures" on their victims' bodies or at the crime scene. Typically, serial murderers act out an intense fantasy relationship with their victims and thereby require their victims to be essentially anonymous props on whom they can inflict torment and death to achieve the exhilaration of sexual gratification. The selection, stalking, and capturing of their victims are essentially their version of foreplay, with the torture and killing culminating in the orgasmic climax (Geberth and Turco, 1997; Johnson and Becker, 1997; Simon, 1996; Starr et al., 1984).

Serial murderers are distinguished from *mass murderers*, who kill multiple victims in a single incident and whose fantasies tend to involve revenge against actual or imagined persecutors. Whereas the torture and murder activities of serial killers tend to be slow and close-up, involving low-tech weapons that gouge, flay, or strangle, the typical goal of mass murderers is to kill as many victims as possible, quickly, efficiently, and all at once using the highest level of lethal technology available to them to do the most damage — handguns, assault weapons, explosives, arson, and so on (Dietz, 1986; Meloy, 1997; Palermo, 1997; Simon, 1996).

PATTERNS OF SERIAL KILLING

The serial killer devotes a lot of energy and intelligence to the planning and execution of his murderous attacks, becoming more proficient each time he kills. Even killers with less-than-average IQs may be extraordinarily cunning and street smart when it comes to their own style of murder (Starr, 1984).

Many serial killers are fascinated by police and detective work and educate themselves in police procedures by reading, taking courses, and watching cop shows. They may impersonate police officers and even insert themselves into the investigations of the very crimes they have committed. John Wayne Gacy had a police radio in his home, Wayne Williams photographed crime scenes, Ted Bundy once worked for the King County Crime Commission, Dennis Nilsen served a year on the London Police Force, and Edmund Kemper hung out at a bar near police headquarters, pestering off-duty officers with questions about murders he had committed (Simon, 1996; Starr, 1984).

Deitz (1986, 1987) proposes a typology that divides serial killers into five categories:

1. *Psychopathic sexual sadists* (e.g., Ted Bundy, John Wayne Gacy)
2. *Crime-spree killers* (e.g., Bonnie and Clyde)
3. *Organized crime functionaries* (e.g., contract killers, gang hits)
4. *Custodial killers* (e.g., nurses who poison or asphyxiate patients)
5. *Psychotic killers* (e.g., David Berkowitz)

Another classification scheme (Holmes and DeBurger, 1985, 1988; Holmes and Holmes, 1996) uses the following typology to describe different types of serial killers: *Spatial mobility serial killers* typically live in one area and confine their murders to a limited geographical area. By contrast, *geographically transient serial killers* travel great distances and scatter their victims over a wide territory, which may include several states or the entire country. The *visionary serial killer* is propelled to kill by psychotic delusions or hallucinations which often "demand" that vengeance be wreaked on members of a certain group, who are usually strangers to the killer. The *mission serial killer* may not actually be psychotic, but feels a self-imposed duty to rid the world of a certain class of people. The *power/control serial killer* receives sexual gratification from the complete domination and control of his victim. Similarly, the *hedonistic serial killer* (a.k.a. the "lust" or "thrill killer") has made a vital connection between personal violence and sexual gratification; killing has become eroticized. His violent activities may include torture, mutilation, dismemberment, anthropophagy, and necrophilia.

The most commonly used classification scheme divides serial killers into *organized* vs. *disorganized* (Geberth, 1990; Geberth and Turco, 1997; Hickey, 1997; Ressler et al., 1986, 1988). Generally, an *organized* serial murderer is above average in intelligence, and his crime is well thought out and carefully planned. The crime is usually committed away from his area of residence or work, and he is quite mobile, often traveling many miles to commit his murders. Fantasy and ritual are important to the organized killer, and he selects a victim, typically a stranger, whom he considers the "right" type in terms of age, physical appearance, behavior, and so on. He typically carries a carefully prepared "torture kit" containing the implements of bondage and mutilation. He may follow and stalk this victim for minutes, hours, or days and may take great pride in verbally manipulating his target into a position of vulnerability. His capture and control of the victim are calculated to afford him maximum power over his hapless prey. He often takes a souvenir or "trophy" from his victim that he may use to relive the event or enhance his fantasies surrounding the killing.

The organized serial killer is familiar with police procedures and often takes pride in thwarting investigations and taunting law enforcement officials by the careful placement or concealment of evidence. He may be a "student" of previous or contemporaneous serial killers, reading up on their exploits and even corresponding with them in prison. He may learn from each of his own crimes and become increasingly sophisticated in his predatory and elusive skills. Although casual observers may describe some serial killers as solitary and strange in their daily behavior, just as commonly he may appear to be normal and a "regular guy" to co-workers, family, and neighbors.

The *disorganized* serial killer is less consciously aware of a plan, and his crime scenes display more haphazard behavior. He is often a loner and a recluse. He is an underachiever, feels sexually and interpersonally inadequate, has a poor self-image, and is considered weird or odd by acquaintances. He typically engages in such sexual activities as voyeurism, exhibitionism, lingerie thefts, and fetish burglaries and uses sadistic and fetish-type fantasy pornography in autoerotic activities. The violent offense is spontaneous, and the victim is usually a target of opportunity. His crimes lack cunning and typically consist of "blitz attacks" that are intended to silence the victim quickly via blunt force trauma. After the sudden sexual and physical violence to the victim, death usually follows quickly. The attack may be characterized by "overkill," with multiple stabs and blows. Postmortem activities with the corpse may include biting, exploratory dissection, mutilation, insertion of foreign objects, or masturbation onto the body. There may not be actual penile penetration of the body. The crime scene is sloppy and disorganized, with little or no effort to conceal the evidence. Trophies are less frequently taken, and there may be a secondary robbery of opportunity. Sometimes an offender has elements of both organized and disorganized categories, and can be called *mixed* (Geberth, 1990; Geberth and Turco, 1997; Hickey, 1997; Ressler et al., 1986, 1988).

PSYCHOLOGICAL DYNAMICS OF SERIAL KILLING

According to many authorities, the prime reason that predatory serial killers stalk, capture, and torture their victims is to obtain a maximal intensity of sexual excitement and orgasm that they are unable to achieve in any other way. Although serial killers typically reach the peak of their activity in their early 20s to mid-30s, their fantasies that fuse cruelty with sexuality usually begin in adolescence, sometimes in childhood.

Many were severely abused physically and sexually as children. A number were illegitimate or adopted and several were sons of prostitutes. A number have had intensely ambivalent, smothering relationships with their mothers that were fueled by both maternal abuse and sexual attraction to the mother. Their play as children often has had a repetitive, stereotyped aggressive pattern. They lie, steal, destroy property, set fires, and are cruel and callous to other children. Many have enjoyed torturing animals from an early age. Odd and isolated since childhood, the future serial killer turns inward and nurtures sadistic sexual fantasies, often accompanied by masturbation, transvestitism, voyeurism, exhibitionism, and other fetishes (Simon, 1996).

The early fantasies may consist of elaborations on certain actual experiences or may be stimulated by "experiments" conceived while viewing various types of movies, magazines, video games, Internet websites, and so on. Some of this material may be integrated into actual sexual experiences or into masturbatory fantasies. At some point, the individual begins to incorporate actual people into his sexually murderous fantasies and begins to mentally rehearse more realistic scenarios for stalking, abducting, and torturing victims to death. In these developing fantasies, as in the later actual killings, the victims become depersonalized, reduced to contemptible objects that exist solely for the gratification of the perpetrator (Malmquist, 1996).

As adolescents and young adults, serial killers often begin their criminal careers with assault, which then escalates to battery, arson, rape, and eventually murder. Once they have fully acted out and gotten away with their sexually violent fantasies, they feel increasingly empowered. The killings feed their fantasies of invincibility and spur further killings. Over time, the abduction, torture, and murder become more ritualized and more refined, and the killers learn from their near-miss mistakes, becoming ever more efficient in their murderous activities and evasion of capture (Simon, 1996).

Simon (1996) believes that in their actions of controlling, torturing, and killing a victim, serial murderers briefly relieve themselves of profound self-loathing. In this view, only the most intensely violent, sexually sadistic exploitation of their victims brings serial sexual killers out of an emotional death, temporarily enabling them to feel calm and relaxed. Many killers report a profound sense of "relief" after carrying out a torture and murder episode, stating that this act is the only way they can feel "normal" — at least until the urge builds toward another murder. Similarly, Malmquist (1996) points to the profound depression and despair reported by many serial killers just prior to their next murderous act, with the subjugation, degradation, and slow destruction of a helpless human being acting as a mood-elevating tonic for these murderers — sort of a perverse "antidepressant" function of serial killing.

According to some clinical-forensic authorities, unlike delusional psychotic murderers, serial sexual murderers do know right from wrong; they are not prey to "irresistible impulses." Rather, serial killers choose not to resist these impulses in their continuing quest for thrilling orgiastic pleasure. In this view, the psychological core of the serial sexual murderer requires the lethal combination of psychopath and sadist or necrophile (Simon, 1996). Other diagnostic considerations include temporal lobe epilepsy, bipolar disorder, schizoid personality, narcissistic personality, and dissociative disorder (Hickey, 1997; Money, 1990).

A common diagnosis in serial killers is some form of *paraphilia*. Nine paraphilias are currently recognized by the *Diagnostic and Statistical Manual of Mental Disorders,* 4th edition (DSM-IV; APA, 1994): fetishism, transvestitism, voyeurism, exhibitionism, sexual sadism, sexual masochism, pedophilia, zoophilia, and frotteurism. Not surprisingly, the paraphilia most commonly associated with serial sexual homicide is sadism (Dietz, 1986; Geberth and Turco, 1997; Meloy, 1988). On the other hand, the term "sexual aggression" may be misleading, because the biological and personality markers associated with antisocial traits as a whole may be quite different from the various DSM paraphilic disorders (Berlin, 1988).

One clinical investigation of the psychological dynamics of future serial sexual murderers comes from a study of adolescents by Johnson and Becker (1997). These authors present the cases of nine 14- to 18-year-old males who had expressed a desire to commit serial killings and were referred to the authors for a forensic evaluation after having committed some non-sexual violent legal offenses. These adolescents reported having repetitive and explicit fantasies of sexual torture, mutilation, and murder, dating from an early age, and increasing over time. Sexually violent fantasies were described as arousing and exciting by these youths. Some of these boys had already begun to practice their sadistic craft on pets and other animals. The types of sexual fantasies reported by these adolescents were strikingly similar to those described in retrospect by established serial killers who have been apprehended and interviewed. The authors propose that the evolving nature of the sexually sadistic fantasy often begins in adolescence and is a possible key factor that must be looked for in identifying youth who are at risk for becoming sexually sadistic serial killers.

Addressing the broader topic of impulsive homicide in general, the contributions of Wertham (1937, 1978) come to us largely through the writings of Schlesinger (1996, 1999). Wertham described the clinical development of what he called the *catathymic crisis*. In this model, a traumatic experience (or set of experiences) creates an unresolvable inner conflict that produces extreme emotional tension. As the individual externalizes the source of this distress to a particular person or class of persons, his thinking becomes increasingly egocentric and disturbed, and at some critical point he concludes that a violent act is the "only way out." He may resist and struggle with this urge for a while, but eventually the act is committed or at least attempted. This is followed by a palpable feeling of relief of emotional tension, in turn followed by a period of superficial normalcy, until the tension begins to build again, reinitiating the cycle.

Schlesinger's expanded model (Revitch and Schlesinger, 1978, 1981, 1989; Schlesinger, 1996, 1999; Schlesinger and Revitch, 1980) specifies five separate categories of violent offenses: (1) sociopathic or environmental, (2) situational, (3) impulsive, (4) catathymic, and (5) compulsive. From the point of view of serial killing, the latter two subtypes appear most relevant. The Schlesinger model of catathymic murder describes it as a psychodynamic process frequently accompanied by disorganization and characterized by an accumulation of tension released through the violent act. This process is divided into two types, acute and chronic, distinguished primarily by whether or not the explosive, psychodynamically driven violent outburst is preceded by a buildup of tension that results in relief.

The compulsive type of murder occupies the extreme endogenous end of the motivational spectrum and is least influenced by external or sociogenic factors; this is the type that appears to be closest to the "classical" type of serial killer. In this homicide subtype, the need to commit the act is very compelling and there is a great likelihood of repetition. In some cases, the urge to commit a sex murder is so strong that the offender's attempt to resist it brings on anxiety and somatic symptoms. Compulsive sex murders are frequently, but not invariably, acted out in a stereotypical and ritualistic manner. The murders may be isolated or occur in clusters, frequent or repeated after long intervals. Typically, sexually violent fantasies precede the homicidal acts by many years, and absence of opportunity to kill does not diminish the urge; for example, even after years of imprisonment, the compulsion persists (Schlesinger,1996, 1999).

Psychodynamically, Schlesinger (1999) believes that in most cases the compulsive sexual murderer has had an unhealthy and disturbed relationship with his mother. The mothers may be rejecting and punitive or, at times, seductive, overprotective, and infantalizing. The young killers-to-be frequently know about, and sometimes actually witness, the mothers' sexual promiscuity. The entire process forges an unhealthy fusion of sexuality and hatred. In response, these young men frequently utilize the defense mechanism of *splitting*: perceiving women as either pure and all good or defiled and all bad. In this conceptualization, repressed incestuous feelings seem to be the main stimulus for sexual homicide. The offender displaces his hatred from the mother to other women; that is, the sexual murders are actually displaced matricide.

While not a sufficient explanation for all cases of serial killing, the catathymic models of Wertham (1937, 1978) and Schlesinger (1996, 1999) may actually help explain many cases of serial and mass murder, as illustrated by a recent study (Hempel et al., 1999) of a sample of 30 mass murderers in the U.S. and Canada during the past 50 years. The data suggest that such individuals are single or divorced males in their 30s with various Axis I paranoid and/or depressive conditions and Axis II personality traits and disorders, usually Clusters A and B. The mass murder is precipitated by a major loss related to employment or relationship. A "warrior mentality" suffuses the planning and attack behavior of the subject, and greater deaths and higher casualty rates are significantly more likely if the perpetrator is psychotic at the time of the offense. Alcohol plays a very minor role. A large proportion of subjects will convey their central motivation in a "psychological abstract," a phrase or sentence yelled with great emotion at the beginning of the mass murder; however, only 20% of these murderers directly threaten their intended victims before the attack. Death by suicide or at the hands of others is the usual outcome for the mass murderer. Interestingly, this homicidal subtype seems to characterize many cases of more recent workplace, school, and church violence (Miller, 1999; Neuman and Baron, 1998).

THE NEUROPSYCHOLOGY OF SERIAL KILLING

Much evidence points to neurological and neuropsychological factors in criminal aggression in general and sadistic serial killing in particular (Pallone, 1996). One problem has been that current theories are too structured and narrowly localized, prompting the need to look for a more psychological/neurobehavioral/ethological theory that blends brain, mind, phylogenesis, and situation. This represents a move away from a reductionistic emphasis and encourages a more systemic and interactive understanding of the brain's role in violent behavior (Martell, 1996; Miller, 1986b, 1998a,b).

AGGRESSION: IMPULSIVE AND PREDATORY

In the animal ethological and neuropsychological literature on aggression, one of the most widely validated behavioral and neuropharmacological distinctions is between *affective* or *impulsive aggression* and *predatory aggression* (Eichelman, 1992; Eichelman et al., 1993; Meloy, 1997; Volavka, 1995). Affective aggression involves high states of emotional and physiological arousal and typically occurs in ritualized intraspecies fighting for food, territory, mates, social status, and so on. One thinks of two wolves in a pack battling over social rank, or two rival gang members signaling, cursing, or threatening each other with gestures, fists, or weapons. Because the usual purpose of affective aggression is to intimidate and dominate within an established social structure, serious physical damage usually does not occur, and actual death of one of the combatants is rare and probably accidental.

Predatory violence is more "cold-blooded," involves low emotional and physiological arousal, usually requires some degree of preparatory stalking, and typically occurs across species, especially between hunter and prey, with the goal clearly being to kill and consume the prey animal for sustenance, not out of feelings of hatred or revenge. One thinks of a leopard quietly and patiently stalking a gazelle for hours before rushing in for the kill, which usually involves a single, efficient bite to the throat, or a professional hit man stalking his subject for days or weeks before quietly and efficiently dispatching him with a garrote, blade, or bullet.

In humans, affective and predatory aggression can be admixed, with the additional complication of more complex planning and socialization. In humans, impulsive aggression in general refers to unplanned aggressive acts that are spontaneous in nature, are either unprovoked or out of proportion to the provocation, and occur among persons who are often characterized as having a "short fuse." Perpetrators may report remorse after the act which, understandably, engenders suspicion about its authenticity. Non-impulsive aggressive acts have been variously labeled as planned, premeditated, instrumental, predatory, or proactive. They are not usually considered to have a significant emotional component but are instead more "cold-blooded" acts.

A long tradition of experimental brain research on cats (the quintessential lone predator) has demonstrated separate neurophysiological pathways mediating predatory vs. affective aggression (Siegel and Pott, 1988). In human children, "reactive aggressives" were found to be much more likely to have a history of physical abuse and social information-processing deficits than "proactive [purposeful] aggressives" (Dodge et al., 1997). Adult criminals diagnosed as "psychopaths" are more likely to engage in predatory violence than non-psychopathic criminals, who commit more affectively violent acts (Meloy, 1988; Serin, 1991; Williamson et al., 1987). Neurophysiologically, human affective-impulsive violent offenders differ from controls on electrophysiological and neuropsychological test measures of impaired information processing (Barratt et al., 1997) and in having lower levels of serotonin and monoamine oxidase A (Brunner et al., 1993; Coccaro et al., 1996; Virkunnen and Linnoila, 1993; Volavka, 1999).

Mass murder is usually a predatory mode of violence — planned, purposeful, emotionless, with minimal autonomic arousal, consistent with the "warrior mentality." Both the psychotic and non-psychotic mass murderer are engaging in predatory violence, even though the reason for the predation may be delusional in the former (Hempel et al., 1999; Meloy, 1999). Meloy (1997) presents a case of predatory violence during mass murder committed by a 35-year-old male, following a week of separation from his spouse and loss of custody of his son. The perpetrator went to his wife's worksite, armed with several powerful weapons, and murdered her and the store manager, wounded a passerby in a car, and killed a police officer arriving at the scene. The obvious pattern of this attack is consistent with a predatory mode of violence — planned, purposeful, emotionless, and not preceded by significant physiological arousal.

Recall that both affective-impulsive and predatory forms of aggression are hardly "pathological" in animal species; on the contrary, such creatures could not survive without these traits. Even in humans, the view toward depathologizing more modal and non-extreme forms of these behavioral traits receives support from a recent study by Barratt et al. (1999) that asked a group of 216 college students to assess their own aggressive acts using a specially designed self-report questionnaire. The results identified four factors: (1) impulsive aggression, (2) mood on the day the act occurred, (3) premeditated aggression, and (4) agitation. Thus, impulsive and premeditated aggression were found to be independent constructs that exist in varying degrees among these normal (i.e., non-clinical sample) college students. In this study, impulsive aggression was characterized in part by feelings of remorse following the acts and by thought confusion. Premeditated aggression was related to more purposeful social gain and dominance.

NEUROCHEMISTRY OF VIOLENCE

Clinical research into the neurobiology of violence typically focuses on the brain's phylogenetically older *limbic system* that mediates the basic experience and expression of emotion, motivation, and physiological arousal. The limbic structures that modulate aggression in rodents include the lateral septum, raphe nuclei, olfactory bulbs, amygdala, and parts of the hypothalamus. Serotonin is the neurotransmitter most clearly implicated in the inhibitory control of aggression. Potentiation of GABA activity also inhibits aggression. Dopamine and norepinephrine generally enhance aggression, and it is possible that the noradrenergic system modulates the relationship between serotonin and aggression in this way by raising the preparedness of the organism to react aggressively. Strong evidence for the inhibitory role of serotonin on aggression stems from neuropharmacological studies of killing behavior in rats. In general, results from animal studies indicate that manipulations that elevate levels of brain serotonin inhibit aggressive behavior, whereas procedures that lower brain serotonin levels induce or increase aggression (Raine, 1993; Raine et al., 1995; Volavka, 1995, 1999).

Testosterone, the male sex hormone, is clearly implicated in aggression, but its effects, particularly in primates, interact with social factors. Persons with a history of violent behavior may have slight elevations in testosterone levels, but this effect is not large. The elevation may be a consequence of the behavior or its antecedent. That is, the influence is two way: social factors influence levels of neurotransmitters and hormones; these substances in turn affect the animal's behavior and thus its social standing. In anatomically intact animals not treated with drugs or other substances, social factors such as dominance appear to be more important than biological factors in regulating aggression, and the preponderance of social factors is more apparent in primates than in lower species (Volavka, 1995, 1999).

Hormones of the hypothalamic-pituitary-adrenal axis, involved in the stress response to threatening situations, also play an important and very intricate role in the regulation of aggression. Hypoglycemia is associated with impulsive, violent behavior, and the link may be mediated via serotonergic mechanisms and alcohol consumption (Volavka, 1995, 1999).

PSYCHOPHYSIOLOGY

Another way to study central nervous system function is through the brain's electrical activity during behavioral tasks, often known as *psychophysiology*. The two most common psychophysiological research methods are the *electroencephalogram* (EEG), which measures the brain's ongoing electrical activity, and the *evoked potential* (EP), which measures how the nervous system processes perceptual stimuli.

One of the most frequently observed EEG abnormalities associated with violence consists of excessive theta activity, an abnormality consistent with the underarousal theory of psychopathy (Raine et al., 1995; Williams, 1969). This theory posits that psychopaths seek excessive stimulation through antisocial behavior to compensate for their constitutionally low levels of physiological arousal. One prospective study (Raine et al., 1990) provided evidence that underarousal may be critically involved in the development of antisocial and criminal behavior. Resting skin conductance, heart rate, and EEG activity were measured in 101 15-year-old schoolboys and were then related to criminality status as assessed 9 years later at age 24. Criminals were found to have significantly lower resting heart rate, reduced skin conductance activity, and more slow-frequency EEG theta activity than non-criminals.

In this study, early EP studies observed long latency *brainstem averaged evoked responses* (BAERs), which psychologically can be interpreted as indicating reduced arousal and excessively high filtering of environmental stimuli. The behavioral consequence of such underarousal and filtering would be stimulus deprivation and chronically low levels of arousal. Findings for middle-latency EPs were much more equivocal, but it was speculated that psychopaths appear to show increased EP amplitudes to stimuli of increasing intensity (visual cortical-augmenting), a phenomenon that has been linked to the trait of *sensation-seeking* (Zuckerman, 1979, 1990). Results from late-latency EPs were more consistent, and they indicated, surprisingly, that psychopaths showed enhanced P300 amplitudes, indicating enhanced attention to stimuli of interest. Psychopaths thus seem to have the ability to attend to stimuli of interest and may in fact become obsessively focused on exciting, thrill-enhancing activities, regardless — or because — of the suffering they cause in others (Raine et al., 1990).

NEUROIMAGING STUDIES

Brain imaging research, utilizing such techniques as *computerized tomography* (CT), *magnetic resonance imaging* (MRI), *regional cerebral blood flow* (rCBF), and *positron emission tomography* (PET), allows direct assessment of structural and functional brain abnormalities, thus providing an improved methodology for studying neurobiological factors predisposing to violent and aggressive behavior (Raine et al., 1995).

Neuropsychological research has shown that the frontal lobes of the brain are crucially involved in behavioral self-awareness and self-control, while the temporal lobes contain many of the limbic structures that mediate emotional and motivation states such as sexuality and aggression (Miller, 1984, 1986a, 1993; Volavka, 1996, 1999). Mills and Raine (1994) reviewed 20 brain-imaging studies using CT, MRI, rCBF, and PET conducted in the study of violent and sexual offending. Based on these findings, the authors suggest the following hypotheses: (1) there is a tendency for frontal lobe dysfunction to be associated with violent offending such as murder; (2) temporal lobe dysfunction may be more associated with less violent sexual offending, including incest and pedophilia; and (3) frontotemporal dysfunction may be associated with both violent and sexual offending, such as rape.

The authors hypothesize the existence of a continuum, with frontal dysfunction and violence at one end and temporal dysfunction and sexual offending at the other. The middle of this continuum may involve some degree of both temporal and frontal dysfunction, as well as a mix of both sexual and violent behavior. As it turns out, both violent and sexual samples were found to have frontotemporal dysfunction, including one study which used a sample made up almost evenly of rapists and incest offenders/pedophiles (Wright et al., 1990). Another study (Volkow and Tancredi, 1987) revealed frontal dysfunction in violent individuals who had no remorse for their actions, a prominent personality trait of psychopaths (Miller, 1989a), which suggests that psychopathy may also be represented at the frontal end of the continuum (Mills and Raine, 1994).

The neuroethologically based categorization of aggressive acts into predatory vs. affective was studied in human murderers by Raine et al. (1998) who assessed glucose metabolism (a measure of regional brain activity) using PET in 15 predatory murderers, 9 affective murderers, and 41 controls in left and right hemisphere prefrontal (medial and lateral) and subcortical (amygdala, midbrain, hippocampus, and thalamus) regions. The key findings in this study were that: (1) affective murderers have lower prefrontal activity and higher subcortical activity than comparisons; (2) predatory murderers have prefrontal activity levels similar to comparisons, but excessive subcortical activity; and (3) the excessive subcortical activity in both affective and predatory murderers was restricted to the right hemisphere (Raine et al., 1998).

The results support the hypothesis that emotional, impulsive murderers are less able to regulate and control aggressive impulses generated from subcortical limbic structures due to deficient prefrontal regulation. The authors hypothesize that excessive subcortical activity predisposes to aggressive behavior, but affective and predatory murderers differ in terms of the regulatory cortical control they exert over aggressive impulses. While the predatory violent offenders have sufficient left prefrontal functioning to modulate such aggressive behavior in a way to intimidate, deceive, and manipulate others to achieve desired goals, affectively violent offenders lack this prefrontal modulatory control over their impulses, resulting in more unbridled, unregulated, aggressive outbursts (Raine et al., 1998).

So far, the emphasis has been on the aggressive component of serial killing. But, insofar as serial sexual homicide has, by definition, a sexual component, it would be useful to explore the neuropsychology of the human sexual response. To this end, Stoleru et al. (1999) allowed normal, adult men to view films that were either humorous or sexually explicit while measuring the electrical activity of their brains via visual EPs. They found that visually evoked sexual arousal was characterized by a threefold pattern of activation: (1) bilateral activation of the inferior temporal cortex, a visual association area; (2) activation of the right insula and right inferior frontal cortex, which are two paralimbic areas that link highly processed sensory information with motivational states; and (3) activation of the left anterior cingulate cortex, another paralimbic area known to control autonomic and neuroendocrine functions. Activation of some of these areas was positively associated with plasma testosterone levels.

To interpret these findings, the authors propose the following neuropsychosexual model. Visually evoked sexual arousal may comprise three coordinated components (Stoleru et al., 1999):

1. *Perceptual-cognitive* component, the function of which is to label and assess visual stimuli as sexual; this component of sexual arousal could be correlated with the observed activation of the right and left inferior temporal cortices, as these regions of visual association cortex are involved in the perception of visual stimuli.
2. *Emotional-motivational* component, which could be correlated with the observed activation of the right insula, right inferior frontal cortex, and left cingulate cortex; these regions associate emotional and motivational content with perceptions.
3. *Endocrine-autonomic* component, which may be related to the observed activation of the left anterior cingulate cortex, a region which also controls the physiological responses to stimuli.

RELATED SYNDROMES

The study of sexuality raises an additional point. Serial sexual homicide may represent a composite neuropsychodynamic entity, combining disordered sexuality and an obsessive stalking-predation pattern of aggression. If so, it might be useful to examine syndromes that appear to contain "elements" or represent "subtypes" of the complete serial killer profile.

Pedophiles

Hucker et al. (1986) have reviewed the evidence for a cerebral abnormality among individuals with paraphilias, such as fetishism, sadism, and transvestitism. These studies usually report abnormalities in the temporal lobes, as indicated by abnormal EEG (Hoenig and Kenna, 1979), CT scans, and neuropsychological testing (Langevin et al., 1985a,b), or the presence of an epileptic seizure focus or brain tumor (Blumer, 1970; Epstein, 1975; Hunter et al., 1963; Mitchell et al., 1954).

Revitch and Weiss (1978) reported that the first manifestation of pedophilia and incest in their four cases arose after the onset of cognitive impairment due to various organic disorders. Scott et al. (1984) reported a comparison of paraphilic men with normal controls using a neuropsychological test battery. Fourteen men had sexually assaulted a prepubescent child, and 22 had assaulted adults. The control group consisted of 31 community volunteers or hospitalized patients with no psychological or neurological history. Results showed that 36% of the pedophiles had neuropsychological impairment, suggesting that cerebral dysfunction might be associated with the expression of a sexual preference for children.

Hucker et al. (1986) used an extensive neuropsychological test battery and CT scans to compare heterosexual, homosexual, and bisexual pedophiles with non-violent, nonsexual offenders. The men were classified into their groups based on criminal history, a standard sex history assessment, and a phallometric test of erotic preference. Pedophiles tended to have lower IQs than controls and showed significantly more impairment on all measures. Left temporoparietal pathology was noted more often for pedophiles. Variations in age or a history of alcohol and drug abuse could not account for the findings.

Erotomania

Erotomania is the delusional belief by someone that another person is passionately in love with him or her. Typically, there is little or no contact between the selected person and the person with erotomania, and the selected person usually is unattainable because of social rank, financial status, or marriage. Often, the erotomaniac preoccupation leads to stalking and harassment of the selected person and/or his or her associates. Erotomania is believed to affect women more than men, although males tend to be over-represented in forensic cases, probably because they tend to be more overtly aggressive in their pursuit. Erotomaniac persons generally are described as being socially inept and having empty lives. Their isolation can result from personality traits of being overly sensitive, suspiciousness, or assumed superiority. A strong desire for relationship is balanced by fears of rejection and intimacy (Harmon et al., 1995; Meloy, 1999; Mullen and Pathe, 1994).

Fujii et al. (1999) examined two patients with erotomania, along with reviewing records of their neurologic examinations and neuropsychological test results. These data were compared with case studies from the literature. Neuropsychological test results suggested that erotomania may be associated with deficits in cognitive flexibility and associative learning that are mediated by frontal-subcortical systems, and with deficits in verbal and visuospatial skills. Neurologic studies suggested abnormalities in temporal lobe regions. The authors conclude that visuospatial deficits or temporal lobe limbic lesions, in combination with isolating and ambivalent romantic experiences, may contribute to misinterpretations in erotomania, Concomitant deficits in cognitive flexibility may contribute to maintenance of the delusional belief.

Despite sex, personality, cultural, and age differences, the two patients demonstrated similar neuropsychological profiles. Both subjects appeared to have weaker left hemisphere functioning, as demonstrated by poorer verbal reasoning skills compared with perceptual organizational skills. A similar pattern was found for memory, where verbal recall was much worse than expected, given their estimated intellectual functioning. Both patients also demonstrated deficits on the Wisconsin Card Sorting Test (WCST) and the Verbal Paired Associates subtest of the Wechsler Memory Scale. These results, along with scores on other neuropsychological tests, suggest deficits in working memory, cognitive flexibility, and the ability to form new associations. Overall, the neuropsychological findings suggested general dysfunction to frontal-subcortical and possibly temporal areas, particularly in the left hemisphere. These neuropsychological findings were corroborated by EEG and MRI.

Dysfunction in frontotemporal and left hemisphere regions has also been implicated in disorders commonly associated with delusional symptoms and syndromes in general (Miller, 1984; 1986a). For example, two of the most consistent neurologic findings in patients with schizophrenia are hypoperfusion in the left dorsolateral frontal area during performance of the WCST (Rubin et al., 1991) and structural abnormalities in the temporal areas on MRI (Jernigan et al., 1991). Similarly, studies have found that psychiatric patients with psychosis secondary to traumatic brain injury generally have lesions in one or both temporal lobes and frontal areas, particularly on the left side (Fujii and Ahmed, 1996). Other studies have demonstrated that delusions, including those involving misidentification, are associated with left and right temporal lobe dysfunction (Flor-Henry, 1969; Malloy and Richardson, 1994; Miller, 1984, 1986a; Signer, 1992).

Fujii et al. (1999) propose that deficits in cognitive flexibility and new learning contribute to erotomania by preventing the development of alternative cognitions. In erotomania, the delusional belief by a person that another person is passionately in love with him or her is staunchly maintained despite repeated evidence to the contrary, including not only direct confrontation by the target of the delusion, but also legal action (the obtaining of a restraining order) that is often taken by the targeted person to prevent future harassment. Given the preponderance of evidence that the target is not in love with the erotomaniac, the unwillingness or inability to alter beliefs possibly could be secondary to neuropsychological deficits in flexibility of forming new associations.

CRAVINGS, COMPULSIONS, AND KINDLING

The sudden, explosive, paroxysmal nature of some forms of violence has led to the idea that such acts of violence may represent a variant of seizure disorder. According to Money (1990), there is, in fact, a parallel between episodes of sexual sadism and epileptic seizures of the non-convulsive type known as *psychomotor* or *temporal lobe seizures*. Psychomotor seizures most commonly have their origin in the temporal lobe, within the limbic system of the brain. As in other paraphilias, sexual sadism and epilepsy do, in some patients, coexist as a double diagnosis.

Paroxysmal brain activity, however, need not represent frank seizures *per se*. Research has identified an electrophysiological process that investigators have named *kindling*, as an analogy to combustible material that must be heated to a certain temperature before igniting. In experimental research, repeated stimulation of temporal lobe limbic structures, particularly the *amygdala,* produces a cumulative increase in excitability and a lowering of seizure threshold, so that a subsequent minor stimulus, insufficient in itself to evoke a seizure-like response, incites the already cumulatively primed brain into paroxysmal activity with correspondingly uncontrolled behavior. Kindling has been used as a model for the slow, progressive buildup of angry or dysphoric feelings in humans that eventually flashes over into full blown violence or depression (Adamec, 1990; Adamec and Stark-Adamec, 1983; Goddard, 1967; Miller, 1997b; Post, 1980; Racine, 1978).

Several researchers have proposed kindling as a neurophysiological model for predatory violence (Niehoff, 1999), and Simon (1996) believes that kindling may have specific applicability to serial sexual murderers because of the escalating pattern of killings, the buildup of dysphoric tension prior to each killing, and the relief felt after the killings. This is particularly true if the killings are understood as being an aspect of recurrent depression or manic-depressive disorder (Post, 1980). It may be that serial killers have an unrecognized, aberrant, or atypical form of mood disorder, so that torturing helpless victims to death literally affords them an exhilarating antidepressant high. Note that the kindling model is also consistent with, and may represent a neurophysiological substrate for, the catathymic process described by Wertham (1937, 1978) and Schlesinger (1996, 1999).

This compulsive aspect of serial killing may actually represent an extreme subtype of a more general typology of cravings, addictions, compulsions, and "irresistible impulses" (Soutullo et al., 1998). In DSM-IV (APA, 1994), the essential feature of an *impulse control disorder* is the failure to resist an impulse, drive, or temptation to perform an act that is harmful to the person or to others. DSM-IV further stipulates that for most impulse control disorders, the individual feels an increasing sense of tension or arousal before committing the act and then experiences pleasure, gratification, or relief at the time of committing the act. After the act is performed, there may or may not be regret, self-reproach, or guilt. Thus, impulse control disorders may be ego-syntonic when relief or pleasure is experienced during the act, but they may also be ego-dystonic when the impulses are associated with tension or anxiety and the behaviors generate self-reproach, shame, or guilt.

Many patients with impulse control disorders may thus be said to be "addicted" to their harmful behaviors. Such actions are often associated with pleasurable feelings, described as feeling "high," "euphoric," "a thrill," or "a rush." There may be tolerance and withdrawal symptoms. It has been hypothesized that serotonergic abnormalities underlie some of the impulsive (and/or compulsive) features of impulse control disorders, noradrenergic or dopaminergic abnormalities underlie their pleasurable or euphoric features, and abnormalities in all three systems underlie the affective disregulation of these disorders (Simon, 1996; Soutullo et al., 1998; Stein et al., 1993).

Soutullo et al. (1998) propose that the impulse control disorders may vary along a dimension of compulsivity vs. impulsivity (see also Miller, 1989a). One extreme of this dimension would consist of purely compulsive disorders further characterized by performance of harm-avoidant behaviors, insight into the senselessness of the behaviors, resistance to performing the behaviors, and the absence of pleasure when the behaviors are performed. Examples would include obsessive-compulsive disorder and such putatively related disorders as body dysmorphic disorder and anorexia nervosa. The other end would consist of purely impulsive disorders further characterized by performance of exciting but harmful behaviors, little insight into the consequences of the behaviors, automatic enactment of the behaviors, and pleasure when the behavior is performed. Examples would include the classic impulse control disorders and substance abuse disorders. Various mixed compulsive-impulsive forms would be situated in between.

On this dimension, we would not situate serial killers on the extreme impulsive end, because, unlike the "pure" psychopath whose numerous and varied antisocial acts are impelled by the whim of the moment, serial killers are locked in to a particular form of violent expression; they cannot adequately release their tension in any way *but* the sadistic act. However, the compulsive quality of their murderous behavior lacks the overly self-reflective, ego-dystonic, anhedonic quality of true obsessive-compulsives; serial killers may say they are "driven" to kill, but they certainly enjoy doing it, feel entitled to do it, and rarely regret it. Thus, in the present view, serial sexual homicide would represent a mixed type of disorder on the impulsivity-compulsivity dimension, but more on the impulsive side of the scale due to the egocentric self-gratification that drives the behavior, accompanied by a large dose of narcissistic entitlement.

NEUROPSYCHOLOGICAL MECHANISMS OF SERIAL KILLING

BRAIN PATHOLOGY OR VARIANT ON A CONTINUUM?

In line with the view of this chapter, serial sexual homicide can be conceptualized as an extreme antisocial variant of phylogenetic predation. As such, it is pathological only in terms of degree, not the nature of the act, and the brain mechanisms involved are on the same continuum as those related to more "normal" forms of hunting, group combat, romantic pursuit, entrepreneurial "go-getting," and other highly motivated, interpersonally confrontational behaviors. While acquired brain injury syndromes may produce elements or analogs of the impulsivity, aggressiveness, or sexual preoccupation that characterize serial killers, the full predatory serial sexual murder behavior pattern is a neurodevelopmentally extreme variant on the continuum of natural predation.

It might be useful to contrast this view with a more radically pathogenic interpretetation. According to Money (1990), sexual sadism is a brain disease that affects the limbic centers and pathways in the brain responsible for sexual arousal, mating behavior, and reproduction of the species, including the amygdala, hippocampus, and hypothalamus. However, he does point out that the limbic region of the brain is also responsible for predation and attack in defense of both the self and the species. In the disease of sexual sadism, the brain becomes pathologically activated to transmit messages of attack simultaneously with messages of sexual arousal and mating behavior. In this overtly pathogenic view, the "pathological mix-up" of these messages in the brain is brought into being by "faulty functioning of the brain's own chemistry." This faulty functioning may be triggered by something as grossly identifiable as brain damage resulting from the growth of a tumor, or from an open or closed head injury. Alternatively, the trigger may be submicroscopic and too subtle to be easily identified on the basis of current brain scanning technology (Money, 1990).

BRAIN INJURY, AGGRESSION, AND CRIMINAL VIOLENCE

Elliott (1992) has reviewed the experimental work in animals and clinical studies in man that have delineated the brain's regulatory systems involved in the expression and control of aggression. As noted above, these structures and pathways are located bilaterally in the *limbic system,* which consists of the septal area, hippocampus, amygdala, head of the caudate nucleus, thalamus, ventromedial and posterior hypothalamic nuclei, midbrain tegmentum, pons, and the fastigial nuclei and anterior lobe of the cerebellum. Normally, the orbitofrontal cortex modulates limbic control of aggression, but this inhibitory control is susceptible to breakdown or override caused by overwhelming internal drive states or excessive outside provocation, even in healthy individuals. Focal lesions confined to specific areas of the cortex may cause deficits in language, spatial reasoning, memory, or sensorimotor functioning, but are not typically followed by significantly heightened aggressive behavior.

Volavka (1995) notes that, although lesions in the temporal lobes or the hypothalamus may elicit aggressive behavior, this is not the usual effect of such brain injury in man. Historically, psychosurgical procedures involving primarily the amygdala, thalamus, or hypothalamus have been carried out to control aggression in a small number of patients. While some decrease in aggression has been reported, methodological problems confound the interpretation of these studies; for example, it is possible that the decrease in aggressive behavior was due to lethargy and fatigue, a common side-effect of such surgeries.

According to Hall (1993), brain lesions that may be associated with violent behavior are often located in the ascending inhibitory component of the *reticular activating system* (RAS), limbic system structures (such as the amygdala, hippocampus, and septum), the dorsomedial and anterior thalamic nuclei, the ventromedial hypothalamus, and the baso-orbital and posteromedial frontal lobe. Damage to these sites may alter self-regulatory abilities in complex person-environment interactions, including violent one-on-one encounters.

MAJOR SYNDROMES OF AGGRESSION FOLLOWING BRAIN INJURY

The irritability, impulsivity, and proneness to aggressive behavior of many individuals who have sustained organic brain damage have led to the use of brain injury as a neuropsychological model of criminal violence (Miller, 1987, 1988, 1990, 1993,

1994, 1997a, 1998a). Whether such a model, or elements of it, can be applied to the neuropsychology of serial killing must be evaluated in light of the available data on established syndromes of impulsive, aggressive behavior.

Explosive Aggressive Disorder, or Episodic Dyscontrol

The type of behavioral disorder known as the *episodic dyscontrol syndrome* (EDS) is typically described as a pattern of intermittent attacks of violence attributed to an electrophysiological disturbance in the brain. It corresponds to the *intermittent explosive disorder* of DSM-IV (APA, 1994) and has been associated with cases of impulsive, unpremeditated homicide, "senseless" attacks on strangers, spouse battery, child abuse, criminally aggressive driving, destruction of property, and even attacks on animals and inanimate objects (Elliott, 1990, 1992).

Episodic dyscontrol syndrome cuts across several diagnostic classifications, such as psychoses, personality disorders, epilepsy, mental retardation, toxic-metabolic disorders, attention-deficit hyperactivity disorder (ADHD), and conduct disorder in children and therefore may occur without a prior history of traumatic injury or other acquired brain damage. When episodic rage does follow a brain injury, a particularly common site of damage is the medial portion of the temporal lobes which contain many of the limbic structures that modulate emotion and motivation. However, while the neuropathology in some cases of organic aggression can be documented by radiological or EEG abnormalities, many cases lack objective neurologic signs. In such cases, the association between aggression and brain injury can only be made by comparing the present state with the patient's premorbid personality and behavioral functioning (Elliott, 1982, 1984; Mark and Ervin, 1970; Miller, 1990, 1992a, 1993, 1994, 1998a; Monroe, 1982; Pincus and Tucker, 1978; Williams, 1969; Wood, 1987).

The clinical presentation in episodic dyscontrol varies in severity and form. More severe aggressive behaviors can appear as sudden, often unprovoked, "storm-like" outbursts that are primitive and poorly organized — flailing, spitting, scratching — and usually directed at the nearest available person or object. The act itself can be quite destructive to furniture, pets, or people who happen to get in the way, but serious injury to bystanders is usually the result of misguided efforts by observers to subdue the patient during an episode. In such cases, the wild thrashing that inflicts the injurious blows probably represents a desperate attempt to escape restraint, rather than a directed assault against a particular individual — although sudden, directed, but usually unsustained attacks may occur.

The outbursts are typically short-lived and may be followed by feelings of regret and remorse when the individual becomes aware of what he has done. Actual murder carried out in such states may be characterized by "overkill," such as an assailant stabbing his victim dozens or even hundreds of times, often in what witnesses describe as a "frenzy." Such uncontrolled violence is likely to be further fueled by alcohol or drugs. Indeed, EDS can often be triggered by even small amounts of these substances, producing the syndrome of *pathological intoxication* which is characterized by uncontrolled violence following seemingly trivial substance ingestion (Elliott, 1992; Miller, 1985, 1989b, 1991, 1992a, 1997a; Pincus and Tucker, 1978).

Another category of dyscontrol syndrome may resemble the type of aggressive response familiar in individuals known for having a "short fuse," that is, for whom it takes less than the usual degree of irritation, frustration, or provocation to elicit a violent response. Observers may agree that there appears to be some connection or "sense" to the eliciting confrontation, but the reaction appears premature and excessive for the relatively mild nature of the provocation, as when, for example, the person starts a fistfight over a relatively minor argument. In such cases, the behavior may appear more in control, more organized, and more clearly directed against the source of the antagonism.

Self-awareness of the actual period of violent behavior varies from patient to patient, usually in association with the severity of the dyscontrol episode itself. Some patients claim total amnesia for the episode, while others report a vague, fugue-like recollection. Still others maintain clear awareness of the outburst but report being powerless to stop it; these are often the patients who express the greatest remorse after the attack. In many cases, the individual may retain sufficient control to momentarily suspend or redirect the violence ("take the fight outside") or switch the target of the attack from a spouse or child to a chair or wall (Miller, 1990, 1992a, 1994, 1998a).

The relationship between episodic dyscontrol and paroxysmal electrophysiological disorders is not yet entirely clear but probably reflects a continuum between normal behavior with normal EEG findings on one end and frank seizures with clearly epileptiform EEG patterns on the other. In fact, EEG patterns of patients with EDS often show this "in-between" pattern of electrophysiological irregularities (Mark and Ervin, 1970; Pincus and Tucker, 1978) that other researchers have identified as neurophysiological kindling (Miller, 1997b, 1998a).

Probably more common, but less easily recognizable, is the type of organic temporal lobe abnormality that does not produce an immediate outburst of physical aggression, but causes an abrupt change of mood (Miller, 1993, 1998a; Wood, 1987). Some brain-injured patients describe mood swings, occurring with no apparent external stimulus, that produce a marked change in behavior, attitude, and frustration tolerance. This change in mood may make the patient more vulnerable to even scant provocation, leading to an outburst of rage that later leaves the individual feeling bewildered, remorseful, and depressed. As discussed above, this may be related to the phenomenon of kindling (Adamec and Stark-Adamec, 1983; Miller, 1997b; Racine, 1978).

Aggression Due to Frontal Lobe Impairment

The frontal lobes in humans have traditionally been conceptualized as the seat of higher abstraction, judgment, planning, sustained motivation, and self-regulation: the so-called "executive functions" of the brain (Luria, 1980; Mattson and Levin, 1990; Nauta, 1971; Stuss and Benson, 1984). Formal, psychometrically assessed tests of intelligence may be relatively unaffected by brain damage confined to the frontal lobes, as many routine skills and items of previously acquired knowledge are largely retained. More commonly seen in such frontal lobe cases are less easily documented disturbances of attention, planning, judgment, self-monitoring, self-control, and initiating and completing activities in the real world, especially in complex, non-routine situations where greater degrees of cognitive flexibility and novel problem-solving are called for (Lezak, 1983; McFie, 1975; Miller, 1992b, 1992c; Rosenthal, 1987; Stuss and Benson, 1984).

From a social and interpersonal perspective, the frontal lobes, particularly the orbitomedial frontal areas, are involved in the inhibitory control of maladaptive and inappropriate behaviors. Patients with orbitomedial frontal injury may become irritable, short-tempered, hostile, and impulsive (Volavka, 1995). This disinhibitory dimension of frontal lobe aggression is what distinguishes it from the EDS syndrome discussed above. EDS seems to be actively generated by a paroxysmal electrophysiological event, whereas frontal aggression seems to represent an "escape," "release," or "misdirection" of aggression due to the brain's impaired ability to maintain emotional equilibrium or to control the behavioral expression of changes in mood. It is because of this disinhibition factor that frontal patients egocentrically or "childishly" overreact to minor provocations or frustrations. Of course, the two processes may interact: impaired frontal functioning may weaken control and lower the threshold to a violent behavioral outburst kindled by an accumulation of electrophysiological tension.

In its most usual clinical presentation, an external irritant or frustration — a thwarted goal, an annoying person — provokes an emotional response from the frontal lobe patient which quickly escalates beyond what most people would regard as "appropriate" to the degree of seriousness of the situation. Once started, such patients seem to have little or no control over their behavior. Serious sustained violence and destructiveness are seldom seen in frontal lobe outbursts. Rather, shouting, crying, cursing, fist-pounding on furniture, and throwing of reachable objects are the most common manifestations; the overall impression is more of a tantrum than a concerted aggressive attack. Insight into, and remorse over, the outburst is rare, and the patient's labile emotional state can easily switch from rage to sadness to mirth with the right kind of prodding and cajoling (Miller, 1990, 1992a,b, 1993, 1994, 1998a).

Similarly, Volavka (1995) argues that while the occasional frontal lobe patient may attack and injure another person, serious violent crime rarely emerges in previously nonaggressive persons following an acquired lesion limited to the frontal lobes. Additionally, although frontal lobe dysfunction is suggested by neuropsychological testing in many persons characterized by criminal or violent behavior, many of these tests are not specific for frontal lobe dysfunction and may suggest longstanding developmental cognitive impairment related to several brain regions and systems. And, even if one accepts that these tests accurately assess impaired frontal lobe functioning, this by itself would be insufficient to prove a causal connection between such localized impairment *per se* and criminal violence. Finally, it may be that aggression following frontal lobe damage occurs only or primarily when other areas, such as the limbic system, are injured as well. Again, great care must be taken in clinical evaluation and forensic case formulation when applying neuropsychological techniques, concepts, and arguments to issues of complex behavior such as violent criminal activity (Miller, 1986b; 1993; 1998a; Volavka, 1995, 1999).

Premorbid Aggression and Antisocial Personality

Perhaps the single most vexing clinical and theoretical issue with brain-injured patients is the relationship between behavior disorder, acquired brain damage, and premorbid personality and cognitive style. Indeed, the short list of behavioral and psychosocial consequences of brain injury, many attributed to frontal lobe damage, includes concreteness, cognitive inflexibility, impulsivity, poor organization and planning, impaired problem-solving, lack of self-control, irritability, emotional lability, problems in sustaining motivation, egocentricity, lack of empathy, unawareness of personal impact on others, and general socially inappropriate behavior (Eslinger, 1998; Miller, 1993, 1996; Stuss and Benson, 1984).

Clinicians, however, have begun to recognize that these impulsive, egocentric, and sometimes aggressive behavioral tendencies and personality characteristics may in fact have predated the brain injury and perhaps contributed to it (Bond, 1984; Miller, 1989b, 1990, 1992a, 1993, 1994, 1997a, 1998a). In such cases, post-injury frontal lobe disinhibition or paroxysmal electrophysiological disturbances may merely further disinhibit or exacerbate a behavioral pattern that has already existed for some time. Demographic data suggest a high incidence of impulsive, even criminal, behavior in this patient group prior to injury, and many of these same supposedly "organic" traits are found in groups of uninjured individuals clinically identified as psychopaths or antisocial personalities (Begun, 1976; Cleckley, 1982; Miller, 1987, 1988; Millon, 1981; Sperry, 1995), in whom there is, in turn, an associated high rate of substance abuse and other impulse-control disorders (Cloninger, 1987; Craig, 1982; Miller, 1985, 1989b, 1991, 1992a, 1997a).

Indeed, there seems to be a relatively small segment of the population that is characterized by recurrent violence and other antisocial behavior since childhood or early adolescence. *Psychopathy,* or *antisocial personality disorder,* is found to involve approximately 3 to 5% of the male population, but compared to other criminals, psychopaths are responsible for a disproportionate amount of crime, and their offenses are more violent and aggressive than those of other criminals (Elliott, 1992). Psychopathic aggression is typically cold, callous, and plotting — that is, predatory — but psychopaths are also prone to spontaneous outbursts of impulsive rage. In both cases, violence often occurs as a response to minor or trivial provocations. The full clinical psychopathic personality profile, which may not appear in every subject, includes a mask of superficial charm concealing fantasies of inflated self-worth, a need for constant thrill-seeking stimulation, marked impulsivity, low reflectivity, poor self-control, shallow affect, impaired empathy, lack of remorse, manipulative behavior, a parasitic and exploitive lifestyle, social irresponsibility, and multiple short-term sexual relationships (APA, 1994; Cleckley, 1982; Elliott, 1992; Miller, 1989a; Millon, 1981; Sperry, 1995).

Correspondingly, many of the observed neuropsychological and personality patterns seen in some brain-injured patients may reflect this premorbidly impulsive, stimulation-seeking, emotionally and behaviorally labile, and antisocial cognitive style, as opposed to being solely or primarily attributable to the effects of brain damage itself. Premorbid deficits in "executive control," therefore, may characterize the thought and behavior of those individuals most likely to incur a traumatic brain injury in the first place, and in fact may be a common risk factor for incurring traumatic injuries of all types (Miller, 1989b, 1992a, 1993, 1998a).

Elliott (1992) delineates the neuropsychological substrate in aggressive psychopathy as consisting of nonspecific EEG abnormalities, resistance to aversive conditioning, low levels of serotonin metabolites in the cerebrospinal fluid of adult psychopaths, low levels of serotonin in the platelets of children with aggressive conduct disorder (a precursor to an antisocial adult), the presence of minor neurologic abnormalities, or "soft signs," and impairment on neuropsychological testing.

Concerning the neuropsychology of violence, a number of studies have observed that neuropsychological deficits in groups of violent offenders tend to involve primarily left hemisphere functions of language and verbal comprehension and expressive speech articulation. This is consistent with a large number of studies on delinquent and conduct-disordered children that suggest that lowered IQ in these groups is a function of lowered verbal (left hemisphere) IQ, as opposed to lowered performance or spatial (right hemisphere) IQ (Brickman et al., 1984; Hart, 1987; Moffitt, 1990; Mungas, 1988; Raine et al., 1995; Tarter et al., 1984).

On neuropsychological testing, adjudicated male delinquents were found to be impaired in their ability to comprehend, manipulate, and utilize conceptual material (Berman and Siegal, 1976). Violent male penitentiary prisoners were more impaired than nonviolent prisoners on measures of cognitive, language, perceptual, and psychomotor abilities (Spellacy, 1978), and assaultive delinquents had a greater number of EEG abnormalities, poorer verbal memory, and increased perseveration, as compared to non-assaultive delinquents (Krynicki, 1978). The significant finding of frontal-like impairment in another series of delinquents led to the hypothesis that antisocial individuals have particular problems in planning their actions, perceiving the consequences of those actions, and altering those actions in the face of changing circumstances (Yeudall et al., 1982). The presence of frontal-like deficits was further established in a group of adult psychopaths, using a variety of neuropsychological measures (Gorenstein, 1982).

More impulsive, assaultive subjects in an adult, male prison population showed significant impairment, when compared to less violent prisoners, on tasks requiring complex integration of information from the visual, auditory, and somesthetic processing systems, as well as impaired ability to create, plan, organize, and execute goal-directed behaviors and to sustain attention and concentration, similar to findings with frontal lobe patients (Bryant et al., 1984). This work was replicated in a non-prison population, showing that psychopathic inpatients at a Veterans Administration alcohol and drug treatment program performed more poorly than non-psychopathic inpatients on a variety of measures sensitive to frontal lobe impairment, even when overall IQ was controlled for (Sutker and Allain, 1987). Overall, replication of this neuropsychological research has not been unanimous (Hare, 1984, 1986; Smith et al., 1992), but the bulk of the data supports the hypothesis of predominant left hemisphere and frontal lobe neuropsychological impairment in non-brain-injured but impulsively antisocial populations (Miller, 1987, 1988, 1998a).

Characteristically impulsive, antisocial individuals probably do not have injured frontal lobes in the same pathophysiological sense as a stroke, gunshot, or head trauma concussion victim. Rather, they most likely possess a particular constitutional neuropsychodynamic organization underlying their impulsive cognitive style (Gorenstein and Newman, 1990; Miller, 1989a, 1992b,c), one important component of which is an underdevelopment of, or deficiency in, frontal lobe control over behavior. To the extent that this neuropsychodynamic pattern affects test performance, we may see "frontal"-like deficits on some neuropsychological measures, as well as in their general behavior.

TOWARD A NEUROPHYLOGENETIC MODEL OF SERIAL SEXUAL HOMICIDE

Serial sexual homicide is a non-socialized and consensually criminalized form of solitary human predation that occurs out of the context of, and without the communal validation of, the individual's social group as an acceptable, temporary extension of combat or other socialized aggression against an out-group. In essence, like a star football player who is expelled from the team for repeatedly tackling fans or the rogue cop who habitually and gratuitously brutalizes suspects, the predatory serial killer "doesn't play by the rules." He stalks and kills the wrong people and does not get our permission first. So we stalk and pursue and try to apprehend him as part of our law enforcement "manhunt."

The neuropsychodynamics of serial killing depend upon the subtype. Impulsive, violent, "disorganized" murders probably involve sudden episodes of disinhibition related to weakened frontal lobe control over limbically evoked violence or the ability to postpone or deflect it or conceal the crime afterwards. Personality correlates would probably involve some permutation of antisocial and schizoid dynamics.

But the planning and calculating capacities of the frontal lobes appear to function only too well in the cunningly efficient "organized" subtype of the predatory serial killer, who shows, if anything, uncommon cleverness in stalking victims and eluding capture himself. Here, hyperactive temporal lobe-limbic mechanisms give the behavior its stereotyped, repeated, and "driven" quality. The predatory serial killer is literally a limbically kindled "engine of destruction." He won't stop and doesn't want to, because nothing in life could possibly replace the thrill of dominating and destroying another human being. His intact cognitive planning skills are utilized in the service of his well-honed murderous craft. His personality correlates probably involve combinations of narcissistic and schizoid traits; he is the lone killer who is more clever than all of us; he is "entitled" to kill, and, aside from his penchant for a specific type of brutal murder, he may not be classically "antisocial."

Finally, the sexual element of serial killing derives from the limbic fusion of sex and aggression that occurs commonly in many forms of "sexual play," that becomes magnified during the rape frenzies of warfare, that may become permanently warped by an abusive but hypersexualized maternal upbringing, and that remains a stable feature in the neuropsychodynamics of the serial killer. Sexuality implies vulnerability, and that vulnerability can either be shared for the purposes of enhanced human intimacy or exploited for the infliction of human cruelty and horror.

These neuropsychodynamic characterizations are, of course, oversimplified and preliminary; however, they serve to illustrate the importance of developing a "unified field theory" of human behavior that sees normal and psychopathological variants of thought, feeling, action, and socialization as points along a continuum of human adaptation. By pathologizing something, we hope to achieve a certain intellectualized distance from it and cognitive control of it — that is one of the reasons that many clinicians are so fascinated by this topic and why you are reading this book.

Serial sexual homicide, however, is no more a "brain disease" than bipolar disorder or borderline personality; it is a neurodevelopmental variation that, under other circumstances, would be adaptive to the survival of the small, tribal, loyal, predatory hunting groups in which most of human evolution occurred. When we study serial killers, that very twinge of admixed fascination and revulsion we feel should remind us that the human capacity for empathic attunement to others is what allows police detectives or FBI agents to say goodbye to their families before going off to work where they will try to "think like a criminal" in order to increase the likelihood of capturing and removing those true predators whose own sadistic pleasures are their only imperative.

REFERENCES

Adamec, R.E. (1990). Does kindling model anything clinically relevant? *Biological Psychiatry,* 27:249–279.

Adamec, R.E. and Stark-Adamec, A.C. (1983). Limbic kindling and animal behavior: implications for human psychopathology associated with complex partial seizures. *Biological Psychiatry,* 20:269–293.

APA (1984). *Diagnostic and Statistical Manual of Mental Disorders,* 4th ed. Washington, D.C.: American Psychiatric Association.

Barratt, E.S., Stanford, M.S., Kent, T.A., and Felthous, A. (1997). Neuropsychological and cognitive psychophysiological substrates of impulsive aggression. *Biological Psychiatry,* 41:1045–1061.

Barratt, E.S., Stanford, M.S., Dowdy, L., Liebman, M.J., and Kent, T.A. (1999). Impulsive and premeditated aggression: a factor analysis of self-reported acts. *Psychiatry Research,* 86:163–173.

Begun, J.H. (1976). The sociopathic or psychopathic personality. *International Journal of Social Psychiatry,* 14:965–975.

Berlin, F.S. (1988). Issues in the exploration of biological factors contributing to the etiology of the "sex offender," plus some ethical considerations. *Annals of the New York Academy of Sciences,* 528:183–192.

Berman, A. and Siegal, A.M. (1976). Adaptive and learning skills in juvenile delinquents: a neuropsychological analysis. *Journal of Learning Disabilities,* 9:583–590.

Blumer, D. (1970). Changes in sexual behavior related to temporal lobe disorders in man. *Journal of Sexual Research,* 6:1173–1180.

Brickman, A.S., McManus, M., Grapentine, W.L., and Alessi, N.E. (1984). Neuropsychological assessment of seriously delinquent adolescents. *Journal of the American Academy of Child Psychiatry,* 23:453–457.

Bryant, E.T., Scott, M.L., Golden, C.J., and Tori, C.D. (1984). Neuropsychological deficits, learning disability, and violent behavior. *Journal of Consulting and Clinical Psychology,* 52:323–324.

Cleckley, H.M. (1982). *The Mask of Sanity,* rev. ed. St. Louis: Mosby.

Cloninger, C.R. (1987). Neurogenetic adaptive mechanisms in alcoholism. *Science,* 236:410–416.

Coccaro, E.F. (1989). Central serotonin and impulsive aggression. *British Journal of Psychiatry,* 155:52–62.

Coccaro, E.F., Kavoussi, R.J., Sheline, Y.I., and Lish, J.D. (1996). Impulsive aggression in personality disorder correlates with tritiated paroxetine binding in the platelet. *Archives of General Psychiatry,* 53:531–536.

Craig, R.J. (1982). Personality characteristics of heroin addicts: empirical research 1976–1979. *International Journal of the Addictions,* 11:227–248.

Dietz, P.E. (1986). Mass, serial, and sensational homicides. *Bulletin of the New York Academy of Medicine,* 62:492–496.

Dietz, P.E. (1987). Patterns in human violence. *Psychiatric Update: American Psychiatric Association Annual Review,* 6:465–490.

Dodge, K.A., Lochman, J.E., Harnish, J.D., and Bates, J.E. (1997). Reactive and proactive aggression in school children and psychiatrically impaired chronically assaultive youth. *Journal of Abnormal Psychology,* 106:37–51.

Eichelman, B.S. (1992). Aggressive behavior: from laboratory to clinic. *Archives of General Psychiatry,* 49:488–492.

Eichelman, B.S. and Hartwig, A. (1993). The clinical psychopharmacology of violence. *Psychopharmacology Bulletin,* 29:57–63.

Elliott, F.A. (1982). Neurological findings in adult minimal brain dysfunction and the dyscontrol syndrome. *Journal of Nervous and Mental Disease,* 170:680–687.

Elliott, F.A. (1984). The episodic dyscontrol syndrome and aggression. *Neurologic Clinics of North America,* 2:113–125.

Elliott, F.A. (1990). Neurology of aggression and episodic dyscontrol. *Seminars in Neurology,* 10:303–312.

Elliott, F.A. (1992). Violence: the neurologic contribution: an overview. *Archives of Neurology,* 49:595–603.

Epstein, A.W. (1975). The fetish object: phylogenetic considerations. *Archives of Sexual Behavior,* 4:303–308.

Eslinger, P.J. (1998). Neurological and neuropsychological bases of empathy. *European Neurology,* 39:193–199.

Flor-Henry, P. (1969). Schizophrenia-like reactions and affective psychoses associated with temporal lobe epilepsy: etiological factors. *American Journal of Psychiatry,* 126:400–404.

Fujii, D.E.M. and Ahmed, I. (1996). Psychosis secondary to traumatic brain injury. *Neuropsychiatry, Neuropsychology, and Behavioral Neurology,* 9:133–138.

Fujii, D.E.M., Ahmed, I., and Takeshita, J. (1999). Neuropsychological implications in erotomania: two case studies. *Neuropsychiatry, Neuropsychology, and Behavioral Neurology,* 12:110–116.

Geberth, V.J. (1990). *Practical Homicide Investigation: Tactics, Procedures, and Forensic Techniques,* 2nd ed. New York: Elsevier.

Geberth, V.J. and Turco, R.N. (1997). Antisocial personality disorder, sexual sadism, malignant narcissism, and serial murder. *Journal of Forensic Science,* 42:49–60.

Goddard, G.V. (1967). Development of epileptic seizures through brain stimulation at low intensity. *Nature,* 214:1020–1021.

Gorenstein, E.E. (1982). Frontal lobe functions in psychopaths. *Journal of Abnormal Psychology,* 91:368–379.

Gorenstein, E.E. and Newman, J.P. (1980). Disinhibitory psychopathology: a new perspective and a model for research. *Psychological Review,* 87:301–315.

Guze, S.B. (1999). Phenomenology of psychiatric illnesses with special reference to risk of violence and other criminal behavior. In Botkin, J.R., McMahon, W.M., and Francis, L.P. (Eds.), *Genetics and Criminality: The Potential Misuse of Scientific Information in Court* (pp. 99–105). Washington, D.C.: American Psychological Association.

Hall, H.V. (1993). Criminal-forensic neuropsychology of disorders of executive functions. In Hall, H.V. and Sbordone, R.J. (Eds.), *Disorders of Executive Functions: Civil and Criminal Law Applications* (pp. 37–77). Winter Park: PMD Publishers.

Hare, R.D. (1984). Performance of psychopaths on cognitive tasks related to frontal lobe function. *Journal of Abnormal Psychology,* 93:133–140.

Hare, R.D. (1986). Twenty years of experience with the Cleckley psychopath. In Reid, W.H., Dorr, D., Walker, J.I., and Bonner, J.W. (Eds.), *Unmasking the Psychopath* (pp. 3–27). New York: Norton.

Harmon, R.B., Rosner, R., and Owens, H. (1995). Obsessional harassment and erotomania in a criminal court population. *Journal of Forensic Science,* 40:188–196.

Hart, C. (1987). The relevance of a test of speech comprehension deficit to persistent aggressiveness. *Personality and Individual Differences,* 8:371–384.

Hempel, A.G., Meloy, J.R., and Richards, T.C. (1999). Offender and offense characteristics of a nonrandom sample of mass murderers. *Journal of the American Academy of Psychiatry and Law,* 27:213–225.

Hickey, E.W. (1997). *Serial Murderers and Their Victims,* 2nd ed. Belmont: Wadsworth.

Hoenig, J. and Kenna, J. (1979). EEG abnormalities and transsexualism. *British Journal of Psychiatry,* 134:293–300.

Holmes, R.M. and De Burger, J. (1985). Profiles in terror: the serial murderer. *Federal Probation,* 39:29–34.

Holmes, R.M. and De Burger, J. (1988). *Serial Murder.* Newbury Park, CA: Sage.

Holmes, R.M. and Holmes, S.T. (1994). *Murder in America.* Thousand Oaks, CA: Sage.

Holmes, R.M. and Holmes, S.T. (1996). *Profiling Violent Crimes: An Investigative Tool.* Thousand Oaks, CA: Sage.

Hucker, S., Langevin, R., Wortzman, G., Bain, J., Handy, L., Chambers, J., and Wright, S. (1986). Neuropsychological impairment in pedophiles. *Canadian Journal of Behavioral Science,* 18:440–448.

Hunter, R., Logue, V., and McMenemy, W.H. (1963). Temporal lobe epilepsy supervening on longstanding transvestism and fetishism: a case report. *Epilepsia,* 4:60–65.

Jernigan, T.L., Zissok, S., and Heaton, R.K. (1991). Magnetic resonance imaging abnormalities in lenticular nuclei and cerebral cortex in schizophrenia. *Archives of General Psychiatry,* 48:881–890.

John, S. and Osview, F. (1996). Erotomania in a brain-damaged male. *Journal of Intellectual Disability Research,* 40:279–283.

Johnson, B.R. and Becker, J.V. (1997). Natural born killers? The development of the sexually sadistic serial killer. *Journal of the American Academy of Psychiatry and Law,* 25:335–348.

Krynicki, V.E. (1978). Cerebral dysfunction in repetitively assaultive adolescents. *Journal of Nervous and Mental Disease,* 166:59–67.

Lezak, M.D. (1983). *Neuropsychological Assessment,* 2nd ed. New York: Oxford University Press.

Malloy, P.F. and Richardson, E.D. (1994). The frontal lobes and content-specific delusions. *Journal of Neuropsychiatry and Clinical Neuroscience,* 6:455–466.

Malmquist, C.P. (1996). *Homicide: A Psychiatric Perspective.* Washington, D.C.: American Psychiatric Press.

Mandel, H.P. (1997). *Conduct Disorder and Underachievement: Risk Factors, Assessment, Treatment and Prevention.* New York: Wiley.

Mark, V.H. and Ervin, F.R. (1970). *Violence and the Brain.* New York: Harper & Row.

Martell, D.A. (1996). Organic brain dysfunctions and criminality. In Schlesinger, L.B. (Ed.), *Explorations in Criminal Psychopathology: Clinical Syndromes with Forensic Implications* (pp. 170–186). Springfield, IL: Charles C Thomas.

Mattson, A.J. and Levin, H.S. (1990). Frontal lobe dysfunction following closed head injury. *Journal of Nervous and Mental Disease,* 178:282–291.

McFie, J. (1975). *Assessment of Organic Intellectual Impairment.* New York: Academic Press.

Meloy, J.R. (1988). *The Psychopathic Mind: Origins, Dynamics, and Treatment.* Northvale: Jason Aronson.

Meloy, J.R. (1997). Predatory violence during mass murder. *Journal of Forensic Science,* 42:326–329.

Meloy, J.R. (1999). Erotomania, triangulation, and homicide. *Journal of Forensic Science,* 44:421–424.

Miller, L. (1984). Hemispheric asymmetry of cognitive processing in schizophrenics. *Psychological Reports,* 55:932–934.

Miller, L. (1985). Neuropsychological assessment of substance abusers: review and recommendations. *Journal of Substance Abuse Treatment,* 2:5–17.

Miller, L. (1986a). The subcortex, frontal lobes, and psychosis. *Schizophrenia Bulletin,* 12:340–341.

Miller, L. (1986b). "Narrow localizationism" in psychiatric neuropsychology. *Psychological Medicine,* 16:729–734.

Miller, L. (1987). Neuropsychology of the aggressive psychopath: an integrative review. *Aggressive Behavior,* 13:119–140.

Miller, L. (1988). Neuropsychological perspectives on delinquency. *Behavioral Sciences and the Law,* 6:409–428.

Miller, L. (1989a). Neurocognitive aspects of remorse: impulsivity-compulsivity-reflectivity. In Stern, E.M. (Ed.), *Psychotherapy and the Remorseful Patient* (pp. 63–76). New York: Haworth.

Miller, L. (1989b). Neuropsychology, personality, and substance abuse: implications for head injury rehabilitation. *Cognitive Rehabilitation,* 7(5), 26–31.

Miller, L. (1990). Major syndromes of aggressive behavior following head injury. *Cognitive Rehabilitation,* 8(6), 14–19.

Miller, L. (1991). Predicting relapse and recovery in alcoholism and addiction: neuropsychology, personality, and cognitive style. *Journal of Substance Abuse Treatment,* 8:277–291.

Miller, L. (1992a). Neuropsychology, personality, and substance abuse in the head injury case: clinical and forensic issues. *International Journal of Law and Psychiatry,* 15:303–316.

Miller, L. (1992b). The primitive personality and the organic personality: a neuropsychodynamic model for evaluation and treatment. *Psychoanalytic Psychology,* 9:93–109.

Miller, L. (1992c). Cognitive rehabilitation, cognitive therapy, and cognitive style: toward an integrative model of personality and psychotherapy. *Journal of Cognitive Rehabilitation,* 10(1):18–29.

Miller, L. (1993). *Psychotherapy of the Brain-Injured Patient: Reclaiming the Shattered Self.* New York: Norton.

Miller, L. (1994). Traumatic brain injury and aggression. In Hillbrand, M. and Pallone, N.J. (Eds.), *The Psychobiology of Aggression: Engines, Measurement, Control* (pp. 91–103). New York: Haworth.

Miller, L. (1996). Neuropsychology and pathophysiology of mild head injury and the post-concussion syndrome: clinical and forensic considerations. *Journal of Cognitive Rehabilitation,* 14(1):8–23.

Miller, L. (1997a). Traumatic brain injury, substance abuse, and personality: facing the challenges to neuropsychological testimony. *Neurolaw Letter,* 6:137–141.

Miller, L. (1997b). Neurosensitization: a pathophysiological model for traumatic disability syndromes. *Journal of Cognitive Rehabilitation,* 15(6):12–23.

Miller, L. (1998a). Brain injury and violent crime: clinical, neuropsychological, and forensic considerations. *Journal of Cognitive Rehabilitation,* 16(6):2–17.

Miller, L. (1998b). Child abuse brain injury: clinical, neuropsychological, and forensic considerations. *Journal of Cognitive Rehabilitation,* 17(2):10–19.

Miller, L. (1998c). *Shocks to the System: Psychotherapy of Traumatic Disability Syndromes.* New York: Norton.

Miller, L. (1999). Workplace violence: prevention, response, and recovery. *Psychotherapy,* 36:160–169.

Millon, T. (1981). *Disorders of Personality: DSM III, Axis II.* New York: Wiley.

Mills, S. and Raine, A. (1994). Neuroimaging and aggression. In Hillbrand, M. and Pallone, N.J. (Eds.), *The Psychobiology of Aggression: Engines, Measurement, Control* (pp. 145–158). New York: Haworth.

Mitchell, W., Falconer, M.A., and Hill, D. (1954). Epilepsy with fetishism relieved by temporal lobectomy. *Lancet,* 2:626–630.

Moffitt, T.E. (1990). The neuropsychology of juvenile delinquency: a critical review. In Tonry, M. and Morris, N. (Eds.), *Crime and Justice: A Review of the Literature.* Chicago: University of Chicago Press.

Money, J. (1990). Forensic sexology: paraphilic serial rape (blastophilia) and lust murder (erotophonophilia). *American Journal of Psychotherapy,* 44:26–36.

Monroe, R.R. (1982). Limbic ictus and atypical psychoses. *Journal of Nervous and Mental Disease,* 170:711–716.

Mullen, P.E. and Pathe, M. (1994). The pathological extensions of love. *British Journal of Psychiatry,* 165:614–624.

Mungas, D. (1988). Psychometric correlates of episodic violent behavior: a multidisciplinary neuropsychological approach. *British Journal of Psychiatry,* 152:180–187.

Nauta, W.J. (1971). The problem of the frontal lobe: a reinterpretation. *Journal of Psychiatric Research,* 8:167–187.

Neuman, J.H. and Baron, R.A. (1998). Workplace violence and workplace aggression: evidence concerning specific forms, potential causes, and preferred targets. *Journal of Management,* 24:391–419.

Niehoff, D. (1999). *The Biology of Violence.* New York: Free Press.

Palermo, G.B. (1997). The berserk syndrome: a review of mass murder. *Aggression and Violent Behavior,* 2:1–8.

Pallone, N.J. (1996). Sadistic criminal aggression: perspectives from psychology, criminology, neuroscience. In Schlesinger, L.B. (Ed.), *Explorations in Criminal Psychopathology: Clinical Syndromes with Forensic Implications* (pp. 187–211). Springfield, IL: Charles C Thomas.

Paris, J. (1999). *Nature and Nurture in Psychiatry: A Predisposition-Stress Model of Mental Disorders.* Washington, D.C.: American Psychiatric Press.

Pincus, J.H. and Tucker, G.J. (1978). *Behavioral Neurology,* 2nd ed. New York: Oxford University Press.

Post, R.M. Intermittent versus continuous stimulation: effect of time interval on the development of sensitization or tolerance. *Life Sciences,* 26:1275–1282.

Racine, R. (1978). Kindling: the first decade. *Neurosurgery,* 3:234–252.

Raine, A. (1988). Evoked potentials and antisocial behavior. In Moffitt, T.E. and Mednick, S.A. (Eds.), *Biological Contributions to Crime Causation* (pp. 14–39). Dordrecht: Nijhoff.

Raine, A. (1993). *The Psychopathology of Crime: Criminal Behavior as a Clinical Disorder.* San Diego, CA: Academic Press.

Raine, A. and Liu, J.-H. (1998). Biological predispositions to violence and their implications for biological treatment and prevention. *Psychology, Crime, and Law,* 4:107–125.

Raine, A., Venables, P.H., and Williams, M. (1990). Relationship between central and autonomic measures of arousal at age 15 and criminality at age 24. *Archives of General Psychiatry,* 47:67–77.

Raine, A., Lencz, T., and Scerbo, A. (1995). Antisocial behavior: neuroimaging, neuropsychology, neurochemistry, and pathophysiology. In Ratey, J.J. (Ed.), *Neuropsychiatry of Personality Disorders* (pp. 50–78). Cambridge: Blackwell Science.

Raine, A., Meloy, J.R., Bihrle, S., Stoddard, J., LaCasse, L., and Buchsbaum, M.S. (1998). Reduced prefrontal and increased subcortical brain functioning assessed using positron emission tomography in predatory and affective murderers. *Behavioral Sciences and the Law,* 16:319–332.

Ressler, R.K., Burgess, A.W., Douglas, J.E., Hartman, C.R., and D'Agostino, R.B. (1986). Serial killers and their victims: identifying patterns through crime scene analysis. *International Journal of Violence,* 1:288–308.

Ressler, R.K., Burgess, A.W., and Douglas, J.E. (1988). *Sexual Homicide: Patterns and Motives.* New York: Free Press.

Revitch, E. and Schlesinger, L.B. (1978). Murder: evaluation, classification, and prediction. In Kutash, I.L., Kutash, S.B., and Schlesinger, L.B. (Eds.), *Violence: Perspectives on Murder and Aggression.* San Francisco, CA: Jossey-Bass.

Revitch, E. and Schlesinger, L.B. (1981). *Psychopathology of Homicide.* Springfield, IL: Charles C Thomas.

Revitch, E. and Schlesinger, L.B. (1989). *Sex Murder and Sex Aggression.* Springfield, IL: Charles C Thomas.

Revitch, E. and Weiss, R. (1978). The pedophilic offender. *Diseases of the Nervous System,* 23:73–78.

Rosenthal, M. (1987). Traumatic head injury: neurobehavioral consequences. In Caplan, B. (Ed.), *Rehabilitation Psychology Desk Reference* (pp. 247–280). Rockville, MD: Aspen.

Rubin, P., Holm, S., and Friberg, L. (1991). Altered modulation of prefrontal and subcortical brain activity in newly diagnosed schizophrenia and schizophreniform psychosis: a regional blood flow study. *Archives of General Psychiatry,* 48:987–995.

Schlesinger, L.B. (1996). The catathymic process: psychopathology and psychodynamics of extreme aggression. In Schlesinger, L.B. (Ed.), *Explorations in Criminal Psychopathology: Clinical Syndromes with Forensic Implications* (pp. 121–141). Springfield, IL: Charles C Thomas.

Schlesinger, L.B. (1999). Murder and sex murder. In Hall, H.V. (Ed.), *Lethal Violence: A Sourcebook on Fatal, Domestic, Acquaintance, and Stranger Violence* (pp. 383–401). Boca Raton, FL: CRC Press.

Schlesinger, L.B. and Revitch, E. (1980). Stress, violence, and crime. In Kutash, I.L. and Schlesinger, L.B. (Eds.), *Handbook on Stress and Anxiety.* San Francisco, CA: Jossey-Bass.

Scott, M.L., Cole, J.K., McKay, S.E., Golden, C.J., and Liggett, K.R. (1984). Neuropsychological performance of sexual assaulters and pedophiles. *Journal of Forensic Science,* 29:1114–1118.

Serin, R. (1991). Psychopathy and violence in criminals. *Journal of Interpersonal Violence,* 6:423–431.

Siegal, A. and Pott, C.B. (1988). Neural substrates of aggression and flight in the cat. *Progress in Neurobiology,* 31:261–283.

Signer, S.F. (1992). Capgras syndrome and delusions of reduplication in neurologic disorders. *Neuropsychiatry, Neuropsychology, and Behavioral Neurology,* 5:138–143.

Signer, S.F. and Cummings, J.L. (1987). Erotomania and cerebral dysfunction. *British Journal of Psychiatry,* 151:275.

Simon, R.I. (1996). *Bad Men Do What Good Men Dream: A Forensic Psychiatrist Illuminates the Darker Side of Human Behavior.* Washington, D.C.: American Psychiatric Press.

Soutullo, C.A., McElroy, S.L., and Goldmith, J. (1998). Cravings and irresistible impulses: similarities between addictions and impulse control disorders. *Psychiatric Annals,* 28:592–600.

Spellacy, F. (1978). Neuropsychological discrimination between violent and nonviolent men. *Journal of Clinical Psychiatry,* 34:49–52.

Starr, M., Raine, G., Pedersen, D., Shapiro, D., Cooper, N., Morris, H., King, P., and Harris, J. (1984). The random killers: an epidemic of serial murder sparks growing concern. *Newsweek,* November 26, pp. 100–106.

Stein, D.J., Hollander, E., and Liebowitz, M.R. (1993). Neurobiology of impulsivity and impulse control disorders. *Journal of Neuropsychiatry and Clinical Neuroscience,* 5:9–17.

Stoleru, S., Gregoire, M.-C., Gerard, D., Decety, J., Lafarge, E., Cinotti, L., LaVenne, F., Le Bars, D., Vernet-Maury, E., Rada, H., Cillet, C., Mazoyer, B., Forest, M.G., Magnin, F., Spira, A., and Comar, D. (1999). Neuroanatomical correlates of visually evoked sexual arousal in human males. *Archives of Sexual Behavior,* 28:1–21.

Stuss, D.T. and Benson, D.F. (1984). Neuropsychological studies of the frontal lobes. *Psychological Bulletin,* 95:3–28.

Sutker, P.B. and Allain, A.N. (1987). Cognitive abstraction, shifting, and control: clinical sample comparisons of psychopaths and nonpsychopaths. *Journal of Abnormal Psychology,* 96:73–75.

Tarter, R.E., Hegedus, A.M., Winston, M.E., and Alterman, A.I. (1984). Neuropsychological, personality, and family characteristics of physically abused children. *Journal of the American Academy of Child Psychiatry,* 23:668–674.

Virkkunen, M.E. and Linnoila, M. (1993). Serotonin in personality disorders with habitual violence and impulsivity. In Hodgins, S. (Ed.), *Mental Disorders and Crime* (pp. 194–207). Newbury Park: Sage.

Volavka, J. (1995). *Neurobiology of Violence.* Washington, D.C.: American Psychiatric Press.

Volavka, J. (1999). The neurobiology of violence: an update. *Journal of Neuropsychiatry and Clinical Neuroscience,* 11:307–314.

Volkow, N.D. and Tancredi, L. (1987). Neural substrates of violent behavior: a preliminary study with positron emission tomography. *British Journal of Psychiatry,* 151:668–673.

Wertham, F. (1937). The catathymic crisis: a clinical entity. *Archives of Neurology and Psychiatry,* 37:974.

Wertham, F. (1978). A catathymic crisis. In Kutash, I.L., Kutash, S.B., and Schlesinger, L.B. (Eds.), *Violence: Perspectives on Murder and Aggression.* San Francisco, CA: Jossey-Bass.

Williams, D. (1969). Neural factors related to habitual aggression: consideration of difference between those habitually aggressive and others who have committed crimes of violence. *Brain,* 92:503–520.

Williamson, S., Hare, R.D., and Wong, S. (1987). Violence: criminal psychopaths and their victims. *Canadian Journal of Behavioral Science,* 19:454–462.

Wood, R.L. (1987). *Brain Injury Rehabilitation: A Neurobehavioral Approach.* Rockville, MD: Aspen.

Wright, P., Nobrega, J., Langevin, R., and Wortzman, G. (1990). Brain density and symmetry in pedophilic and sexually aggressive offenders. *Annals of Sex Research,* 3:319–328.

Yeudall, L.T., Fromm-Auch, D., and Davies, P. (1982). Neuropsychological impairment in persistent delinquency. *Journal of Nervous and Mental Disease,* 170:257–265.

Zuckerman, M. (1979). *Sensation Seeking: Beyond the Optimum Level of Arousal.* Hillsdale: Erlbaum.

Zuckerman, M. (1990). The psychophysiology of sensation seeking. *Journal of Personality,* 58:313–345.

Zuckerman, M. (1991). *Psychobiology of Personality.* Cambridge: Cambridge University Press.

8 Serial Stalkers: Recent Clinical Findings

Robert Lloyd-Goldstein

CONTENTS

INTRODUCTION

Stalking has been described as the quintessential crime of the 1990s. A recent report indicated that an estimated 1 million adult American women and 0.4 million adult American men are stalked annually (with a lifetime risk of 8% for women and 2% for men) (Tjaden and Thoennes, 1998). Stalking has various definitions in legal, law enforcement, and clinical contexts, reflecting the wide spectrum of behaviors that are encountered. The broad and sometimes hazy use of the term overlaps with a myriad of behaviors associated with other demarcated areas of scientific study (e.g., domestic violence, serial murder, serial rape, erotomania), even merging on occasion into the extremes of exaggerated "normal" social interactions. Stalkers are indeed a heterogeneous group. As Simon (1996, pp. 48–49) observed:

0-8493-2236-7/00/$0.00+$.50
© 2000 by CRC Press LLC

"The man who cases a woman's home before a sexual assault is often dubbed a stalker. Is the contract killer who follows his victim to determine the best point of attack a stalker? What about the rejected husband or lover who cannot let go? Is the egotistical person who writes a movie star for a date a stalker? What are called stalkers present a wide spectrum of behaviors. Nor is there a stalker syndrome, only a common behavioral pathway to the victim for a broad variety of motives."

In a legal context, stalking has been defined as "willful, malicious, and repeated following and harassing of another person that threatens his or her safety" (California Penal Code Section 646.9). The FBI classification manual defines a stalker as "a predator who stalks or selects a victim based on a specific criterion of the victim" (Simon, 1996, p. 48). Clinicians have defined stalking as "an abnormal or long-term pattern of threat or harassment directed toward a specific individual" (Meloy and Gothard, 1995, p. 259).

Behavioral scientists have investigated the psychopathology, motivations, disordered behavior, and other associated clinical features of stalkers (Meloy, 1996; Mullen and Pathé, 1994; Zona et al., 1993). Although still very much in its infancy, the scientific study of stalking has grown exponentially in the relatively brief span of the last decade, giving rise to a plethora of serious clinical research studies and a scholarly book devoted to this important topic (Kienlen et al., 1997; Meloy 1998; Mullen et al., 1999) From a historical perspective, the study of stalkers was misleadingly equated with the study of erotomania in past years. In a review of preliminary research studies between 1978 and 1995, Meloy (1996) was able to identify only five studies in the stalking literature that did not focus exclusively on subjects diagnosed with erotomania. It is now recognized that only a small proportion of stalkers overall suffer from erotomania (Kienlen et al., 1997)

To date, no published study on stalking has addressed the phenomenon of serial stalking *per se*. A computer-generated search of the literature on stalking and erotomania reveals no references on serial stalking. This chapter represents the first attempt to focus on this subject and present the available clinical findings that have emerged. In the first part of the chapter, the typology, demographics, psychopathology, psychodynamics, motivations, behavior patterns, management strategies, and forensic dimensions of stalking will be reviewed. The second part of the chapter presents an overview of the current state of knowledge and recent clinical findings regarding serial stalkers, which are addressed in depth, and a clinical vignette of a serial stalker from the author's private forensic practice.

TYPOLOGY OF STALKERS

There have been several attempts to classify and categorize the various stalking behaviors and relationships into useful typologies. The many complexities of the stalking phenomenon and its heterogeneous nature make it unlikely that any one classification system will be adopted as definitive and authoritative at any time soon. Each of the leading investigators has propounded his or her own typology in an attempt to further scientific investigation and clinical understanding and provide answers to the daunting questions of who stalks, why they stalk, and, most important, how to stop them (Mullen et al., 1999, p. 1249). Zona et al. (1993) classified stalkers into three distinct groups: erotomanic, love obsessional, and simple obsessional. Only the latter group was characterized by an actual, prior relationship with the victim. Harmon et al. (1995) formulated a classification scheme using two axes: the first defining the nature of the attachment (either affectionate/amorous or persecutory/angry) and the second describing the previous relationship (personal, professional, employment, media, acquaintance, none). Kienlen et al. (1997) proposed a simple dichotomy between psychotic and non-psychotic stalkers. Mullen et al. (1999) developed a classification system based on context and motivation which was composed of five groups: rejected, intimacy seeking, incompetent, resentful, and predatory. A recent *Notre Dame Law Review* article suggested that four basic categories of stalkers exist: erotomania and de Clérambault's syndrome, borderline erotomania, former intimate stalkers, and sociopathic stalkers (McAnaney et al., 1993).

For heuristic purposes, I have incorporated elements of these various classification systems to describe the following major categories of stalkers. (This is not intended to be an exhaustive or comprehensive new classification scheme.)

EROTOMANIC STALKERS

As noted above, until recently there was an ill-founded tendency to equate stalking with erotomania (Kienlen et al., 1997). de Clérambault (1942) described *primary* erotomania as a circumscribed monodelusional disorder in which the subject holds the delusion that a person (often of elevated social status, a celebrity, political leader, even the patient's own psychiatrist[*]) is passionately in love with the subject, communicates in subtle and indirect ways, and often acts in a paradoxical manner (e.g., appearing disinterested or rejecting in order to test the subject's love or throw others off the track). The *Diagnostic and Statistical Manual of Mental Disorders,* 4th ed. (DSM-IV) diagnosis of delusional disorder, erotomanic type, is the current official nosological designation for this condition. *Secondary* erotomania refers to a more generalized psychotic condition, in which the distinctive erotomanic delusion is but one manifestation of widespread, severe psychopathology. Erotomanic symptoms may occur in 22 different DSM-IV diagnostic categories. In two thirds of these cases of secondary erotomania, the underlying diagnosis is schizophrenia; the second most common diagnosis is a mood disorder (often with manic symptoms). Traditionally, primary erotomania was deemed to occur exclusively among women, and Hart (1921) referred to the condition as "old maid's insanity." It has become increasingly clear, however, that erotomanic patients in a forensic setting are more likely to be men (Goldstein, 1986, 1987; Taylor et al., 1983). It has been suggested that this is a function of the vast over-representation of men in the violence-prone offender population (Goldstein, 1987). The research on stalking is generally in agreement that approximately 10% of stalkers have a primary diagnosis of delusional disorder, erotomanic type, contrary to earlier misconceptions (Kienlen et al., 1997; Meloy and Gothard, 1995).

---

[*] Stalking of psychiatrists and other mental health personnel has been reported in various contexts (e.g., Brown et al., 1996; Raskin and Sullivan, 1974; Sandberg et al., 1998).

CELEBRITY STALKERS

There is little doubt that we live in a culture that is fascinated and obsessed with celebrity to an extent that borders on rampant social pathology. The media glare and lurid sensationalism associated with the tragic deaths of Princess Diana and John F. Kennedy, Jr., are two recent examples of this phenomenon. It is not surprising, therefore, that celebrities frequently are singled out as targets of stalkers (often mentally ill, socially isolated individuals who become enmeshed in fantasy relationships with actors, rock singers, star athletes, political leaders, and other icons of our society). The ensuing association with a celebrity that is fantasized and acted out (in the absence of any reality-based personal relationship) often serves to bolster the defective self-image of the perpetrator. Some stalkers believe that their association with a celebrity will transform them into celebrities in their own right (Mark David Chapman, who fatally shot John Lennon, expressed such a conviction).

Although celebrity stalkers comprise a small fraction of stalkers overall, it is hardly surprising that they generate the most attention and notoriety, based on the fame of their targets (Table 1). The celebrity stalkers of John Lennon (Mark David Chapman), Jodie Foster (John Hinckley, Jr.[*]), and David Letterman (Margaret Ray), among others, have themselves become part of the folklore of our global village. It was the tragic murder of a television star, Rebecca Schaeffer, by a deranged fan who had stalked her and become enraged by her rejection that resulted in the raising of public awareness about the widespread incidence of stalking behavior (most commonly victimizing non-celebrities) and the substantial public health and criminal justice concerns that are involved. This in turn led to enactment of the first anti-stalking law in California in 1990. Over the years, sometimes in response to other high-profile cases, anti-stalking legislation has been passed in every jurisdiction in the U.S., as well as in Canada, Great Britain, and Australia.

FORMER INTIMATE STALKERS

In contrast to the foregoing categories, in which an actual, prior personal relationship has never existed between the stalker and victim, in this group a past real-life relationship of an intimate nature has existed, but for some reason or another has turned sour. These relationships include intimately shared life relationships (marriage, cohabitation) and other intimate relationships of various duration (dating, affairs). Most typically, a former or estranged spouse or ex-lover does the stalking, refusing to accept that the relationship has ended or seeking retribution for perceived rejection or infidelity. These ex-partners may be determined to win back their "loved one" or alternatively to get even for what they view as a betrayal. These individuals fixate on their victims and refuse to let go (or more accurately, refuse to be rejected by them) (McAnaney et al., 1993). These stalkers are highly rejection sensitive, emotionally overdependent on their victims, ambivalent about the overdependency, and jealous over real or imaginary infidelities, and they exhibit a powerful need to control or dominate their ex-partner, by force if necessary. A number of these

---

* Hinckley attempted to assassinate President Reagan, an act that he described as "historic," in order to impress Ms. Foster and win her love (Goldstein, 1995).

TABLE 1
Selected Stalkers and Their Victims

Stalkers	Victims
Joni Penn	Sharon Gless, actress
Mark David Chapman	John Lennon, musician
Arthur Jackson	Teresa Saldana, actress
	John F. Kennedy, president
	Theresa Berganza, singer
John Hinckley, II	Jodie Foster, actress
Tina Ledbetter	Michael J. Fox, actor
Stephen Stillabower	Madonna, musician
	Sean Penn, actor
Ken Gause	Johnny Carson, TV host
Nathan Trupp	Michael Landon, actor
	Sandra Day O'Connor, Supreme Court Justice
Ralph Nau	Olivia Newton-John, singer
	Marie Osmond, singer
	Cher, singer
	Farrah Fawcett, actress
John Smetek	Justine Bateman, actress
Robert Bardo	Rebecca Schaeffer, actress
Billie Jackson	Michael Jackson, singer
Margaret Ray	David Letterman, television host
Roger Davis	Vanna White, television star
Brook Hull	Teri Garr, actress
Ruth Steinhagen	Eddie Waitkus, baseball player
Daniel Vega	Donna Mills, actress
Robert Keiling	Anne Murray, singer

Source: Reprinted from Holmes, R.M. and Holmes, S.T. (1998). *Contemporary Perspectives on Serial Murder* (p. 140). Thousand Oaks, CA: Sage Publications. With permission.

---

individuals have a history of domestic violence (battering). No data are currently available regarding the incidence of subsequent stalking behavior among individuals with a history of domestic violence (Kurt, 1995).

These stalkers demonstrate a gross disorder of attachment and bonding, involving intense feelings toward the victim, with the simultaneous realization that these feelings are *not* reciprocated (in contrast to the erotomanic stalker, who harbors the delusion that the victim reciprocates feelings of love, despite the absence of any actual, prior personal relationship or emotional reciprocity). These stalkers are, therefore, not delusional. They are unable to tolerate the abandonment anxiety that develops when their ex-partner leaves the relationship. There is a significant incidence of violence perpetrated by this group of stalkers, mostly by men, but also by former female intimates. There are estimates that "as many as ninety percent of the women killed by (former) husbands or boyfriends were stalked before a murder occurred"

(McAnaney et al., 1993, p. 838). Six risk markers for violence found in men involved in intimate relationships have been identified: low self-esteem, low income level, low occupational status, alcohol abuse, a history of physical abuse as a child, and a history of witnessing parental violence as a child (Sugarman and Hotaling, 1989).

CASUAL-ACQUAINTANCE STALKERS

In this category, the actual, prior relationship between the stalker and victim has been a more casual personal relationship (in which the stalker oftentimes misinterpreted the meaning or depth of the interaction). Meloy (1989) coined the term "borderline erotomania" to describe a group of non-psychotic individuals who are intensely fixated on a love object but who are not delusional (they are fully aware that their love is not reciprocated by the victim). There is typically a history of passing emotional engagement with the object of their fantasy, albeit sometimes a most trivial one (e.g., a friendly but innocuous glance or some similar expression of warmth or openness may suffice). These individuals exhibit a profound disturbance of attachment or bonding. Findings include ego fragility, over-utilization of primitive defense mechanisms (splitting, projective identification), narcissistic character pathology, and a clingy emotional desperation in the face of potential abandonment. Overwhelming narcissistic rage (abandonment rage) may develop when the victim fails to reciprocate feelings of love. These individuals usually have underlying character pathology or a personality disorder of the cluster-B type (histrionic, narcissistic, or borderline subgroups, significantly more frequently than antisocial personality disorder) (Meloy and Gothard, 1995). They are emotionally needy and morbidly infatuated would-be lovers, who are "seeking intimacy with the object of their unwanted attention" (Mullen et al., 1999, p. 1246).

PREDATORY/SOCIOPATHIC STALKERS

These stalkers sometimes suffer from paraphilias and often have a history of prior sexual offenses. Their victims are usually strangers, although ideal victim types are often selected based on specific personal, physical, or occupational attributes. These stalkers enjoy a sense of power obtained through tracking their victims and anticipating and rehearsing their planned sexual attack. Escalation into gratuitous violence (including murder) is an associated feature. Serial killers (usually of the hedonistic or power/control type) and serial rapists would logically fit into this group, although these two categories of offenders are conspicuously absent from the stalking literature. Although the behavior of these individuals is often characteristic, no data are currently available regarding the incidence of stalking behavior in either of these two categories. It is likely that future research will address this issue and uncover a significant relationship. These individuals do not appear to be seeking a personal relationship with their victims, but may be displacing their childhood rage at being abused or rejected onto a substitute victim in adulthood. In some cases, their fantasies are suggestive of borderline erotomania. For example, one serial murderer "began to follow women down the street fantasizing that they would love him" (Leibman, 1989, p. 44).

Miscellaneous Types of Stalkers

Incompetent stalkers are socially inept and/or intellectually limited individuals who are attracted to their victims but are not delusional (they are aware that that their feelings are unreciprocated). They persistently pursue the object of their affection in the hope of achieving an intimate relationship, despite their longstanding history of clumsy interactions with the opposite sex (Mullen et al., 1999).

Resentful stalkers aim to frighten their victims and inflict emotional distress. There may be a vendetta against a particular victim or a generalized grievance directed at victims selected at random. One stalker relentlessly targeted a young woman he had passed in the street after he had just suffered a distressing personal humiliation. He selected her simply because she seemed to be attractive, well-to-do, and happy (Mullen et al., 1999).

Other categories would include the political stalker (who tracks, sometimes assaults or even assassinates, political figures on the basis of paranoid delusions or ideology) and the hit stalker (the professional killer-for-hire).

Psychiatric Status

In a study of 145 stalkers in a forensic population, Mullen et al. (1999) found that 43% had an Axis I diagnosis, and 41% suffered from a psychotic disorder (delusional disorders, schizophrenia, and bipolar disorder). Three quarters of the psychotic group had a diagnosis of delusional disorder, less than half of which were of the erotomanic type (13.8%, which is slightly higher than in previous studies). Fifty-one percent had personality disorders (mostly falling into cluster B), and 25% had comorbid substance abuse/dependence.

Kienlen et al. (1997) studied a forensic population of 25 stalkers, of which 78% had an Axis I psychiatric disorder. Nearly one third of all subjects had a psychotic disorder and were delusional. Only one patient manifested erotomanic delusions. Stalking in the other psychotic patients was associated with non-erotic delusions and other manifestations of the psychosis. (Other diagnoses in the psychotic group included schizophrenia, bipolar disorder, and psychotic disorder NOS). The majority of the non-psychotic stalkers had an Axis I diagnosis (major depression, adjustment disorder, substance abuse/dependence). Seventy-three percent of the non-psychotic stalkers were diagnosed with personality disorders (most often with a cluster B or dependent personality disorder).

In a study of 20 stalkers, Meloy and Gothard (1995) found a plethora of Axis I disorders: 35% were diagnosed with substance abuse/dependence; 25%, with mood disorders; 15%, with adjustment disorder; 10%, with delusional disorder; 5%, with schizophrenia; and 5%, with paraphilias. Eighty-five percent of the stalkers were suffering from personality disorders (mostly from cluster B, but with significantly less antisocial personality disorder).

Schwartz-Watts et al. (1997) reported on a forensic cohort of 18 stalkers, of which 78% had an Axis I diagnosis. Fifty percent had psychotic conditions (28% suffered from mood disorders with psychotic features, 11% from delusional disorders, and

11% from schizophrenia). Fifty percent of the stalkers had some degree of organicity, and 61% of the group were substance abusers.

Of the subjects in Meloy and Gothard's study (1995), 51% had a prior criminal history. Kienlen et al. (1997) found that 63% of their sample had a prior criminal history, with non-psychotic stalkers more likely to have a history of prior violent offenses. Mullen et al. (1999) reported that 39% of their group of stalkers had previous criminal convictions (28% for interpersonal violence, 7% for sexual offenses, and 4% for other types of criminal offenses). The consensus of virtually all studies is that stalking is not "an aberrant behavior committed by an otherwise law-abiding and mentally healthy individual" (Meloy and Gothard, 1995).

DEMOGRAPHICS AND ASSOCIATED BEHAVIORS

The prototypical stalker tends to be an older, unmarried male, with a better than average education but with a very unstable work history. For example, Kienlen et al. (1997) found that 84% of their sample was male (they suggested that there may have been more men in their population because men are more prone to violence and hence are over-represented in a forensic context); the median age of their subjects was 34; the highest educational level achieved by two thirds of the group was beyond high school; 60% of the group was unemployed at the time of the alleged offense, and 56% had unstable work histories (nearly half of the group had lost their jobs within seven months of the onset of their stalking behavior).

Most stalkers have been unsuccessful in establishing or maintaining intimate relationships. Most have never married or are not married at the time of the stalking behavior. In one study, 72% were separated or divorced from a spouse or recently separated from an intimate partner (Kienlen et al., 1997). Meloy and Gothard (1995, p. 261) reported that many of their subjects whose victims were strangers "never had a significant intimate relationship and consistently failed in their courtship attempts. This appeared to heighten their social isolation."

Harassing contacts are characteristically multiple and various. The most common method of communication is by telephone (one subject made more than 200 telephone calls in a 24-hour period; Mullen et al., 1999). Other preferred methods include letter writing, e-mail messages, graffiti, sending gifts, surveillance (one subject hired a helicopter to maintain observation), persistent following, visits to the victim's home, and repeated approaches in public situations. Psychotic stalkers were significantly more likely to visit the victim's home. Non-psychotic stalkers were more likely to make contact in public places. The latter, being highly resourceful and manipulative, were able to acquire a detailed knowledge of the victim's movements and whereabouts in order to track him or her. One stalker coordinated her vacations with those of her love object, arranging to sit next to him on the airplane and booking adjoining hotel rooms. Ninety-eight percent of stalkers employ multiple methods of harassment. Stalking behavior is reported to have a duration of anywhere from several weeks to over 20 years (Anderson, 1993; Kienlen et al., 1997; Mullen et al., 1999).

The overwhelming majority of victims are female. All stalkers are more likely to target members of the opposite sex, although same-sex stalking, formerly believed to be quite infrequent, occurred in 44% of a group of stalkings by strangers in one study (Hall, 1998). Homosexual men are significantly more likely to be stalked than heterosexual men (Tjaden and Thoennes, 1998). Mullen et al. (1999) found that in a cohort of 145 stalkers, 30% were ex-partners of the victim, 23% had had a professional relationship with the victim (most often a medical practitioner), 11% had a work-related interaction, 19% were casual acquaintances, 14% had no previous contact, and only 2% stalked celebrities. Kienlen et al. (1997) reported that 58% stalked ex-partners, 20% stalked casual acquaintances, 12% stalked a parent, 8% targeted public figures, and 4% pursued strangers. Non-psychotic subjects most often pursued former intimates, and psychotic perpetrators more frequently targeted individuals with whom they had never had intimate relations, such as casual acquaintances or strangers.

Meloy (1996) found that while one half of the stalkers made threats, only one fourth acted on their threats with violence. Kienlen et al. (1997) reported that 76% of their subjects made threats, while 32% acted on their threats. Non-psychotic stalkers are more likely to make threats and to act out violently, not infrequently using a weapon. There is a significant relationship between threats and prior intimacy. Stalkers are more likely to threaten a former spouse or intimate partner than a stranger. While the specter of mentally ill strangers may evoke the most fear in victims, those who actually do act out violently are most likely to be former intimates. A history of prior offenses, comorbid substance abuse, and the issuance of threats are predictive markers for assaultiveness. A significant percentage of stalkers had sustained head injuries and exhibited some degree of organicity, which may account for their final loss of control and possible acts of violence (Kienlen et al., 1997; Schwartz-Watts et al., 1997). Most stalkers are not violent, but those who do resort to violence usually assault the victim without using a weapon. Less frequently, the assaults are primarily sexual in nature. Homicide has been reported in a very small percentage of cases (less than 2%). The most common target of violence is the love object (80% of victims). Third parties (perceived as standing in the way of pursuit) were assaulted much less frequently (Meloy, 1996).

Many stalkers experienced significant psychosocial stressors in the months immediately preceding the onset of stalking behavior (e.g., the breakup of an intimate relationship, loss of employment, death of a loved one, loss of child custody). They may attempt to compensate for the loss through the pursuit of a love object or express their anger through stalking as a means of revenge. Non-psychotic stalkers are more likely to act out violently and to possess a weapon when stalking their victims. Their pursuit has been described as "more emotionally charged," as it is related to reality-based attachment issues or a sense of mistreatment by the victim. The high incidence of personality disorders in this group is also associated with a greater likelihood of threatening and assaultive behavior (Kienlen et al., 1997). It is noteworthy that stalkers are 2.5 times more likely to have served in the armed forces and more likely to have fathers who were career military (Schwartz-Watts et al., 1997).

PSYCHODYNAMICS AND MANAGEMENT

In many cases, stalking behavior is best viewed as a "gross disturbance of attachment or bonding" (Meloy, 1989, p. 480). Disturbances in early childhood relationships and attachments (e.g., separation from a trusted primary caretaker, emotional absence of a parent caused by illness or substance abuse, parental abuse) may contribute to the disturbed pattern of attachment manifested in stalking behavior. In one study, 63% of the subjects experienced a change or loss of their primary caretaker during childhood, and 55% were the victims of parental child abuse. As adults, these individuals are extraordinarily rejection sensitive and are reliving the emotional or physical abandonment experienced in childhood (Kienlen et al., 1997). The borderline-level defensive operations of many stalkers and their narcissistic character pathology have been described in a series of papers by Meloy (1989, 1990, 1992, 1996). Violent outbursts in these individuals are triggered by narcissistic rage (abandonment rage) in response to rejection by the love object. For those stalkers who have had a prior relationship with the victim (Meloy and Gothard, 1995, p. 262):

> "Abandonment rage arising out of a narcissistic sensitivity appears to defend against the grief of object loss, which then drives the obsessional pursuit. For those subjects without a prior relationship with the victim, fantasy or delusion defends against feelings of loneliness or isolation. When the subject seeks actual contact…a rebuff then stimulates abandonment rage."

Character traits that contribute to stalking behaviors include narcissism, hysteria, paranoia, and psychopathy. (Many of these individuals are diagnosed with Axis II personality disorders, typically from cluster B.) Primitive defense mechanisms (e.g., splitting, projective identification) and borderline personality organization may result in confusion regarding the origin of the stalker's own internal mental processes. According to Meloy (1996, p. 159), "They will often attribute their own internal stimuli to the victim, and vice versa." In some cases, this has led the stalker to seek an order of protection against the victim and level accusations of harassment and stalking against the object of their own pursuit (Mullen et al., 1999). Many stalkers minimize or deny their pattern of misconduct and show no remorse for their actions (Kienlen et al., 1997).

There is a paucity of data regarding effective management of stalkers and long-term followup of various approaches. In general terms, treatment of psychotic stalkers is directed at the delusional symptomatology. The clinical course is quite variable. The disorder may be chronic, with a waxing and waning of the delusional preoccupation. Periods of full remission may be followed by subsequent relapses. Psychotic stalkers, intimacy seeking stalkers, love obsessionals, and borderline erotomanics require assertive psychiatric management, because they are relatively impervious to judicial sanctions. Treatment of the non-psychotic former intimate stalker is likely to be difficult, requiring long-term psychotherapy for maladaptive personality disturbances, in combination with appropriate legal sanctions. Mullen et al. (1999, p. 1248) offer the following assessment of current management strategies:

> "[Stalkers] with major mental disorders require treatment, but given that delusional disorders predominate in this population, this is no easy matter and requires considerable psychotherapeutic skill in addition to pharmacotherapy and more general support. Those with personality disorders are a disparate group, but most can benefit from a combination of support, social skills training, and psychotherapy."

A discussion of the impact of stalking on victims, the effect of anti-stalking legislation, and the various threat-management approaches to protect victims is beyond the scope of this chapter and has been addressed elsewhere (e.g., Anderson, 1993; Hall, 1998; McAnaney et al., 1993; Toobin, 1997). Despite the fact that most stalkers are not violent, they nonetheless (Goldstein, 1998, pp. 203–204): "invariably bring chaos to the lives of their victims. The merciless harassment and pursuit inflict enormous psychological and social disruption and damage, often escalating over a period of many years. Victims may be reduced to living in an unrelieved state of siege."

SERIAL STALKERS

Despite the burgeoning interest in stalking as a serious subject for scientific study and research during the past decade, there has been virtually nothing written about the phenomenon of *serial* stalking. As mentioned previously, a computer-generated database search of the literature on both stalking and erotomania from 1960 to the present revealed no references on the subject of serial stalking *per se*. We are truly at a very beginning stage in the empirical scientific study and analysis of this important phenomenon. Meloy (1999), a noted authority on stalking summarizes the current state of knowledge as follows:

"There is very little science anywhere on serial stalking. A few people allude to it in various pop books and everyone speculates that it's done, but [there is] not much research."

Perhaps one reason for the meager research in this area is that the concept of serial stalking on its very face seems to be inherently counter-intuitive and paradoxical. The central hallmark of the stalker is his or her unyielding fixation on a single love object who is pursued, even in the face of continuing rejection. In a world of casual romance, sexual promiscuity, and escalating divorce rates, the stalker stands out as a paragon of absolute fidelity, single-mindedly and relentlessly devoted to his or her "loved one" (however irrational or hopeless the pursuit may be and however insurmountable the obstacles that are strewn in the stalker's path). The intensity of this morbid passion is conveyed by the remarks of a patient suffering from erotomania who referred to her victim in the following terms (Enoch et al., 1967, p. 13):

"No person or circumstance will be able to separate us, not even death, because this exists solely for those who love by the body; I will be united to him eternally because I love with my mind, as he loves me. ...I shall never be complete until I can live with him always."

In view of the stalker's "eternal" devotion and undying love for the chosen object, it may never have occurred to most investigators that serial stalking even existed, much less that it merited serious scientific study. No standards or criteria have been established or recognized as authoritative to define serial stalking. Compare this, for example, to the recognized standard for serial murder: the killing of three or more people over a period of more than 30 days, with a significant cooling-off period between the murders (Holmes and Holmes, 1998).

I propose that serial stalking should be defined as the *sequential* stalking of discrete victims at different times. Subsequent victims should not be linked to the original individual or organization on which the stalker initially became fixated. (A stalker who becomes fixated on a victim may also sometimes concurrently stalk third parties who are somehow related to the initial victim; likewise, a stalker who becomes fixated on an organization may harass multiple victims who are employees of that organization. These examples would not constitute serial stalking.) Stalkers with multiple love objects on a concurrent basis should be distinguished from true serial stalkers.

Although there are no published reports devoted to the subject of serial stalking, a handful of papers contains incidental data indicating that there have been recorded instances of past victims, multiple victims, or sequential victims of stalkers. I have gleaned these data from the stalking literature and will present and analyze the findings and their implications (see Table 2).

In the overwhelming majority of studies on stalking, the stalker focuses tenaciously on one and only one victim. In accordance with this fundamental observation, the "one victim" hypothesis stands for the proposition that by and large the stalker restricts his pursuit to one exclusive victim. However, Meloy (1996) cautioned that the "one victim" hypothesis is not necessarily conclusive, because the natural course of stalking is often interrupted by arrest and prosecution, and, furthermore, many researchers may simply be unaware of the existence of prior victims (or fail to inquire about them).

ALLUSIONS TO MULTIPLE OBJECTS AND SERIAL STALKING IN THE LITERATURE

In his 1942 paper, de Clérambault included one somewhat atypical male case in his series of otherwise female patients with erotomania. Unusually, the man held the delusional conviction that he was loved by at least two women at once (multiple love objects of a concurrent nature), and he believed that everyone was conspiring to procure a wife for him. The first study that alluded to the existence of sequential victims of stalking was a report by Taylor et al. (1983). In a small sample of men with erotomania in a forensic context, three out of their four cases (75%) directed their amorous attentions at different women (including Princess Caroline of Monaco) in a sequential pattern. All of the subjects had been diagnosed with paranoid schizophrenia, but the authors suggested that delusional disorder may have been a more appropriate diagnosis in the serial stalkers.

Zona et al. (1993) reviewed a forensic sample of 74 stalkers from the case files of the Threat Management Unit (TMU) of the Los Angeles Police Department. Six subjects (8%) had a history of sequential stalking with one prior victim (one subject in the erotomanic subgroup [n = 32], five subjects in the love obsessional subgroup [n = 32], and none in the simple obsessional subgroup [n = 35]).

Harmon et al. (1995) analyzed a forensic cohort of 48 cases referred to a court clinic because of charges related to stalking types of behavior. The most common diagnoses in this group were delusional disorder (14 cases, 6 of the erotomanic subtype), schizophrenia (10 cases), and personality disorders (9 cases, none of the

TABLE 2
Research Studies Containing Incidental Data on Stalkers with Multiple Love Objects

Study	Population	N	Subjects with Multiple Victims	Associated Clinical Findings
Taylor et al. (1983)	Violent male offenders with erotomania (England)	4	75% (all sequential)	All paranoid schizophrenics (more likely all delusional disorder erotomanic subtype)
Zona et al. (1993)	Stalkers from case files of LAPD Threat Management Unit (U.S.)	74	8% (all sequential)	Occurs in erotomanic and love obsessional subgroups (not in simple obsessional subgroup)
Mullen and Pathé (1994)	Forensic population of erotomanic stalkers (Australia)	14	21% (all sequential)	All schizophrenics
Harmon et al. (1995)	Stalkers referred to court clinic (U.S.)	48	33% (most concurrent)	No specific clinical correlations
Menzies et al. (1995)	Men with erotomanic delusions in mixed forensic/general psychiatric population (Canada)	13	31% (all concurrent)	All schizophrenics with antisocial personality disorder
Mullen et al. (1999)	Stalkers referred to forensic psychiatric center for treatment (Australia)	145	No percent given (all sequential)	Occurs in incompetent stalker and predatory stalker subgroups
Meloy et al. (2000)	Stalkers referred to court clinic (U.S.)	65	18% (all sequential)	No specific clinical correlations

Note: Total studies = 7; total N = 363.

antisocial personality disorder subtype). In 16 of the 48 cases studied (33%), there were multiple victims of the harassment. However, in almost all cases, it appears that the multiple victims were stalked on a concurrent basis. For example, one stalker targeted a law firm, because of his grievance over the loss of his lawsuit; he stalked various lawyers, their families, and secretarial staff from the firm. A vague statement is made to the effect that "some" of the stalkers had a prior history of the same charge, *sometimes with different objects*, but no quantitative breakdown is given to establish the percentage of serial stalkers in the recidivist group. Only one of the clinical vignettes that is presented appears to meet the criteria for serial stalking conclusively. No correlation is made in the study between clinical diagnoses and those cases involving multiple victims.

Mullen and Pathé (1994, p. 471) studied a forensic group of 14 psychotic stalkers with erotomanic symptoms. Three subjects (21%) had multiple victims and appeared to be serial stalkers; that is, they had "at *different times* directed their affections at *different women*" [emphasis added], although one subject believed that his subsequent victims were in fact his "first love" in disguise. All of the serial stalkers were middle-aged men with a diagnosis of schizophrenia. Two of these subjects had three serial victims; one had two serial victims.

Menzies et al. (1995) described the clinical and behavioral features of 13 men with erotomanic delusions in a mixed forensic/general psychiatric population. Four of the subjects (31%) had multiple victims (three of these cases had more than two victims). All four of these subjects were diagnosed with schizophrenia on Axis I and antisocial personality disorder on Axis II. However, none of these cases appeared to be serial stalkers. Attachments to different victims were concurrent in all cases.

Mullen et al. (1999), in a study of a forensic population of 145 stalkers, constructed five subgroups on the basis of context and motivation: rejected, intimacy seeking, incompetent, resentful, and predatory. Reference is made to serial stalking in two of these subgroups. It is noted that incompetent stalkers (15% of the overall sample) tend to abandon the pursuit of current victims with "relative ease" in the face of judicial sanctions but typically go on to choose others. The incompetent stalkers in the study had often previously stalked others. No specific figures are given for the incidence of serial stalking in this subgroup, nor is any correlation made with psychiatric diagnoses on Axes I or II. They also note that predatory stalkers (4% of the overall sample) were the most likely of all the other subgroups to have a history of previous convictions for sexual offenses. Presumably (although this is not stated explicitly), many of these subjects (who were diagnosed predominantly with paraphilias) were serial stalkers who had planned and executed sexual attacks on prior victims whom they had also stalked.

Meloy et al. (2000), in a study of 65 stalkers, report that 12 of the subjects (18%) had 17 prior stalking victims overall. Half of these subjects reported prior stalking of strangers (although only two had been previously criminally charged with stalking).

These occasional references in the stalking literature to multiple victims describe a recurring phenomenon in various populations of stalkers. When instances of multiple victims do occur, they are for the most part concurrent in nature and not sequential (i.e., not true cases of serial stalking). However, the findings do serve to confirm Meloy's supposition (Meloy, 1996) that the "one victim" hypothesis is not conclusive. It has been established that a significant proportion of stalkers do pursue multiple victims. Most of these cases involve concurrent multiple victims; a smaller percentage involves sequential victims. Only the latter are true cases of serial stalking. Serial stalking does exist, in a small but significant number of cases. Furthermore, the data indicate that serial stalking is observed in both psychotic and nonpsychotic stalkers.

Discussion

Stalking subjects with multiple victims (whether concurrent or sequential) are, like all stalkers in general, predominantly men and fall into a number of psychotic and non-psychotic diagnostic categories (e.g., delusional disorder, erotomanic subtype and other delusional subtypes, schizophrenia, paraphilias, etc.). Many of these subjects have an Axis II diagnosis of personality disorder (not infrequently antisocial personality disorder).

There is no clearcut explanation for the fact that a small subset of stalkers fixates on multiple objects (either concurrently or sequentially). Menzies et al. (1995) speculate that the development of multiple objects is a function of personality. The four subjects in their study with multiple victims were all schizophrenics with an Axis II diagnosis of antisocial personality disorder. The authors hypothesize that antisocial traits may be central to the development of multiple objects, as individuals with antisocial personality disorder tend to develop unstable superficial relationships devoid of emotional commitment. Such individuals are often sexually promiscuous, quick to project blame for their own shortcomings (including infidelity), and prone to jealousy, suspiciousness, and violence. The authors suggest that it is plausible that when such antisocial individuals also demonstrate stalking behavior, they are more likely to develop multiple objects. This is theoretically consistent with findings that a predominance of typical stalkers with one victim suffers from a personality disorder *other than antisocial personality disorder* (Meloy and Gothard, 1995, p. 261):

"If personality disorder is understood as a disorder of *attachment*, with antisocial personality disorder representing a chronic *detachment* from others, our finding of significantly less antisocial personality disorder among obsessional followers [i.e., stalkers] makes theoretical sense. Those who obsessively follow others, relentlessly seeking proximity to an unwilling and often angry and frightened object, would similarly be expected to have a personality disorder other than antisocial personality disorder." [emphasis added]

This suggests that when personality disorder is a significant factor in stalking behaviors, the "typical" stalker has an intense and pathological attachment to one and only one object of pursuit and usually does *not* suffer from antisocial personality disorder (but most often from other cluster B personality disorders) (Meloy and Gothard, 1995). In contrast, when personality disorder plays a key role, the "atypical" stalker more often suffers from antisocial personality disorder and may go on to develop multiple objects (either concurrently or sequentially).

CLINICAL VIGNETTE

S.S. is a 41-year-old woman who worked as a peep-show model in Manhattan. She had previously been a travel agent and a freelance medical writer. For almost 10 years, she had stalked the director of cancer surgery at a prestigious New York City hospital. She pursued him relentlessly, placing innumerable telephone calls to his office and home, bombarding him and his family with letters and notes, trailing him to medical conferences all over the world (and arranging to sit next to him on the airplane, booking adjoining rooms at his hotel, and even trying to force her way into taxis to be at his side).

She grew up in an affluent New York suburb, attended college, and applied for admission to a human genetics and physiology master's program after college. She attempted to pass herself off as a physician and read medical texts and journals, even between sets at the Honey Buns Club where she worked. She often impersonated a doctor at her victim's hospital, wearing a white coat and bogus medical identification, in order to take meals at the hospital cafeteria and attend his clinical conferences on colorectal cases. She even came to be known as "the colorectal groupie" (Franzini and Grossberg, 1995, p. 14).

She was arrested on at least four occasions for harassment and aggravated harassment. Her pursuit of the doctor and his family included obscene phone messages, increasingly threatening letters and calls, and escalating public approaches. After her arrest, police found numerous airline frequent-flyer cards and club memberships; the doctor's travel itinerary; detailed personal data about his family, friends, and colleagues; and a rubber glove in her possession. She steadfastly maintained the delusional conviction that she had been the doctor's lover and became threatening toward her victim and his family after repeated advances over many years remained unrequited.

There was a long history of prior erotic delusional attachments in her past. At least 20 individuals connected with the case involving the doctor were forced to take out orders of protection against her (including four judges who removed themselves from her case because of harassment directed toward them). She followed one of these judges, wrote erotic letters to him, and visited his wife in disguise to obtain details about his personal life.

After I was retained by her lawyer to prepare a pre-sentence psychiatric report, she began to harass me, as well. On one occasion, she invited me with great fanfare to attend a "victory celebration" at Tavern on the Green, a deluxe Manhattan restaurant. She continued to write to me occasionally for several years. After her re-arrest for stalking a new victim, she wrote to request that I once again serve as her psychiatric expert. She insisted that I was the only one who could help her, because, as she put it, "Compared to the many other psychiatric evaluations which I've undergone, yours was the most accurate." She took pains to remind me that, "Although you saw me at my worst, when I was incarcerated, you might recall that I am blessed with extraordinary good looks and style sense." She has persistently refused any psychiatric treatment, complaining that the psychiatrists in any institutional setting "will take particular sadistic delight in destroying my beauty and brains with those poisons known as 'psychotropics' and 'neuroleptics' in the pseudoscience of psychiatry." I have managed to resist her blandishments and avoid further personal contact or involvement with her since the original criminal proceedings. There have been no further communications from her for the past 4 years.

CONCLUSION

A state-of–the-art review of stalking has been presented that includes proposed typologies, demographic characteristics, psychopathology, psychodynamics, behavior patterns, management strategies, and forensic dimensions. An overview of the current state of knowledge and recent clinical findings regarding serial stalking has been addressed in depth, and a clinical vignette of a serial stalker from the author's private forensic practice has been presented. This chapter represents the first attempt to focus on the subject of serial stalking *per se* and to assemble existing data from disparate sources in order to present the sum total of clinical research data that is currently available. This marks a first step in the empirical scientific study of serial stalking. No data are currently available regarding the incidence of serial stalking behavior among individuals who habitually engage in domestic violence (Kurt, 1995). Likewise, serial murderers and serial rapists are notably absent from the stalking literature, despite the fact that they exhibit the pathognomonic behavioral characteristics of watching, tracking, and stalking their intended victims with precision before they strike. Anecdotal and clinical reports abound that these groups routinely engage in what functionally may be called serial stalking. The need for more research in this area is paramount. Another fertile area for future research is cyber-stalking. The computer revolution inevitably "will serve to quicken and potentiate the twisted fixations of the stalker, thereby creating a new and more challenging set of problems in the years to come" (Goldstein, 1998, p. 209). The specter of the serial cyber-stalker is likely to loom on the forensic horizon at the dawn of this new millennium. As more data become available from these related areas of inquiry, more focused and methodologically sophisticated studies promise to enhance and refine our understanding of serial stalking. This will have important implications for the development of more effective management strategies, introduction of scientific rigor into the early identification of serial stalkers, and more informed decision-making about conditions of release.

REFERENCES

Anderson, S.C. (1993). Anti-stalking laws: will they curb the erotomanic's obsessive pursuit? *Law and Psychology Review*, 17:171–191.

Brown, G.P., Dubin, W.R., Lion, J.R., and Gary, L.J. (1996). Threats against clinicians: a preliminary descriptive classification. *Bulletin of the American Academy of Psychiatry and the Law*, 24:367–376.

de Clérambault, G. (1942). Les Psychoses passionelles. In *Oeuvres Psychiatriques* (pp. 323–443). Paris: Presses Universitaires de France.

Enoch, M.D., Trethowan, W.H., and Barker, J.C. (1997). *Some Uncommon Psychiatric Syndromes*. Bristol: John Wright & Sons.

Franzini, L.R. and Grossberg, J.M. (1995). *Eccentric and Bizarre Behaviors*. New York: John Wiley & Sons.

Goldstein, R.L. (1986). Erotomania in men [letter to the editor]. *American Journal of Psychiatry*, 143:802.

Goldstein, R.L. (1987). More forensic romances: de Clérambault's syndrome in men. *Bulletin of the American Academy of Psychiatry and the Law*, 15:267–274.

Goldstein, R.L. (1995). Paranoids in the legal system: the litigious paranoid and the paranoid criminal. *The Psychiatric Clinics of North America*, 18:303–315.

Goldstein, R.L. (1998). de Clérambault on line: a survey of erotomania and stalking from the old world to the world wide web. In Meloy, J.R. (Ed.), *The Psychology of Stalking* (pp. 193–212). San Diego, CA: Academic Press.

Hall, D.M. (1998). The victims of stalking. In Meloy, J.R. (Ed.), *The Psychology of Stalking* (pp. 113–137). San Diego, CA: Academic Press.

Harmon, R., Rosner, R., and Owens, H. (1995). Obsessional harassment and erotomania in a criminal court population. *Journal of Forensic Sciences*, 40:188–196.

Hart, B. (1921). *The Psychology of Insanity*. Cambridge: Cambridge University Press.

Holmes, R.M. and Holmes, S.T. (1998). *Contemporary Perspectives on Serial Murder*. Thousand Oaks, CA: Sage Publications.

Kienlen, K.K., Birmingham, D.L., Solberg, K.B., O'Regan, J.T., and Meloy, J.R. (1997). A comparative study of psychotic and nonpsychotic stalking. *The Journal of the American Academy of Psychiatry and the Law*, 25:317–334.

Kurt, J.L. (1995). Stalking as a variant of domestic violence. *Bulletin of the American Academy of Psychiatry and the Law*, 23:219–231.

Liebman, F.H. (1989). Serial murderers: four case histories. *Federal Probation*, 53:41–66.

McAnaney, K., Curliss, L., and Abeyta-Price, C. (1993). From jurisprudence to crime: anti-stalking laws. *Notre Dame Law Review*, 68:819–909.

Meloy, J.R. (1989). Unrequited love and the wish to kill: The diagnosis and treatment of borderline erotomania. *Bulletin of the Menninger Clinic*, 53:477–492.

Meloy, J.R. (1990). Nondelusional or borderline erotomania [letter to the editor]. *American Journal of Psychiatry*, 147:820–821.

Meloy, J.R. (1992). *Violent Attachments*. Northvale, NJ: Jason Aronson.

Meloy, J.R. (1996). Stalking (obsessional following): a review of some preliminary studies. *Aggression and Violent Behavior*, 1:147–162.

Meloy, J.R. (1998). *The Psychology of Stalking*. San Diego, CA: Academic Press.

Meloy, J.R. (1999). Personal communication to the author.

Meloy, J.R. and Gothard, S. (1995). Demographic and clinical comparison of obsessional followers and offenders with mental disorders. *American Journal of Psychiatry*, 152:258–263.

Meloy, J.R., Rivers, L., Siegel, L., Gothard, S., Naimark, D., and Nicolini, R. (2000). A replication study of obsessional followers and offenders with mental disorders. *Journal of Forensic Sciences*, in press.

Menzies, R.P.D., Fedoroff, J.P., Green, C.M., and Isaacson, K. (1995). Prediction of dangerous behavior in male erotomania. *British Journal of Psychiatry*, 166: 529–536.

Mullen, P.E. and Pathé, M. (1994). Stalking and the pathologies of love. *Australian and New Zealand Journal of Psychiatry*, 28:469–477.

Mullen, P.E., Pathé, M., Purcell, R., and Stuart, G.W. (1999). Study of stalkers. *American Journal of Psychiatry*, 156:1244–1249.

Raskin, D.E. and Sullivan, K.E. (1974). Erotomania. *American Journal of Psychiatry*, 131:1033–1035.

Sandberg, D.A., McNiel, D.E., and Binder, R.L. (1998). Characteristics of psychiatric inpatients who stalk, threaten, or harass hospital staff after discharge. *American Journal of Psychiatry*, 155:1102–1105.

Schwartz-Watts, D., Morgan, D.W., and Barnes, C.J. (1997). Stalkers: the South Carolina experience. *Journal of the American Academy of Psychiatry and the Law*, 25:541–545.

Simon, R.I. (1996). *Bad Men Do What Good Men Dream*. Washington, D.C.: American Psychiatric Press.

Sugarman, D.B. and Hotaling, G.T. (1989). Violent men in intimate relationships: an analysis of risk markers. *Journal of Applied Social Psychology*, 19:1034–1051.

Taylor, P., Mahendra, B., and Gunn, J. (1983). Erotomania in males. *Psychological Medicine*, 13:645–650.

Tjaden, P. and Thoennes, N. (1997). *Stalking in America: Findings from the National Violence Against Women Survey*. Denver, CO: Center for Policy Research.

Toobin, J. (1997). Stalking in L.A. *The New Yorker*, LXXIII:72–83.

Zona, M., Sharma, L., and Lane, J. (1993). A comparative study of erotomanic and obsessional subjects in a forensic sample. *Journal of Forensic Sciences*, 38:894–903.

9 Serial Burglary: A Spectrum of Behaviors, Motives, and Dynamics

Louis B. Schlesinger

CONTENTS

New College Nottingham
Learning Centres

0-8493-2236-7/00/$0.00+$.50
© 2000 by CRC Press LLC

In the past several years, the overall rates for burglary (defined as the unlawful entry or attempted entry of a structure with intent to commit a felony or theft) have declined, as have all categories of crime in the U.S. (FBI *Uniform Crime Reports*, 1998). Nevertheless, more than 2.5 million burglaries were committed in 1997, and burglary has become the second most common crime, behind larceny-theft and ahead of motor vehicle thefts. One burglary took place every 13 seconds in 1997, and two out of three burglaries were residential. Contrary to popular belief, about half of all residential burglaries occurred in the evening, when the occupants might likely be home. Only 14% of all burglaries were cleared by law enforcement in 1997, and burglary arrests were even down 4% from the prior year.

Despite the pervasiveness of burglary, the topic only rarely is treated in the forensic psychiatric/psychological literature (Revitch, 1978, 1997; Schlesinger and Revitch, 1999). Because most burglaries are a result of social, environmental, or situational factors, rather than an outgrowth of psychogenesis, most of the studies on burglary have been conducted by sociologists, criminologists, and law enforcement officers, who rely mainly on the legal classification of crime. Legal definitions of crime — based mostly on degree of intent — treat all burglaries as fundamentally alike. In these legal definitions, only superficial and seemingly logical phenomena are considered as motivational factors; consequently, what might seem to be premeditation could actually be a compelling, irrational drive, with reasons obscure even to the offender.

Psychiatric diagnosis, *per se*, cannot be used as a common denominator in the classification of crime, as only crimes committed under the influence of psychotic delusions, organic disorders, or toxic states are diagnostically relevant. In fact, as Pallone and Hennessy (1994) have persuasively argued, the vast majority of crime is attributable not to psychopathology but to opportunity, inclination, anticipation of reward, or expectation of impunity. Therefore, psychoanalytic penetration into the deeper levels of personality is often too theoretical, frequently esoteric, and often not relevant in understanding all criminal behavior. To obviate this problem, Revitch and Schlesinger (1981, 1989; Schlesinger, 1999a) developed a classification system of criminal/antisocial behavior that is based not on personality diagnosis or dynamics but on an analysis of the motivational stimuli leading to the criminal act itself. Excluding the small number of offenses that are direct outgrowths of a psychiatric or neurological disorder, the motivational stimuli are spectrally distributed, with the purely exogenous on one end of the scale and the purely endogenous at the other end. Offenses prompted by a psychotic disorder or a toxic or neurological condition form a group of their own.

Thus, offenses are divided into: (1) environmental or sociogenic, (2) situational, (3) impulsive, (4) catathymic, and (5) compulsive (see Figure 1). This classification is not intended to be rigid, as borderlines, with characteristics belonging to the adjoining areas, are inevitable. Exogenous or environmental factors play less and less of a role as one approaches the extreme end of the scale, occupied by the compulsive offenses. Psychogenic or internal factors play a lesser role in the sociogenic offenses, where environmental influences dominate. Burglary, like any other crime, can occupy any spot along the motivational spectrum. For example, burglary might be an act motivated by strong environmental pressures, such as peer group

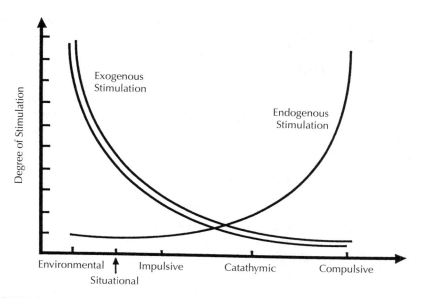

FIGURE 1. The motivational spectrum.

influence on adolescents; it might be a situational act solely to obtain money, or an impulsive act, or the result of a sexually driven compulsion that is often ego-dystonic or outright bizarre.

BURGLARY RESULTING FROM PSYCHOSIS, SUBSTANCE ABUSE, OR ORGANIC DISORDERS

PSYCHOSIS

Although psychiatric or neurological diagnoses are inadequate as the sole means for classification of crime, certain criminal acts, including some rare cases of burglary, are an outgrowth of such conditions. An example of burglary resulting from a psychosis is the complex case of Richard Trenton Chase (Ressler and Shachtman, 1992). Chase believed that his blood was evaporating and that he must drink the blood of others in order to continue to live. Thus, he killed animals, including dogs, cats, rabbits, and birds, and drank their blood. At one point, in his early 20s, he injected rabbit blood into his veins. He was subsequently sent to a convalescent center, but he continued to kill small animals in order to drink their blood and, in his mind, prevent his death. Several years later, following his release, he began breaking into homes, stealing objects, and on several occasions defecating and urinating in the residences. Finally, he decided to kill humans so he could drink their blood and hence preserve his life. When searching for victims he would walk randomly down a street to a nearby home and rattle the door. If the door was open, he went in; if it was locked, he simply went on to another house. Chase wound up killing ten people. He claimed he was responding to auditory hallucinations commanding him to kill. In this case, the break-ins were a means to obtain victims in order to carry out behavior consistent with his obvious psychosis.

In some cases, burglary may be an indirect result of a psychosis. Delusional jealousy, for example, is a form of paranoia characterized by accusations of infidelity and aggressive attitudes toward the partner, coupled with feelings of insecurity and dependency. The accusations may have some basis in reality, but the truth is distorted and "evidence" is frequently fabricated (Revitch, 1954). The disorder is sometimes confused with severe jealousy (Morenz and Lane, 1996), and the delusional nature of the condition is missed (Silva et al., 1999). Diagnosis also can be rendered difficult because the perpetrator seems to have an intact personality, is able to work, and can convince others of his rationality. Family members, and even mental health clinicians, therefore make incorrect assessments, taking what is actually a delusion at face value and regarding the healthier partner as the one who is mentally disturbed (Revitch, 1960; Revitch and Hayden, 1955). The delusional partner, most frequently the male, may search for clues to bolster his notion of unfaithfulness. He may check the partner's underwear, looking for traces of semen, or he may follow her in order to catch her with a nonexistent paramour. The urge to search for "evidence" led to the arrest for burglary in the following strange case.

Case 1

A 44-year-old male was arrested for burglary of a neighbor's home. In a statement to the police, he revealed that the reason for the break-in was to obtain "evidence" of his 36-year-old wife's sexual affair with the 74-year-old male neighbor. While in the neighbor's home, he observed wet bathroom towels, which indicated to him that his wife and the neighbor had taken a shower together. He admitted to entering the house on two other occasions so that he could find "evidence" to bolster his delusional belief about his wife's unfaithfulness. He was also suspected of burglarizing the home of his wife's co-worker, also a man about 30 years her senior.

Psychological evaluation revealed a clear case of delusional jealousy that had persisted for the entire length of their 8-year marriage. This man would not have committed the burglaries if he had not been delusional. He had no prior criminal record and was employed as an engineer for a local oil refinery. He and his wife had seen two marital therapists, both of whom incorrectly evaluated the wife as being more disturbed than the husband. The husband maintained a calm and compliant demeanor when discussing his wife's suspected infidelities, whereas the wife became extremely upset, proclaiming her innocence and impressing the therapists as being out of control.

SUBSTANCE ABUSE

There is clearly a relationship between substance abuse (particularly alcohol, heroin, and cocaine) and crime, but in most cases (except for impulsive aggression) the relationship is indirect (Bradford et al., 1992). A review of the overall rates of substance abuse among prisoners indicates that 20 to 80% are dependent on one substance or another (Halleck, 1971). While many burglars are alcohol and drug dependent, only a small minority have been acutely intoxicated during the burglary. A study by Bennett and Wright (1984) found that about one third of all burglars committed their offenses under the influence of alcohol, but the majority of these offenders saw no causal relationship between drinking and their criminal behavior. Many offenders stated that they had no reason to change their normal drinking pattern simply because they intended to commit a burglary. Similarly, cocaine and opiate addicts often indulge in criminal activities, such as burglary, in order to obtain money to support their need (Mott, 1986; Nurco, 1987), but the drug itself rarely stimulates the act. The following case of burglary, indirectly related to substance abuse, is quite typical.

Case 2

After serving several years in prison for burglary, a 50-year-old male (B.B.) was referred by the court to a substance abuse rehabilitation program. The offender had been dependent on alcohol for 35 years and had taken heroin intravenously for 30 years and cocaine for about 20 years. In his early 20s, he began burglarizing his own family members to obtain money to purchase drugs. "They knew I did it," he said, "but for some reason they let me go." In his late 20s, he committed home burglaries. Almost all his victims were individuals whom he knew; he rationalized that "somebody owed me money, so I broke into their house." On one occasion, he burglarized his AA sponsor's home: "I was working at my friend's house, who was actually my AA sponsor. I was painting. I went there to work and gathered things up inside. I thought I could steal something so I could just get some money. The neighbors saw my car."

The final series of burglaries occurred at a pharmaceutical distribution plant where he briefly worked: "I broke in with another guy to steal cases of barbiturates. I was around the system. I knew how to get in through the door and windows that weren't armed. I checked them. I was also stealing drugs while I was there." In all of B.B.'s burglaries, the primary motivation was to obtain money to buy heroin and cocaine.

ORGANIC DISORDERS

Only very rarely is a burglary committed as a direct result of an organic disorder. There have been cases of criminal behavior, usually of a violent nature, associated with various organic conditions, such as brain tumors (Nevin, 1966), brain injuries (Mark and Southgate, 1971), encephalopathies (Bachet, 1951), and epilepsy (Mark and Ervin, 1970). A close analysis of these reported cases, however, often reveals a strong psychosocial component; organicity — if it plays a role at all — serves primarily to weaken inhibitory controls (Juul-Jensen, 1974). The effects of mild neuropsychological abnormalities on criminality have been studied carefully over the past 20 years (Adams et al., 1990; Nestor, 1992; Pontius and Yudowitz, 1980). There is often an inverse relationship between the degree of brain impairment and the importance of personality/social factors in accounting for criminal behavior in such cases. Even in cases where brain damage is severe, however, such as in mental retardation, there is rarely a direct relationship between the mental deficiency and the crime (Smith and Kunjukrishnan, 1986).

It is sometimes very difficult to determine whether a criminal act has been committed as a result of postictal confusion or in an ambulatory automatism associated with a seizure. Juul-Jensen (1974) reviewed the case histories of individuals who alleged that their crimes were committed during such postictal cloudy states. He concluded that (p. 811): "The possibility exists ... but the number of such crimes is very small, and the differential diagnosis is therefore extremely difficult when epilepsy is pleaded in extenuation of a serious crime." The following case involves the questionable role of organicity in a burglary.

Case 3

A 20-year-old male was apprehended for a series of burglaries committed primarily to obtain money to procure drugs. He was evaluated by a consulting psychiatrist, who concluded that the offender was not criminally responsible because he was subject to complex partial seizures and, as a result, was unable to recall the break-ins. The offender's history of childhood attention deficit hyperactivity disorder and learning disability, according to the psychiatrist, bolstered the diagnosis of complex partial seizures. Complete neurological and neuropsychological evaluation, including EEGs and an MRI, showed no abnormalities. The psychiatrist, who had little experience in forensic matters, was more concerned with proving his neurobiological explanation (for just about every type of behavior) than attempting to understand the case. He had based his conclusion on the offender's own statements, apparently without realizing that it is extremely common for criminal defendants to claim that they have no recall for events. The court found no credibility to the consultant's opinion.

BURGLARY RESULTING FROM SOCIAL-ENVIRONMENTAL CONDITIONS

The sociological study of crime is chiefly concerned with statistical trends and the relationship of crimes to other variables, such as socioeconomic status, race, age, and region. Most crime, including burglary, takes place among the economically disadvantaged (Gibbons, 1968). Poverty alone, however, cannot explain all crime or the fluctuation in crime rates, particularly in western industrialized society. In fact, sometimes crime increases during economic prosperity (Cohen and Felson, 1979), and burglaries, for example, often result more from greater criminal opportunity than from economic strain or social disorganization (Stack, 1995).

JUVENILE CRIME

Group pressure and subgroup values are major contributing factors to crime, particularly juvenile crime. Adolescents who lack success in more socially desirable avenues or feel alienated, angry, and insecure because of family disruption are especially vulnerable to the suggestions, contagion, and feelings of power generated by a group. According to Cohen (1969, p. 52): "These problems are chiefly status problems; certain children are denied status in the respectable society because they cannot meet the criteria of the respectable status system. The delinquent subculture deals with these problems by providing criteria of status which these children can meet." In fact, most burglaries committed by juveniles are committed within a group; adolescents who burglarize alone are likely motivated by more pathological factors (Revitch, 1978). The following case demonstrates the influence of a juvenile peer group in the commission of burglaries.

Case 4

A 17-year-old male (C.C.), along with four of his friends, was arrested for burglary of a liquor store. He explained, "We hung out together and played basketball. Some of the guys had different ways of doing criminal things. Some sold drugs. We started talking and then we decided to break into a house. One night, me and a few of my friends did it. We took jewelry, took a gun, and took money. We knew who lived there. Nobody was home. It was in our neighborhood. We were just wild. We were into a criminal lifestyle. We had no burglar tools. We pushed in the side door."

C.C. and his friends committed about ten residential burglaries, for which they were not arrested. They eventually broke into a liquor store and were arrested. C.C. entered the store through the roof. Earlier that day, he was in the store with his friends. They waited for it to close, and a few hours later they broke in through a vent. They took liquor and cash "just to have money." C.C.'s juvenile criminal career, prior to the burglaries, involved three to four episodes of shoplifting, also with friends, and a number of school behavioral problems. He explained, "I wanted to get an image to be a burglar to prove to my friends that I was down with it. Let's go ahead and do it. We were a wild bunch of teenagers. It was a bad experience in my life that shouldn't have happened. I was with the wrong crowd."

BURGLARY AS A PROFESSION

Sutherland's (1947) theory of differential association argues that people learn criminal behavior and attitudes through interaction with others who have such beliefs. This concept would clearly apply to the semiprofessional or professional burglar, who is a direct product of the values of a subculture and not necessarily the product of urbanization and poverty as stressed by some (Bulloch, 1955). The burglaries of the semiprofessional or professional burglar are logical, adaptive, and purposeful — the goal being to obtain money. In contrast, the adolescent burglar's goal is to achieve a sense of belonging, with money being a secondary goal, often rationalized. Professional and semiprofessional burglars steal because it is their job. Lindesmith (1941) believed that both the professional criminal and the businessman are in pursuit of material success and differ only in the means they employ and the services they render.

Semiprofessional burglars have a life pattern marked by instability, poor school and work adjustment, long criminal records, many fleeting relationships, and substance abuse; thus, they lack the sophistication of the professional burglar. One semiprofessional burglar referred to himself as "a smash and go burglar. I'd smash the window, stick my hand through there and turn the doorknob" (Hills, 1992, p. 48). The professional burglar, as distinguished from both the juvenile and the adult semiprofessional, often specializes in such objects as jewels, coins, furs, or silver (Green et al., 1976).

Semiprofessional serial burglars can be generally divided into the marginal offenders and a smaller number of the more sophisticated (Eskridge, 1983), who target only certain residences or certain types of businesses. The more sophisticated semiprofessional merges with the professional and often displays an astute awareness of the vulnerability of the dwelling selected as a target (Logie et al., 1992; Taylor and Nee, 1988; Wright et al., 1995). Some semiprofessional serial burglars hold legitimate jobs in the labor force and essentially "moonlight" in burglary as a means of additional income (Holzman, 1983). The following case is illustrative.

Case 5

D.D., a 42-year-old male charged with multiple burglaries, was a substance abuser (heroin and cocaine) and a semiprofessional burglar with a fairly sophisticated method of operation, which he had developed over the years. D.D. would primarily burglarize construction sites: "I'd do it by myself because if I got caught someone could tell on me, and I don't want any co-defendants." He would apply for a job at a construction site and, while there, would observe where the power tools were kept and what security was in place. Shortly after closing time he would return, break into the construction site, and steal power tools. He would bring bolt cutters as well as a bag for carrying the tools away. "I'd do this only for financial gain. I know tools and I know their value. I had a fence. I used him for years."

He provided the following details to defend and explain his actions: "I wasn't robbing people; it was insurance companies. I wasn't comfortable doing a house burglary, although I did a few. It's easy to get into a house, but it's hard to leave. If you walk out with someone's TV, it looks funny. ...[When I burglarized construction sites,] I'd blend in and steal during the day also, right in front of you. The construction site closes around 3:30. It takes about one hour for security to settle down, and I blended right in. If I used someone to help me carry something, the person didn't know what I did, nothing; so he couldn't tell on me. I did it for my drug addiction. When I was doing this, I was thinking about burglary almost all the time. I did the burglary to feed an addiction. The burglary and the addiction was a 24-hour-a-day job."

The professional burglar has less psychopathology than the semiprofessional, is less frequently involved with substance abuse, and takes his job of burglary more seriously. He often views conventional jobs as demeaning and regards burglary as a dignified way of earning a living — not just as a device for getting money to buy drugs. Maguire and Bennett (1982, p. 59), in studying professional burglars, were struck by the frequent use of terms that imply a close parallel between professional burglary and a legitimate occupation. "Thefts are referred to as 'jobs,' from which one can 'earn well.' Burglars 'work' particular areas. There is a 'market' for stolen property, with regular 'dealers' or 'buyers.' There are 'pros,' 'experts,' and 'specialists' in various areas who gain status from their skill or earning ability. Those who no longer steal are sometimes referred to as 'retired.' ...Most of the offenders ... believe they were members of a 'profession' in which those who reach the top could expect substantial rewards."

Shover (1972) has studied the structure and careers of professional burglars. He found that the behavior of professional serial burglars supported Sutherland's (1937) theory — namely, that the burglar "could not exist except for his location in a structured and collective network of social relationships which included members of the host society" (Shover, 1972, p. 540). Thus, the professional burglar learns his criminal techniques from more experienced burglars, develops fences (buyers for his wares), and learns how to use bondsmen and attorneys. A professional burglar must also establish relationships with "tipsters" (such as night watchmen, prostitutes, delivery men, or jewelers) whose information about certain premises or their occupants can assist the burglar in planning his activity. "He must establish relationships with those kinds of people who can teach him and assist him in coping with the problems endemic to burglary" (Shover, 1972, p. 542).

Some professional burglars are so sophisticated that they operate in several states and target only those locations where they are certain that valuables will be present. The following case of a professional burglar is illustrative.

Case 6

A 47-year-old male (E.E.) earned his living from the proceeds of burglary. He began stealing at age 12 but did not commit his first burglary until age 27, when he broke into a store on the street where he lived. "I wanted money, I was poor, so I planned it out for several weeks. I stole before, but I never broke in. It was all for money." From this point on, E.E. began burglarizing "as a way of life. It was like my job. You have a need and you have to figure a way to fill it. I had to maintain a lifestyle, and burglary was an option for me."

Jailed a number of times, E.E. learned burglary techniques from other inmates "that I selected." By talking with other burglars, he learned how to inactivate alarms by cutting wires. He then began to specialize in residential burglary. He emphasized, "I learned from my mistakes. I became very adept at how to get in. I brought tape for the windows, cotton so you wouldn't get cut, knee pads, surgical gloves for no prints. I would take anything of value that was carriable." He became proficient at targeting houses: "I saw one guy drive a Mercedes home [and thought,] 'There must be money in there.' I got $15,000 in that house: cash, rings, and watches. I would go straight to the bedrooms, take a pillowcase, turn the mattress over, look under the bed, in the closets there are furs. I had Iranian fences that taught me what to look for. I never took a gun, I'd only go so far. I'd never hurt anybody. I would go to a house early in the morning, usually around 9 o'clock. I'd drive around, I'd stop, knock on the door. If someone came to the door, I'd say I am lost. Sometimes I'd call the house. I'd get the name from the door and look up the telephone number. Rich people are proud to put their name out."

E.E. was eventually apprehended when he committed a burglary with an associate who got into a violent confrontation with the occupant, who had a gun. For this offense E.E. served 8 years in prison but continued to burglarize when released. "I went back to work, but by myself!"

SITUATIONAL BURGLARIES

Situational crimes occur as a result of particular circumstances present at a given time that either directly or indirectly stimulate the act. Situational acts of burglary may be premeditated or sudden and usually are triggered by a stressful life event. Depression, despair, helplessness, fear, and anger are the kinds of stressful emotions that can stimulate the behavior. One offender explained that his motivation to burgle stemmed from anger and hatred toward police, authority, and society at large:

"Burglary provided an outlet for the spirit of revenge that rose within me. …I had been grievously wronged and I was imposing a just retribution on the creatures who had persecuted me" (Booth, 1929, p. 126). All types of personalities may resort to situational crimes; however, inadequate and immature personalities with few inner resources are most vulnerable. Situational burglaries are typically, but not always, one-time events. The following case of a singular situational burglary, triggered by financial stress, serves as an example.

Case 7

A 42-year-old professional financial planner (F.F.), son of a major political figure in the state, was arrested for burglary of a neighbor's home. The following events led to the burglary: F.F. had acquired $640,000 from clients, to whom he promised 7 or 8% returns on their investment. Instead of investing the money in fairly secure instruments, which he had agreed to do, he invested in highly speculative accounts. F.F. planned to make about 20 to 25%, pay his clients, and keep the remainder for himself. Unfortunately, the anticipated high profits did not materialize as expected, and about $300,000 was lost. In an act of desperation, he broke into a wealthy neighbor's home to steal art, jewelry, and other valuables that he knew would be there. F.F. was arrested when he tried to sell the merchandise. A local fence called the police because he thought F.F. was an undercover investigator. F.F. had never been involved in criminal behavior previously. The burglary was clearly a situational event, triggered by a desperate need for money to pay off his clients.

IMPULSIVE OFFENDERS WHO COMMIT BURGLARY

Impulsive offenders are individuals with a lifestyle characterized by lack of direction, randomness of actions, and unpredictability (Revitch and Schlesinger, 1978). These individuals may have chronic feelings of anger, vindictiveness, and low self-esteem with compensatory strivings for recognition. They also may be emotionally explosive or over-reactive to external stimuli, although they are usually passive and easily led. Impulsive offenders can commit aggressive acts, including homicide, or non-aggressive criminal acts such as burglary. The burglaries are usually poorly structured, unpremeditated, or only partially planned.

Impulsive offenders differ from situational offenders by the multiplicity of prior antisocial acts, although each individual act may have a strong situational connotation. On occasion, impulsive offenders are recruited into semiprofessional crime, but they are typically not successful, because they lack purposefulness and their involvement is casual. In some instances, the mere prospect of money fuels the burglary, as the following case demonstrates.

Case 8

A 31-year-old male with a long history of minor antisocial acts committed an amateurish burglary under the following circumstances: "I was hanging out at 10 p.m. in the area. I had no money and no way to get money. A guy said, 'I know what you can do.' He said he'd done a lot of burglaries. He said it was easy. He told me what I had to do. He'd checked it out and said this was easy. He gave me the tools. He wanted some of the money if I got any, a piece of what I made. I took a cloth bag and a pry bar and a hammer. I was anxious to do it to get some money. It was a nail salon; I was gonna break in and take the money. I jumped on the roof because the guy said there was a weak spot. I pried the roof off and climbed down and went inside. They had no money. I saw a phone and broke it open and took the change out. I looked around and I saw nail polish, so I took that. I put it in the bag. I had about two hundred bottles of nail polish. The guy said to keep moving around. He said money should be in the drawers where they sit at. I looked but found nothing. I climbed back up and left. I had about sixty dollars worth of change. I was carrying around the nail polish. I was on my way to sell it the next morning when the police caught me because they had my description. They had an eye-witness. When I was arrested, I confessed. I had the stuff in my hands, there was no need to say anything else."

This offender had committed several previous burglaries and had used drugs but was not an addict. He was an unemployed laborer at the time of this impulsive burglary, which he committed just because a friend had said "it was an easy way to get money."

CATATHYMIC OFFENSES

The concept of catathymic crisis was introduced into forensic psychiatry by Wertham (1937) in an attempt to explain certain acts of violence without apparent motivation. Wertham defined catathymic crisis as "a transformation of the stream of thought as the result of certain complexes of ideas that are charged with a strong affect, usually a wish, a fear, or an ambivalent striving" (p. 975). In Wertham's view, the central feature of the disorder is the idea that violence must be committed. The need to commit the violent act is compelling, although the individual may resist the urge for some time. Revitch and Schlesinger (1981, 1989; Schlesinger, 1996a,b) refocused the concept and divided the process into two general types: acute and chronic. The acute type is an explosive outburst triggered by a sudden, overwhelming emotion attached to underlying emotionally charged conflicts. For example, a 16-year-old male suddenly killed his mother, in a dissociative state, following years of mother-son incest. The outburst was triggered by his attempt to discontinue the sexual involvement, which had been initiated and prolonged by the mother (Schlesinger, 1999a).

The chronic catathymic process involves the buildup of tension over a period of time, with the emergence of the idea that the way to gain relief from the discomforting state is to commit a violent act — usually against a close relation, a family member, or sometimes the entire family. Schlesinger (2000) reports the case of a 36-year-old male who finally decided that he had to kill his entire family, in order to spare them from experiencing the humiliation he felt when he could not solve a problem associated with a home-improvement project.

Burglary is hardly ever associated with the catathymic process. In the following case, however, a burglary was substituted for an urge to commit arson. Clear sexual underpinnings were involved in the urge to set a fire and in the perpetrator's feeling of relief after committing the burglary.

CASE 9

A 22-year-old male (G.G.), charged with burglary, was evaluated in the county jail. During the examination, he revealed that he had set about seven fires, in a 2-year period, for which he had not been caught. The firesetting began shortly after he learned of his mother's sexual indiscretions following his father's death. He described a state of tension that was released once the fire was set, plus feelings of guilt and fear: "I wanted to get caught because I knew I needed help."

On the day of the burglary, G.G. had planned to set fire to a home in his neighborhood. Once he got the idea to set a fire, it "took hold of me." He obsessed about the idea for several hours and had a strong urge "to do it." He approached the house, but, for some reason, "rather than set it on fire, I thought of breaking in through the window to look around. I looked around, took a clock radio, and left." Following the burglary he "felt better," and the urge to set the fire temporarily dissipated. He was quickly arrested for the burglary, because a neighbor had spotted him leaving the home through a window.

In this case, the urge to set a fire was transformed to an urge to break in, and a feeling of relief followed the burglary. A sexual element is noted, typical in many chronic catathymic offenses. This transformation of the urge to set a fire into the urge to commit burglary is quite unusual; both were probably fueled by underlying sexual dynamics related, in part, to anger at his mother for her sexual conduct.

COMPULSIVE SEXUALLY MOTIVATED BURGLARIES

Although most burglaries are committed for material gain, law enforcement has always recognized a much smaller group of burglars who differ in criminal technique, psychological makeup, and motivation from the traditional gain-oriented burglar (Gibbons, 1968). The more the burglary is symbolic, maladaptive, compelling, without logic, and sometimes outright bizarre, the more likely it is sexually motivated (Revitch, 1978). Banay (1969, p. 24) remarked that, "Some burglars ... tell of achieving orgasm at the moment of entering a window or breaking a locked door." Guttmacher (1963) and Banay (1969) have argued that many crimes — such as burglary, arson, and some assaults — may on the surface seem nonsexual but are in fact sexually driven, although the sexual dynamics remain covert.

FETISH BURGLARY AND VOYEURISTIC BURGLARY

Schlesinger and Revitch (1999) have described two types of sexual burglaries: (1) fetish burglary, with overt sexual dynamics, where the offender steals objects such as female underwear; and (2) voyeuristic burglary, with covert sexual dynamics, stimulated by voyeurism and a generalized urge to look around (see Table 1). Fetish burglaries have been recognized by law enforcement for many years and are defined by Ressler and Shachtman (1992, p. 8) as "breaking and entering cases in which the items stolen or misused are articles of women's clothing, rather than jewelry or other items of marketable value; often, the burglars take these for autoerotic purposes."

TABLE 1
Differentiating Characteristics of Fetish and Voyeuristic Burglaries

Type of Burglary	Sexual Dynamics	Behaviors
Fetish	Overt; stimulated by sexual attraction to non-living objects	Fetishism (begins in late childhood). Burglary to get fetish objects (begins in adolescence). Steals objects, commonly female underwear, shoes, hairbrushes. Sometimes soils premises.
Voyeuristic	Covert; stimulated by urge to look	Voyeurism (begins in late childhood). Burglary with urge to look and inspect premises (begins in adolescence). Steals objects of minimal value; stealing is rationalized.

A classic case of a fetish burglar is that of William Heirens, who developed a fetish for female underwear at age 9. He began to steal and collect female underwear and then burglarized to obtain them. Heirens committed hundreds of fetish burglaries and later killed two women and a child in their apartments. He became so sexually aroused by burglary that, "He had … an erection [and emission] at the sight of an open window" (Kennedy et al., 1947). Another fetish burglar, Jerome Brudos, developed a foot fetish as a young child and at age 16 began breaking into houses in order to steal women's shoes, and later their underwear. On several occasions, he confronted the occupants and choked them unconscious; he eventually went on to murder four women (Rule, 1983). Sometimes the fetish burglar will rip and destroy female clothing, and in very rare instances he will soil the premises by defecation, urination, or ejaculation. The following case of fetish burglary by an adolescent is illustrative.

Case 10

A 19-year-old female called the police to report that her parents' home had been burglarized. When the police arrived, they noticed that "each of the bedrooms was messed up, and the individual who broke into the house had defecated on the bed." The victim reported that her and her sister's underwear drawers were thrown on the floor, and she believed that some of their underwear was missing. Several weeks later, another intruder broke into the same house and hit a 17-year-old female occupant over the head with a bottle. He called the victim several hours later and said, "Next time you'll be pregnant." After a third attempted break-in, on a Sunday morning, the burglar was apprehended by a neighbor while on his way to church.

When interviewed, the 16-year-old offender stated that he knew the victim, a fellow classmate about whom he had fantasized. He said he became preoccupied with her underwear, "what it looked like; I wanted to have it." He also revealed, upon questioning, rape fantasies, fantasies of having sex with the victim, a history of being teased by his older brother, and fantasies of attacking people: "I'd pull them to the ground and knock them out; it could be a girl." He was unable to explain "why I went to the bathroom on her bed." In this case, there is a clear relationship between the burglary and the offender's sexual fantasies, fetishism for female underwear, aggressive acts of defecation, and assault on the female occupant.

Voyeuristic burglaries are stimulated by the urge to look, often with a fantasy of seeing a naked woman. Here, sexual items are not taken; instead, offenders may steal something of minimal value to help them rationalize why they are there. One offender stated, "I'd feel stupid if I broke in and didn't take nothing." Frequently, the sexual motivation of these burglaries is missed, as the dynamics are covert and not understood by the offender or the authorities. Albert DeSalvo, the "Boston Strangler" (Rae, 1967); the infamous Ted Bundy (Rule, 1988); Richard Ramirez, the "Night Stalker" (Lindecker, 1991); and Danny Rolling, the "Gainesville Ripper" (Ryzuk, 1994) were all voyeurs as adolescents. Their voyeurism progressed to voyeuristically motivated burglary and eventually to serial homicide. In the following case, a serial voyeuristic burglary led to assault on a female occupant.

Case 11

A 20-year-old male (J.J.) was charged with burglarizing about 40 homes and assaulting one female occupant. The offender began breaking into homes at 18 years of age: "I did it for the excitement and urge to do it, to see if I can get away with it. It made me feel happy, an evil happy feeling. I couldn't stop. I don't know why I was doing it. It was like taking drugs, I was addicted to burglarizing. There was a thrill about it." J.J. had been a voyeur since age 15; he also developed bulimia around this time and engaged in ten acts of arson. His compulsion to burglarize became so strong that for the past several months, before being apprehended, he was completely out of control. He took some money from various homes he broke into, but he "really did not need the money."

J.J. connected his anger and emotional conflicts to his relationship with his parents: "There was a competition for my mother between me and my father. He would get mad at me, my mom would take my side, and he'd get more mad. There was a competition for my mom's love. There were glances and stares by my father. I got more attention from my mom and he got mad. Maybe he thought I'd become the head of the household." J.J. had thoughts of killing his father, and on at least one occasion he even attempted to poison him. To J.J. the break-ins somehow proved that he was "more of a man [than his father] because I had the guts to do it. He had a gun, so I got a bigger gun. I was afraid he'd kill me, so I got a gun. I didn't kill him because my mom would be too upset." These burglaries clearly were compulsive, sexually motivated, and connected to a voyeurism that began in late adolescence. In addition, an escalating amount of aggression was evident.

BURGLARY AND SEXUAL AGGRESSION

Forensic practitioners have long noted a strong association between burglary and subsequent sexual aggression. Guttmacher (1963) studied a group of 36 aggressive sexual offenders and found that eight (22%) had a history of burglary. He concluded that the underlying personality makeup of the rapist and the burglar is similar and noted that the legal term "breaking and entering" itself suggests a sexual assault at some level. Guttmacher's findings were confirmed several years later by Revitch

(1965) in his study of 43 men who had made serious attacks on women, including instances of beating, choking, and knifing and nine murders. Here, only three offenders had a history of prior sexual offenses, whereas 12 (28%) had a history of burglary, and four out of 12 (33%) combined burglary with assault on the female occupant.

Ressler et al. (1983) reported the case of a 24-year-old who committed 12 rapes and rape-murders over a 4-year period. His criminal record began at age 12 with burglary. At age 14, he was charged with burglary and rape, and his offenses escalated until he committed numerous burglaries and five rape-murders. In an FBI-sponsored study of 36 sexual murderers, Ressler et al. (1988) found that at least two of the offenders had committed sexual burglaries days or hours before they committed a sexual homicide. Unfortunately, this report did not include the total number or details of the burglaries.

Recently, Davies and Dale (1996) studied the behavior patterns and geographical aspects of serial rapists. Although these authors were not focusing on the criminal histories of their subjects, they did, nevertheless, note a significant number of burglaries among their rape cases. For example, one offender "was believed to have carried out hundreds of burglaries, was relatively affluent, [and also committed] six known sexual offenses during two years" (p. 150). Another serial burglar attacked seven elderly women in their homes; yet another committed burglary, robbery, and two sexual assaults within a 5-month period. Several other cases of "burglar-rapists" were reported without any details. Additionally, seven "prolific rapists" who committed their sexual assaults in victims' homes all had a history of burglary.

Schlesinger and Revitch (1999), in their summary of 14 notorious contemporary sexual murderers with a history of burglary (see Table 2), noted that six out of the 14 (43%) were apprehended not for murder but for committing a burglary. These authors also studied 52 sexual murderers and found that 42% had a history of burglary (32% fetish burglary; 68% voyeuristic burglary). In their sample, 77% of the women murdered in their homes were killed by an offender with a history of burglary.

DISCUSSION

Antisocial behavior, including burglary, may have a variety of causes, as illustrated by the motivational spectrum in the classification of crime. Unfortunately, in the official statistics on burglary, all offenses are grouped together for actuarial purposes. Even burglaries with overt sexual motives are not classified separately, just as definite sex murders, with distinct overt manifestations of genitality, are listed merely as homicide. As a result, the true incidence of the various types of burglaries, including sexual burglary, remains unknown. Nevertheless, the vast majority of burglaries seem to be gain-oriented, with sexual burglaries occurring much less frequently. Most burglaries are repetitive and remain unsolved. In 1996 and 1997, 86% of all burglaries were not cleared by law enforcement (FBI *Uniform Crime Reports*, 1998).

The financial loss from burglaries in 1997 was approximately $3.3 billion, and the average loss per residential victim was $1334. (The financial loss for larceny theft, the most frequent crime, was $4.5 billion, and $7 billion for motor vehicle theft, which follows burglary in frequency of occurrence.) In addition to financial

TABLE 2
Notorious Sexual Murderers Who Committed Burglaries

Offender	Type of Burglary[a]	Number Murdered and Location of Murder[b]
Jerome Brudos	Fetish burglary began at age 16; shoe and foot fetish.	Murdered four women in his home and outside of home.
Ted Bundy	Voyeurism in adolescence led to voyeuristic burglary and "cat" burglary.	Murdered 30 to 40 women in and outside of their residences.
Richard Trenton Chase[c]	Committed fetish burglary and soiled premises.	Murdered 10 women in their homes; engaged in vampirism.
Nathaniel Code	Numerous undescribed "cat" burglaries; ejaculated on premises.	Murdered eight victims in their homes.
Albert DeSalvo[c]	Voyeurism began in adolescence, voyeuristic burglaries began during military service; ejaculated on premises.	Murdered 13 women in their homes.
Robert Hansen	Undescribed burglaries began in early 20s.	Murdered four prostitutes outside and inside residences.
William Heirens[c]	Fetish burglary began at age 13; soiled premises by defecation and urination.	Murdered three women in their homes; dismembered a child.
Cleophus Prince[c]	Found guilty of 21 undescribed daytime "cat" burglaries.	Murdered six women in their homes.
Richard Ramirez	Voyeurism since childhood; numerous voyeuristic burglaries.	Murdered 13 women and men, mostly in their homes.
Monte Rissell	Numerous undescribed burglaries began at age 12.	Murdered five women, prostitutes and others, outside their homes.
Danny Rolling	Voyeurism, voyeuristic burglaries, and regular burglaries.	Murdered five women plus three men and a child in their homes.
George Russell[c]	Numerous undescribed burglaries began in early adolescence.	Murdered three women, two in their homes, one outside.
Arthur Shawcross	Numerous undescribed burglaries.	Murdered three women, two in their homes, one outside.
Timothy Spencer[c]	Numerous undescribed burglaries began at age 14; considered a "cat burglar extraordinaire."	Murdered four women in their homes.

[a] In various reports of these cases, the details of the burglaries were not provided.

[b] The number of victims usually represents what the offender was legally charged with; in many cases, this number underestimates the actual murders committed.

[c] Apprehended while committing a burglary; subsequently charged with murder.

Source: From Schlesinger, L.B. and Revitch, E. (1999). Sexual burglaries and sexual homicide, *Journal of the American Academy of Psychiatry and Law*, 27:227–238. With permission.

loss, burglary victims also experience enormous psychological distress, including generalized feelings of fear and anger, a long-term sense of insecurity, fear of future victimization, and negative impact on children (Brown and Harris, 1989; Kobayashi, 1996; Mawby and Walklate, 1996; Rountree and Land, 1996; Winkel and Vrij, 1995).

In view of these deleterious effects, the remarkable lack of interest in the study of burglary by forensic practitioners is perplexing. Most research on burglary is done by sociologists, focusing on statistical trends and relationships; however, the many and varied levels of motivation in burglaries are often missed in such analyses. For example, Warr (1988) noted the frequent association between burglary and rape, and he even coined the term "home intrusion rape." He concluded, however, that the rapes were an unfortunate "opportunistic event." In fact, it is not opportunity that rape and burglary have in common; it is the underlying sexual motivation. The professional or semiprofessional burglar, with gain-oriented motivation, would hardly rape a woman just because she is there and the opportunity to rape presents itself. The last thing a professional burglar, in search of valuables, wants is a confrontation with the occupant. One professional burglar commented that he has "nothing in common with those who commit sex crimes or other emotional crimes and would not even be courteous to them if he should by chance meet them in prison" (Sutherland, 1937, p. 4).

A prospective and cooperative study, by individuals and centers, needs to be undertaken in order to get a further understanding of the psychological underpinnings of the various types of serial burglary. A purely legal approach to burglary, rigidly applied, takes into account only the definition of the offense and does not deal with the offender. Although the concept of retribution for misdeeds is necessary for the environmentally stimulated, situationally stimulated, and impulsive burglar, it will not deter the pathologically motivated burglar or offer protection to the public. Nor will the strictly punitive approach help in rehabilitation before acts of sexual burglary escalate to sexual assault or gynocide.

The forensic practitioner needs to be aware of the different levels of motivation of the various types of burglary. Those committed solo and under bizarre circumstances, where material gain is minimal or rationalized, often have a strong underlying sexual basis. Not every sexually motivated burglar will assault or kill a woman; nevertheless, the ominous significance of compulsive sexually motivated burglary must be recognized and such cases thoroughly evaluated. An understanding of the different types of burglary and their differing behavioral characteristics, motives, and dynamics will assist in such assessments.

REFERENCES

Adams, J.J., Meloy, J.R., and Moritz, M.S. (1990). Neuropsychological deficits and violent behavior in incarcerated schizophrenics. *Journal of Nervous and Mental Disease*, 178:253–256.

Bachet, M. (1951). The concept of encephaloses criminogenes (criminogenic encephalosis). *American Journal of Orthopsychiatry*, 21:794–799.

Banay, R.S. (1969). Unconscious sexual motivation in crime. *Medical Aspects of Human Sexuality*, 3:91–102.

Bennett, T. and Wright, R. (1984). The relationship between alcohol use and burglary. *British Journal of Addictions*, 79:431–437.

Booth, E. (1929). *Stealing Through Life*. New York: Knopf.

Bradford, J., Greenberg, D.M., and Motayne, G.G. (1992). Substance abuse in criminal behavior. *Psychiatric Clinics of North America*, 15:605–622.

Brown. B.B. and Harris, P.B. (1989). Residential burglary victimization: reaction to the invasion of a primary territory. *Journal of Environmental Psychology*, 9:119–132.

Bulloch, H.A. (1955). Urban homicide in theory and fact. *Journal of Criminal Law, Criminology and Police Science*, 45:565–575.

Cohen, A.K. (1969). The delinquent subculture. In Cavan, R.S. (Ed.), *Juvenile Delinquency*, 2nd ed. Philadelphia: Lippincott.

Cohen, L.E. and Felson, M. (1979). Social change in crime rate trends: a routine activity approach. *American Sociological Review*, 44:588–608.

Davies, A. and Dale, A. (1996). Locating the stranger rapist. *Medicine, Science, and the Law*, 36:146–156.

Eskridge, C.W. (1983). Predicting burglary: a research note. *Journal of Criminal Justice*, 11:67–75.

Gibbons, D.C. (1968). *Society, Crime, and Criminal Careers*. Englewood Cliffs, NJ: Prentice-Hall.

Green, E.J., Booth, C.E., and Biderman, M.D. (1976). Cluster analysis of burglary MOs. *Journal of Police Science and Administration*, 4:382–388.

Gutttmacher, M.S. (1963). Dangerous offenders. *Crime and Delinquency*, 9:381–390.

Halleck, S.L. (1971). *Psychiatry and the Dilemmas of Crime*. Berkeley: University of California Press.

Hills, S.L. (1992). *Tragic Magic: The Life and Crimes of a Heroin Addict*, Chicago: Nelson-Hall.

Holzman, H.R. (1983). The serious habitual property offender as "moonlighter": an empirical study of labor force participation among robbers and burglars. *Journal of Criminal Law and Criminology*, 73:1174–1192.

Juul–Jensen, P. (1974). Epilepsy: social prognosis. In Vinken, P.J. and Bruyn, G.W. (Eds.), *Handbook of Clinical Neurology*, New York: Elsevier.

Kennedy, F., Hoffman, H., and Haines, W. (1947). A study of William Heirens. *American Journal of Psychiatry*, 104:113–121.

Kobayashi, J. (1996). A study of post incident maladjustments of burglary victims: the relationship between police responses to victims and their psychological maladjustments. *Report of the National Research Institute of Police Science*, 37:1–20.

Lindecker, C.L. (1991). *Night-Stalker*. New York: St. Martin's Press.

Lindesmith, A.R. (1941). Organized crime. *Annals of the American Academy of Political and Social Science*, 217:119–127.

Logie, A., Wright, R., and Decker, S. (1992). Recognition memory performance and residential burglary. *Applied Cognitive Psychology*, 6:109–123.

Maguire, M. and Bennett, T. (1982). *Burglary in a Dwelling: The Offense, the Offender, and the Victim*. London: Heinemann.

Mark, V.M. and Ervin, F.R. (1970). *Violence and the Brain*. New York: Harper & Row.

Mark, V.M. and Southgate, T.M. (1971). Violence and brain disease. *Journal of the American Medical Association*, 216:1025–1034.

Mawby, R.I. and Walklate, S. (1996). The impact of burglary: a tale of two cities. *International Review of Victimology*, 4:267–291.

Morenz, B. and Lane, R.D. (1996). Morbid jealousy and criminal conduct. In Schlesinger, L.B. (Ed.), *Explorations in Criminal Psychopathology: Clinical Syndromes with Forensic Implications.* Springfield, IL: Charles C Thomas.

Mott, J. (1986). Opioid use and burglary. *British Journal of the Addictions,* 81:671–678.

Nestor, P.G. (1992). Neuropsychological and clinical correlates of murder and other forms of extreme violence in a forensic psychiatric population. *Journal of Nervous and Mental Disease,* 180:418–423.

Nevin, D. (1966). Charlie Whitman: The Eagle scout who grew up with a tortured mind. *Life,* 11:28–31.

Nurco, D.N. (1987). Drug addiction and crime: a complicated issue. *British Journal of the Addictions,* 82:7–9.

Pallone, N.J. and Hennessy, J.J. (1994). *Criminal Behavior.* New Brunswick, NJ: Transaction Publishers.

Pontius, A.A. and Yudowitz, B.S. (1980). Frontal lobe system dysfunction in some criminal actions shown in the narratives test. *Journal of Nervous and Mental Disease,* 168:111–117.

Rae, G.W. (1967). *Confessions of the Boston Strangler.* New York: Pyramid Books.

Ressler, R.K. and Shachtman, T. (1992). *Whoever Fights Monsters.* New York: St. Martin's Press.

Ressler, R.K., Burgess, A.A., and Douglas, J.E. (1983). Rape and rape murder: one offender and twelve victims. *American Journal of Psychiatry,* 140:36–40.

Ressler, R.K., Burgess, A.A., and Douglas, J.E. (1988). *Sexual Homicide: Patterns and Motives.* New York: Free Press.

Revitch, E. (1954). The problem of conjugal paranoia. *Diseases of the Nervous System,* 15:271–277.

Revitch, E. (1960). Diagnosis and disposition of the paranoid marital partner. *Diseases of the Nervous System,* 21:117–118.

Revitch, E. (1965). Sex murder and the potential sex murderer. *Diseases of the Nervous System,* 26:240–248.

Revitch, E. (1978). Sexually motivated burglaries. *Bulletin of the American Academy of Psychiatry and Law,* 6:177–283.

Revitch, E. (1997). Burglaries with sexual dynamics. In Schlesinger, L.B. and Revitch, E. (Eds.), *Sexual Dynamics of Antisocial Behavior,* 2nd ed. Springfield, IL: Charles C Thomas.

Revitch, E. and Hayden, J.W. (1955). The paranoid marital partner: counselors' client, psychiatrists' problem. *Rutgers Law Review,* 9:512–527.

Revitch, E. and Schlesinger, L.B. (1978). Murder: evaluation, classification, and prediction. In Kutash, I.L., Kutash, S.B., and Schlesinger, L.B. (Eds.), *Violence: Perspectives on Murder and Aggression.* San Francisco, CA: Jossey-Bass.

Revitch, E. and Schlesinger, L.B. (1981). *Psychopathology of Homicide.* Springfield, IL: Charles C Thomas.

Revitch. E. and Schlesinger, L.B. (1989). *Sex Murder and Sex Aggression.* Springfield, IL: Charles C Thomas.

Rountree, P.W. and Land, K.C. (1996). Burglary victimization, perception of crime risk, and routine activities: a multi-level analysis across Seattle neighborhoods and census tracks. *Journal of Research in Crime and Delinquency,* 33:147–180.

Rule, A. (1983). *Lust Killer.* New York: Signet.

Rule, A. (1988). *The Stranger Beside Me.* New York: Signet.

Ryzuk, M. (1994). *The Gainesville Ripper.* New York: St. Martin's Press.

Schlesinger, L.B. (1996a). The catathymic crisis (1912–present): a review and clinical study. *Aggression and Violent Behavior,* 1:307–316.

Schlesinger, L.B. (1996b). The catathymic process: psychopathology and psychodynamics of extreme aggression. In Schlesinger, L.B. (Ed.), *Explorations in Criminal Psychopathology: Clinical Syndromes with Forensic Implications.* Springfield, IL: Charles C Thomas.

Schlesinger, L.B. (1999a). Adolescent sexual matricide following repetitive mother-son incest. *Journal of Forensic Sciences,* 44:746–749.

Schlesinger, L.B. (1999b). Murder and sex murder: psychopathology and psychodynamics. In Hall, H.V. (Ed.), *Lethal Violence: A Source Book on Fatal Domestic, Acquaintance, and Stranger Violence.* Boca Raton, FL: CRC Press.

Schlesinger, L.B. (2000). Familicide, depression and catathymic process. *Journal of Forensic Sciences,* 45:200–203.

Schlesinger, L.B. and Revitch, E. (1999). Sexual burglaries and sexual homicide: clinical, forensic, and investigative considerations. *Journal of the American Academy of Psychiatry and Law,* 27:227–238.

Shover, N. (1972). Structures and careers in burglary. *Journal of Criminal Law, Criminology and Police Science,* 63:540–549.

Silva, J.A., Ferrari, M.M., Leong, G.B., and Penny, G. (1999). The dangerousness of persons with delusional jealousy. *Journal of the American Academy of Psychiatry and Law,* 26:607–623.

Smith, S.M. and Kunjukrishnan, R. (1986). Medicolegal aspects of mental retardation. *Psychiatric Clinics of North America,* 9:699–712.

Stack, S. (1995). The effect of temporary residences on burglary: a test of criminal opportunity theory. *American Journal of Criminal Justice,* 19:197–214.

Sutherland, E.H. (1937). *The Professional Thief.* Chicago: University of Chicago Press.

Sutherland, E.H. (1947). *Principles of Criminology.* Philadelphia: Lippincott.

Taylor, M. and Nee, C. (1988). The role of cues in simulated residential burglary: a preliminary investigation. *British Journal of Criminology,* 28:396–401.

Warr, M. (1988). Rape, burglary, and opportunity. *Journal of Quantitative Criminology,* 4:275–288.

Wertham, F. (1937). The catathymic crisis: a clinical entity. *Archives of Neurology and Psychiatry,* 37:974–977.

Winkel, F.W. and Vrij, A. (1995). Coping with burglary: the effects of a police service on victims' emotional readjustment. In Davies, G. and Lloy-Bostock, S. (Eds.), *Psychology, Law, and Criminal Justice,* Berlin: Walter Dee Gruyer.

Wright, R., Logie, R.H., and Decker, S.H. (1995). Criminal expertise and offender decision-making: an experimental study of the target selection process in residential burglary. *Journal of Research in Crime and Delinquency,* 32:39–53.

10 Men Who Sexually Harass Women

John B. Pryor and Adena B. Meyers

CONTENTS

"That in 1981, in the basement of the Capitol, Senator Packwood walked a former staff assistant into a room, where he grabbed her with both hands in her hair and kissed her, forcing his tongue into her mouth…" —One of .17 specific incidents of sexual misconduct described in the U.S. Senate Select Committee on Ethics 1994 Report on allegations of sexual misconduct by Senator Bob Packwood.

"I cannot imagine anything that I said or did to Anita Hill that could have been mistaken for sexual harassment." —Clarence Thomas, October 11, 1991, testimony before the Committee on the Judiciary, U.S. Senate, on the nomination of Clarence Thomas to be Associate Justice of the Supreme Court of the U.S.

"(Lois) Robinson encountered particularly severe verbal harassment from a shipfitter … while assigned to work with him on a number of different nights … [the shipfitter] regularly expressed his displeasure at working with Robinson, making such remarks as 'women are only fit company for something that howls,' and 'there's nothing worse than having to work around women.' " ——*Robinson v. Jacksonville Shipyards, Inc.* (1991).

0-8493-2236-7/00/$0.00+$.50
© 2000 by CRC Press LLC

Over the last 20 years, sexual harassment has become recognized as an issue of social and political importance. Sexual harassment is generally understood as a form of gender-based discrimination. Although sexual harassment is conceivably gender neutral, research shows that most targets of sexual harassment are women and most perpetrators are men. Surveys in the U.S. indicate that the sexual harassment of women by men is widespread in business (Fitzgerald et al., 1997), academic (Fitzgerald et al., 1988), government (U.S. Merit Systems Protection Board, 1980, 1988, 1995), and military settings (Bastian et al., 1996). While men also have been found to be negatively affected by sexual harassment (Berdahl et al., 1996; Waldo et al., 1998), most research has focused upon the impact of sexual harassment upon women. The experience of sexual harassment has been found to have a negative impact upon both the professional and personal lives of targeted women, damaging both their achievement opportunities and their psychological well-being (Fitzgerald et al., 1997; Gutek and Koss, 1993; Murdoch and Nichol, 1995; Pryor, 1995a,b).

Why do men sexually harass women? Pryor et al. (1993) have suggested that both person factors (relatively stable personality and attitudinal characteristics) and situational factors (e.g., local social norms) may contribute significantly to repeated sexually harassing behavior. This chapter reviews evidence about the roles that both person and situation factors play in predicting and explaining sexual harassment. Within this context, our primary focus is upon person factors: Specifically, what are the psychological characteristics of men who are predisposed to commit sexual harassment against multiple women or in multiple contexts? As implied in the quotes at the beginning of the chapter, an essential first step in this analysis is the acknowledgment that there are different kinds of sexual harassment. We review the differentiation of distinct types of sexual harassment from both a legal perspective and a social science perspective. From extensive social science research, consistencies in victims' descriptions of their experiences have given rise to a theory of male propensities that may underlie different forms of sexual harassment. Of these varying male propensities, a proclivity for sexual exploitation has been examined most extensively. Previous research exploring the behavioral, attitudinal, nonverbal, and social cognitive correlates of sexual exploitation proclivities are examined, and new research linking these proclivities to general personality dimensions is reported.

TYPOLOGY OF SEXUAL HARASSMENT

LEGAL DEFINITIONS

From a legal perspective, two general forms of sexual harassment are recognized: (1) *quid pro quo* sexual harassment, where sexual or gender-based behavior becomes a term or condition of employment or advancement, and (2) *hostile environment* sexual harassment, where sexual or gender-based behavior creates an intimidating, hostile, or offensive work environment (Equal Employment Opportunity Commission, 1980). Two additional elements are also important in a legal understanding of sexual harassment. First, it is not enough to prove that such behaviors simply occurred in order to build a legal case for sexual harassment. One must also establish that such behavior had some sort of adverse effect upon the work environment. Proof of an adverse effect is usually rooted in evidence about its pervasiveness or severity. Second, sexual harassment is legally defined as *unwelcome behavior*. Whether a behavior is deemed unwelcome is a subjective judgment on the part of the person who experiences the behavior. In judging whether some specific behavior fits the legal definition of *unwelcome behavior*, the courts make a determination as to whether a reasonable person in the same social setting with characteristics like those of a particular plaintiff would view the potentially harassing behavior as unwelcome. In making such determinations, it is generally recognized that what is viewed as unwelcome is subject to individual variation. For example, women are thought to generally view sexual overtures at work as more threatening than men (Equal Employment Opportunity Commission, 1990). While most of the case law in the U.S. involves sexual harassment in work contexts, similar discrimination cases have arisen in fair housing (Roos, 1998) and equal education cases (Peckman, 1999).

DEFINITIONS FROM SOCIAL SCIENCE

Developing parallel to the legal perspective has been a social science perspective on sexual harassment. From the onset of social science research on this subject in the late 1970s, the victims' experiences have been the focus of most sexual harassment studies. An emerging measurement standard for assessing sexually harassing experiences is found in the work of Fitzgerald and her colleagues (1995). The Sexual Experiences Questionnaire (SEQ) provides a reliable and valid instrument to measure the incidence and prevalence of sexual harassment in the academic workplace. Factor analysis studies suggest that the SEQ measures three general forms of sexually harassing behavior: gender harassment, unwanted sexual attention, and sexual coercion. With regard to gender harassment, Gelfand et al. (1995, p. 8) state: "This category encompasses a wide range of verbal and nonverbal behaviors not aimed at sexual cooperation; rather, they convey insulting, hostile, and degrading attitudes about women." Unwanted sexual attention includes repeated requests for dates and persistent attempts to establish unwelcome sexual relationships. Sexual coercion includes the use of threats or bribes to solicit sexual involvement. Research has shown consistently that gender harassment is the most common form of sexual harassment, followed by unwanted sexual attention and then by sexual coercion. This same rank order pattern holds across many organizational and cultural settings (Fitzgerald et al., 1995; Schneider and Swan, 1994). Reliable and valid versions of the SEQ exist in Portuguese (Gelfand et al., 1995), Turkish (Wasti et al., 1999) and Hebrew (Barak et al., 1995), as well as in English.

PERSON AND SITUATION VARIABLES AS PREDICTORS OF VARIOUS TYPES OF HARASSMENT

Pryor and Whalen (1997) have suggested that the consistencies in women's experiences found in SEQ research may have potential implications for understanding why men engage in sexual harassment. There are at least three possible explanations for the three-part covariance structure of the SEQ. First, one might cynically conclude that these categories are simply in the minds of the beholders; that is, they represent some sort of bias in how women classify these behaviors. However, there is some evidence that male victims also employ similar categories even though their overall experience of sexual harassment is only a fraction of that of women (Berdahl et al., 1996). If we assume that the three categories represent veridical regularities in women's experiences, then two additional explanations emerge. First, the SEQ categories may reflect consistencies in the behaviors of specific harassers. Thus, the same man who performs one behavior in a given category is more likely to perform others from the same category than behaviors from different categories. For example, the man who makes crude sexist remarks is more likely to perform other kinds of gender harassment such as displaying sexist materials than he is to attempt to establish an unwelcome sexual relationship with a woman or other forms of unwanted sexual attention. Presumably, he also would be more likely to perform other forms of gender harassment than various forms of sexual coercion such as attempting to reward women for sexual cooperation. Another explanation for the observed covariance structure of the SEQ is that certain social situations might give rise to certain kinds of sexual harassment, but not necessarily others. For instance, the social norms in a given work group or organization might foster a climate ripe for a particular kind of sexual harassment. Of course, these possibilities are not mutually exclusive. Some men may be more likely to perform particular forms of sexually harassing behavior than others. At the same time, one might be more likely to observe a particular form of sexual harassment in some social settings than others.

GENDER HARASSMENT

Pryor and Whalen (1997) theorized that individual differences in sexism may contribute to propensities for gender harassment. Recent research by Pryor and his students (Pryor et al., 1999; Hahn et al., 1999) has confirmed this prediction. Men who scored higher on Swim's Modern Sexism Scale (Swim et al., 1995) were found to be more likely to ask women sexist questions in a mock job interview. Situational factors, such as having one's sense of masculinity threatened and being exposed to sexist primes, also contributed to men's propensities to exhibit sexist verbal behaviors in these studies.

UNWANTED SEXUAL ATTENTION

Pryor and Whalen (1997) also theorized that a common contributor to men's persistence in making unwanted sexual advances toward women might simply be a lack of social sensitivity. Consistent with this hypothesis, Pryor (1995a,b) asked women who claimed to be sexually harassed why they were bothered by the harassing behavior. Sixty-one percent said that they were bothered because the harasser was insensitive to their feelings, and 54% added that they were bothered because they were not attracted to the harasser. The social psychological basis of this breakdown in sexual communication may be related to characteristic differences in how men and women interpret cross-gender interactions. Research by Abbey (1982) and others (see Stockdale, 1993) suggests that men often read more sexual intent into women's friendly behaviors toward men than women intend to convey. Abbey (1987) found that 72% of college women had experienced incidents where their intentions had been misperceived by men to be sexual. Even when these women responded with an overt signal that they had been misunderstood, a relatively common response from the men was to keep on "trying." Tuchfarber (1996) found that men's willingness to persist in the face of rejection was related to the perceived receptiveness of the woman's initial behavior (this quality relates to her overall friendliness) coupled with the directness of her rejection. Men were more uncertain about whether they should persist if the rejection to a date request was indirect (e.g., "I don't know. I'll have to think about it.") and she was initially very friendly. Some men may be more adept than others in interpreting women's affective cues and understanding rejection. Those with heterosocial decoding deficits may be more likely to persist in sexual advances when women are resistent (Lipton et al., 1987; McDonel and McFall, 1991).

Some social settings also may increase the likelihood of unwanted sexual behaviors. For example, Gutek (1985) found that sexual harassment was more common in "sexualized work environments." These are work settings where other sexual behaviors are also common. These other "social sexual behaviors" include behaviors that are not viewed negatively by either male or female workers. Similarly, Pryor et al. (1995) found that sexual harassment occurred more often in settings where men observed other sexual stimuli. Specifically, female federal workers' reports of sexual harassment were correlated with their male co-worker's perceptions of the general sexual ambience of their offices. In offices where men reported observing sexually explicit posters, pin-ups, computer software, graffiti, etc., women were more likely to report uninvited sexual attention, such as requests for dates.

SEXUAL COERCION

Pryor and Whalen (1997) also theorized that sexually coercive behaviors such as using threats or bribes to enlist sexual cooperation may be related to male proclivities for sexual exploitation as measured by the Likelihood To Sexually Harass (LSH) Scale (Pryor, 1987). This instrument was designed to measure male proclivities to behave in a sexually exploitive way toward women in professional settings. The LSH scale consists of ten scenarios in which men are asked to imagine being in positions of social dominance over women. The male respondents are asked to rate the likelihood that they would use their social power to sexually exploit the women if they thought they could do so with impunity. For example, one scenario asks men to imagine being the director of a television news service and having the power to promote someone to be the anchor woman on the evening newscast. They were asked to rate the likelihood of their using this power to solicit "sexual favors" from an attractive female reporter given that they feared no professional repercussions. Like this example, the other key behaviors queried in the LSH are all examples of *quid pro quo* sexual harassment.

CHARACTERISTICS OF MEN WHO SCORE HIGH IN LSH

Many studies have shown that the LSH scale holds high reliability, plus good discriminant and convergent validity (Pryor, 1998). With regard to discriminant validity,

Pryor (1987) reported a low correlation between LSH and the Crowne and Marlowe (1955) Social Desirability Scale; however, all previous administrations of the LSH scale have been conducted under conditions of anonymity. The high face validity of the LSH might create demand problems if it were administered in a context where respondents had reasons to describe themselves in a positive light and knew they might be identified. With regard to convergent validity, Pryor et al. (1995a,b) summarized the research correlating LSH and other individual difference scales into three general categories of findings: (1) The LSH shows positive correlations with various measures related to sexual violence. For example, the LSH was found to correlate with Malamuth's (1986) Likelihood To Rape Scale (Pryor, 1987) and to Malamuth's (1989a,b) Attraction to Sexual Aggression Scale (Pryor et al., 1995). (2) The LSH is positively correlated with more masculine self-descriptions on gender role scales. For example, high LSH men tend to value male status and toughness and to believe that men should avoid feminine occupations and activities. These are components of the Brannon and Juni (1984) stereotypic male sex role norm. Pryor (1987) also found that LSH is correlated with general attitudes toward women (Spence et al., 1974), attitudes toward feminism (Smith et al., 1975) and some of the subscales of the Extended Personal Attributes Questionnaire (Spence and Helmreich, 1978). These findings suggest that high LSH men hold negative views about the role of women in society and try to differentiate themselves from female stereotypes. (3) Higher LSH scores are correlated with the functions men ascribe to sexual behavior. For example, Pryor and Stoller (1994) found that high LSH men tend to view sex as serving dominance, novelty (defense against boredom), social recognition, and hedonism functions. In other research, Pryor (1987) also found LSH to be associated with authoritarianism, negative attitudes about sex, and difficulty with perspective taking.

LSH AND BEHAVIOR

Research conducted by Pryor and his colleagues (summarized in Pryor et al., 1995) has consistently shown that the LSH can be used along with some variations in social circumstances to predict sexually harassing behavior. For example, Pryor et al. (1993) found that when high LSH men were exposed to a harassing role model, they sexually harassed a female trainee (a confederate). Sexual harassment in this study was operationally defined as *unsolicited sexual touching*. The high LSH men did not harass when exposed to a role model who behaved professionally. In both conditions, the role model was a graduate student who acted as an experimenter in the study. Low LSH men did not engage in sexual harassment, regardless of their role models. This and other research has suggested that sexual harassment can be predicted from an analysis of individual differences in the predilection for harassment combined with an analysis of social normative factors that encourage or discourage such behavior.

   If they are put into a position where they have some authority and can act freely with relative impunity, research has found that high LSH men typically behave in a sexually exploitive way. In laboratory research by Rudman and Borgida (1995), men were asked to conduct a mock job interview with a female undergraduate (a confederate). These interviews were videotaped and rated by independent judges.

Men who scored high on the LSH scale were rated as behaving in a more dominant and sexualized manner than men who scored low on the LSH. Research by Driscoll et al. (1998) suggests that high LSH men can be reliably differentiated from low LSH men by their nonverbal interactions with women in professional settings. Driscoll and her colleagues videotaped college men who interviewed an attractive female subordinate. Silent clips of these videotaped interviews were shown to men and women who were asked to guess how the male interviewers had completed the LSH scale. Analyses revealed that these naïve judges could accurately estimate the men's LSH scores solely on the basis of their nonverbal behaviors. Subsequent research by Murphy et al. (1999) examined the specific nonverbal behaviors differentiating high and low LSH men in this setting. High LSH men were found to differ primarily from low LSH men in their nonverbal dominance cues, such as the time spent making direct eye contact with the female interviewee and their body orientation (e.g., leaning back). High LSH men also spent less overall time in conducting the interviews, perhaps implying that they were less likely to take the interview seriously.

While most research connecting the LSH to behavior has been conducted in laboratory settings, some studies have connected LSH scores to more naturalistic behaviors. For example, a field study by Barak and Kaplan (1996) demonstrated that the LSH was strongly correlated with admissions of having sexually harassed college women among male university professors. In the Barak and Kaplan study of Canadian college professors, the LSH was strongly correlated with self-reports of gender harassment, uninvited sexual attention, and sexual coercion, the three general types of sexual harassment identified by Fitzgerald and her colleagues from analyses of women's experiences (Fitzgerald et al., 1995).

LSH AND SOCIAL COGNITION PROCESSES

Two recent studies (Bargh et al., 1995; Pryor and Stoller, 1994) explored some of the social cognitive correlates of the LSH. Pryor and Stoller (1994) used an illusory correlation paradigm to investigate the idea that high LSH men may associate ideas about sexuality with ideas about social dominance. Pre-testing was used to select words related to sexuality (climax, sex, etc.), words related to social dominance (boss, dominance, etc.), and neutral words. These words were presented to male participants in pairs for brief durations on a projection screen. Sexuality words were paired equally often with both neutral (control) words and social dominance words. Likewise, social dominance words were paired as often with control as with sexuality words. Participants were told to try to remember as many of the word pairs as they could. Afterward, the participants were asked to estimate the number of times each possible pair had been presented. Analyses of these estimates revealed that participants who scored high on the LSH (the upper quartile of the distribution) tended to perceive an illusory correlation between sexuality and social dominance words, overestimating their co-occurrence relative to control words. Men who scored low on the LSH did not perceive such an illusory correlation. This study suggests that high LSH men cognitively link concepts of sexuality and concepts of social dominance.

The second study examined the possibility that sexuality words could serve as primes for social dominance words and visa versa. Put another way, could brief exposures to sexuality words increase the cognitive accessibility of dominance words and visa versa? Bargh et al. (1995) presented sexuality, social dominance, or control prime words for 90 msec on a CRT screen while the participants were waiting for a word to be presented at a focal point. Their instructions were to pronounce the word appearing at the focal point as quickly as they could. The prime words appeared at a range of 2 cm above or below the focal point, just inside the parafoveal range. A visual mask of random letters appeared for 10 msec following each prime word. The distance between the participant's eyes and the fixation point was approximately 50 cm. This placed the priming words at 2.3° of visual angle. While words presented in this orientation have been shown to activate their semantic representations in memory (Rayner, 1978), the brief duration of presentation and the subsequent mask make it impossible for participants to foveally process the priming stimuli. So, the phenomenal experiences of the primes are as flashes of light upon the screen. Results of this study revealed that high LSH men could pronounce sexuality words more quickly if they were preceded by dominance primes than control words. Likewise, high LSH men could pronounce dominance words more quickly if they were preceded by sexuality primes than control words. Low LSH men evidenced no such facilitation effects related to primes. This study suggests that ideas about sexuality may automatically activate ideas about dominance for high LSH men. Similarly, dominance ideas automatically activate sexuality ideas.

The automatic and bi-directional association between dominance (or social power) and sex suggests that activation of either concept is sufficient to activate the other. So, when men with a proclivity for sexual harassment find themselves in positions of social power over women, ideas about sex come effortlessly to mind. Conversely, when they entertain ideas about sex, thoughts of social power flow into consciousness. Thus, the schematic structure of these bi-directional sex↔dominance associations may create a cognitive readiness for sexually exploitive or harassing behaviors.

There are several possible ways men may come to strongly associate sex and social power. Men who have been power holders may misinterpret the typically friendly and deferential behavior (Jones, 1964) of their female subordinates as signs of sexual interest (Abbey, 1982). Thus, concomitant proclivities for chronic misinterpretation of female friendliness could create associations between sex and social power. Consistent with this idea, Pryor (1987) reported that high LSH men tend to lack certain social skills that may relate to accurate interpersonal interpretation such as perspective-taking abilities. This process could also be played out in men who simply observe other male power-holders interacting with women. In other research, Pryor and his colleagues have found that men who are high in LSH also tend to see social status as an integral part of the masculine sex role (Pryor and Stoller, 1994). Real men need social status according to this view. Finally, some researchers maintain that the connection between sex and male power is not just a figment of males' interpretation but is a fact of evolutionary processes. Evolutionary psychologists have suggested that women have evolved to be attracted to men who possess the social power and resources necessary for the provision of offspring (Buss, 1994;

Kendrick and Keefe, 1992). This analysis may imply that men are constantly exposed to the idea that resources and social status are means to gain sexual access to women. If this analysis is correct, then men who do not associate power and sex may be the exceptions and those who do, the rule. Nevertheless, the evolutionary psychology perspective allows for individual variation in the degree to which women seek partners with social power and men see power as a means to sexual access (see Buss, 1994). Taken collectively, these two studies present strong evidence that men who are high in the likelihood to sexually harass cognitively link concepts of sexuality with concepts of social dominance.

In general, studies using the LSH have contributed significantly to our understanding of the characteristics of men who are likely to commit sexually exploitive forms of sexual harassment. Specifically, it appears that men with this proclivity are prone to other sexually violent behaviors, are hyper-masculine, and view sex in social domination terms. Evidence of these connections provides important theoretical insights regarding the social function of this form of sexual harassment and suggests that it may be appropriate to view this type of sexual harassment as falling along a continuum of sexual aggression and violence against women (e.g., Sheffield, 1987, 1999; Vogelman-Sine et al., 1979).

LIKELIHOOD TO SEXUALLY HARASS AND PERSONALITY

What the existing body of research using the LSH scale does not provide is a practical way for organizations to identify men who are likely to commit sexual harassment. The LSH is a useful research instrument with well-documented construct validity and reliability; however, because of its high face validity, this measure is probably not appropriate for use in applied contexts in which personnel decisions are made. It seems unlikely that employees with sexual harassment proclivities would respond honestly to the LSH items if they knew that the results could affect their employment status. Costa and McCrae (1992) have argued that the five-factor model that has been used to summarize and describe personality dimensions in normal samples may be of theoretical and practical use in predicting and explaining dysfunctional behavior. Measures of these five personality factors are often used in organizational settings and have been shown to predict job performance and related desirable and undesirable behavior in a variety of occupations (see Tokar et al., 1998, for a review). An exploration of the relationship between LSH and the "big five" personality factors may thus prove useful.

THE "BIG FIVE" PERSONALITY FACTORS AND DYSFUNCTIONAL BEHAVIOR

A number of scales have been developed to assess the five-factor model (e.g., Costa and McCrae, 1992a,b; John et al., 1991). The five dimensions they measure are *neuroticism* (N), which refers to emotional maladjustment, marked by a tendency to experience anxiety and/or depression; *extraversion* (E), which refers to a high activity level, sociability, assertiveness, and liking to be the center of attention; *openness to experience* (O), which involves intellectual curiosity and creativity, as opposed to narrow-mindedness; *conscientiousness* (C), which describes people who are organized, dependable, productive, careful, and hard-working; and *agreeableness* (A), which taps cooperation, likeability, gentleness, and trust and is negatively associated with interpersonal conflict.

Widiger (1997) argues that extreme scores on any of the five dimensions (or their component facets) may be evidence of maladjustment. For example, high neuroticism is associated with anxiety and depression and is present in many psychotherapy clients, but extremely low neuroticism suggests a lack of emotional reactivity that may be a sign of psychopathy. Although low agreeableness implies suspiciousness, exploitation, and low empathy, high agreeableness may be associated with unhealthy levels of docility and gullibility. The extremes of the conscientiousness dimension include perfectionism and rigidity on the one hand, and carelessness and negligence on the other, while the two poles of openness include such problems as alexythymia and prejudiced beliefs (low openness) and peculiar behavior and odd beliefs (high openness). Finally, high levels of extraversion may be related to mania, while low extraversion is related to depressive symptomology (low energy, social withdrawal, and anhedonia).

Although a proclivity to engage in sexual harassment does not constitute a mental disorder, it appears to represent a dysfunctional behavioral disposition that may be better understood through an examination of its association with these underlying personality factors. Previous research has demonstrated associations between the big five and problematic employee behavior. For example, low conscientiousness is related to poor job performance, involuntary turnover, and employee criminality (Tokar et al., 1998), and absenteeism is positively related to extraversion and inversely related to conscientiousness (Judge et al., 1997). To explore possible connections between the big five and sexual harassment proclivities, the following study was conducted.

THE "BIG FIVE" PERSONALITY FACTORS AND LSH

Participants were 122 male college students enrolled in psychology courses at Illinois State University. They received extra credit for participating in the study. Participants ranged in age from 18 to 50, with a mean age of 20.7. Nine percent were freshmen, 25% were sophomores, 40% were juniors, and 26% were seniors.

An abbreviated version of the LSH scale (Pryor, 1987) was administered. This two-item measure presents respondents with two of the ten scenarios found in the original LSH scale. After each scenario, participants rate on a scale of 1 to 5 the likelihood that they would use their power to help an attractive woman in exchange for sexual favors. The reliability of this abbreviated version of the LSH has been demonstrated in previous research (e.g., Pryor and DeSouza, 1999) and in this particular sample the internal consistency was high (alpha = .78).

Neuroticism, extraversion, openness to experience, conscientiousness, and agreeableness were assessed using the Big Five Inventory (BFI) of John et al. (1991). The reliability and validity of this measure have been reported elsewhere (e.g., Benet-

Martínez and John, 1998). In our sample, the internal consistencies of the five scales were high, with coefficient alphas ranging from .79 to .84.

In order to explore the relationship between LSH scores and BFI personality factors, hierarchical regression analyses were conducted. The BFI factors were Z-transformed, and all possible two-way interaction terms were computed. Three participants were dropped from the regression analyses due to incomplete responses. LSH was regressed on the BFI factors and interaction terms. All main effect terms were entered into the model in the first step, and a step-wise algorithm was used to explore the incremental contributions of the interaction terms. (Additional hierarchical regression analyses were performed to explore the potential contributions of higher order interaction terms, but none of these yielded statistically significant results.) The first step (main effects) yielded a statistically significant change in R-squared (multiple $R = .31$; $F [5113] = 2.46$; $p < .05$). Univariate analyses revealed that the main effect of conscientiousness contributed significantly to the model ($t [118] = -2.06$; $p < .05$). The only interaction term that significantly improved the model was conscientiousness × openness (multiple $R = .39$; $F [1112] = 3.37$; $p < .01$).

To further explore this interaction, the sample was divided into groups above and below the medians for conscientiousness and openness. Then a 2 (high vs. low conscientiousness) × 2 (high vs. low openness) analysis of variance was performed. Paralleling the results from the regression analyses, the ANOVA revealed a significant conscientiousness main effect and an openness × conscientiousness interaction. *Post hoc* comparisons of LSH means across each of these four groups using the Duncan's procedure indicated men who were both low in conscientiousness and low in openness manifested higher LSH scores than those in the other three groups (see Figure 1).

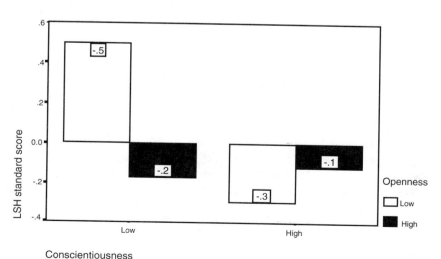

FIGURE 1. Likelihood To Sexually Harass (LSH) scores as a function of conscientiousness and openness.

In general, these results suggest that men who are high in LSH tend to be low in conscientiousness, and the relationship between LSH and conscientiousness is moderated by openness. Low openness appears to exacerbate the association between low conscientiousness and LSH. In other words, men who lack conscientiousness are predisposed to sexually harass women, and this is especially true among men who are closed-minded or closed to their own feelings.

As noted above, low conscientiousness is associated with a variety of undesirable employee characteristics, and as a result its association with LSH is neither surprising nor especially unique. The implication is that men who are disorganized, inefficient, unreliable, easily distracted, lazy, or careless are more likely than their co-workers to engage in repeated sexual harassment, just as they are at risk for other work-related problems. However, in addition to measuring a proclivity for undesirable job-related behavior, LSH seems to be related to interpersonal functioning. Interestingly, in their study examining the connection between the big five personality factors and social interactions, Barrett and Pietromonaco (1997) found that conscientiousness was unrelated to indices of the quality and quantity of social interactions. Nevertheless, there is evidence that conscientiousness is predictive of impairments in interpersonal functioning as reflected by its inverse association with borderline and antisocial personality disorders (Dyce, 1997), both of which are marked by a proclivity for impulsive behavior.

What appears to differentiate high LSH men from other employees low in conscientiousness is their tendency to also be low in openness. Tokar et al. (1998) describe research linking openness to intrinsic motivation and to positive responses to employee training, and they report that openness is inversely related to job performance in samples of blue-collar workers such as machine operators and police officers. This latter association may be due to the fact that low openness implies pragmatism and a preference for work that is routine. In the interpersonal domain, openness is associated with higher levels of intimacy in interpersonal relationships (Barrett and Pietromonaco, 1997).

These findings provide useful insights regarding the vocational and interpersonal functioning of men who are likely to engage in repeated sexual harassment. At the intersection of low conscientiousness and low openness, it appears that high LSH men tend to be generally unreliable employees at risk for a variety of work-related difficulties (low conscientiousness), who may be extrinsically motivated, difficult to train, and relatively rigid in their work style (low openness). In addition, LSH men may exhibit a variety of interpersonal difficulties such as impulsive behavior and problems with intimacy.

While more research needs to be undertaken to firmly establish the links between LSH and personality factors, this preliminary study suggests that such links do indeed exist. It is possible that general personality tests such as the Big Five Inventory could be used to identify men in organizational settings who might be at risk for sexually harassing behaviors. Once identified, these high-risk individuals might be targeted for training designed to reduce the likelihood of such behavior. As we shall see in the next section, such training may hold hope for curbing some forms of sexually harassing behavior. One advantage of using scales like the Big Five Inventory for these purposes is that such scales seem relatively impervious to social desirability pressures, even in applied settings (Ones et al., 1996).

PREVENTION OF SEXUAL HARASSMENT

Most sexual harassment prevention efforts have been focused upon workplace interventions. While workers who attend training/education programs often seem to feel that such programs have a positive impact upon sexual harassment in the workplace, research is mixed about such a connection. Studies of federal workers found no connection between agency training and harassment (U.S. Merit Systems Protection Board, 1995). One possible explanation for this finding could be that there is little variability in the prevalence of training across federal agencies (they all do it). Also, the vast majority of federal workers receive training on this topic. Finally, the U.S. Merit Systems Protection Board surveys contained few questions about the specific details of training. In analyses of a large-scale survey of U.S. military personnel, Williams et al. (1999) also found no connections between training and incidence of harassment. One possible problem with this study is that the same respondents who reported whether they had experienced sexual harassment also reported the degree of training their units had experienced. So, some sort of common response bias could have potentially affected both variables. Another perspective on training comes from a large-scale survey of Canadian women conducted by Gruber (1998). Whether respondents' organizations had conducted employee training sessions was part of an index Gruber assembled of *proactive organizational practices* in dealing with sexual harassment. This index also included other variables such as whether the organization had established official complaint procedures for sexual harassment problems. Regression analyses revealed that the extent of contact with men was a key predictor of incidence of sexual harassment. Proactive organizational practices also were significant predictors of sexual harassment and were generally stronger predictors than more passive organizational practices such as just disseminating pamphlets or posters on the topic.

Training/education programs aimed at sexual harassment prevention are sometimes embedded in "diversity training" programs (Hemphill and Haines, 1997) or "awareness training" programs (Meyer et al., 1981). According to the U.S. Bureau of Labor Statistics (1995, http://www.bls.gov/eptover.htm), "Awareness training provides information on policies and practices that affect employee relations or the work environment, including Equal Employment Opportunity practices (EEO), affirmative action, workplace diversity, sexual harassment, and AIDS awareness." While sexual harassment is often covered in diversity training programs, the degree of coverage is subject to wide variation. Also, judging from the vast number of training vendors on the World Wide Web, many training programs have been developed that focus upon sexual harassment, *per se*, leaving other diversity issues to other training efforts. A review of the research literature by Myers (1995) concluded that the effectiveness of training or other interventions that focus on changing diversity-related attitudes and behaviors has not been clearly demonstrated. Thus, many questions about the effectiveness of sexual harassment training in organizations remain to be answered.

There have been several experimental or quasi-experimental attempts to evaluate the effectiveness of short-term training upon harassment-related attitudes and perceptions (for a review, see Pryor and Whalen, 1997). Most of these studies have involved samples of undergraduates. Some of these studies seem to suffer from possible experimenter demand biases (Beauvais, 1986; Thomann et al., 1989). A study by Maurizo and Rogers (1992), while not suffering from the same design problems of the Beauvais (1986) and Thomann et al. (1989) studies, seems to have been directed primarily at potential victims. Research by York et al. (1997) found that a common training technique — asking participants to analyze written cases — can affect undergraduates' sensitivity to sexually harassing behaviors depicted in training films. Participants were more likely to judge "less blatant" videotape episodes as sexual harassment after performing several written case analyses. Research by Blakely et al. (1998) found that undergraduate men who viewed a standard sexual harassment training film subsequently rated ambiguous, hypothetical sexually harassing behaviors (e.g., "making sexually suggestive remarks or gestures around a female subordinate") as more severe than men who had not viewed the film. These researchers found that both men and women rated more openly sexual behaviors (e.g., "touching a female subordinate on a private body part") as more severe after watching the film.

An evaluation study by Moyer and Nath (1998) seems to have been more methodologically sophisticated than most of these studies; however, the scope of what the training/education set out to accomplish in this study was very narrowly defined. Moyer and Nath tried to establish whether and how men and women differed in their ability to discriminate descriptions of sexually harassing behavior from those of nonsexually harassing behavior, and whether any gender differences could be ameliorated by training. Experts were used to categorize a series of short vignettes as examples of sexual harassment (under Maine law) or not. Male and female participants (undergraduate volunteers) were randomly assigned to either a no-training control condition or a training condition in which they learned specifics about the legal definition of sexual harassment in Maine and the university's policies. In some conditions a film depicting examples was also used. Afterwards, all groups judged whether the scenarios constituted sexual harassment. A signal detection analysis was used in comparing women's and men's responses (MacMillan and Creelman, 1991). Without training, women were found to be both more biased (they more often judged sexual harassment when it was not there) and more accurate (they better discriminated harassment from non-harassment) than men. After training, Moyer and Nath found a convergence in women's and men's judgments, which was due to men adopting a response bias similar to that of women.

Results of a recent study by Perry et al. (1998) indicate that training may hold promise for altering the behaviors of men who are particularly high in their risk for sexually harassing behaviors. Perry and her colleagues first pre-tested college men using the LSH scale and then exposed them to either a popular, commercially available, sexual harassment training film (Meyer, 1992) or a control film. Participants were subsequently videotaped while they taught an attractive woman how to putt as part of a training exercise. Previous research by Pryor (1987) used a similar procedure and found that men who scored high in LSH took advantage of the opportunity for physical contact afforded by the putting lesson and touched the female trainee in a sexual way. Perry and her colleagues found that men who scored high on the LSH showed gains in knowledge about sexual harassment after viewing the film and displayed fewer sexual advances to the woman to whom they were assigned to teach a putting lesson. Interestingly, a post-test with the LSH found that LSH levels were essentially unaltered by the training film. Thus, the psychological proclivities measured by the LSH did not seem to change, only men's willingness to act upon these proclivities. The Perry et al. (1998) study seems to be the only experimental research to date that has found sexual harassment training to have an impact on actual behavior. This study suggests that training programs have the potential to influence people's understanding of what is considered to be sexual harassment. The study also suggests that cognitive/educational changes brought about by training may be followed by short-term changes in behaviors. The potential for long-term changes brought about by training remains to be demonstrated.

In summary, sexual harassment prevention efforts seem to span a wide range of goals and strategies. This lack of focus is probably the single leading reason they are difficult to evaluate. It does seem possible to alter people's understanding of what is considered to constitute "sexual harassment" through training. A common part of training also seems to be making employees aware of organizational policies concerning sexual harassment, including what one should do if one experiences sexual harassment in a workplace and what will happen when a complaint has been filed. Thus, training/educational programs in an organization can be viewed as one method that an organization communicates its concerns about this issue to its employees. In this way, training/educational programs could be viewed as contributors to the organizational climate relevant to sexual harassment. This is not to say that all training/educational programs launched by organizations for their employees necessarily have such positive effects upon climates. Employees seem acutely sensitive to disingenuous, "just to cover your rear end" organizational responses to sexual harassment. Such "prevention efforts" could well have a boomerang effect on organizational climate.

In our analysis of different forms of sexually harassing behavior, we identified three potential individual differences that contribute to sexual harassment: sexist attitudes, heterosocial communication deficits, and sexual exploitation proclivities. When one considers that sexual harassment most often represents a pattern of behavior over time, it is clear that acting upon any of these individual differences could be facilitated or inhibited by situational factors. Thus, part of the "serial" quality of sexual harassment would seem to be related to the social pressures experienced by the would be harasser. Such a person × situation model (Pryor et al., 1993) seems useful in understanding sexual harassment as a social behavior.

REFERENCES

Abbey, A. (1982). Sex differences in attributions for friendly behavior: do males misperceive female's friendliness? *Journal of Personality and Social Psychology,* 42:830–838.

Abbey, A. (1987). Misperceptions of friendly behavior as sexual interest: a survey of naturally occurring incidents, *Psychology of Women Quarterly,* 11:173–194.

Barak, A. and Kaplan, N. (January, 1996). Relationships Between Men's Admitted Sexual Harassment Behaviors and Personal Characteristics, paper presented at the 22nd National Consultation on Career Development, Ottawa, Ontario, Canada.

Barak, A., Pitterman, Y., and Yitzhaki, R. (1995). An empirical test of the role of power differential in originating sexual harassment. *Basic and Applied Social Psychology,* 17:497–517.

Bargh, J.A., Raymond, P., Pryor, J.B., and Strack, F. (1995). The attractiveness of the underling: an automatic power sex association and its consequences for sexual harassment. *Journal of Personality and Social Psychology,* 68:768–781.

Barrett, L.S. and Pietromonaço, P.R. (1997). Accuracy of the five-factor model in predicting perceptions of daily social interactions. *Personality and Social Psychology Bulletin,* 23:1173–1187.

Bastian, L.D., Lancaster, A.R., Reyst, H.E. (1996). *Department of Defense 1995 Sexual Harassment Survey.* Arlington, VA: Defense Manpower Data Center.

Beauvais, K. (1986). Workshops to combat sexual harassment: a case of studying changing attitudes. *Signs,* 12:130–145.

Benet-Martínez, V. and John, O.P. (1998). *Los cinco grandes* across cultures and ethnic groups: multitrait multimethod analyses of the big five in Spanish and English. *Journal of Personality and Social Psychology,* 75:729–750.

Berdahl, J., Magley, V., and Waldo, C. (1996). The sexual harassment of men: exploring the concept with theory and data. *Psychology of Women Quarterly,* 20:527–547.

Blakely, G.L., Blakely, E.H., and Moorman, R.H. (1998). The effects of training on perceptions of sexual harassment allegations. *Journal of Applied Social Psychology,* 28:71–83.

Brannon, R. and Junni, S. (1984) A scale for measuring attitudes about masculinity. *Psychological Documents,* 14:6–7.

Buss, D.M. (1994). *The Evolution of Desire: Strategies of Human Mating.* New York: Basic Books.

Costa, P.T., Jr. and McCrae, R.R. (1992a). *NEO PI-R: The Revised NEO Personality Inventory.* Odessa, FL: Psychological Assessment Resources.

Costa, P.T., Jr. and McCrae, R.R. (1992b). Normal personality assessment in clinical practice: the NEO Personality Inventory. *Psychological Assessment,* 4:5–13.

Crowne, D. and Marlowe, D. (1955). *The Approval Motive.* New York:Wiley.

Driscoll, D.M., Kelly, J.R., and Henderson, W.L. (1998). Can perceivers identify likelihood to sexually harass? *Sex Roles,* 38(7–8):557–588.

Dyce, J.A. (1997). The big five factors of personality and their relationship to personality disorders. *Journal of Clinical Psychology,* 53:587–593.

Equal Employment Opportunity Commission. (1980). Guidelines and discrimination because of sex (Sec. 1604.11). *Federal Register,* 45:74676–74677.

Equal Employment Opportunity Commission. (1990). *EEOC Policy Guidance on Current Sexual Harassment Issues,* N-915-050 (BNA) 89, March 19.

Fitzgerald, L., Shullman, S.L., Bailey, N., Richards, M., Swecker, J., Gold, Y., Ormerod, A.J., and Weitzman, L. (1988). The incidence and dimensions of sexual harassment in academia and the workplace. *Journal of Vocational Behavior,* 32:152–175.

Fitzgerald, L.F., Gelfand, M.J., and Drasgow, F. (1995). Measuring sexual harassment: theoretical and psychometric advances. *Basic and Applied Social Psychology,* 17(4):425–445.

Fitzgerald, L.F., Drasgow, F., Hulin, C.L., Gelfand, M.J, and Magley, V. (1997). Antecedents and consequences of sexual harassment in organizations: a test of an integrated model. *Journal of Applied Psychology,* 82:578–589.

Gruber, J.E. (1998). The impact of male work environments and organizational policies on women's experiences of sexual harassment. *Gender and Society,* 12(3):301–320.

Gutek, B.A. (1985). *Sex and the Workplace.* San Francisco: Jossey-Bass.

Gutek, B.A. and Koss, M.P. (1993). Changed women and changed organizations: consequences of and coping with sexual harassment. *Journal of Vocational Behavior (special issue),* 42:1–21.

Hahn, E., Pryor, J.B., Hitlan, R., and Olson, M. (1999). Gender Harassment Conceptualized as a Form of Hostile Outgroup Discrimination against Women, paper presented at the June meeting of the American Psychological Society, Boulder, CO.

Hemphill, H. and Haines, R. (1998). Combat harassment by starting with mind (establish a zero-tolerance policy). *Business Insurance,* 32:16.

John, O.P., Donahue, E.M., and Kentle, R.L. (1991). *The "Big Five" Inventory — Versions 4a and 54.* Berkeley: University of California, Berkeley, Institute of Personality and Social Research.

Jones, E.E. (1964). *Ingratiation.* New York: Appleton-Century-Crofts.

Judge, T.A., Martoccio, J.J., and Thoresen, C.J. (1997). Five-factor model of personality and employee absence. *Journal of Applied Psychology,* 82:745–755.

Kenrick, D.T. and Keefe, R.C. (1992). Age differences in mates reflect sex differences in human reproductive strategies. *Behavior and Brain Sciences,* 15:75–92.

Lippa, R. and Arad, S. (1997). The structure of sexual orientation and its relation to masculinity, femininity, and gender diagnosticity: different for men and women. *Sex Roles,* 37:187–208.

Lipton, D., McDonel, E.C., and McFall, R.M. (1987). Heterosocial perception in rapists. *Journal of Consulting and Clinical Psychology,* 55:17–21.

Loehlin, J., McCrae, R.R., Costa, P.T., Jr., and John, O.P. (1998). Heritibilities of common and measure-specific components of the big five personality factors. *Journal of Research in Personality,* 32:431–453.

MacMillan, N.A. and Creelman, C.D. (1991). Signal detection theory: a user's guide. Cambridge: Cambridge University Press.

Malamuth, N. (1986). Predictors of naturalistic aggression. *Journal of Personality and Social Psychology,* 50:953–962.

Malamuth, N. (1989a). The attraction to sexual aggression scale: part one. *Journal of Sex Research,* 26:26–49.

Malamuth, N. (1989b). The attraction to sexual aggression scale: part two. *Journal of Sex Research,* 26:324–354.

Maurizio, S.J. and Rogers, J.L. (1992). Sexual harassment and attitudes in rural community care workers. *Health Values,* 16:40–45.

McDonel, E.C. and McFall, R.M. (1991). Construct validity of two heterosocial perception skill measures for assessing rape proclivity. *Victims and Violence,* 6:17–30.

Meyer, A. (1992). Getting to the heart of sexual harassment. *HR Magazine,* 37:82–84.

Meyer, M.C., Berchtold, I.M., Oestreich, J.L., and Collins, F.J. (1981). *Sexual Harassment.* New York:Petrocelli Books.

Murdoch, M. and Nichol, K. (1995). Women veterans' experiences with domestic violence and sexual harassment while they were in the military. *Archives of Family Medicine,* 4:411–418.

Murphy, J.D., Driscoll, D.M., and Kelly, J.R. (1999). Differences in the nonverbal behavior of men who vary in the likelihood to sexually harass. *Journal of Social Behavior and Personality,* 14(1):113–128.

Myers, J.G. (March, 1995). Enhancing the effects of diversity awareness training: a review of the research literature. *FAA Office of Aviation Medicine Reports,*10:1–25.

Nelson, P.A. (1979). A Sexual Functions Inventory, unpublished doctoral dissertation, University of Florida.

Ones, D.S., Viswesvaran, C., and Reiss, A.D. (1996). Role of social desirability in personality testing for personnel selection: the red herring. *Journal of Applied Psychology,* 81:660–679.

Peckman, S. (1999). Title IX standards in teacher-student sexual harassment: what are we teaching the teachers? — *Gebser v. Lago VISTA Independent School District. Creighton Law Review,* 32:1805–1831.

Perry, E.L., Kulik, T., and Schmidtke, J.M. (1998). Individual differences in the effectiveness of sexual harassment awareness training. *Journal of Applied Social Psychology,* 28(8):698–723.

Pryor, J.B. (1987). Sexual harassment proclivities in men. *Sex Roles,* 17:269–290.

Pryor, J.B. (1995a). The phenomenology of sexual harassment: why does sexual behavior bother people in the workplace? *Consulting Psychologist: Practice and Research,* 47:160–168

Pryor, J.B. (1995b). The psychosocial impact of sexual harassment on women in the U.S. military. *Basic and Applied Social Psychology,* 17:581–603.

Pryor, J.B. (1998). The Likelihood To Sexually Harass scale. In Davis, C.M., Yarber, W.H., Bauserman, R., Schreer, G., and Davis, S.L. (Eds.), *Sexuality-Related Measures: A Compendium* (pp. 295–298). Beverly Hills, CA: Sage.

Pryor, J.B. and DeSouza, E. R. (1999) Unpublished data. Normal, IL: Department of Psychology, Illinois State University.

Pryor, J.B. and Stoller, L. (1994). Sexual cognition processes in men who are high in the likelihood to sexually harass. *Personality and Social Psychology Bulletin,* 20:163–169.

Pryor, J.B. and Whalen, N.J. (1996). A typology of sexual harassment: characteristics of harassers and the social circumstances under which sexual harassment occurs. In Donohue, W.O. (Ed.), *Sexual Harassment: Theory, Research, and Treatment* (pp. 129–151). Arlington Heights, MA: Allyn & Bacon.

Pryor, J.B., LaVite, C., and Stoller, L. (1993). A social psychological analysis of sexual harassment: the person/situation interaction. *Journal of Vocational Behavior (special issue),* 42:68–83

Pryor, J.B., Giedd, J.L., and Williams, K.B. (1995). A social psychological model for predicting sexual harassment. *Journal of Social Issues,* 51:69–84.

Pryor, J.B., Hitlan, R., Olson, M., and Hahn, E. (April, 1999). Gender Harassment: Some Social Psychological Studies of the Antecedents, invited address at the Meeting of the Midwestern Psychological Association, Chicago, IL.

Rayner, K. (1978). Foveal and parafoveal. In Requin, J. (Ed.), *Attention and Performance VIII* (pp. 149–161). Hillsdale, NJ: Erlbaum.

Robinson v. Jacksonville Shipyards, Inc. (1991). 59 LW 2470 (DC M Fla).

Roos, C. (1998). *DiCenso v. Cisneros:* an argument for recognizing the sanctity of the home in housing sexual harassment cases. *University of Miami Law Review,* 52:1131–1151.

Rudman, L. and Borgida, E. (1995). The afterglow of construct accessibility: the behavioral consequences of priming men to view women as sex objects. *Journal of Experimental Social Psychology,* 31:493–517.

Schneider, K.T. and Swan, S. (April, 1994). Job-Related, Psychological, and Health-Related Outcomes of Sexual Harassment, paper presented at a conference of the Society of Industrial and Organizational Psychology, Nashville, TN.

Sheffield, C.J. (1987). Sexual terrorism: the social control of women. In Hess, B.B. and Feree, M.M. (Eds.), *Analyzing Gender: A Handbook of Social Science Research.* Beverly Hills, CA: Sage.

Sheffield, C.J. (1999). Sexual terrorism: the social control of women. In Hess, B.B. and Feree, M.M. (Eds.), *Analyzing Gender: A Handbook of Social Science Research* (pp. 171–189). Newbury Park, CA: Sage.

Smith, E., Feree, M., and Miller, F. (1975). A short scale of attitudes toward feminism. *Representative Research in Social Psychology,* 6:51–56.

Spence, J.T. and Helmreich, R. (1978). *Masculinity, and Femininity: Their Psychological Dimensions, Correlates, and Antecedents.* Austin: University of Texas Press.

Spence, J.T., Helmreich, R., and Stapp, J. (1973). A short version of the Attitude Toward Women scale. *Bulletin of Psychonomic Society,* 2:219–220.

Stockdale, M.S. (1993). The role of sexual misperceptions of women's friendliness in an emerging theory of sexual harassment. *Journal of Vocational Behavior,* 42:84–101.

Swim, J., Aiken, K.J., Hall, W.S., and Hunter, B.A. (1995). Sexism and racism: old fashioned and modern prejudices. *Journal of Personality and Social Psychology,* 68:199–214.

Thomann, D.A., Strickland, D.E., and Gibbons, J.L. (1989). An organizational development approach to preventing sexual harassment. *CUPA Journal,* 40:34–43

Tokar, D.M., Fischer, A.R., and Subich, L.M. (1998). Personality and vocational behavior: a selective review of the literature, 1993–1997. *Journal of Vocational Behavior,* 53:115–153.

Tuchfarber, J. (1996). A Study of Men's Willingness To Persist in Sexual Advances in the Face of Rejection, unpublished Master's thesis, Illinois State University, Normal, IL.

U.S. Merit Systems Protection Board. (1981). *Sexual Harassment in the Federal Workplace: Is It a Problem?* Washington, D.C.: U.S. Government Printing Office.

U.S. Merit Systems Protection Board. (1988). *Sexual Harassment in the Federal Government: An Update.* Washington, D.C.: U.S. Government Printing Office.

U.S. Merit Systems Protection Board. (1995). *Sexual Harassment in the Federal Government: Trends, Progress, Continuing Challenges.* Washington, D.C.: U.S. Government Printing Office.

Vogelman-Sine, S., Ervin, E., Christensen, R., Warmsun, C., and Ullman, L. (1979). Sex differences in feelings attributed to a woman in situations involving coercion and sexual advances. *Journal of Personality,* 47:420–431.

Waldo, C.R., Berdahl, J.L., and Fitzgerald, L.F. (1998). Are men sexually harassed? If so by whom? *Law and Human Behavior,* 22:59–79.

Wasti, S.A., Bergman, M.E., Glomb, T.M., and Drasgow, F. (1999). Test of the Cross-Cultural Generalizability of a Model of Sexual Harassment, paper presented at the annual meetings of the Society for Industrial and Organizational Psychology, May, 1999, Atlanta, GA.

Widiger, T.A., (1997). Personality disorders as maladaptive variants of common personality traits: implications for treatment. *Journal of Contemporary Psychotherapy,* 27:265–282.

Williams, J.H., Fitzgerald, L.F., and Drasgow, F. (1999). The effects of organizational practices on sexual harassment and individual outcomes in the military. *Military Psychology,* 11:303–328.

York, K.M., Barblay, L., and Zajack, A. (1997). Preventing sexual harassment: the effect of multiple training methods. *Employee Responsibilities and Rights Journal,* 10:277–289.

Part III

Introduction

Part III encompasses serial offenders who display unusual syndromes or in some way constitute a special population. In Chapter 11, David M. Greenberg, Philip Firestone, John M. Bradford, and Ian Broom explain and discuss their research on infantophiles — repetitive offenders who target and sexually abuse children under the age of 5 (pre-elementary school). Except for the research carried out by these authors, there are really no other published data on this category of serial offenders. Their research has led them to conclude that serial infantophiles probably have more psychopathology than non-serial infantophiles, are more likely to deny their sexual offenses, and are more likely to escape detection because their very young victims lack verbal skills and therefore are unable to report molestation. With increased public awareness and perhaps electronic surveillance (for example, in daycare centers), more offenders will be identified and more research on this interesting subgroup of child molesters (who are not as rare as initially believed) will result.

In Chapter 12, Thomas W. Haywood and Jack Green discuss serial offending among the clergy. Over the past several years, considerable media and ecclesiastic attention has been given to clergy who have engaged in repetitive acts of sexual misconduct. The authors of this chapter report their research in which they compare cleric to noncleric offenders. A number of differences emerge. For example, cleric offenders have fewer victims, tend to select older victims, and manifest less serious psychopathology than nonclerics. However, the victims of abuse by clergy are often even more traumatized than victims of nonclerics, because the offender is an individual who occupies a position of trust and responsibility and is expected to be a moral leader. The authors present intriguing and important findings in a sensitive manner and offer approaches to treatment with this group of offenders — a population that has previously been under-researched.

In Chapter 13, A.J. Cooper reviews the available findings on female serial offenders. As some researchers have argued, serial offending — and sexual offending in general — is overwhelmingly a male phenomenon; however, a small subgroup of female offenders has consistently been identified. Dr. Cooper reports on several different types of female serial offenders: female child molesters, female rapists, women who repetitively assault victims along with an adult male, women who sexually molest teenage boys, and women who sexually molest prepubescent children of both sexes. Female exhibitionists as well as female serial murderers are also covered in this chapter. The author concludes by discussing predictor variables for recidivism, problems in making diagnoses and establishing a treatment regimen, and difficulties conducting empirical research with a population of offenders encountered so rarely.

Serial offending by children and adolescents is presented by Wade C. Myers and Marian J. Borg in Chapter 14. The authors enumerate and examine the serial offenses committed by juveniles — offenses including arson, cruelty to animals, various sexual and sadistic crimes, and serial murder. The scientific community has only recently begun to study the problem of serial offending during childhood and adolescence; consequently, there is a paucity of existing literature and even less empirical research on this topic. Drs. Myers and Borg make a strong point that additional research is needed. Because the majority of adult offenders commit their first criminal act during childhood or adolescence, the importance of studying this group of young offenders cannot be overemphasized.

The final chapter of Part III, and the final chapter of the book, is devoted to the survivors of serial crime (the victims themselves or the families and loved ones of victims who did not survive). Laurence Miller and Louis B. Schlesinger show how individuals cope and move on with their lives after being the victim of a serial offense or having a family member or loved one victimized or murdered. The authors note common survivor reactions and symptoms, which are particularly intense if a child is murdered. Survivors and family members often have difficulty in dealing with the criminal justice system, which they frequently accuse of retraumatizing them — from the first step of victim notification and body identification through the arrest, plea bargaining, trial, and appeals process. Drs. Miller and Schlesinger then discuss psychological treatment for survivors and families, which includes crisis intervention, victim advocacy, and individual and family therapy, with special attention to bereaved children. Treatment also is often needed for therapists, criminal investigators, and others who are involved with such traumatic and stress-producing cases and become traumatized themselves. The subject of this chapter — the plight of the survivors of serial crime — is often neglected in discussions of the criminal offender; this chapter attempts to add some balance by illuminating a previously neglected area.

11 Infantophiles

David M. Greenberg, Philip Firestone,
John M. Bradford, and Ian Broom

CONTENTS

INTRODUCTION

Pedophiles, by definition, are individuals who have characteristic symptoms of recurrent, intense sexual fantasies of sexual activity or sexual urges involving prepubescent children (APA, 1994). Hebophiles are similarly sexually aroused but by pubescent rather than prepubescent children. The *Diagnostic and Statistical Manual of Mental Disorders*, 4th ed. (APA, 1994) has excluded perpetrators of pubertal victims. To incorporate offenders of both pre-pubertal and pubertal victims, researchers have adopted the term "child molesters." This term is broad enough to incorporate all perpetrators of child sexual abuse with victim ages ranging from infancy to usually age 16, regardless of whether they acknowledge sexual fantasies or sexual urges involving children or whether they admit to being sexually aroused by children.

0-8493-2236-7/00/$0.00+$.50
© 2000 by CRC Press LLC

Sexual abuse of infants and toddlers has been described in the literature, with victims as young as 2 to 3 months (Cupoli and Sewell, 1988; Dube and Hebert, 1988). Infantophiles is a term adopted for a subcategory of child molesters who sexually abuse children under the age of 5 years (Greenberg et al., 1995). Although age of victim has been adopted for purposes of delineation, strictly speaking in many cases the developmental (sexual, psychological, and physical) stage of the child's development (prior to entering first grade) is the erotic or sexual component of arousal for the perpetrator.

The term "serial" implies arranged in or forming a series (Guralnik, 1978). The number of victims used as criterion for classification of serial offenders varies from study to study. All have a minimum of two victims, but some require three or more victims (Ressler et al., 1988). Unlike serial child molesters, serial murderers, rapists, and arsonists have received the considerable attention of researchers (Kocsis and Irwin, 1988). Geberth (1986) divided serial murderers who have had multiple victims into three categories — namely, mass, spree, or serial offenders. Mass offenders have three or more victims in a single event, spree offenders have three or more victims in different locations, and serial offenders have victims with a significant intermission of time between each offense. Likewise, child molesters could be considered serial if they have multiple victims with intermission periods between each offense. Kocsis and Irwin (1998) argue that the number of victims should not be the defining characteristic but rather "a psychological propensity to continue to commit a series of similar offenses." They report that analysis of psychological characteristics of a serial offender will reveal a propensity profile associated with such offenses.

This chapter will use the term "serial" to incorporate the criteria of a minimum of two victims where there is an intermission of time between the two offenses; the second offense is not dependent on location nor does it occur at the same time period of the initial offense. We will briefly review the literature on the psychological, physiological, and offense characteristics which differentiate recidivistic (serial) child molesters from non-recidivist (non-serial) child molesters. Second, using the age of the victim as a delineating variable, infantophiles will be compared to other non-infantophile extrafamilial child molesters. The authors will then report on the factors which distinguish between the serial and non-serial infantophile groups.

LIMITATIONS WITH RECIDIVISM STUDIES

Research on recidivism of child molesters is fraught with methodological difficulties (Furby et al., 1989). Sample selection with this population has inherent difficulties. Child molesters are notoriously clandestine in their activities, and their self-reports are invariably unreliable (Pollock and Hashmall, 1991). Victims' reports may not be representative of the perpetrator population, as many victims often do not report the sexual abuse. Accused perpetrators may not be prosecuted, or, in order to obtain a conviction, the prosecutor may enter into a plea bargain with the perpetrator to a lesser nonsexual offense. As child molesters, in most cases, do not present for study at community or hospital clinics, samples are invariably drawn from correctional institutions or forensic psychiatric hospitals, where these individuals are usually pre-trial, sentenced, or on probation/parole orders. Therefore, composition of these samples may vary from study to study. Some variables that are known to affect the outcome rates include demographics (age, marital status, employment, geographical area); criminal history (prior arrests, age of the first offense); type of offense; victim characteristics (age and gender); legal status and disposition (hospital or corrections, plea bargaining, amenability to treatment); and family and community support (Greenberg, 1998). Scrutiny of samples selected is, therefore, crucial to the understanding of the differing outcome rates.

The design of the study will also affect recidivism outcome rates. Studies that are retrospective may differ from prospective studies (Furby et al., 1989). The definition of recidivism also varies from study to study, and this criterion will also affect the outcomes rates. For example, does recidivism indicate a repetition of the same act with a child or any sexual offense, or possibly any sexual or physical violent offense or any criminal offense, no matter how minor? Perhaps the most noticeable differences between studies is the variable followup period. The longer the period of followup, the higher the cumulative recidivism rate (Soothill et al., 1976). Ideally, child molesters should be followed up for the remainder of their total life span, after the initial offense, to determine if they are serial offenders. Practically, however, all studies have a beginning and an end. Subjects within the sample have different ranges of followup, and most commonly the mean followup period is reported rather than for individual members of the sample. Finally, analysis of data must also take into account the attrition rate and what statistically significant level is used in the study. These factors, among others, influence the outcome studies that attempt to distinguish recidivist from non-recidivist child molesters.

All recidivism results flowing from this type of research should therefore be regarded as relative recidivism rates rather than absolute or true values. These rates are considered underestimates of the actual recidivism rates. Consequently, predictive variables emanating from the differences between serial and non-serial child molesters currently only have moderate validity. There has been renewed interest in distinguishing child molesters who later perpetrate further criminal acts. In many recent studies, three incremental levels of recidivists have been defined: (1) those child molesters who commit a repeated sexual act involving any sexual offense, (2) a sexual and/or physical violent act, and (3) any criminal act. Cumulative scoring with each successive recidivism level is now being used because, with plea bargaining, sexual charges may be transformed to a nonsexual violent conviction, and for the same reason many researchers are now using both charges or convictions in determining recidivism rates.

RECENT CHILD MOLESTER RECIDIVISM STUDIES

There has been renewed interest in distinguishing child molesters who go on to perpetrate further sexual, violent, or criminal offenses. Hansen and Bussiéré (1998) completed a recent landmark meta-analysis of 61 followup recidivism studies (n = 23,393) which were completed between 1943 and 1995. They reported that 12.7% of extrafamilial child molesters sexually recidivated when they were followed up over a mean 4- to 5-year period. The cumulative nonsexual violent recidivism rates for child molesters was 9.9%, and the recidivism rate for any criminal offense was 36.9% after the same 4- to 5-year followup period.

Subsequently, additional recidivism studies since 1995 have been published. Proulx et al. (1997) reported on a sample of 269 child molesters who were released from a maximum security psychiatric hospital. Their findings showed that, over an average followup period of 64.5 months, 13% of their child molester sample were serial offenders; that is, they were reconvicted for a new sexual offense. Quinsey et al. (1998) reported that, with a mean followup period of 44 months (maximum 17 years), 17% of child molesters sexually recidivated. When any sexual or physical violent offense was included in the definition of recidivism, some 27% of child molesters recidivated.

Few researchers have distinguished between incest child molesters perpetrators and extrafamilial child molesters. One exception is the work by Firestone et al. (1999) who reported that in a sample of 192 convicted extrafamilial child molesters, who were followed up for an average of 7.8 years after their conviction (maximum period of 12 years), the percentage of men who committed a further sexual offense was 15.1%. The percentage of men who committed any sexual and/or physical violent offense was 20.3%; 42% of the extrafamilial sample reoffended with a further criminal offense. Firestone et al. (1999) explored the recidivism rates of 222 incest offenders who were followed up for an average of 6.7 years (maximum period of up to 12 years) after their initial conviction. The percentage of incest child perpetrators who committed a sexual, violent, or criminal offense by the twelfth year was 6.4, 12.4, and 26.7%, respectively.

These recidivism studies allow us to compare the serial recidivist to the non-recidivist group. We have then been able to demonstrate various demographic, psychological, and physiological differences between these groups and the factors that best discriminate the serial offenders. However, as mentioned previously, these recidivism rates are relative rates rather than absolute values due to the various methodological difficulties encountered. Despite these limitations, these distinguishing variables allow clinicians to discriminate and therefore predict recidivist from non-recidivists child molesters.

PREDICTORS OF SERIAL OFFENDERS

Hansen and Bussieré's meta-analysis (1998) reported that various variables distinguished sexual recidivists from non-recidivists in their study population of mixed sex offenders. They reported that the phallometric assessment was the best predictor of sexual recidivism for "sex offenders" (r = .32, where 'r' is the magnitude of the correlation). Other discriminating variables included paraphilic interests (r = 0.22), prior sexual offense (r = 0.19), failure to complete treatment (r = 0.17), antisocial personality disorder (r = 0.14), any prior criminal offense (r = 0.13), age (r = 0.13), never married (r = 0.11), unrelated to the victim (r = 0.11), and any male victim (r = 0.11).

Quinsey et al. (1995) reported that predictive variables that can distinguish recidivist from non-recidivist sex offenders included the following: prior sexual convictions (r = 0.26), prior violent offenses (r = 0.22), never married (r = 0.22), deviant index-phallometric studies (r = 0.21), previous admissions to corrections (r = 0.20), previous male victim (r = 0.20), psychopathy checklist (r = 0.18), previous admissions to maximum-security facility corrections (r = 0.18), previous female victim (r = 0.17), number of male victims (r = 0.17), prior convictions for other offenses (r = 0.14), and previous adult victim (r = 0.13). By ranking sex offenders into six recidivism levels, the authors claim they could correctly classify 77% of sexual recidivists with a 44% rate of improvement over chance.

Proulx et al. (1997) reported that in their sample of sex offenders released from a maximum security psychiatric hospital, penile phallometry studies (Pedophile Index) had predictive validity. In addition, prior sexual offenses, extrafamilial victims, male victims, younger offenders, and living alone were also predictive of a recidivist pattern of behavior.

Most research to date has been done on sex offenders in general. Few researchers have distinguished child molesters or incest perpetrators from other types of sex offenders, such as rapists or exhibitionists. One exception is a body of work done by Firestone et al. (2000) who reported on a group of 192 extrafamilial child molesters who were followed up for an average of 7.8 years after conviction. They found that the Michigan Alcohol Screening Test (MAST) (Selzer, 1971) and the phallometric studies were able to distinguish sexual extrafamilial serial child molesters from non-recidivists. Compared with nonviolent recidivists, serial extrafamilial child molesters who recidivated with a violent offense were more likely to have a history of violence in the families in which they were raised and were rated significantly more psychopathic on Hare's (1991) psychopathy checklist-revised (PCL-R). For criminal recidivism in general, recidivist extrafamilial child molesters were distinguished from non-recidivists by numerous various variables (Table 1). They reported a small number of significant difference between recidivists and non-recidivists in sexual and violent categories which precluded an attempt to determine which combination of factors meaningfully predicted reoffense. However, with criminal recidivism, a discriminate function analysis was able to successfully distinguish between recidivists and non-recidivists using a combination of total criminal offenses, psychopathy checklist (PCL-R), age, and number of previous sexual offenses. The rate of improvement over chance (RIOC) was 31% (Loeber and Dishion, 1983). Interestingly, using the psychopathy checklist alone, the RIOC was 34%.

Likewise, with a group of 222 incest perpetrators who were followed up for an average of 6.7 years after their conviction, the sexual recidivists compared to the non-recidivists scored higher on the MAST and on the PCL-R (Firestone et al., 1999b). Violent recidivists compared to non-recidivists scored higher on the MAST and PCL-R and had more violence in their previous police contact. Compared with non-recidivists, incest perpetrators who reoffended with any criminal offense were older, their families of origin were more turbulent, and they reported high rates of being physically abused or being away from their homes prior to the age of 16. In addition, they demonstrated hostility on the Buss Durkee Hostility Inventory (BDHI) (Buss and Durkee, 1957) and higher scores on the MAST and the PCL-R. They also had more charges of convictions for sexual violent and any criminal acts on their police records. Again, the small number of significant differences between recidivists and non-recidivists in the sexual and violent categories precluded an attempt to

TABLE 1
Prediction Variables in Extrafamilial Child Molesters

	Criminal	Violent	Sexual
Age	X		
Education	X		
History of drug abuse	X		
History of violence	X	X	
Family history of mental illness	X	X	
Physical abuse under age 16	X		
Placed outside home under age 16	X		
Derogatis Sex Function Inventory	X		
Buss Durkee Hostility Inventory	X		
Michigan Alcohol Screen Inventory	X		X
PCL Factor 1	X	X	
PCL Factor 2	X	X	
PCL total	X	X	
Pedophile Assault Index	X	X	X
Rape Index	X		
Previous violent record	X		
Previous criminal record	X		

determine which combination of factors meaningfully predicted reoffending. However, for criminal recidivism, using a stepwise discriminate functional analysis to assess which combination of factors would meaningfully predict recidivism, a combination of total criminal offenses, PCL-R, the number of previous sexual offenses, and age resulted in an RIOC of 27%.

INFANTOPHILES

There is a paucity of research on child molesters who sexually abuse children under the age of 5 years (pre-elementary school). In a preliminary study, Greenberg et al. (1995) reported on a sample of 10 male infantophiles and compared this to a sample of 28 pedophiles who sexually abused older children between the ages of 8 and 12. They reported that the median age for the infantophile group was 23.5 years, which differed significantly from the pedophile group who had a median age of 32 years of age. Of the sample, 63% were single, while 21.1% were either married or in common-law marriages. For the infantophile group, the mean age of the victims was 3.9 years (SD = 0.88); for the pedophile group, 9.29 years (SD = 2.06). For the entire sample, 66% molested female children and 29% molested only male children, with the remainder molesting children from both genders. The number of victims reported per offender for the entire sample ranged from 1 to 5, with 66% admitting molestation of only one victim. There was no difference between the two groups on these factors. For both groups, 47% reported using no threats of violence or physical violence toward their child victims; however, 39% reported using threats with or without a weapon, and 10% reported minor injuries to their victims with or without weapons. Only 2.6% mutilated or murdered their victims, and there were no differences between the two groups. Likewise there were no statistical differences between the two groups with regard to relationship to the victim; 63% reported they were acquaintances or friends, while 21% reported that they were strangers to the victims, 10.5% were stepfathers, and 5.3% were relatives (uncles, grandfathers, cousins, brothers, etc.).

For the total sample, 29% reported having been sexually abused in their own childhoods. Two members of the infantophile group reported being sexually victimized in their own childhood when they were 6 years of age, while the pedophile group reported being sexually abused when they were 7.5 years old (SD = 2). Rates of alcohol dependency and drug abuse did not differ between the groups; 29% of the sample reported that they had a history of alcohol dependency, and 18% reported a similar history of drug abuse. On the MAST, 29% reported scores suggestive or indicative of alcoholism. Almost 90% of the total sample had no history of violence, and 72% had no previous convictions for criminal offenses with no differences between the groups. Overall, the two groups did not differ on the BDHI score, although 26% of the total sample had scores above the cut-off point of 38. Finally, with the Derogatis (1978) Sexual Functioning Inventory (DSFI), low t-scores indicated a poorer level of functioning in 27%, who scored below the cut-off point for the Sexual Functioning Index.

FOLLOWUP STUDY OF INFANTOPHILES

The authors conducted a followup study to compare infantophiles to other extrafamilial (non-infantophile) child molesters and their recidivism rates and to investigate the factors that predict which infantophile offenders go onto perpetrate serial sexual offenses. The assessment process and data collection at the Sexual Behaviors Clinic at a university teaching psychiatric hospital have been well described previously (Bradford and Greenberg, 1998; Firestone et al., 1998). Subjects were assessed between 1980 and 1992. Offense information was gathered from the national database of criminal charges and convictions called the Canadian Information Center. For the offender to be considered eligible for recidivism, he must have been free to commit a crime. All subjects were males and at least 16 years old. The child molester group self-reported or had been convicted of molesting extrafamilial children between the ages of 6 and 16 years old, while the infantophile group similarly reported or had been convicted of a sexual act of against children 5 years of age or younger. Subjects who reported molesting children from both groups were excluded from the study. Written informed consent was obtained from all subjects.

MEASUREMENT OF SEXUAL AROUSAL

Changes in penile circumference in response to audio/visual stimuli were measured by means of an indium-gallium strain gauge and monitored with a Farrell Instruments CAT200. These data were then processed on an IBM-compatible computer for storage and printout.

STIMULI PRESENTATION

The order of stimulus presentation, held constant for all subjects, was computer controlled using MPV-Forth Version 3.05 software provided by Farrell Instruments. Videotapes of explicit heterosexual and/or homosexual consensual adult sex were presented first, followed by a set of slides. Finally, subjects were presented with one or more of the three series of audiotapes, according to the nature of the subject's sexual offense. The audiotapes consisted of 120-second vignettes which described sexual activities varying in age, gender, and degree of consent, coercion, and/or violence portrayed (Abel et al., 1981). Each subject was presented with a full set containing one vignette from each category following instructions to allow normal arousal to occur. The female child series consisted of descriptions of sexual activity with a female partner/victim for eight categories. The male child series consisted of eight corresponding vignettes involving a male partner/victim but also included one scenario involving an adult female partner. For each of the female child and male child series, two equivalent scenarios for each category were included. Categories were (1) child initiates, (2) child and adult mutually engage, (3) nonphysical coercion of child, (4) physical coercion of child, (5) sadistic sex with child, (6) nonsexual assault of child, (7) consenting sex with female adult, and (8) sex with female child relative (incest). The audiotape series used to identify sexual attraction to rape included two scenarios of 2-minute duration for each of three categories: (1) consenting sex with adult female, (2) rape of adult female, (3) nonsexual assault of adult female.

SCORING

The Pedophile Index was computed by dividing the highest response to the child initiates or child mutual stimulus by the highest response to an adult consenting stimulus. The Rape Index was computed by dividing the response to a rape stimulus involving an adult female victim by the response to a stimulus of adult consensual sex. The Assault Index was computed by dividing the response to a physical nonsexual assault by the response to adult consenting stimulus.

ANALYSES

Before performing statistical tests, the data were screened to ensure that the assumptions underlying the tests were not violated. Outlying cases were detected by using a criterion of ±3 standard deviations from the mean or by visual inspection of normal probability plots. Values of outlying cases were adjusted upward or downward according to the direction of the problem. This method is appropriate when case retention is desirable and does not unduly influence the group mean (Tabachnick and Fidell, 1989).

RESULTS

DEMOGRAPHIC AND SELF-REPORTED HISTORICAL CHARACTERISTICS

With regard to demographic data and self-reported personal histories, as indicated in Table 1, there were no significant differences between infantophiles and child molesters, with the exception of age and admission to the index offense. Infantophiles were significantly younger at the time of assessment than were child molesters (M = 30.11 vs. 37.69), and they were less likely to admit to perpetrating the offense (M = 29.4 vs. 56.1%). There was evidence of a trend with infantophiles reporting fewer family histories of alcoholism than child molesters and fewer infantophiles admitting to being sexually abused in their own childhood. There was no significant difference between the groups with regard to the reported use of substances at the time of the index offense and family history of mental illness, criminality, or drug abuse.

There were no significant differences between the two groups with regard to relationship with the victim. The outstanding feature was that, for both infantophiles and child molesters, the majority of victims were acquaintances of the offender rather than strangers. In no cases were the victims relatives of the perpetrator, as by definition such perpetrators were categorized as incest offenders and not as infantophiles or child molesters (see Table 2).

PSYCHOLOGICAL TEST SCORES FOR THE
INFANTOPHILE AND CHILD MOLESTER GROUPS

Psychological maladjustment was represented by three variables: (1) alcohol abuse, as measured by the total MAST score; (2) general hostility, as measured by the total BDHI score; and (3) degree of psychiatric disturbance, as measured by the total Brief Psychiatric Rating Score (BPRS) (Overall and Gorham, 1962). As indicated in Table 3, there were no statistically significant differences between the infantophile and child molester groups with regard to alcoholism. The outstanding feature on the MAST was that the child molester group met the criterion of 7 or higher, considered strongly indicative of alcohol abuse (M = 7.35). Similarly, there were no significant differences in general hostility, with neither group meeting the criterion for clinical hostility. There was also no significant difference between groups in the degree of psychiatric disturbance.

In terms of sexual functioning, as assessed by the Sexual Functioning Index (SFI) of the DSFI, there were no significant differences between the two groups. The outstanding feature on the SFI was that both the infantophile and the child molester groups demonstrated below-average sexual functioning in general (M = 29.60, 2nd percentile, and M = 32.48, 4th percentile, respectively). Two psychological scales eliciting attitudes and beliefs regarding sexual deviance and aggression were administered — namely, the Cognition Scale (Abel et al., 1989) and the Rape Myth Acceptance Scale (RMAS) (Burt, 1980). With regard to the Cognition Scale, there were no statistically significant differences between the two groups.

TABLE 2

Demographic and Self-Reported Characteristics of Infantophiles and Child Molesters

Variable	Infantophiles (n)	Child Molesters (n)	τ or χ^c	df	p <
Age[a]	30.11 ± 11.13 (18)	37.69 ± 123.20 (192)	5.559	209	0.019
Education[a]	10.50 ± 2.92[a] (16)	11.31 ± 3.60[a] (184)	0.763	199	0.383
Full-scale IQ[a]	79.80 ± 20.45[a] (5)	92.04 ± 17.32[a] (74)	2.291	78	0.134
Married[b]	44.5% (8)	46.8% (89)	0.038	1	1
Admit to index offense[b]	29.4% (5)	56.1% (106)	4.466	1	0.035
History of drug abuse[b]	14.3% (1)	18.9% (10)			1.0003
History of sexual abuse[b]	22% (4)	42% (80)	2.593	1	0.084
Outside placement before 16 years[b]	40% (4)	30.4% (35)			0.5013
Family history of alcohol abuse[b]	0% (0)	37% (20)			0.0843
Family history of drug abuse[b]	0% (0)	13% (7)			0.5863
Family history of mental illness[b]	0% (0)	7.4% (4)			1.0003
Family history of criminality[b]	0% (0)	18.5% (10)			0.5873
Substance use at time of index offense[b]	14.3% (1)	24.1% (13)			1.0003
Victimization by stranger[b]	25% (2)	19% (23)			0.6523
Victimization by acquaintance[b]	75% (6)	82.6% (100)			0.6323

[a]Mean responses ± standard deviations.

[b]Percentage of subjects is presented first followed by the number of subjects in parentheses.

[c]Fisher's Exact Test (2-sided).

However, with regard to the RMAS, there was evidence of a trend, with the infantophiles scoring lower than the child molesters ($M = 57.21$ and 62.67, respectively), indicative of acceptance of sexual coercion. Psychopathy was assessed using the PCL-R. There were no significant differences between groups on the PCL-R total score, with neither group scoring above the cutoff score for psychopathy (30).

TABLE 3
Psychological Test Scores of Infantophiles and Pedophiles

Variable	Infantophiles (n)	Child Molesters (n)	t	df	p <
Michigan Alcohol Screening Test	3.00 ± 5.68 (15)	7.35 ± 10.48 (135)	2.489	149	0.117
Buss Dirkee Hostility Inventory	26.81 ± 14.71 (16)	26.65 ± 13.37 (186)	0.002	201	0.962
Brief Psychiatric Rating Scale	5 ± 5.10 (7)	8.85 ± 7.64 (53)	−1.291	58	0.202
Derogatis Sexual Functioning Inventory	29.60 ± 10.34 (16)	32.48 ± 12.09 (184)	0.854	199	0.357
Cognition Scale	4.58 ± 0.36 (16)	4.41 ± 0.58 (150)	1.237	165	0.268
RMAS	57.21 ± 11.72 (14)	62.67 ± 9.57 (92)	3.72	105	0.056
Psychopathy Checklist-Revised Total	22.28 ± 7.05 (9)	17.96 ± 7.83 (122)	2.575	130	0.111
Factor 1	9.56 ± 2.60 (9)	8.28 ± 3.13 (122)	1.424	130	0.235
Factor 2	12.27 ± 3.50 (7)	7.69 ± 5.43 (86)	4.797	92	0.031

An exploratory consideration of the two major factors into which the PCL-R items can be grouped indicated that the infantophiles scored significantly higher on Factor 2 (criminal lifestyle) than the child molesters ($M = 12.27$ vs. 7.69). There were, however, no group differences on Factor 1 (psychopathic personality).

PHALLOMETRIC ASSESSMENT

As indicated in Table 4, there were no statistically significant differences between infantophiles and child molesters on any of the phallometric measures. The outstanding feature on phallometric testing was that both the infantophile and the child molesters groups scored within the clinical range on the PI ($M = 1.54$ and 1.60, respectively), while neither group scored within the clinical pedophile range on either the Rape Index or the Assault Index.

TABLE 4
Phallometric Measures for Infantophiles and Pedophiles

Variable	Infantophiles (n)	Child Molesters (n)	t	df	p <
Pedophile Index	1.54 ± 1.53 (11)	1.60 ± 1.42 (131)	0.02	141	0.886
Rape Index	0.56 ± 0.59 (14)	0.53 ± 0.64 (176)	0.03	189	0.854
Assault Index	0.21 ± 0.37 (14)	0.28 ± 0.47 (176)	0.323	189	0.57

OFFENSE HISTORIES AND RECIDIVISM

As indicated in Table 5, there were no statistically significant differences between infantophiles and child molesters with regard to criminal offense histories in any of the categories of sexual, violent, and criminal. As indicated in Table 6, there were no statistically significant differences between infantophiles and child molesters with regard to sexual, violent, and criminal recidivism. Figures 1 and 2 show the survival rates for the two groups.

TABLE 5
Criminal Offense History of Infantophiles and Child Molesters

Variable	Infantophile (n)	Child Molester (n)	t	df	< p
Number of previous sexual offenses	0.27 ± 0.65 (11)	0.50 ± 1.25 (138)	0.075	148	0.784
Number of previous violent offenses	0.46 ± 0.82 (11)	0.78 ± 1.55 (138)	0.084	148	0.772
Number of previous criminal offenses	3.00 ± 3.69 (11)	2.51 ± 3.79 (138)	0.322	148	0.571

TABLE 6
Recidivism Records of Infantophiles and Pedophiles

Variable	Infantophiles	Child Molesters	p <[a]
Sexual recidivism	9.1% (1)	13.7% (19)	1.000
Violent recidivism	18.2% (2)	18.1% (25)	1.000
Criminal recidivism	63.6% (7)	37.7% (52)	0.114

[a] Fisher's Exact Test (2-sided).

PREDICTORS OF SERIAL INFANTOPHILES

The recidivist and non-recidivist infantophiles were compared on the same demographic and historical characteristics, psychological tests, and phallometric measures as the preceding study. A total sample of 18 infantophiles was included in the following analysis. There were no significant differences between the two groups with the variables of age, education, full-scale intelligence quotient, marital status, admission to index offense, history of their own sexual abuse, placement outside the home before the age of 16, or family history of alcohol abuse, mental illness, and criminality. The serial infantophile group more often reported a history of drug abuse than non-serial offenders (80 vs. 0%); however, there was no difference between the groups in consumption of drugs at the time period surrounding the offense. There was no difference between the groups with regard to the proportion of perpetrators who were strangers vs. acquaintances.

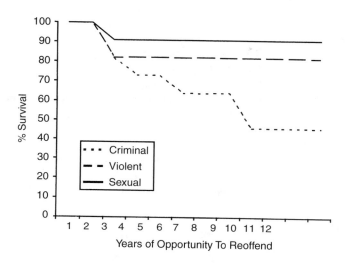

FIGURE 1. Survival rates for infantophiles.

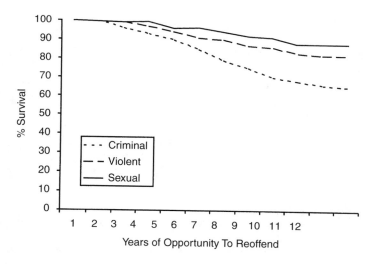

FIGURE 2. Non-infantophile child molester survival rates.

Using the psychological test scores of the serial and non-serial infantophiles, no differences were found on the MAST, BDHI, DSFI, Cognition Scale, RMAS, and the total Factor 1 score of the PCL-R. The BPRS was significantly higher in the serial infantophile group (16.6 vs. 7.09). Although the total PCL-R did not differ in the serial and non-serial groups, Factor 2 was significantly higher (M = 13.8 vs. 8.45) in the serial offenders (see Tables 7 and 8).

TABLE 7
Demographic and Self-Reported Characteristics of Serial and Non-Serial Infantophiles

Variable	Serial Infantophiles (n)	Non-Serial Infantophiles (n)	t or χ[b]	df	p <
Age[a]	27.50 ± 5.32 (6)	31.42 ± 13.15 (12)	−.693	16	.498
Education[a]	10.00 ± 1.10 (6)	10.80 ± 3.65 (10)	−.517	14	.613
Full-scale IQ[a]	93.00 ± 12.12 (3)	60.00 ± 8.49 (2)	3.273	3	.047
Married[b]	50% (6)	41.7% (12)	.113	1	.563
Admit to index offense[b]	20% (5)	33.3% (12)	.302	1	.528
History of drug abuse[b]	80% (5)	0% (5)	6.667	1	.024
History of sexual abuse[b]	0% (6)	16.7% (12)	2.571	1	.276
Outside placement before 16 years[b]	50% (6)	25% (4)	.429	1	.452[3]
Family history of alcohol abuse[b]	40% (5)	20% (5)	.476	1	.500[c]
Family history of drug abuse[b]	40% (5)	20% (5)	.476	1	.500[3]
Family history of mental illness[b]	25% (4)	20% (5)	.032	1	.722[c]
Family history of criminality[b]	40% (5)	0% (5)	2.500	1	.222[3]
Substance use at time of index offense[b]	25.0% (4)	0% (3)	.875	1	.571[3]
Victimization by stranger[b]	20% (5)	33.3% (3)	.178	1	.643[c]
Victimization by acquaintance[b]	80% (5)	66.7% (3)	178.	1	.643[c]

[a] Mean responses ± standard deviations.
[b] Percentage of subjects is presented first followed by the number of subjects in parentheses.
[c] Fisher's Exact Test (2-sided).

Phallometric analysis showed no differences using the Pedophile Index, although the outstanding feature is that both groups had a positive index for pedophilic arousal ($M = 1.75$ vs. 1.24, respectively). Although the Rape Index was less than one, the serial infantophiles had a small trend towards having a higher scores ($M = .86$ vs. 0.33). There was no difference in the assault index between the two groups.

Finally, the previous criminal record of sexual and violent charges or convictions was not different between the two groups. There was, however, a significant difference between the groups, with the serial infantophiles having a criminal record with more previous criminal offenses (see Tables 9 and 10).

TABLE 8
Psychological Test Scores of Serial and Non-Serial Infantophiles

Variable	Serial Infantophiles (n)	Non-Serial Infantophiles (n)	t	df	p <
Michigan Alcohol Screening Test	5.80 ± 9.55 (15)	1.60 ± 1.78 (135)	1.394	13	.187
Buss Dirkee Hostility Inventory	31.00 ± 14.68 (6)	24.30 ± 14.90 (10)	.875	14	.396
Brief Psychiatric Rating Scale	16.60 ± 8.88 (5)	7.09 ± 6.80 (11)	2.365	14	.033
Derogatis Sexual Functioning Inventory	27.08 ± 11.66 (6)	31.10 ± 9.792 (10)	−.741	14	.471
Cognition Scale	4.62 ± .38 (6)	4.55 ± .37 (10)	.386	14	.705
RMAS	51.75 ± 18.10 (4)	59.40 ± 8.40 (10)	−1.114	12	.287
Psychopathy Checklist-Revised Total	24.45 ± 7.55 (6)	17.93 ± 3.74 (3)	1.378	7	.211
Factor 1	9.67 ± 3.14 (6)	9.33 ± 1.53 (3)	.170	7	.870
Factor 2	13.8 ± 2.83 (5)	8.45 ± .78 (2)	4.797	92	.031

TABLE 9
Phallometric Measures for Serial and Non-Serial Infantophiles

Variable	Serial Infantophiles (n)	Non-Serial Infantophiles (n)	t	df	p <
Pedophile Index	1.75 ± 1.82 (6)	1.24 ± 1.25 (5)	.532	9	.608
Rape Index	0.86 ± 0.69 (6)	0.33 ± 41 (8)	1.796	12	.098
Assault Index	0.28 ± 0.45 (6)	0.158 ± 0.33 (8)	.598	12	.564

TABLE 10
Previous Criminal Record of Serial and Non-Serial Infantophiles

Variable	Serial Infantophile (n)	Non-Serial Infantophile (n)	t	df	< p
Number of previous sexual offenses	0.50 ± 0.84 (6)	0 ± 0 (5)	1.324	9	.218
Number of previous violent offenses	0.83 ± 0.94 (6)	0 ± 0 (5)	1.878	9	.093
Number of previous criminal offenses	5.17 ± 3.82 (6)	0.40 ± 0.55 (5)	2.86	9	.023

CONCLUSION

Except for the studies carried out by the authors over the past 4 years, there are no other published data on these offenders. It has been assumed that these infantophile child molesters are a relatively small novel group. An important finding from our results indicate that this may not be true, as infantophiles are far more likely to deny their sexual offenses and thus escape detection. Furthermore, their victims are less verbal and therefore far less likely to report the sexual molestation. The majority of these offenders in our sample were acquaintances and therefore more likely to escape detection, as they have more access to infants than strangers. Successful arrest and conviction may prove equally difficult with infant preschool victims unless there is obvious trauma or overt detection by a responsible adult. They have many features similar to extrafamilial child molesters but tend to be younger, more often deny the offense, and have a higher Factor 2 PCL-R score. The differences between the serial infantophiles and the non-recidivistic group include a history of drug abuse, a higher Factor 2 PCL-R score, and a larger number of previous criminal offenses. The significance of the higher BPRS is unknown, but it would seem to suggest that the recidivists have more psychopathology. A limitation of investigating the serial vs. non-serial infantophiles is the relatively small number of subjects; therefore, some of these findings may be unreliable. Increased public awareness and electronic surveillance, such as daycare video monitoring, may in time shed more light on this under-researched group of child molesters.

REFERENCES

Abel, G.G., Blanchard, E.B., and Barlow, D.H. (1981). Measurement of sexual arousal in several paraphilias: the effects of stimulus modality, instructional set and stimulus content on the objective. *Behaviour Research on Therapy,* 19:25–33.

Abel, G.G., Gore, D.K., Holland, C.L., Camp, N., Becker, J.V., and Rathner, J. (1989). The measurement of cognitive distortions of child molesters. *Annals of Sex Research,* 2:135–152.

APA (1994). *Diagnostic and Statistic Manual of Mental Disorders,* 4th ed., rev. Washington, D.C.: American Psychiatric Association, 1994.

Brooks, P., Devine, M., Green, T., Hart, V., and Moore, M. (1988). Serial murder: a criminal justice response. *Police Chief,* 54:37–45.

Bradford, J.M. and Greenberg, D.M. (1998). Treatment of adult male sex offenders in a psychiatric setting. In Marshall, W.L., Hudson, S.M., Ward, T., and Fernandes, T.M. (Eds.), *Sourcebook of Treatment Programs for Sexual Offenders.* New York: Plenum Press.

Burt, M. (1980). Cultural myths and supports for rape. *Journal of Personality and Social Psychology,* 38:217–230.

Buss, A.H. and Durkee, A. (1957). An inventory for assessing different kinds of hostility. *Journal of Consulting and Clinical Psychology,* 21, 343–349.

Cupoli, J.M. and Sewell, P.M. (1988). 1049 children with a chief complaint of sexual abuse. *Child Abuse and Neglect,* 12:151–162.

Derogatis, L.R. (1978). *Derogatis Sexual Functioning Inventory.* Baltimore, MD: Clinical Psychometrics Research.

Dube, R. and Hebert, M. (1988). Sexual abuse of children under twelve years of age: a review of 511 cases. *Child Abuse and Neglect,* 12:321–330.

Firestone, P., Bradford, J.M., McCoy, M., Greenberg, D.M., Curry, S., and Larose, M.R. (1998). Recidivism in court referred rapists. *Journal of American Academy of Psychiatry and the Law,* 26(2):185–200.

Firestone, P., Bradford, J.M., Greenberg, D.M., and Larose, M.R. (1999a). Homicidal sex offenders: psychological, phallometric and diagnostic features. *Journal of the American Academy of Psychiatry and the Law,* 26(4):537–552.

Firestone, P., Bradford, J.M., Greenberg, D.M., McCoy, M., Larose, M., and Currie, S. (1999b). Prediction of recidivism in incest offenders. *Journal of Interpersonal Violence,* 14:511–531.

Firestone, P., Bradford, J.M., McCoy, M., Greenberg, D.M., Currie, S., and Larose, M. (2000) Prediction of recidivism in extrafamilial child molesters based on court related assessments. *Sexual Abuse: A Journal of Research and Treatment,* (in press).

Furby, L., Weinrott, M.R., and Blackshaw, L. (1989) Sex offender recidivism: a review. *Psychological Bulletin,* 105:3–30.

Geberth, V.J. (1986). Mass, serial and sensational homicides: the investigative perspective. *Bulletin of the New York Academy of Medicine,* 62:492–496.

Greenberg, D.M. (1998). Sexual recidivism of sex offenders. *Canadian Journal of Psychiatry,* 43:459–465.

Greenberg, D.M., Bradford, J.M., and Curry, S. (1995). Infantophilia — a new subcategory of pedophilia? A preliminary study. *Bulletin of the American Academy of Psychiatry and Law,* 23:63–71.

Guralnik, D.B., Ed. (1978). *Collins Concise English Dictionary.* Glasgow: William Collins Sons & Co.

Hanson, R.K. and Bussiére, M.T. (1998). Predicting relapse: a meta-analysis of sexual offender recidivism studies, *Journal of Consulting and Clinical Psychology,* 66:348–362.

Hare, R.D. (1991). *Manual for the Revised Psychopathy Checklist.* Toronto: Multi-Health Systems.

Kocsis, R.N. and Irwin, R.H.J. (1998). The psychological profile of serial offenders and redefinition of the misnomer of serial crime. *Psychiatry, Psychology and Law,* 5:197–213.

Loeber, R. and Dishion, T. (1983). Early predictors of male delinquency: a review. *Psychological Bulletin,* 94:68–99.

Overall, J.E. and Gorham, D.R. (1962). Brief Psychiatric Rating Scale. *Psychological Reports,* 10:799–812.

Pollock, N.L. and Hashmall, J.M. (1991). The excuses of child molesters. *Behavioral Science and the Law,* 9:53–59.

Proulx, J., Pellerin, B., Paradis, Y., McKibben, A., Eaubut, J., and Oumiet, M. (1997). Static and dynamic predictors of recidivism in sexual aggressors. *Sexual Abuse: A Journal of Research and Treatment,* 9:7–28.

Quinsey, V.L., Lalumiere, M., Rice, M.E., and Harris, G.T. (1995). Predicting sexual offenses. In Campbell, J.C. (Ed.), *Assessing Dangerousness: Violence by Sexual Offenders.* Thousand Oaks, CA: Sage.

Quinsey, V.L., Rice, M.E., and Harris, G.T. (1995). Actuarial prediction of sexual recidivism. *Journal of Interpersonal Violence,* 10:85–105.

Quinsey, V.L., Khanna, A., and Malcom, P.B. (1998). A retrospective evaluation of the Regional Treatment Centre Sex Offender Treatment Program. *Journal of Interpersonal Violence,* 13:621–644.

Ressler, R.K., Burgess, A., and Douglas, J.E. (1988). *Sexual Homicide: Patterns and Motives.* New York: Lexington Books.

Selzer, M.L. (1971). The Michigan Alcohol Screening Test: the quest for a new diagnostic instrument. *American Journal of Psychiatry,* 127:1653–1658.

Soothill, K.L., Jack, A., and Gibbens, T. (1976). Rape: 22-year cohort study. *Medicine, Science and the Law, 16*:62–69.

Tabachnick, B.G. and Fidell, L.S. (1991). Software for advanced ANOVA courses: a survey. *Psychological Issues in Radical Therapy International Journal,* 23:208–211.

Wilkes, G.A. and Krebs, W.A., Eds. (1992). *Collins English Dictionary,* 3rd ed. Sydney: Harper-Collins.

12 Cleric Serial Offenders: Clinical Characteristics and Treatment Approaches

Thomas W. Haywood and Jack Green

CONTENTS

The problem of cleric sexual misconduct has received attention from the news media (Berry, 1992; Ostling, 1991; Press, 1993) over the past several years. Cases of cleric sexual misconduct from the Roman Catholic Church are often sensationalized by the media, who have frequently reported on priests who are serial offenders and have stimulated public outrage with these glaring reports of cleric malfeasance. Clergy occupy positions of responsibility and trust and are expected to be moral leaders. In fact, clergy have been rated higher in caring, stability, interpersonal skills, and professionalism than both psychologists and psychiatrists (Schindler et al., 1987).

When victims of cleric sexual misconduct report the emotional trauma associated with being sexually abused by clergy, they often indicate that they have lost faith in the church and God as a result of this abuse (McLaughlin, 1994; Rossetti, 1995). Victims groups especially are calling for cleric accountability and for a responsible and pastoral response from the institutional church (Miller, 1991; Stiles, 1987). Thus, church authorities have directed considerable attention and resources to deal with the problem of cleric sexual misconduct. Berry (1992) estimates that the Catholic

Church alone has spent over $400 million in medical and legal fees as well as victim settlements over a 10-year period.

Sexual abuse of children is not a problem unique to the 20th century; in fact, there have been reports of child sexual abuse dating back to the time of ancient Greece and Rome. The Council of Elvira in 305 A.D. forbade molesters of boys from ever receiving communion (Quinn, 1989). St. Basil ordered strict punishments for monks who molested children (Payer, 1982) which included shorning of hair, smearing spit on the face, and public flogging. St. Basil's reprimands included binding in chains and imprisonment, fasting, prayers, and special supervision. Monks were not allowed to interact with youths in counseling or socially.

In this chapter, we review prevalence estimates of cleric sexual misconduct and discuss a variety of opinions relating to this problem. We also describe the institutional church's responses, policies, and procedures in dealing with allegations of cleric sexual misconduct. In addition, we review the research relating to cleric offense and victim characteristics, as well as cleric offender clinical characteristics. We also present case examples of cleric offenders who are dangerous serial offenders, and, finally, we discuss evaluation and treatment protocols for alleged cleric offenders and research necessary for development of prevention programs for cleric sexual misconduct.

Opinions relating to the extent of the problem of cleric sexual misconduct and church handling of the problem run the spectrum. Opinion polls indicate that 50 to 70% of the public feels the church is not handling the problem properly, is not solving the problem, is protecting its own image, and is even covering up ("Sexual abuse by priests?", 1993; Franklin, 1992). Similarly, victims groups claim the church often minimizes the extent of the problem and can be intimidating and harassing, even to the point of attacking victims and their families through countersuits and release of information to the press. Victims groups claim churches are not intervening effectively to control risk of cleric misconduct. In contrast, Jenkins (1996) claims that radical feminists, liberals, and anti-Catholic forces are distorting the extent of the problem to make it appear more widespread and heinous than it actually is. He describes victims as being motivated to exaggerate claims of damage to earn settlements for high-priced psychotherapy and hefty fees for court testimony.

Geoly (1999) reports that churches are actively given legal advise on what needs to be done to control risk among their clergy, including information about the basis for church legal liability, litigation and public relations strategy, the role of mental health professionals, church misconduct policies, and in-service training. Geoly (1999) also describes decisive and multi-level church responses to the problem of cleric misconduct, including removal of the cleric during investigations, a pastoral approach toward both alleged clergy and victim, deployment of parish response teams, and public relations strategies. Churches are developing more conservative policies, including dismissal from the clerical state, toward clergy involved in sexual misconduct to minimize victimization and to guard against church legal liability (National Catholic Conference of Bishops, 1995).

Recently, churches have spent considerable time and resources in establishing administrative guidelines for dealing with the problem of cleric sexual misconduct. Extensive analysis and reports relating to church procedures and mechanisms for handling allegations of cleric sexual misconduct have been developed and considered for implementation in both Catholic and Protestant churches (Australian Conference, 1996; Canadian Conference of Catholic Bishops, 1992; Dempsey et al., 1992; Hopkins, 1991; National Catholic Conference of Bishops, 1995). One report includes comprehensive multifactoral consideration of pastoral, legal, psychiatric, and psychological dimensions of alleged sexual misconduct for both the priest and the victim (Dempsey et al., 1992). Church policy and procedure guidelines for processing cases of sexual misconduct also include mention of church procedural mechanisms for screening of priests, continuing education of priests, and priest assignments (Dempsey et al., 1992); however, prevention programs for clergy have not been thoroughly developed or studied and are not being deployed on a regular basis.

PREVALENCE OF SEXUAL MISCONDUCT AMONG CLERGY

There are approximately 412,000 Jewish and Christian clergy, including 4000 rabbis, 55,000 Catholic priests, 255,000 Protestant pastors, and 100,000 Roman Catholic nuns, according to the U.S. Department of Labor (1992). Yet, data relating to prevalence of offensive behavior (or paraphilia disorder) among clergy are exceedingly scarce; hence, the scope of the problem of cleric sexual offending is somewhat unclear. Sipes (1990) estimates that 2 to 6% of priests are pedophiles or ephebophiles, and 20 to 40% of priests get involved in sexual misconduct with adults; however, Sipes (1990) made it clear that his estimates are not based on empirically verifiable data sources. Loftus and Camargo (1993) noted in an empirical study of clergy with psychiatric problems (n = 1322) that 8.4% of clergy indicated they had, or were reported as having, sexual difficulties with minors. In this same sample of clergy with psychiatric problems, 16% were noted to have sexual difficulties with women and 12% indicated having sexual difficulties with men. Estimates of prevalence of sexual misconduct among Protestant ministers involving sexual boundary violations with adults have ranged from 5.8 to 24%, depending on the report (Friel and Friel, 1988; Goetz, 1992; Seat et al., 1993). The variance in incidence and prevalence rates of cleric sexual misconduct is partly due to unreliable source data and, in part, to research design variability and limitations. For example, cleric offenders are known to more frequently deny and minimize problems, psychopathology, and offenses than noncleric offenders (Haywood et al., 1994b; Wasyliw et al., 1998).

The cleric and psychological professions have been noted to be similar in that both groups spend a significant amount of time counseling, with the average cleric estimated to spend 15% of their time in counseling activity (Weaver et al., 1997). Robinson (1994, 1999) described the cleric sexual abusing situation as similar to mental health professional sexual misconduct cases in that professional boundaries are crossed. Data are exceedingly scarce relating to a history of paraphilia disorder among clerics who have crossed professional boundaries. Abel (1988) reports that sexual deviates who cross one boundary of sexual deviance are likely to cross others. Warberg et al. (1996) reported that approximately 20% of professional sexual misconduct (PSM) cases were known to have histories of prior paraphilias. In another report, clerics were shown to be less likely to report multiparaphilic behaviors than noncleric alleged offenders (Kelly et al., 1991). However, clerics have also been shown to more frequently deny and minimize problems (Haywood et al, 1994; Wasyliw et al., 1998). Again, the true incidence and prevalence rates of sexual misconduct and paraphilia disorder among clergy are unclear.

OFFENSE AND VICTIM CHARACTERISTICS AMONG CLERIC PERPETRATORS

Loftus and Camargo (1993) noted that clerics were more likely to be involved in sexual misconduct with adults than minors. They found in a psychiatric population of 1322 priests and brothers that 27.8% had sexual relations with adult women or men, while 8.4% were involved with underage persons. Similarly, Robinson (1999) found, in an Australian sample of clergy, a 2:1 ratio of clergy sexual misconduct with adults vs. children. In Tables 1 and 2, we compare cleric to noncleric perpetrators and victim characteristics.

TABLE 1
Cleric Offenders Victim Characteristics

		Victim Age	
		<14	14–17
Research Study	n	(%)	(%)
Haywood et al. (1996a)	107		
Cleric child molesters	30	36	63
Noncleric incestuous	13	100	0
Noncleric extrafamilial	26	85	15
Loftus and Camargo (1993)	1322		
Cleric child molesters	111	32	68
Abel et al. (1988)	561		
Noncleric paraphiles	561	25	7
Bradford et al. (1992)	443		
Noncleric paraphiles	443	32	26

Clerics involved in child molestation are more likely than noncleric child molesters to molest adolescents and males (Abel, 1999; Abel et al., 1988; Bradford et al., 1992; Haywood et al., 1996a; Loftus and Camargo, 1993). Homosexual pedophiles are known to engage in more frequent paraphilic acts, have more victims, and more frequently recidivate than all other types of molesters of minors (Abel et al., 1987; Bradford et al., 1992; Furby et al., 1989; Hansen and Bussiere, 1998). Given that clerics' victims are often male minors and the way in which the media sensationalize coverage of cleric perpetrators, depicting them as having multiple victims, there ought to be heightened concern about this type of activity. However, both Haywood et al. (1996a) and Loftus and Camargo (1993) found that cleric offenders who come to the attention of authorities often present with having only

TABLE 2
Cleric Offenders Victim Characteristics

Research Study	n	Victim Gender	
		Girl (%)	Boy (%)
Haywood, et al. (1996a)	107		
Cleric child molesters	30	23	77
Noncleric incestuous	13	62	38
Noncleric extrafamilial	26	50	50
Loftus and Camargo (1993)	1322		
Cleric child molesters	111	4	96
Abel et al. (1998)	1363		
Prepubescents		42	15
Adolescents		26	10
Prepubescents, incest		35	9
Adolescents, incest		14	3
Bradford et al. (1992)	443		
Pedophiles		22	10
Ephebophiles		17	9

one or two minor victims (53%, and 30%, respectively). In addition, Kelly et al. (1991) reported that cleric offenders are less likely to engage in multiple paraphilic behaviors than noncleric offenders. However, these findings should be interpreted with caution, given the more frequent and pervasive denial demonstrated by clerics alleged to be involved in sexual misconduct (Haywood et al., 1994b; Wasyliw et al., 1998).

In summary, available data suggest unique offense and victim characteristic among cleric perpetrators. Clerics are more likely to engage in sexual misconduct with adults than minors. Of those involved with minors, the victims are more likely to be adolescent males. Cleric offenders are less likely than nonclerics to be serial offenders or to have multiple paraphilias.

CLINICAL AND PSYCHOSEXUAL CHARACTERISTICS

There is a paucity of research into cleric offender clinical characteristics. In a series of studies relating to denial, minimization, and cognitive distortions among sex offenders (Grossman et al. 1992; Haywood and Grossman, 1994; Haywood et al., 1993, 1994a,b; Wasyliw et al., 1994, 1998), cleric offenders have been noted to demonstrate unique patterns. Haywood et al. (1998) noted that cleric offenders are more likely to demonstrate extreme minimization of personal problems and to lack insight into personal problems than are noncleric sex offenders. Nonclerics were more likely to use cognitive distortions to rationalize and justify child molestation. Wasyliw et al. (1998) noted in a study of minimization among cleric and noncleric alleged offenders that clerics showed more extreme minimization on the MMPI than did nonclerics. In this sample of cleric and noncleric sex offenders, the Rorschach was found to be insensitive to minimization.

Haywood et al. (1996b) noted in a sample of cleric and noncleric admitted child molesters and cleric and noncleric normal controls a significant association between abuse in childhood and becoming a child molester for both clerics and noncleric; however, different psycho-etiologies of offending among cleric and noncleric offenders were suggested. On the MMPI, noncleric offenders, in comparison to cleric offenders, were noted to demonstrate more sociopathy and psychopathology in general, while clerics indicated more sexual conflictedness.

Haywood et al. (1996a) examined self-reported sexual functioning among cleric and noncleric alleged sex offenders. Clerics indicated lower sexual drive, fewer sexual experiences, and a more conservative attitude toward sex than normal controls. This was attributed, in part, to the unique training and socialization experience of clergy. Noncleric offenders demonstrated more significant sexual inadequacy than clerics when compared to normal controls. The need for normative data relating to psychosexual functioning among nonoffending clergy was highlighted.

A few studies have been conducted comparing clinical characteristics of clerics sexually involved with age-inappropriate persons to cleric patients who have not been sexually abusive. Loftus and Camargo (1993) researched a sample of 1322 clerics and examined clinical characteristics on the MMPI and WAIS in clerics involved with age-inappropriate persons in comparison to clerics involved in sexual abuse with adults and nonabusing cleric patients. They noted that clerics involved in sexual misconduct with minors were more shy, passive, and lonely than the other cleric psychiatric patients. In addition, clerics involved with minors (n = 117) were less anxious, less introverted, and less obsessive than the nonabusing cleric patients. In a second report based on the same patient population, Camargo (1997) found that clerics involved with minors demonstrate higher verbal scores and lower performance scores on the WAIS in comparison to other cleric patients. In addition, clerics involved with minors were described as being more passive and scored low in expressing anger. The significance of these results were qualified, and difficulties in developing sex offender taxonomies from psychological variables were highlighted. The Loftus and Camargo (1993) and Camargo (1997) studies were limited in that normal clergy and noncleric offender comparison groups were not included.

Plante et al. (1996) studied a sample of 80 clerics involved in sexual misconduct with minors and 80 nonabusing cleric patients and compared cleric clinical characteristics on the MMPI-2 and the WAIS-R. Similar to Camargo (1997), they found that verbal IQs were higher for clerics who abused minors than for the other clerics, although this was related to age of the priests. Over-controlled hostility (O-H) was the most significant differentiator between clerics who abused minors and the nonoffending clerics. The Plante et al. (1996) study was limited in that clerics with substance abuse problems were excluded from the sample. Importantly, in the main finding relating to hostility scores, they did not consider that self-reported hostility inventories have been found to be influenced by minimization (Wasyliw et al., 1994).

The following are two case examples of cleric offending behavior, evaluation, and treatment outcome.

CASE 1

Fr. A was a developer and supervisor of youth programs for 7th and 8th grade junior high students. Approximately every 6 weeks, Fr. A would take the youth camping. Fr. A coordinated campsite sleeping arrangements, which put him in frequent and close contact with the children at the campsite. As the coordinator of these camping trips, on more than one occasion Fr. A planned a shortage of sleeping bags or mattresses. He would then use this situation to share sleeping accommodations with the youths at bedtime. He would have a few drinks before bed and then snuggle in with the youngsters. When the children were asleep, he would fondle their genitals and masturbate himself. The young men he would bunk with were not special friends and he would not extend a special relationship with them after the camping event. Other activities on these same camping trips were also sexual in nature. Fr. A would routinely have the boys swim naked in the campsite lake, and he would often play-wrestle with the boys but not actually touch their genitals. Fr. A did this on several camping trips and molested dozens of young boys.

Fr. A would sometimes bring young men from one of the youth groups to a trailer that he kept in a rural area. The youths would sleep in tents around the trailer, and in the evening, before going to bed, Fr. A would tell stories, one of which was an especially frightening story about camping. If one of the boys was afraid at bedtime, he was allowed to sleep in the trailer with Fr. A. Again, when the boys were asleep, Fr. A would masturbate the boys and himself.

Fr. A also had his own van with a number of interesting devices, such as a radar detector, a compact disc player, a refrigerator, and so on. He would cruise around and lure teenage boys that interested him into his vehicle. They would express interest in his devices, and he would take them out to dinner. He would bring the boys back to his van and eventually proposition them for sexual contact.

Fr. A stopped the camping trips because he feared his sexual behaviors would get him in trouble. He also began therapy for his feelings of depression and anxiety. Five years after disengaging from youth group activities, one of the young men came forth with complaints, and the diocese vicar required Fr. A to undergo psychiatric evaluation. In the course of psychiatric assessment, Fr. A was fully cooperative. On psychological testing, he was noted to be emotionally guarded, and he denied emotional difficulties and psychological problems. He attempted to present himself as psychologically healthy, controlled, and competent. Based on testing results, it was found that Fr. A guarded and restricted his feelings through intellectualization. It was concluded that Fr. A may be vulnerable to impulses or needs which he poorly understood, and that his guardedness could lead to problems in judgment in unstructured, emotionally challenging situations. Further interviewing and review of treatment records indicated that Fr. A had shown limited insight into himself, that he was chronically depressed and anxious, and that he used alcohol to cope with his loneliness and feelings of depression and anxiety.

It was recommended Fr. A not have contact with minors, that he live in a structured setting, and that he continue in individual and group treatment and with monitoring of alcohol use. Fr. A determined that the priesthood was what he wanted no matter the assignments. Fr. A was a skilled mechanic and had janitorial experience, thus he was able to gain and maintain employment within the church. As part of a cognitive restructuring approach to treatment, a number of rules had to be set up to prevent his sexual acting out. These included selling his trailer and compliance with the treatment schedule. He had to check in by phone twice daily and complete weekly psychosexual inventories and weekly group and individual therapy sessions. In cognitive behavioral therapy, it became clear that Fr. A lacked the original learning associated with inhibiting his sexual behaviors with minors. He grew up with an absent father and his mother was very lenient. Fr. A adjusted well in that he cooperated with all archdiocese requirements.

Case 2

In his first assignment as an ordained priest 10 years ago, Fr. B became sexually involved with a 13-year-old he was counseling. He masturbated this boy, as well as another youngster in the parish. Fr. B took a third boy to a movie and tried to touch him, but this boy reported Fr. B to the diocese chancellor office. Fr. B was called in to see the bishop and was soon transferred to another parish.

Fr. B was stationed at the second parish for 2 years. There he got involved with six high school boys, individually, not as a group. Activities included masturbation and performing oral sex on them, but these incidents were not reported. For unrelated reasons, Fr. B was transferred to another parish, where he stayed 3 years. He was involved sexually with some of the 7th and 8th grade boys with whom he had contact as basketball coach. The individual sexual contacts involved masturbation, oral sex, and, in one case, sodomy (the boy inquired about sodomy and indicated he would like to have it done). These incidents were reported, and the bishop was informed. Fr. B at first denied it, but later admitted to all of it.

Fr. B was again transferred to a different parish. In this re-assignment, he got too close to a family and molested two of the children. The younger boy was in 8th grade, and the touching involved masturbation and, on a couple of occasions, oral sex and sodomy. While Fr. B was watching television one night at the family's house, the 16-year-old sister came home after the parents had gone to bed. She had been drinking and approached Fr. B. They had intercourse.

Shortly after, Fr. B began to follow the counsel of his confessor and refrained from sexual contact with minors for the next few years; however, when Fr. B was considering a transfer to another parish, he was ordered to undergo psychiatric evaluation due to new diocesan-mandated policies and procedures. Fr. B denied having inappropriate sexual activities with minors over the previous few years. He did admit to sexual contact with an adult woman he had been counseling, which included sexual intercourse on a couple of occasions. He also admitted to contacts with adult males in bookstores on several occasions.

In the course of psychiatric evaluation, Fr. B denied that alcohol or stress had anything to do with his sexual behaviors. He also denied being depressed or that his actions were related to feeling depressed. Fr. B did express significant cognitive distortions in the interview and on questionnaires. He indicated he thought he was showing the children love and an expression of affection when he had sexual contact with them. Fr. B stated that the boys sometimes encouraged sexual activity and that he was interested in the children's sexual growth and development.

Psychological testing revealed that Fr. B strongly minimized emotional and characterological problems and had a marked tendency for intellectualization and denial. Testing also indicated that Fr. B had limited resources for coping with stresses and frustration and that he was emotionally fragile and needy. Fr. B was noted to be emotionally immature with strong needs for attention, affection, and acceptance. He tended to be dramatic, exhibitionistic, and attention seeking and was at risk for impulsive, inappropriate actions and judgments.

Fr. B was given a diagnosis of paraphilia NOS: ephebophilia and dependent personality disorder. It was recommended that he enter into cognitive behavioral therapy on a weekly basis which would include monitoring of all sexual activities and fantasies. Pharmacologic therapy with Depo-Provera® was also recommended.

In the course of therapy with Depo-Provera®, Fr. B's testosterone levels were lowered and he consistently reported having a low sex drive and infrequent sexual thoughts and fantasies. He was transferred to a community situation where he lived with adults and had no contact with children. Fr. B was noted to be easy to work with, candid, and almost childlike. Past problem behaviors were reviewed, and Fr. B began to recognize his pattern of using poor judgment and developed strategies to avoid those situations.

EVALUATION AND TREATMENT PROTOCOLS FOR CLERIC OFFENDERS

EVALUATION PROTOCOLS

Thorough evaluation of cleric sex offenders should include interview, objective and projective personality testing, assessment of cognitive distortions, sexual preference profiling, sexual history, and polygraph. The MMPI-2, the Millon-2, and the 16PF are well researched instruments for assessment of personality and psychopathology and have special scales for identifying minimization of personal problems and psychopathology, which are of special relevance for clergy. Projective testing may be especially indicated because of its resilience to minimization effects (Wasyliw et al., 1996). Evaluation of cleric offenders should include assessment of cognitive distortions that sex offenders commonly use, such as the Abel-Becker cognition scales or the rationalizations and cognitive distortion indices on the MSI.

Sexual preference profiling is also an important dimension to assess, either with the Abel assessment of sexual interest or phallometry. Sexual preference profiling is important because cleric offenders, like other offenders, may attempt to conceal their deviant interest or may not appreciate the scope of their deviant propensities. However, church personnel working with the mental health agency may have high moral sensitivity to use of sexually explicit stimuli with their priests and may favor use of the Abel assessment rather than phallometry. The Abel assessment is a less intrusive testing procedure than phallometry and is less sexually explicit. Clinicians may argue for testing with phallometry if priests are willing to give informed consent. More research is necessary to clarify whether visual reaction time techniques or phallometry are more efficient at identifying deviant sexual interest (Haywood et al., 1999). Sexual history questionnaires should also be administered, although clerics are likely to give a minimized self-report of deviant sexual interest. Polygraph may be especially indicated because of the high level of denial noted among cleric alleged offenders.

TREATMENT OF CLERIC OFFENDERS

Data relating to treatment of cleric offenders are also scarce. A number of reports describe various conceptual and psychoanalytical therapeutic approaches based on clinician observations from working with the cleric population (Blanchard, 1991; Hopkins, 1991; Laasar 1991; Muse and Chase 1993; Steinke 1989). One study describes policies and procedures relating to establishing a treatment program and church/treatment provider relationship (Kelly, 1998). Camargo (1999) described a comprehensive inpatient treatment approach which included pharmacologic, psychotherapeutic, physical therapy, and spirituality components. Warberg et al. (1996) described a cognitive behavioral approach to treating clergy.

Green (1999) described unique aspects of cognitive behavioral treatment of clergy and the "being a person" (BAP) paradigm used at the Isaac Ray Center's Sexual Behaviors outpatient clinic. Clinicians described clerics as demonstrating naiveté and a sense of entitlement. In the course of treatment of clergy, it became apparent that seminary training usually failed to address the most basic human interaction scenarios and the possibilities of what could go wrong. A recurring theme that therapists encountered was the almost *ad lib* component the priests utilized in dealing with others.

The BAP treatment paradigm is based on a cognitive behavioral and relapse prevention theory of treatment and includes a list of over 100 items to alter the nature of patient beliefs and actions (see Figure 1). The list provides a basic set of formulae that assist the therapist and the patient in reviewing what has been learned, what needs to be learned, and how to deal with people in a social setting. Many of these items allow therapists to identify behaviors that are missing from a functionally adequate repertoire. The BAP list is also useful in identifying the interactional content that an individual requires to communicate and problem solve in complex social interactions. Learning is operationally defined as a reasonably permanent change in response potentiality based on information and practice. The BAP utilization effects new learning.

In Table 3 we detail 12 items used in the treatment of Fr. A and Fr. B. All of these items were selected from the BAP list (Figure 1). Items selected were based on the individual's belief system and the individual's personality (items 1, 2, 3, 6, 8, and12 for Fr. A; items 2, 4, 5, 7, 8, 10, 12 for Fr. B). It was decided to use these items for these individuals because they represented aspects of social learning not imparted by their family or not learned from personal experience in each case.

Green (1999) described further unique aspects of treating clergy. He notes the clinical efficacy of using learning schemas commonly utilized in treating developmentally disabled when used with the cleric population. Both developmentally disabled patients and cleric offenders had problems with internal repertoire in that

Happy
Coping
Proactive
Self-Actualizing
Organized

Level of responsibility commensurate with our cognitive skills
Capacity to function "as if you're being scrutinized"
Job   Capacity to be functionally selfish
Friends   Ability to utilize what is in your repertoire
Family   Awareness that the organism strives for "action"
Energy   Capacity to accept second best alternatives
Empathy   Ability to put theories into practice
Sexuality   Sense of what constitutes closure
Credentials   Ability to listen and be receptive
Judgment   Deal with functional frustration
Appearance   Positive (realistic) concept of self
Information   Ability to alter behavior as required by shifting scenarios
A conscience   Ability to create and sustain relationships
Memberships   Ability to recognize and factor out self-limiting behaviors
Mobility   Awareness of an Rx having constructed our own lifestyle
Impulse control   Remove from others the ability to control your emotions
Ethnic awareness   Awareness of how to reduce drives in acceptable ways
Ability to change   Ability to utilize leisure time to re-energize
Ability to network   Ability to recognize the rights of others
Sense of reality   Ability to identify and utilize resources
Anger management skills   Access to things (and awareness of how they work)
Sense of identity   Positive milieu out of which to operate
Sense of integrity   Awareness of domain (one's own space)
Ability to communicate   Ability to relate to others
Sense of humor   Ability to factor out errors/mistakes
Sense of history   Recognize superstitious learning
Ability to take risk   Recognize cause and effect
Ability to start over   Ability to deal with unfairness
Ability to listen   Ability to establish hierarchies
Ability to keep contracts   Awareness of successive approximation
Ability to delay gratification   Ability to be flexible
Ability to construct strategies   Re-establish homeostasis ↑↓
Ability to recognize deficits   Ability to be managed
Ability to establish perspective   Ability to be mobile
Good physical and emotional health   Ability to request assistance
Ability to get and utilize money   Ability to celebrate
Awareness of *quid pro quo*   Positive perception (capacity for)
Awareness of how the world works   Ability to relax
Ability to operate within time frames   Ability to negotiate
Ability to compromise without feeling defeat   Ability to forgive
Ability to review the results of past behaviors   Sense of spirituality
Capacity to shift paradigms   Sense of limits
Ability to recover   Sense of reciprocity
Sense of "possibility"   Sense of proportion
Ability to get what you want   Sense of how the body works
Ability to create novelty in your life   Ability to shut up
Ability to sustain commitment   Ability to review
Ability to live like this is it   Ability to control anger
Awareness of moral, legal, and ethical responsibilities   Memory
Ability to know that "our thoughts create our world"   Capacity to be
Awareness of our "quality of interactions with others"   selfish
Awareness of the "standard to which we are held"   Capacity for
Awareness of having some autonomy, "not being stuck"   loyalty
Awareness of "what the rules are"

Disorganized
In conflict
Unhappy
Disabled
Reactive

FIGURE 1. BAP treatment paradigm.

TABLE 3
Sample of Being a Person (BAP) Items Used in Treating Priests

1. Empathy
2. Sexuality
3. A conscience
4. An ability to listen
5. Ability to objectively review one's past behavior
6. Ability to deal with functional frustration
7. Ability to create and sustain positive relationships
8. To remove from others the ability to control your emotions
9. Ability to recognize the rights of others
10. Awareness of domain (one's own and other)
11. The ability to request assistance
12. The ability to recognize rationalizations

it often did not include a sufficient inhibition component to regulate their sexual actions. Treatment intervention involved utilizing the red-light/green-light paradigm (Figure 2). The red-light/green-light concept or function is based on the assumption that an individual has not learned sufficient internalized rules of order to prevent an urge from becoming an aberrant action. The concept teaches simplifying the judgment process to the universal and simple language of the red-light/green-light paradigm. A red-light situation may be a child asking an unrelated adult to pull up his underwear after going to the washroom. The decision should be a verbal response such as, "I'll go get your brother or mother to help you." The red-light/green-light paradigm introduces a simplified judgment and decision process to avoid aberrant behaviors.

Among developmentally disabled patients, a 95% improvement in response efficiency is not uncommon. Among priests, red-light situations may include being within 40 inches of youth, having physical contact with parishioners, engaging in suggestive conversation with youth, and planning one-to-one encounters where boundaries could be crossed with either adults or youth. We view this procedure as "externalizing the cue system" rather than relying on one's own internalized system of behavioral cues. The red-light/green-light paradigm can also be applied to thoughts for a more proactive approach to avoiding abusive behavior. Hence, cognitive behavioral reprogramming can be effective treatment intervention to prevent further abusive behavior.

SUMMARY

Sexual abuse by clergy is egregious behavior that has stimulated public outrage. True prevalence of cleric misconduct is unknown. Research indicates that clerics tend to be involved in misconduct with adults more often than minors, and when abuse involves minors the victims are most likely to be adolescent males. Preliminary

Thoughts → Urges → Offensive Actions → Consequences

Proactive approaches

Thoughts → Consequences → Diminished Urges

FIGURE 2. Red-light/green-light paradigm.

data suggest that clerics are less likely than noncleric sex offenders to be serial offenders or have multiple paraphilias. The data available from evaluation and treatment of clergy, though sparse, could provide information for better prevention strategies within the churches.

REFERENCES

Abel, G.G., Becker, J.V., Mittleman, M., Cunningham-Rathner, J. Rouleau, J.L., and Murphy, W. (1987). Self-reported sex crimes of nonincarcerated paraphiliacs. *Journal of Interpersonal Violence,* 2:3–25.

Abel, G.G., Becker, J.V., Mittleman, M., Cunningham-Rathner, J., and Rouleau, J.L. (1988). Multiple paraphilic diagnosis among sex offenders. *Bulletin of the American Academy Psychiatry Law,* 16:153–168.

Abel, G.G. (1999). The Assessment and Treatment of Child Molesters, presented at the 30th Annual Meeting of the American Academy of Psychiatry and Law, October14–17, Baltimore, MD.

Australian Catholic Bishops' Conference and the Australian Conference of Leaders of Religious Institutes (1996). *Towards Healing.* Melborne: National Capital Printing.

Australian Catholic Bishops' Conference & the Australian Conference of Leaders of Religious Institutes (1997). *Integrity in Ministry.* Melborne: National Capital Printing.

Berry, J. (1992). *Lead Us Not into Temptation: Catholic Priests and the Sexual Abuse of Children.* New York: Doubleday.

Blanchard, G.T. (1991). Sexually abusive clergymen: a conceptual framework for intervention and recovery. *Pastoral Psychology,* 38:237–246.

Bradford, J., Boulet J., and Pawlak A. (1992). The paraphilias: a multiplicity of deviant behaviors. *Canadian Journal of Psychiatry,* 37:104–108.

Camargo, R.J. (1997) Factor, cluster, and discriminant analyses of data on sexually active clergy: the molesters of youth identified. *American Journal of Forensic Psychology,* 15:5–24.

Camargo, R.J. (1999). Residential Treatment of Sex Offending Clergy at the Southdown Institute, paper presented at the 18th Annual Meeting of the Association for the Treatment of Sexual Abusers, September 22–25, Lake Buena Vista, FL.

Canadian Conference of Catholic Bishops (1992). *From Pain to Hope: Report on the Ad Hoc Committee on Child Sexual Abuse.* Ottawa: Author.

Dempsey, J.Q., Gorman, J.R., Madden, J.P., and Spilly, A.P. (1992). *The Cardinals Commission on Clerical Sexual Misconduct with Minors,* report to Cardinal Bernardin Archdiocese of Chicago.

Franklin, F.L. (1992). Catholics fault church on handling of sex charges. *The Boston Globe,* July 26, pp. 1, 8.

Friel, J. and Friel, L. (1988). *Adult Children.* Deerfield Beach, FL: Health Communications, Inc.

Furby, L. Weinrott, M.B., and Blackshaw, L. (1989). Sex offender recidivism: a review. *Psychological Bulletin,* 105:3–30.

Geoly, J. (1999). Cleric Sexual Misconduct: Legal Liability and Church Responses, paper presented at the 18th Annual Meeting of the Association for the Treatment of Sexual Abusers, September 22–25, Lake Buena Vista, FL.

Geotz, D. (1992). Is the pastor's family safe at home? *Leadership,* 13(4):38–44.

Green, J. (1999). Unique Aspects of Cognitive Behavioral Treatment, paper presented at the 18th Annual Meeting of the Association for the Treatment of Sexual Abusers, September 22–25, Lake Buena Vista, FL.

Grossman, L.S., Haywood, T.W., and Wasyliw, O.E. (1992). The evaluation of truthfulness in alleged sex offenders' self reports: 16PF and MMPI validity scales. *Journal of Personality Assessment,* 59:264–275.

Hansen K. and Brussiere, M.T. (1998). Predicting relapse: a meta-analysis. *Journal of Consulting and Clinical Psychology,* 66:348–362.

Haywood, T.W. and Grossman L.S. (1994). Denial of deviant sexual arousal and psychopathology in child molesters. *Behavior Therapy,* 25:327–340.

Haywood, T.W., Grossman, L.S., and Hardy, D. (1993). Assessment of denial and personality in psychiatric evaluations of sex offenders. *Journal of Nervous and Mental Disease,* 181:183–188.

Haywood, T.W., Grossman, L.S., Kravitz, H.M., and Wasyliw, O.E. (1994a). Profiling psychological distortion in alleged child molesters. *Psychological Reports,* 75:915–927.

Haywood, T.W., Hardy, D.W., Kravitz, H.M., and Cavanaugh, J.L. (1994b). Cleric Misconduct with Minors: Minimization and Self-Reported Sexual Functioning, paper presented at the Annual Meeting of the Association for the Treatment of Sexual Abuser, November, San Francisco, CA.

Haywood, T.W., Kravitz, H.M., Grossman, L.S., Wasyliw, O.E., and Hardy, D.W. (1996a). Psychological aspects of sexual functioning among cleric and noncleric alleged sex offenders. *Child Abuse & Neglect,* 20:527–536.

Haywood, T.W., Kravitz, H.M., Wasyliw, O.E., Goldberg, J., and Cavanaugh, J.L. (1996b). Cycle of abuse and psychopathology in cleric and noncleric molesters of children and adolescence. *Child Abuse & Neglect,* 20:1223–1243.

Haywood, T.W., Liles, S., and Kravitz, H.M. (1998). Minimization and Cognitive Distortion in Cleric and Noncleric Alleged Child Molesters, paper presented at the 18th Annual Meeting of the Association for the Treatment of Sexual Abusers, Oct., Vancouver, B.C.

Haywood, T.W., Kravitz, H.M., and Cavanaugh, J.L. (1999). Profiling Sexual Deviance VRT and PPG Technologies, paper presented at the 30th Annual Meeting of the American Academy of Psychiatry and Law, October 14–17, Baltimore, MD.

Hopkins, N.M. (1991). Congregational intervention when the pastor has committed sexual misconduct. *Pastoral Psychology,* 39:247–255.

Jenkins, P. (1996). *Pedophiles and Priests: Anatomy of a Contemporary Crisis.* Oxford: Oxford University Press.

Kelly, A.F. (1998). Clergy offenders. In Marshall, W.L., Fernandez, Y.M., and Ward, T. (Eds.), *Sourcebook of Treatment Programs for Sexual Offenders.* New York: Plenum Press.

Kelly, J., Cavanaugh, J.L., Liles, S., Serritella, J., and Goedert, R. (1991). *Clergy and Sexual Misconduct: Clinical, Legal, and Divine Intervention,* Scientific Proceeding of the Annual Meeting of the American Academy of Psychiatry and Law, October 17–20, Lake Buena Vista, FL.

Laaser, M.R. (1991). Sexual addiction and clergy. *Pastoral Psychology,* 39:213–235.

Loftus J. and Camargo, R. (1993). Treating the clergy. *Annals of Sex Research,* 6:287–303.

McLaughlin, B.R. (1994). Devastated spirituality: the impact of childhood sexual abuse on the survivor's relationship with God and the church. *Sexual Addiction and Compulsivity: The Journal of Treatment and Prevention,* 1:145–158.

Miller, J. (1991). *Pedophilia in the Priesthood: A Church in Crisis,* unpublished manuscript. Victims of Clergy Abuse Linkup (VOCAL).

Muse, S. and Chase E. (1993). Healing the wounded healers: "soul" food for clergy. *Journal of Psychology and Christianity,* 12:141–150.

National Catholic Conference of Bishops (1995). *Canonical Delicts Involving Sexual Misconduct and Dismissal from the Clerical State,* Washington, D.C.:Author.

Ostling, R.N. (1991) Sins of the fathers. *Time,* August 19, p. 15.

Payer, P.J. (1982). *Book of Gomorrah: An Eleventh Century Treatise Against Clerical Homosexual Practices.* Waterloo: Wilfried Laurer University Press.

Plante, T.G., Manuel, G., and Bryant, C. (1996). Personality and cognitive functioning among hospitalized sexual offending Roman Catholic priests. *Pastoral Psychology,* 45:129–139.

Press, A. et al. (1993). Priests and abuse. *Newsweek,* August 16, pp. 42–43.

Quinn, P.A. (1989). *Better Than the Sons of Kings.* New York: Peter Lang Publishing.

Robinson, E.A., Greer, J.M., Estadt, B., and Thompson, G. (1994). *Shadows of the Lantern Bearers: A Study of Sexually Troubled Clergy.* Ann Arbor, MI: UMI Dissertation Services.

Robinson, T., Taylor, G., and Watson, D. (1999). Clinical Trends Noticed in a Group of Australian Clergy Who Committed Sexual Boundary Violations Against Children or Adults in Their Care, paper presented at the 18th Annual Meeting of the Association for the Treatment of Sexual Abusers, September 22–25, Lake Buena Vista, FL.

Rossetti, S.J. (1995). The impact of child sexual abuse on attitudes toward God and the Catholic Church. *Child Abuse & Neglect,* 19:1469–1481.

Schindler, F., Berren, M.R., Hannah, M.T., Beigal, A., and Santiago, J.M. (1987). How the public perceives psychiatrists, psychologists, nonpsychiatric physicians, and members of the clergy. *Professional Psychology: Research and Practice,* 18:371–376.

Seat, J. Trent, J., and Kim J. (1993). The prevalence and contributing factors of sexual misconduct among Southern Baptist pastors in six southern states. *Journal of Pastoral Care,* 47(4):363–372.

Sexual abuse by priests? (1993) *Emerging Trends,* 15(18):5.

Sipes, R. (1990). *A Secret World: Sexuality and the Search for Celibacy.* New York: Bruner/Mazel Publishers.

Steinke, P.L. (1989). Clergy affairs. *Journal of Psychology and Christianity,* 8:56–62.

Stiles, H. (1987). *Assault on Innocence.* Albuquerque, NM: B&K Publishers.

U.S. Department of Labor (1992). *Occupational Outlook Handbook.* Washington, D.C.: Bureau of Labor Statistics.

Warberg, B.W., Abel, G.G., and Osborn, C. (1996). Cognitive behavioral treatment for professional sexual misconduct among the clergy. *Pastoral Psychology,* 45:49–63.

Wasyliw, O.E., Grossman, L.S., and Haywood, T.W. (1994). Denial of hostility and psychopathology among alleged child molesters. *Journal of Personality Assessment,* 63:185–190.

Wasyliw, O.E., Haywood, T.W., and Grossman, L.S. (1995). *Denial in Priests Accused of Sex Offenses,* Scientific Proceeding of the Annual Meeting of the American Academy of Psychiatry and Law, October 17–20, Lake Buena Vista, FL.

Wasyliw, O.E., Benn, A.F., Grossman, L.S., and Haywood, T.W. (1998). Detection of minimization of psychopathology on the Rorschach in cleric and noncleric alleged sex offenders. *Assessment,* 5(4):389–397.

Weaver, A.J., Samford, J.A., Kline, A.E. Lucas, L.A., Larson, D.B., and Koenig, H.G. (1997). What do psychologists know about working with the clergy? An analysis of eight APA journals: 1991–1994. *Professional Psychology, Research and Practice,* 28:471–474.

13 Female Serial Offenders

A.J. Cooper

CONTENTS

0-8493-2236-7/00/$0.00+$.50
© 2000 by CRC Press LLC

Females committing serial crimes (e.g., sexual murder and other criminal activities) is not new but remains uncommon, probably underestimated, and clearly underreported. As a corollary, information on these women is sparse and of uneven quality and comes from widely disparate sources. For example, reports of various cases often come from sketchy biographies of notorious women murderers, often based on dubious historical writings, while more recent cases are of greater journalistic accuracy and enhanced detail. Systematic controlled studies on this population and objective replicated data relating to causation, typologies, motives, assessment, and treatment are mostly lacking — an omission that is becoming increasingly evident as female serial offenders apparently proliferate and (possibly) become more violent (Hickey, 1997).

In addition to a dearth of quality data, the definition of "serial" is problematic. The FBI has designated a male "serial rapist" as an individual who has ravished 10 or more women and a "serial killer" as having perpetrated three or more homicides with at least a 30-day interval between each (Hazelwood et al., 1993); the term has not otherwise been delineated. In this chapter, following the FBI's numerical precedent, a female killer will be identified as "serial" if she has killed at least three victims, although the 30-day interregnum (the FBI's second criterion) will be waived to increase the database. For other types of criminal behaviors, "serial" is defined more diversely as chronic, driven, recalcitrant, persistent, and (re)-offending, regardless of the number of victims (which would be viewed by a probable majority of experts in the field as representing an extreme along a continuum of the behavior in question). Thus, a woman who molests a single child repeatedly over months or years is considered to be a "serial offender," as is one who molests several children if only on a single occasion. Of course, some females, depending on the circumstance, may abuse a particular child once and another several times. As more research information accrues, it may well be that there is merit (treatment and prognostic implications) in subdividing female child molesters into single vs. multiple victim dichotomies. However, currently there is insufficient support for such a distinction.

This chapter relies heavily on detailed single-case histories presented from various points of view, as well as a handful of more formal psychosocial and forensic investigations on groups of female offenders. However, the cumulative information, being derived from diverse populations, often precludes generalizations or conclusions. Despite the aforementioned limitations, the author hopes to stimulate interest in a subject that, until now, has been largely ignored, at least by serious researchers. The female serial offender may finally be coming of age. This chapter deals with sexual offenders, murderers, psychopathy, recalcitrance, assessment, and treatment.

FEMALE CHILD MOLESTERS

As it becomes dismayingly more clear that females can and do molest children, more cases are being reported; however, the number of offenses is low — between 5 and 8% of the total (Dubé and Hébert, 1988; Green and Kaplin, 1994; Thomlinson et al., 1991; Wakefield and Underwager, 1991). Women abuse children of both sexes but recent information suggests that girls are targeted more often (Faller, 1987; Rudin et al., 1995). The victims may range in age from babyhood to adolescence, but no age is immune (Margolin, 1991; Rudin et al., 1995). Offenders may be arbitrarily divided into juvenile and adult types (Hunter and Matthews, 1997).

JUVENILE OFFENDERS

Matthews et al. (1997) found that over half of 67 young female sex offenders had more than one victim, with some having ten; 25% of these offenders had engaged in intercourse (vaginal and/or anal) and nearly one half in oral sexual behaviors, while 20% admitted to using "force" during the commission of their crimes.

Psychopathology

Matthews et al. (1997) observed that approximately 50% of their sample of juvenile female offenders displayed generalized emotional and behavioral disturbances. Individual and family psychopathology and dysfunction were rife. Many of these youthful perpetrators manifested significant levels of anxiety and depression, and some were diagnosed as suffering from post-traumatic stress disorder (PTSD). Other workers (Hunter et al., 1993) not only found a high incidence of PTSD in residentially treated juvenile female sex offenders but also high levels of homicidal ideation and affective disturbances. The group studied by Matthews et al. (1997) significantly abused drugs, and approximately 50% had a history of suicidal preoccupation or attempts. Many of these youthful offenders demonstrated nonsexual antisocial decorum, including chronic lying, petty theft, and physical assault.

Etiology

These female juveniles often exhibited prolonged histories of maltreatment and/or exposure to interpersonal violence. For instance, Fehrenbach and Monastersky (1988) elicited evidence of prior sexual abuse in 50% of their sample of adolescent female sex offenders and previous physical abuse in 20%. Knopp and Lackey (1987), who studied both prepubescent and adolescent females, noted early sexual victimization in almost all. Matthews et al. (1997) found a similar history of sexual exploitation in a majority of their subjects. They also observed that these girls tended to be younger than juvenile male sex offenders when first victimized, and more often coercive force was used against them.

Johnson (1993) noted that all of the sexually aggressive young females with whom she worked had been molested, and that they generally seemed anxious and confused about their sexuality. Johnson opined that such offenders act out sexually and aggressively as a means of reducing the painful emotions which they repeatedly experience as a result of their own trauma. However, other workers (Gill and Johnson, 1992; Johnson, 1993; Yates, 1991) found that some sexually victimized children exhibited precocious signs of erotic interest; a number became aroused by physical closeness or emotional intimacy regardless of the age and sex of the other person.

Matthews et al. (1997) delineated a small group of more highly disturbed female adolescent perpetrators who were deviant in their sexual fantasies and arousal patterns. The majority of these girls reported extensive early sexual activities, during which they had become highly aroused. Hunter et al. (1993) also found that deviant sexual fantasizing before they acted out was common. A case previously reported by Cooper et al. (1990) details a young woman who was both a victim of sexual abuse and a hypersexual child molester. She displayed many of the features reported by Matthews et al. (1997), Gill and Johnson (1992), Johnson (1993), and Yates (1991). The girl acted alone and was not suffering from a psychosis during the commission of her multiple offenses. In addition to a detailed clinical evaluation, she undertook psychometric, endocrinologic, electroencephalographic, and vaginal photoplethysmographic testing. It was considered that a multi-measure protocol, of a type similar to that employed in male sex offenders, might generate useful data, with possible etiologic treatment and prognostic implications.

CASE EXAMPLE

Ms. K. was an unmarried, Caucasian, 20-year-old who was referred for a pre-trial examination, having been charged with sexually assaulting two sisters ages 4 and 5 years. Molestation had occurred repeatedly over several months during babysitting. Abusive acts included slapping the children, inserting pencils and other objects into their vaginas, and performing oral sex on them. During these activities, Ms. K. usually felt angry towards the victims, although not always. She had become increasingly preoccupied with violent sexual fantasies involving the children and was fearful that she might act these out. She also acknowledged fondling several other young boys and girls during the previous 2 to 3 years, also while babysitting; however, these incidents did not come to police attention.

Developmental History

Ms. K. was the youngest of four children and the only daughter. She was born six weeks premature, weighing 5 pounds, 6 ounces, and required blood transfusions secondary to a Rhesus factor incompatibility. As a preschooler, she had frequent temper tantrums which she attributed to parental overprotection and lack of consistent discipline. The family had moved often, and the children were not encouraged to socialize outside the home. Her school grades were generally good, despite the many relocations. She had few friends during her childhood. She reached puberty at age 12.

Sexual History

Ms. K. alleged that she was repeatedly raped by a maternal uncle from the time she was 3 years old. He was later imprisoned for molesting his own child. When she was 12, her 14-year-old brother began to engage her in a variety of sexual activities. These included mutual genital fondling, oral genital stimulation, and, later, sexual intercourse. On the one hand, she viewed this involvement as "morally wrong," but at the same time she derived considerable emotional and physical pleasure from it. She recognized that she had intense sexual cravings. When she was 14, her second older brother also began sexually exploiting her but in a much more aggressive manner. They began to experiment with sado-masochistic practices such as bondage, which she found particularly exhilarating. Her sexual fantasies became increasingly more violent. The abuse by her brothers continued until she left home at 17. Ms. K. admitted to initiating manual-genital and oral-genital stimulation with a dog and a cat, both male family pets, during her childhood. Sex with animals was a recurring fantasy for her.

Significant Medical and Psychiatric History

At the age of 15, Ms. K. was diagnosed as suffering from grand mal epilepsy; however, as a result of recent, more extensive evaluations (including serial waking-and-sleeping EEGs over 2 years), this diagnosis was revised to "hysterical seizures." Ms. K. had an extensive psychiatric history. Since early adolescence, she had experienced frequent depression with suicidal ideation. She had attended many crisis centers, usually following suicidal gestures, and had been twice hospitalized.

Clinical Assessment

She presented as a mixed personality disorder with borderline and sociopathic features, multiple paraphilias (notably pedophilia, sexual sadism, and zoophilia, with hypersexuality and somatization disorder). Her most prominent complaints were continuous preoccupation with violent sexual fantasies involving adults and children of both sexes, plus unremitting sexual tension and prolonged compulsive masturbation.

Psychometric Testing

Ms. K. completed the Wechsler Adult Intelligence Scale-Revised (WAIS-R), the MMPI, the Derogatis Sexual Functioning Inventory (DSFI), and the Luria Nebraska Neuropsychological Battery (LNNB). On the WAIS-R, she scored in the average range of intelligence (verbal IQ = 96; performance IQ = 88; full-scale IQ = 92). There was no suggestion of defective memory or attention, although some slight impairment of visual-motor coordination was evident. All of her scores on the LNNB were within the normal range. However, consistent with findings in the WAIS-R, she exhibited some mild difficulties in motor coordination and rhythm. Overall, neither of these tests elicited evidence of significant cerebral dysfunction.

The MMPI showed several markedly elevated clinical scales indicating depression, anxiety, somatic preoccupation, chronic hostility and resentment, social alienation, and isolation. Individuals manifesting this type of profile are typically naive, immature, and eccentric, with poor impulse controls. They also tend to be distrustful, sensitive, and emotionally labile, with inner conflicts about sexuality and dependency, plus deep feelings of insecurity and inadequacy and an exaggerated need for affection and attention. They often respond to stress with increased somatic preoccupation or withdrawal into fantasy and daydreams.

The Derogatis Sexual Function Inventory (Derogatis, 1980; Derogatis et al., 1981) revealed limited sexual knowledge, low self-esteem, negative and conservative attitudes towards sex, and extreme dissatisfaction with her physical appearance (body image). Coupled with a high sex drive and an extremely high sexual fantasy score, these findings suggested an individual obsessively preoccupied with sex.

Sexual Arousal Studies

Arousal studies were conducted in a standard sexual laboratory using the vaginal photoplethysmograph (Henson et al., 1979; Morokoff and Heiman, 1980; Wincze et al., 1976) and a Gras Model 8 polygraph. The system allows four arousal-dependent measures: vaginal blood volume (VBV), vaginal pulse rate (VPR), vaginal pulse amplitude (VPA), and response duration. Ms. K. was shown a battery of sexual slides comprising nude males and females of different ages, plus adults and children engaging in a variety of sexual activities. The essential slide contents and order of presentation are depicted in Figure 1. Testing began after 5 minutes of baseline recording during which there was minimal fluctuation (baseline = 0 cm of pen deflection; see Figure 1). Each slide was displayed for 30 seconds, and the interval between successive stimuli was as long as it took for Ms. K. to return to baseline. The peak responses (centimeters of pen deflection) occurring during the presentation of each slide and in the 30 seconds immediately following (post-stimulus response) are seen in Figure 1.

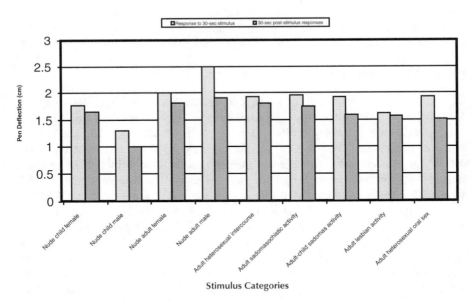

FIGURE 1. Peak vaginal pulse amplitude (VPA) to erotic slides. (From Cooper, A.J. et al. (1990). *Canadian Journal of Psychiatry*, 35:334–337. With permission.)

There were some early difficulties with movement artifacts. Nevertheless, Ms. K. showed substantial levels of undifferentiated "physiological sexual arousal" (e.g., up to 2.5 cm of pen deflection to an adult nude male). This was consistent with both her subjective experiences reported continuously throughout the testing and her admitted sexual fantasies. During the evaluation, Ms. K. frequently responded to the point of orgasm. Overall, the data suggested polymorphous eroticism with sadistic, masochistic, and pedophiliac elements, in addition to considerable hostility and aggression. The findings were congruent with Ms. K.'s earlier and current sexual predilections and behaviors. Ms. K. admitted feeling anger toward the models in some of the slides. She observed that this enhanced, rather than diminished, her subjective sexual pleasure.

A word of caution on plethysmography: this non-routine procedure is contentious, even when employed on male sex offenders from which virtually all the research data are derived (Barker and Howell, 1992; Simon and Schouten, 1991). The possibility of false-positive, false-negative, and other confounding elements may seriously compromise the test's diagnostic and predictive power. Plethysmography has been used infrequently in females (Henson and Reuben, 1979; Morokoff and Heiman, 1980; Winczeet al., 1979). Not only are normative data lacking, but the methodology is more problematic, and interpretation of the findings more difficult. Despite the aforementioned limitations, plethysmography is possibly the most promising objective approach in defining an offender's sexual responsiveness and preferences (children vs. adults, same sex vs. opposite sex, violent vs. nonviolent sex, etc.). Together with detailed clinical, psychometric, and historical data (e.g., an established and clear history of repeated sexual offenses against children, admission of sexual urges towards children or strong presumptive evidence of such, confirmed use of child pornography, etc.), test results may support (correlate with) a diagnosis of pedophilia or other paraphilias. Clearly, further work with this potentially informative tool is necessary before it can confidently be included in a "standard" sex-offender assessment of either gender.

Endocrine Studies

Serum levels of testosterone, progesterone, 17 B-estradiol, follicle stimulating hormone, Latinizing hormone, and prolactin were assayed on four occasions during her hospitalization. Thyroid function was assessed twice. All of the results were within the normal range.

Comment

Why some females such Ms. K. develop into recalcitrant serial sex offenders is incompletely understood but is likely the result of several overlapping elements including polygenetic predisposition, biological (e.g., deviant hypersexuality, the genesis of which is also unknown), and serendipitous or premeditated psychological factors (e.g., a multiplicity of vicissitudinous life experiences), or imitation. And, if the immediate and subsequent consequences of the particular sexual activity are predominantly positive (immediate sexual gratification, dominating/controlling a victim, later masturbating while fantasizing a prior experience vs. feelings of guilt, fear of detection, punishment, etc.), then it may become entrenched, cyclical, and potentially life-long. Typically with increasing age, as the strength of the sex drive wanes, the behavior becomes overtly less aggressive. In Ms. K's case, factors could not be unequivocally identified and weighted commensurably; however, it is reasonable to suggest that the extensive sexual abuse at the hands of family members when she was a young and susceptible child resulted in precocious sexual conditioning which later became deviant as she was exposed to sado-masochistic and other types of stimulation. Thus, by early adolescence, her extensive childhood sexual experiences had become fixated as paraphilias, and her dominant sociopathic traits, notably the absence of guilt and empathy, made it possible for Ms. K. to continue, with apparent equanimity, to offend against young children until apprehended.

ADULT OFFENDERS

The literature on adult female serial child molesters is scant and pales in comparison to available data for adult males. Although there are certain similarities between men and women who commit these types of sexual crimes, Matthews et al. (1994) point to significant differences. For instance, females are less likely to use force and are not as frequently involved with the criminal justice system as are their male counterparts. Moreover, almost twice as many men as women have criminal records for other offenses. It is imputed that because of a number of cultural and biological factors — notably, social modeling, genetic, and hormonal differences — males are more likely to be aggressive and psychopathic, thereby perpetrating more crimes and accruing more charges and convictions. Despite the heterogeneity of the population, for the purposes of description, three main categories have been proposed (Hunter and Matthews, 1998), although overlap may occur. It is not yet known whether such a classification has etiological or prognostic implications: (1) women who co-offend with a male, (2) women who sexually molest teenaged boys, and (3) women who sexually molest prepubescent children of both sexes.

Although a rudimentary attempt has been made to subdivide female child molesters into a number of categories, there is overlap, and the genesis of ostensibly similar offending behaviors (especially motivation) may vary across cases. For instance, one woman may be driven by powerful aberrant urges; another may transgress primarily because an age-appropriate sexual partner (an adult) is not available, and a third may offend out of revenge. Because many other factors may come into play, each case must be evaluated holistically to foster understanding and to optimize management.

Females Who Assault with an Adult Male

The victim is usually a family member, friend, or acquaintance, rarely a stranger. The male accomplice is typically a husband or boyfriend (Faller, 1987; Kaufman et al., 1995; O'Connor, 1987; Solomon, 1992). The molestation is generally initiated by the male, who is more often the dominant partner; often the woman is passive and emotionally dependent on him. At first, she may participate reluctantly out of fear of being left by him and/or otherwise threatened or beaten into compliance. As the behavior becomes entrenched, she may be able to rationalize ego-dystonic feelings of guilt and shame and become more sanguine in her role, even deriving a measure of sexual/emotional gratification. Many of these women have longstanding insecurity, and low self-esteem, are socially isolated, and are often poorly educated. A significant proportion of them report having been sexually abused during childhood, either within or outside the nuclear family. In a minority of cases, the woman assumes a more aggressive role. She may procure victims for her mate and actively engage in the abuse (Green and Kaplin, 1994). These offenders may be viewed as co-equal with the male. Such partnerships are potentially more dangerous than those in which the woman is largely passive.

Case Example

A serial female sexual offender, without a previous criminal record, and her male companion were caught just in time before they murdered. Apparently copying the notorious Canadian killers of two school-girls, 38-year-old James Bennett and 20-year-old Crystal Hendricks used drugs and physical force to subdue their numerous victims, ranging in age from 3 to 17 years (which included family, friends, acquaintances, and teenage prostitutes). Hendricks pled not guilty, maintaining that she had been under Bennett's control; however, after 5 days of deliberation, a jury found her culpable on several counts of sexual assault, administering a stupefying drug, and making child pornography.

Acting on a number of tips late in the summer of 1997, the police traced Bennett's previous spouse, Deborah, who, fearing for her life, had moved to Idaho. Deborah admitted that in 1994 she and her (then) husband had drugged and sexually assaulted Crystal Hendricks, who was 15 at the time. Soon, however, Hendricks became Bennett's favorite sexual partner, and Deborah, apprehensive that her husband might kill her, preemptively left him, taking along videotapes of the sexual assault on Hendricks. Deborah reasoned that she could use these to keep Bennett at bay if he ever decided to harass her.

Based on the information furnished by Bennett's ex-wife, the police obtained a warrant to search Bennett's and Hendrick's trailer. They found it was outfitted with hidden cameras and a variety of paraphernalia for use in sadistic sexual practice. They also discovered extensive notes and descriptions of the couple's activities and future plans, as well as videotapes depicting the victimization of at least 22 young persons, mostly female, many of whom had been incapacitated by sedative drugs. One tape featured Hendricks having sex with a dog.

Hendricks, who took the stand in her own defense, told the Court that she had been a childhood victim of sexual abuse. She had been raped at the age of 5 by one of her mother's boyfriends and later molested by another. She claimed that she had fallen totally under Bennett's control and became his sex slave. Hendricks insisted that she did not know the tapes even existed and claimed amnesia for the events recorded on them; however, she had kept a diary detailing the couple's activities which was introduced as evidence. The minutiae were graphic and included two scripts for pornographic movies. The plots revolved around the forcible kidnapping of a 10- to 15-year-old girl who was to be raped and tortured, then "finished off." This material contrasted starkly with Hendricks' insistence that her actions were those of an automaton, under the domination of Bennett, who master-minded the project. Hendricks and Bennett were both found guilty and face lengthy prison terms.

Women Who Sexually Molest Teenage Boys

These women are generally less disturbed in a conventional psychological sense. They often hold positions of trust (e.g., teachers), have more intact egos, and may be relatively functional. Their sexual acting out may be related to dissatisfaction or failure in an adult relationship or marriage. They may be attracted physically and psychologically to a teenager. He is likely to be initially flattered and, as she becomes overtly seductive, the couple "fall in love" and the relationship becomes intimate. There appears to be strong physical and emotional rewards for both individuals, and usually the liaison is characterized as consensual. A number of these women are apparently immature, being sensitive to rejection and dependent. They find it easier to relate to younger persons who may be more malleable.

There are several instances of an infatuated woman deliberately becoming pregnant by her teenage lover, conjecturally to strengthen her hold over him by boosting his ego. If the woman is charged with a sexual offense and ordered not to associate with the youth, she may ignore the proscription. Some couples may flee a jurisdiction in an attempt to stay together. However, other motives have been invoked for the sexual exploitation of teenage boys by adult women, including "revenge." O'Connor (1987) described the case of mature female who repeatedly had sex with a 13-year-old unrelated boy as retaliation against her unfaithful husband.

Sarrel and Masters (1982) provide an example of incestuous mother-son abuse which apparently impaired the son's adult sexual performance. He was unable to consummate his marriage for 3 years. The son was an only child whose parents divorced when he was 2 years old. He did not recall ever seeing his father. His mother began playing with his genitals when he was 13; shortly after, he experienced his first nocturnal emission. Within a few months, the genital play progressed to fellatio and then intercourse. Sexual interaction continued at his mother's instigation several times a week until he left for college. Although he never initiated sex, he always responded to her overtures. He was completely devoted and especially enjoyed her "obvious pleasure" during their sexual activities; this was more important to him than his own satisfaction.

In his first year at college, he failed to achieve an erection during an initial sexual opportunity with a girl of his own age. He was suffused with guilt at the thought of being "unfaithful" to his mother. When at home during vacations, he continued to be sexually active with her until she died in his senior year. He was "devastated," and when he resumed dating, he was unable to maintain an erection. After several failures, he began to feel that his "sex life" had ended with the death of his mother. Sarrel and Masters (1982) do not comment on putative psychiatric diagnoses or psychopathology in either the mother or son; however, the narrative description minimally suggests pathologic co-dependency but within a grossly uneven relationship: the mother being dominant, controlling, and exploitive; the son seemingly passive and compliant. Neither had been deterred by society's supposed incest taboo. Only the mother's death brought the sexual relationship to an end.

WOMEN WHO SEXUALLY MOLEST
PREPUBESCENT CHILDREN OF BOTH SEXES

Like adolescent serial offenders, adult women who molest prepubescent children of both sexes tend to be pervasively dysfunctional and to have been physically and sexually abused themselves by caregivers from an early age (Allen, 1991; Faller, 1988). Their sexual acting-out has been characterized as compulsive, often with a strong deviant theme. Matthews et al. (1989) opined that this population cognitively distorts the meaning of their sexual transgressions in a similar manner to that seen in adult male offenders. They may continue to recidivate even if apprehended and charged with a criminal offense. Neither punishment nor treatment may deter them.

FEMALE SERIAL EXHIBITIONISM

Genital exposure, which is among the most common of sexual offenses in men, is disproportionately rare in women. Thus, in England, between 1975 and 1984, of the 21,217 cases of indecent exposure recorded in criminal statistics, only two women were convicted and neither was jailed. One case, a 21-year-old single woman of borderline intelligence, had started to strip in public places, partly to impress and seek the admiration of a group of newly acquired friends. Subsequently, the behavior became more frequent and it was often accompanied by exhibitionistic masturbation. She had several admissions to a psychiatric hospital for drug overdosing and short-lived depressions, and she had served four short prison sentences for theft and threatening behavior. Despite being brought before the Court several times for her indecent exposures, she was never imprisoned (O'Connor, 1982). Another case was a 40-year-old separated woman of West Indian origin. On three consecutive days, she was arrested for "outraging public decency." She called at people's houses and asked to use the telephone. When admitted, she took all her clothes off and asked the man of the house to have sex with her. On the fourth day, she exposed her breasts in public and held them close to a young boy who was passing with his mother. This woman had a long history of recurrent hypomanic episodes, which seemed temporally related to her sexually disinhibitory conduct. The Court recognized that she was mentally ill and discharged her for psychiatric treatment (O'Connor, 1987).

A much more interesting case, psychopathologically, was described by Grobe (1985). A 43-year-old divorced woman presented to the psychiatric clinic complaining that she was losing control over her life. She had been dismissed, approximately 2 years before, from a prominent position in a male-dominated profession in which she had received much adulation. Unfortunately, she had not been able to obtain similar employment and became depressed with feelings of hopelessness. She had become emotionally entangled with a male co-worker. This relationship involved marathon erotic activities of such intensity that she felt she was disintegrating; sometimes she had experienced up to 50 orgasms in a single night. Unhappily, the liaison was unsatisfactory in all other respects. She became increasingly aware that she was being exploited sexually which further reduced her self-esteem.

Immediately following the onset of this relationship, she began to engage in exhibitionistic behaviors. At times she sunbathed in the nude, comporting herself so she could be observed. Subsequently, she started to drive on the highway in search of large trucks. If there were no other cars in the vicinity, she would disrobe, revealing her breasts to the male driver, and then if the evoked response was appreciative, exposing her genitals. During these displays she experienced "marked sexual arousal" and "occasional orgasms." She also began to feel much better about herself. Subsequently, she became bolder and began to take burgeoning risks. She would spend up to 30 minutes with a particular truck, playing cat-and-mouse exhibitionistic teasing games before suddenly turning off on an exit ramp where trucks were not permitted. Over a weekend, to satisfy her urge, she might drive up to 600 miles.

During analysis, Grob interpreted that his patient's exhibitionistic proclivities were based on early fragmented development and emotional deprivation, including maternal loss and a manipulative, rejecting father which resulted in an enhanced need for attention and narcissistic gratification. Initially, this was satisfied by public recognition of a successful professional career; however, after being dismissed, she developed exhibitionistic behavior with addiction-like power, in an attempt to satisfy her need for acclaim. Grob also intimates that she sought to frustrate and control her male audience with her particular method of exhibitionism as a possible outlet for her anger, envy, and frustrated identification with men. After many months of psychoanalytic support, her exposures became less frequent but did not stop entirely. She was never apprehended.

The putative motives compelling this woman's behavior, seem similar to those that may be inferred in males, although the genesis of the urge to expose (e.g., distant and proximal causes) may differ in detail (e.g., inherent gender dissimilarities; different family, interpersonal dynamics, personality structure, etc.). Paralleling male exposures, other possible motives in females might include misanthropy (e.g., hatred and/or contempt for men), a need to be in control, a wish to insult, an amorphous sense of exhilaration (e.g., roller-coasting), or an ambiguous sexual invitation (in some males, genital exposure has culminated in consensual sexual activity with the targeted woman). Additionally, the individual's *modus operandi* (e.g., characteristics of the victims, method of exhibitionism, preferred location, and other idiosyncrasies) may reflect important personality variables. These might have treatment and prognostic implications if a particular individual seeks help. Detailed case analysis (Grob, 1985) can be invaluable in unraveling the complexities of what, on the face of it, would seem to be inexplicable and extraordinary behavior.

FEMALE SERIAL KILLERS

Women who murder serially (defined as killing three or more victims) are not a new phenomenon; however, according to U.S. data, since 1950 there has been a marked escalation in their numbers. In part, this may be due to increasing public awareness that, contrary to cultural stereotypes, women can and do kill multiple victims. As well, there might be a higher percentage of criminal apprehension because of greater forensic knowledge and more sophisticated investigative methods, including DNA typing. Notwithstanding the aforementioned, it has been intimated that the figures may reflect a real increase in female-perpetrated multicide. And, some authorities who embrace this proposition have further conjectured that it could be due to a powerful women's liberation movement which, since the mid-1970s, has increasingly championed female emancipation and empowerment in various domains (Adler, 1975; Demming, 1977). Others have dismissed this opinion as being unestablished and alarmist (Chapman, 1980; Schur, 1984; Weisheit, 1984).

The current empirical data are insufficient to support a link between feminism and criminality. Further, the number of women who kill multiple victims is relatively few in comparison to men who do so. However, there is no doubt that in some respects female serial killers are becoming more like their male counterparts. Thus, there has been an increasing tendency for women to kill strangers, using methods that are inherently more violent (e.g., shooting, bludgeoning, stabbing). Females who kill serially may either have an accomplice (usually a dominant male initiator) or act alone, often in a subtle and surreptitious manner so that the victim remains oblivious to the end. The preferred *modus operandi* of female perpetrators, who act singly, is poisoning. FBI data (1975–1999) reveal that 26 women dispatched an estimated range of 173 to 214 victims for an average of 7 to 9 per perpetrator. Most of the females were in their early 30s and went on killing for several years until detected.

Victim Selection

Consistent with the heterogeneity of the genre, victims are also miscellaneous; however, the majority are family members. Females demonstrate a proclivity toward age-specific groups of victims. For instance, nurses or other healthcare professionals, working in a pediatric unit of a hospital, focus on babies or young children undergoing treatment, while a healthcare worker employed in a nursing home would choose old and frail individuals. In both cases, the victims are vulnerable and unsuspecting.

"Place-specific" offenders are responsible for a disproportionate number of serial killings. Typically, these are perpetrated in hospitals, nursing homes, and private residences — locations that would simply not be conceived as high risk. It may only be after several "unexpected" similar deaths over months or years that the authorities incredulously begin to think the unthinkable and launch an investigation. These women are the "quiet killers" who, early in their careers, are quintessentially careful. They behave in an exemplary manner so as not to attract attention. However, emboldened by their success at avoiding detection and, with a burgeoning sense of ego-boosting invincibility, they begin to take more chances, kill one time too many, and are caught.

Typologies, Motives, and Psychopathology

An analysis of 400 cases suggests that male serial murderers may be subdivided into four main types, although there is some overlap (Holmes and deBurger, 1985). A similar taxonomy has been proposed for females; however, because the latter are few in number, this classification should be viewed as tentative. As more data accumulate, it may require modification.

Comfort Killers

The inferred motive for this type of killer is material gain (money, property, jewelry, etc.). The victims are usually family members and close acquaintances. Mostly these individuals literally wish to make a "financial killing" and, after a "decent interval" to allow for any police or family suspicion to abate, move on to the next victim. These crimes are carefully planned and completed with such finesse that the victim may not appreciate what is happening. The most common vehicle is poison. Despite the increased availability of potentially lethal pharmaceuticals and other substances (e.g., potassium chloride, muscle-relaxants, insulin, etc.), arsenic remains the first choice. It may be administered insidiously over a long period of time, producing a variety of gastrointestinal and neurological symptoms, the significance of which is rarely recognized, or it may be given acutely as a single, fatal dose.

On psychological evaluation, comfort killers may show relatively little psychopathology and are usually not psychotic; however, given their history of repeated homicides and other antisocial behaviors, most women would probably satisfy DSM-IV criteria for personality disorders of an antisocial or mixed type. Medico-legally, the available information suggests that the majority of comfort killers would be judged as culpable for their actions. Accordingly, they would be disposed of as per the criminal code of a specific jurisdiction.

Visionary Killers

In contrast to comfort killers, subjects comprising this group are more obviously mentally ill. Clinical and behavioral analyses suggest that the majority of them display features of a major psychiatric disorder, notably schizophrenia and/or a drug psychosis. These women are often impelled to kill by command, auditory hallucinations fueled by paranoid ideation. They may attack perfect strangers impulsively, without apparent reason. The motivation is intrinsic to the psychosis. For example, Priscilla Ford claimed to have heard the voice of God exhorting her to kill certain people who were "evil" and therefore deserving of death. These auditory directives also told her how to recognize a target. She killed without compunction several innocent individuals. It was recognized that she suffered from a psychosis; nevertheless, she was convicted and condemned to death.

Another visionary killer was Lillian Edwards, who suffered from manic depression. In December, 1940, she was released from a California State Hospital on a month's home leave. During Lillian's hospitalization, her husband had employed a housekeeper to take care of the couple's three children. She would remain overnight when his job as a salesman took him out of town. Unfortunately, due to an apparent misunderstanding, the housekeeper left the children alone with Lillian. After bathing them and putting them to bed, Lillian strangled her 9-year-old daughter, 6-year-old son, and 11-month old daughter with bed sheets. When examined subsequently, she claimed no recollection for the murders. She insisted that a big black car had come to the house and a man and a woman dressed in white got out and took the children away to operate on them. Lillian Edwards was found to be insane and was returned to the same hospital from which she had been released less than one month before.

Finally, some psychotically depressed mothers, driven by delusions and hallucinations, may murder their entire families to "save them from the evils and
hypocrisy of this life." In their deranged thinking, they are sending them to heaven
and eternal bliss. These unfortunate women are generally recognized as being
mentally ill and not criminally responsible. They are often sent to psychiatric
hospitals for treatment.

Hedonistic Killers

Hedonistic female serial killers, although few in number, are principally motivated
by overwhelming deviant sexual urges. Carol Bundy was alleged to have killed a
male and several young female prostitutes. She also assisted her male accomplice,
Douglas Clark, to abduct and decapitate victims. The heads were often used for
deviant sexual acts. Behavioral analyses of their crimes pointed to the importance
of sexual sadism as a motivating force.

Another lethal hedonistic partnership was that of the Canadian killers, Paul
Bernardo and Carla Homolka. Bernardo was probably a serial rapist, although he
was never apprehended before he enlisted Homolka and turned to murder. They first
caused the death of Homolka's younger sister while sexually assaulting her. Later,
the couple abducted, imprisoned, raped, tortured, and finally killed two teenage girls,
recording the details on videotape for their subsequent pornographic pleasure. They
completed their gruesome work by dismembering the bodies and disposing of the
parts in different locations to mislead the police. Fortunately, Bernardo and Homolka
were caught before they killed again, which would have been inevitable.

Although details of the extensive psychological and physiological assessments
are not generally available, and Homolka dissimulated in an attempt to save her own
skin, trial and historical data suggest that initially Bernardo was the dominant partner
and that Homolka was infatuated with him. However, later, as their conduct escalated
to include sexual torture and murder, it appears that Homolka assumed a much more
significant role; indeed, on some occasions, she may well have been the instigator
and the main perpetrator. The paraphilias, as defined in the DMS-IV, generally apply
to males, but sufficient information emerged during the couple's trial to suggest that
both of them would have satisfied current criteria for sexual sadism.

A Bernardo-Homolka type of synergistic partnership is to be sharply distinguished from a scenario in which a male psychopathic sexual sadist compels a
"brain-washed" woman, such as a wife, an acquaintance, or even a kidnapped victim,
to assist in the abduction, torture, and murder of other women. This phenomenon
has been comprehensively described by Hazelwood et al. (1993). Seven females,
who were "transformed" by a systematic program of physical, emotional, and sexual
abuse into being the compliant appendages of their sexually sadistic partners, were
evaluated. Three of them had been married to sexual sadists for between 2 and 13
years; the other four had dated sadists exclusively for between 3 and 18 months. All
women were victimized sadistically by the men. As children, four of these women
were abused sexually, two were abused physically, and six were psychologically
traumatized. None of them reported previous knowledge of sadomasochism. All had
low self-esteem. One attractive victim confided that she let herself be seduced

because she could not believe that the sadist found her physically appealing. All berated themselves for "being so stupid." They could neither accept nor comprehend that they had been manipulated to such a degree by the men. All the women suffered physical mistreatment during their relationship with their sadistic partners. They reported being frequently beaten with fists and blunt objects. One woman reported that her boyfriend kept her in captivity for three days, during which she was bound in adhesive tape. Other forms of abuse included whippings, being burned, and having their nipples and labia painfully clamped.

All the women were sexually traumatized by their partners. Three victims were violently penetrated by large foreign objects. Anal insertion was favored over vaginal. Forced fellatio was reported by all women. The men particularly relished ejaculating on their bodies or into their mouths. Some of the females were compelled to have sex with others, two were raped by friends of the sadist while he watched, and one was forced to engage in various sexual acts with another woman who had been kidnapped by her husband. The sexual sadists were described by their partners as insatiable, with sexual exploitation dominating their lives.

Several women were forced to write and sign articles of slavery. Some were compelled to describe, in minutiae, various degrading sexual activities while they were taking place; yet others were cajoled by the men to plead for sexual or physical mistreatment which was then cynically inflicted. The women were constantly verbally harangued and demeaned by their sexually sadistic partners. They were kept in a permanent cowed and fearful state. In all cases, these women went through a similar process of transformation from relatively normal patterns of living to relating to bizarre, destructive, and dangerous forms of exploitation and perversion.

Hazelwood et al. (1993) hypothesized that male sexual sadists can intuitively identify a naive, vulnerable woman who they then systematically manipulate into compliantly submitting to their dominance and sexual perversity. These authors believe that sadistic men have previously attempted such activities unsuccessfully with other women. The researchers also imply that the sadists' behaviors reflect malignant male chauvinism, with all women ultimately being typed as "bitches and whores." The men tend to select "nice" middle-class females who have never before been exposed to aberrant sexual practices. The sadists are zealously committed to transforming these "nice" women into humiliated victims.

Initially, the sadists are charming, considerate, unselfish, and attentive to their partner's needs, relating to them in a romantic, seductive manner; however, once they have manipulated the women into total dependency, they begin to shape their partner's sexual conduct to satisfy their own brutal and deviant needs. Typically, sexual sadists alternatively coax and coerce the women to engage in a range of sexual behaviors, way beyond their prior experiences or even what they could imagine — notably, being forced to perform fellatio, often to the point where they gag or vomit, or submitting to bondage and anal intercourse and allowing themselves to be vaginally and anally penetrated with foreign objects. Typically, the sadists film these sadomasochistic activities for their subsequent pornographic titillation. The women are required to watch these demeaning rituals, which also serves to remind them that their sole purpose in living is to submit to the sadist's every whim. Once the sadists have molded the women to their specific narcissistic requirements, they ensure total surrender by isolating them from other than a few, carefully selected deviant friends.

Punishment is an essential ingredient in the process that allows sexual sadists to control and dominate their women. In addition to the already mentioned range of physical and mental tortures that sadists inflict on their victims, the latter may also be forced into participating in serial criminal activities, including torture, rape, and murder of other women. Despite the fact that these hapless individuals have been "transformed" by "brainwashing" from decent human beings to "compliant appendages," if apprehended as a co-offender, they have usually been deemed to be legally culpable, although they may receive shorter sentences because of their subordinate role to that of the dominant male.

Power Serial Killers

These women, who often work as nurses or health-aides in hospitals or nursing homes, are motivated by the potential "power" they wield over the lives of children, the aged, and others incapacitated by sickness who have no alternative but to put their trust in the caregiver's hands. Terry Rachels, a registered nurse, was indicted in 1986 on six counts of murder and 20 counts of aggravated assault. It was alleged that she killed six patients in the surgical intensive care unit of the hospital where she worked by injecting them with potassium chloride. The victims ranged in age from 3 to 89 years. Nurse Rachels had been employed at the hospital since 1981; she had an unblemished record and was considered to be an excellent surgical intensive-care specialist. She had no previous criminal record, was married with children, and was an active church-goer. One month after the last victim died (February 11, 1986), she confessed to the police that she had injected five of the patients with a potentially lethal substance, three of whom later died. Subsequently she recanted, stating that the intensity of the interrogation had confused her.

She underwent a comprehensive forensic psychiatric evaluation and was found fit to stand trial. In Court, defense counsel argued that she had been sexually abused as a child by her stepfather and had later developed a dissociative personality disorder that rendered her susceptible to "fugue-type states" during which she did things that she could not subsequently remember. However, the Court-appointed psychologist, while agreeing that Ms. Rachels suffered from a personality disorder, insisted that she knew the difference between right and wrong. The Court found her guilty of administering potassium chloride to an 89-year-old, thereby causing his death. She was sentenced to 17 years imprisonment, but because of recently introduced judicial guidelines was paroled after serving only 24 months. Thereafter, she was managed as an outpatient at a women's correctional institute.

Disciple Serial Killers

These, extremely few in number, are less understood than other types of female murderers. They apparently kill on the personal whim of a charismatic and narcissistic male, who selects not only the victim but also the manner of death. Typically these women are somewhat confused and dissatisfied with their lives. They eschew a conventional lifestyle that lauds career, the acquisition of wealth, and a respect for tradition. They seek an alternative and are enticed into communes, families, or cults. They tend to be extremely suggestible and are easily molded by the leader into obedient minions, only too willing to execute his every wish. They hope thereby to attract favored attention and be rewarded.

Women in these "families" may vie to be chosen by the dominant male for sexual and/or procreative purposes, which is especially valued. The women have no sense that they are being manipulated or misused. Some of these "families" have a pseudo-religious flavor; however, it is the male leader, not the Almighty, who demands to be worshipped and followed without question. The male leader controls the destiny of his disciples. Although these female followers may be considered to have undergone a type of "brain-washing," this is not the same as that inflicted on the female collaborators of the sexual sadists described previously, whose hold on their female partners is based more on "fear and punishment" than out of desire to win approval and be preferred over other potential consorts. A recent infamous example of disciple killing involve the female followers of Charles Manson. Leslie Van Houten and others willingly butchered victims at Manson's command. They claimed to be in a state of ecstasy during the slayings, which were particularly brutal.

ATYPICAL FEMALE SERIAL MURDERER

Finally, a description of an atypical serial female killer is warranted. Aileen Carol Wuornos apparently murdered for a number of overlapping motives, including hatred of men, revenge, sexual sadism, and robbery. Aileen was born in Michigan to a 16-year-old girl and a 19-year-old handyman. The marriage ended prematurely, and later her father was imprisoned for kidnapping, rape, and other crimes; he eventually committed suicide while in jail. Aileen claimed that she was raped at age 13 and became pregnant; subsequently, her child was placed in an adoptive family. At the age of 15, Wuornos took to the streets and earned money from prostitution and importuning. She dropped out of school after being warned by the authorities about her misuse of street drugs. She stated she was raped and beaten many times as a teenager. At 25, she was convicted of robbery and served 14 months of a 3-year sentence. She was disruptive in jail and was frequently disciplined. Approximately one year after being released, the bisexual Aileen had a lesbian relationship which ended when her partner, without warning, abruptly departed because of Aileen's unpredictable propensity to be violent. At the age of 33, Wuornos murdered seven men within an 11-month period. At her trial, she insisted that she had killed only in self-defense, when the men had become dangerously aggressive during sex. Several of her victims were found nude or partially clad; they had all been robbed and shot several times in the torso.

Like male serialists, Aileen was peripatetic, targeted only strangers, and left very little evidence. Although her motives were mixed, material gain was clearly important. Thus, she carefully selected men driving expensive cars. She conjectured that the "pickings" were likely to be better. Aileen, more like a male serial killer than the prototypical female, was diagnosed as an extremely violent and dangerous psychopath. She was sentenced to die in Florida's electric chair.

PSYCHOPATHY, CRIMINALITY, AND RECIDIVISM

There is relatively good agreement by psychiatrists, psychologists, and individuals working in the criminal justice system as to the key features of psychopathy. For example, Cleckley (1976) proposed 16 characteristics of psychopathy. The revised psychopathy checklist (PCL-R) devised by Hare and Colleagues (Hare, 1980; Hare and Harper, 1991; Hare and Hart, 1992; Hare et al., 1993) is one of the most widely researched and valuable psychometric instrument in current practice. The PCL-R was originally developed for clinical use in adult male forensic populations; however, recent research has validated it for the assessment of adult female offenders. The PCL-R has excellent psychometric properties in adult male offenders and forensic psychiatric patients, with high internal consistency and inter-rater and test/re-test reliability. Moreover, the psychometric properties of the PCL-R appear to be stable across those cultures in which it has been standardized. The PCL-R has a clear and replicable two-factor structure. Factor 1 reflects interpersonal affective symptoms and has been labeled the "callous and remorseless use of others." Factor 2 indicates socially deviant behavior that has been designated as a "chronically unstable and antisocial lifestyle."

The research on psychopathy has been conducted primarily on male prison inmates. Notwithstanding the dearth of information on females, although there may be differences in degree, male and female psychopaths are expected to manifest a broad range of similar criminal behaviors (including sexual offenses, homicide, offenses against property, etc.). However, female psychopaths, in general, are less aggressive, commit fewer criminal acts, are less likely to recidivate, and more often will present co-morbidly with histrionic personality disorder and somatization (Cloninger and Guze, 1970). Salekin et al. (1998) suggest that the current PCL-R may not be as useful in predicting recidivism in females as it is in males. However, despite the fact that there may be some differences in degree between male and female psychopaths, the diagnosis has clear implications. Gender notwithstanding, psychopaths begin criminal activities earlier, commit more types of offenses (violent and nonviolent), and have a higher offense rate than non-psychopaths (Cooke, 1995; Forth et al., 1990; Hare et al., 1988; Serin, 1991; Smith and Newman, 1990). There is some evidence that psychopaths "burn out" in their middle 30s, but this is true only for nonviolent transgressors, and even then psychopaths still commit crimes at a rate equivalent to that of serious and persistent non-psychopathic offenders (Harris et al., 1991; Hart and Hare, 1997a; Hare et al., 1992). In general, psychopaths recidivate at a rate three or four times higher than that of non-psychopaths, although female psychopaths re-offend less than their male counterparts and typically in a less violent fashion (Forth et al., 1990; Harris et al., 1993; Hart and Hare, 1997b). Further, while incarcerated or institutionalized, regardless of gender, psychopaths are more disruptive than non-psychopaths (Cooke, 1994; Forth, 1990; Rice et al., 1992).

Even allowing for lower recidivism rates and less assaultive/dangerous behavior in females, psychopathy predicts violence and violent recidivism in offenders. Additionally, psychopaths tend to engage in instrumental violence (less so in females). Typically, they threaten strangers with weapons and are motivated by vengeance, retribution, sadism, or money. Motives may overlap or change in emphasis, depending upon the dynamic context of a specific crime (Cornell et al., 1996; Serin, 1991). Psychopathy is associated with sexual sadism and violent recidivism among sex offenders, but again less so in females.

Despite the fact that there have been few controlled studies of treatment responses in well-defined populations of psychopaths, milieu therapy has often been recommended as the method of choice (Dolan and Coid, 1993; Meloy, 1995); however, there is no consensus that any type of management is predictably successful. Indeed, some observers have suggested that certain treatments (of incarcerated or institutionalized psychopathic offenders) make them worse (e.g., more dangerous). Highly adaptable and consummate actors, they simply become more efficient psychopaths. For instance, Hemple and Wong (1991) and Rice et al. (1992) observed that following intensive milieu exposure, the recidivism rate of the treated psychopaths increased.

Clearly, the treatability of psychopaths (males and females alike) is an extremely important societal issue. If, currently, therapies for dangerous repeat offenders are ineffective, then ensuring community safety (by incarcerating the psychopath) may be the single most important consideration. Of course, not all psychopaths are dangerous, although they may still engage in a variety of criminal and unethical behaviors.

A group of sub-criminal or white-collar psychopaths (both sexes) motivated by financial rewards, power, and prestige, may be found in the workplace, including politics and the professions. These individuals are able to manipulate, scheme, deceive, and charm potential benefactors, and they also intimidate, confuse, and isolate detractors. However, these individuals are rarely labeled "criminals." Frequently, their connections, extreme subtlety, high intelligence, charm, and mental agility— unlike the violent psychopathic criminal — may allow them to avoid dire legal consequences, even when they do transgress.

CASE EXAMPLE OF A FEMALE PSYCHOPATH

Ms. X., a 30-year-old woman of Native Canadian lineage, was remanded to a Canadian hospital's forensic unit for pre-trial assessment. She was facing charges of murdering her cell mate while serving a 4-year sentence for armed robbery at a women's penitentiary. It was alleged that there was a sexual motive to the killing. She was prematurely returned to a correctional facility as a result of verbally aggressive behavior in the hospital and at least one attempt to sexually victimize another patient. Additionally, a visitor was apprehended with a concealed weapon and a number of illicit drugs presumably procured for Ms. X.

Ms. X. was the middle of nine siblings. She was born prematurely and apparently spent several weeks in an incubator. Only two of her siblings were full biological relatives, the remainder having different fathers. At age 6, she was removed from her home due to alleged sexual abuse and neglect. She was moved to several foster homes and was reportedly continually sexually abused for the next 3 years. At age 9, she absconded from her foster home, joined a street gang, and engaged in theft and narcotics trafficking to subsist. It was also likely that she engaged in prostitution. While attending public school at age 6, she was noted to be impulsive and attention-seeking. At the time of her pre-trial assessment, Ms. X. claimed to have completed grade nine. She started to take drugs regularly from the age of 9. Her substance abuse included the regular intravenous administration of cocaine and heroin. Her parents were drug users, and at least one of her sisters died of an accidental overdose. Ms. X. admitted to having engaged in numerous short-term homosexual and hetero-sexual relationships. She indicated only two serious affiliations, both lasting less then 1 year. She admitted to sado-masochistic sexual traits, as well as being preoc-cupied with violent sexual fantasies.

Ms. X. perpetrated her first crime at age 9. Since then, she had accumulated numerous charges and convictions for breaking-and-entering, automobile theft, com-mon assault, narcotics-related offenses, and armed robbery. She had also been charged with murder but was acquitted; her attorney successfully presented a "bat-tered woman syndrome" defense. Additionally, she had a history of cruelty to animals; she had also engaged in bestiality. She served 15 terms of incarceration for a cumulative total of 16 years (she had spent over half her life in jail). All of her immediate family members have criminal records and all have been incarcerated at one time or another. On the PCL-R, Ms. X. produced a total score of 34, which places her at the 94 percentile in relation to a normative group of male prison inmates. Compared to the male normative groups, her two factor scores placed her at the 89 percentile and 83 percentile, respectively. Gender notwithstanding, her score indi-cated severe psychopathy. Psychological testing, augmented by clinical evaluation, failed to reveal evidence of a serious psychotic disorder. She manifested transient paranoid ideation and features of an hysterical personality. Overall, she appeared as a chronically angry, hypersexual individual, preoccupied with sexual sadism and inclining toward explosive emotional outbursts. She was singularly aggressive and showed a marked propensity to lose herself in an erotic fantasy world.

COMMENT

Female psychopaths are apparently relatively rare and there is little information on them. The aforementioned case summary was culled from a comprehensive report which claims to be the first intensive case study of this phenomenon. It is generally argued that male psychopaths engage in more criminal behavior, are more violent, and recidivate more than their female counterparts. Ms. X., however, might be viewed as being somewhat atypical of female psychopaths, as she engaged equally in criminally dangerous behavior as did her male counterparts. Her extensive repertoire of illegal behaviors, including homicide, sexual assault, armed robbery, thefts, and misuse of drugs, may be partially attributed to her exposure as a child to the pervasive antisocial conduct of her immediate family and acquaintances. These experiences became integral to her personality by the time she reached early adolescence. The prognosis in this case would seem to be poor. It is likely that she will continue to offend in various ways and will spend more time in jail or other secure institutions.

DISCUSSION

For practical purposes, the assessment of female serial offenders is to evaluate risk and to guide management. Because these women are few in comparison to males, there is as yet no specific protocol available; however, there are more similarities than differences between the sexes, which makes it possible to apply selected male assessment procedures, albeit with some sensible modifications, if an experienced clinician (in the field of offending behaviors) considers such to be appropriate. Until there is much more empirically derived data to support a different approach, this would seem a reasonable compromise.

A comprehensive assessment of a serial female perpetrator may include some or all of the following: a detailed description of the nature of the offenses; characteristics of the victim; prior transgressions; psychopathology; psychiatric diagnoses (if any); and past history, including educational background, social history, sexual history, IQ, religious beliefs, occupational history, and previous therapies (if undertaken). The single most important assessment tool remains a detailed clinical history compiled flexibly by an experienced practitioner. However, before embarking, the interviewer should obtain informed consent and be aware of any limits of confidentiality or child-abuse reporting requirements and any other germane matters pertaining to a particular jurisdiction. Any collateral information (from police, probation reports, victim statements, previous evaluations, and medical records) should be obtained and reviewed prior to the initial interview. Psychological testing may usefully augment clinical data. The Personality Assessment Inventory and the Hare psychopathy checklist have been found to be moderately useful in predicting recidivism in women and should be administered. The Derogatis Sexual Functioning Inventory (DSFI) may generate data relative to a female offender's adequacy of sexual functioning. This test is an omnibus-type scale with separate scores on eight sub-tests, including information, experience, drive, attitudes, symptoms, affects, gender-role, and fantasy (Derogatis, 1980).

Plethysmography has been used only rarely in female sex offenders, but, if available, the procedure can be applied by an experienced operator to generate data that usefully complements information derived from multiple other sources. However, it should be emphasized that female plethysmography is still experimental, and the uses and limitations of the test remain to be established. Although, to date, the Registrant Risk Assessment Scale (Witt et al., 1996) and the Predictor Variable List for Sexual Recidivism (Hanson and Bussier, 1998) have been employed exclusively with male sex offenders, they would seem potentially informative in female sex offenders.

FINAL THOUGHTS

This chapter reviewed a representative sample of the existing literature on female serial offenders, notably sexual offenders and murderesses. As far as is known, overwhelmingly men commit more serious crimes of all types than women do, although percentages and gender comparisons are either not available or the figures are incomplete, non-representative, and/or suspect. Therefore, from the information generated to date, future trends cannot be accurately predicted. Moreover, although it has been stated that both sexual offenses and homicides perpetrated by females are increasing, for a number of reasons it is not clear whether this is real or apparent.

Female sex offenders tend to be less intrusive and passive than their male counterparts, but they appear to chose similar victims — a preponderance of females over male children, although both sexes may be exploited by a specific perpetrator. Although the data are limited, serial female killers appear to be more heterogeneous than female sex offenders. This population is less violent in their *modus operandi* than male serial killers; they tend to use inherently less aggressive methods of dispatching victims, poison still being the preferred vehicle. However, a minority of women are killing more like men, using extremely violent methods.

Why an infinitely small minority of women develop into sex offenders or serial murderers remains substantially unknown, and the eventuality cannot be predicted purely on the basis of a stereotypical set of antecedents. Although being raised in a dysfunctional family and witnessing and participating in violence of various types may influence a person's future behavior, only a fraction of females exposed to such an environment evolve into recalcitrant perpetrators. Clearly, there must be other factors at play, including variable genetic predisposition and biological elements, notably hormones. Serendipity may also be involved, at least initially, and imitation may play a role in some cases.

Similarly, the motives for sexual offending and committing murder may not be immediately clear or may otherwise be willfully obfuscated by a particular individual. The reasons may have to be inferred by detailed examination and analysis of the behaviors in question. Only with a clear understanding as to the causes that impel and perpetuate the behavior may it become possible to develop appropriate remedies. Furthermore, motives may be multiple and overlapping. They may also change in emphasis during the execution of the behavior, depending on victim response — for instance, an overriding physical sexual gratification motive being subordinated by a psychological need to humiliate, demean, or even to kill.

Risk-assessment protocols for female offenders are currently not available; however, because there are many similarities between male and female offenders, until female-specific instruments are constructed it would seem an acceptable compromise to deploy some validated male instruments (e.g., the psychopathic checklist, revised; PCL-R) with gender-driven modifications, if these seem reasonable. The management of both male and female recidivates is still experimental. Currently, the public's security in regard to these predators is the paramount concern. Axiomatically, it seems that, like their male counterparts, female serial offenders (after serving whatever sentence is imposed) require a mix of treatment ingredients tailored to their needs. It is not currently known whether these populations benefit from such interventions. Obviously, the message for the future is research and more research. However, if repetitive female sex offenders and murderers continue to be encountered so rarely, hypothesis-based studies may be difficult or impossible to conduct. These individuals, especially the most extreme examples, may best be viewed as dangerous psychologic curios to be studied on an intensive case-by-case basis.

REFERENCES

Adler, F. (1975). *Sisters in Crime: The Rise of the New Female Criminal.* New York: McGraw Hill.

Barker, J.G. and Howell, R.J. (1992). The plethysmography: a review of recent literature. *Bulletin of the American Academy of Psychiatry and Law,* 20(1):13–25.

Chapman, J. (1980). *Economic Realities and the Female Offender.* Lexington, MA: Lexington Books.

Chasnoff, I.J. Burns, W.J., Schnoll, S.H., Burns, K., Chisum, G., and Kyle-Spore, L. (1986). Maternal-neonatal incest. *American Journal of Orthopsychiatry*, 56:577–580.

Cleckley, H. (1976). *The Mask of Sanity*, 5th ed. St. Louis, MO: Mosby.

Cloninger, D., and Guze, S. (1970b) Psychiatric illness and female criminality: the role of sociopathy and hysteria in the antisocial woman. *American Journal of Psychiatry*, 127:303–311.

Cooke, D.J. (1994). *Psychological Disturbance in the Scottish Prison System: Prevalence, Precipitants and Policy.* Edinburgh: Scottish Home and Health Department.

Cooke, D.J. (1995). Psychopathic disturbance in the Scottish prison population: cross-cultural generalizability of the Hare Psychopathy Checklist. *Psychology, Crime and Law*, 2:101–118.

Cooper, A.J., Swaminath, S., Baxter, D., and Poulin. C. (1990). A female sex offender with multiple paraphilias: a psychologic, physiologic (laboratory sexual arousal) and endocrine case study. *Canadian Journal of Psychiatry*, 35:334–337.

Cornell, D., Warren, J., Hawk, G., Stafford, E., Oram, G., and Pine, D. (1996). Psychopathy in instrumental and reactive violent offenders. *Journal of Consulting and Clinical Psychology*, 64:783–790.

Demming, R. (1977). *Women: The New Criminals.* Thames: Nelson.

Derogatis, I.R. (1980). Psychological assessment of psychosexual functioning. *Psychiatric Clinic of North America*, 3:113–131.

Derogatis, I.R., Meyer, J.K., and King, K.M. (1981). Psychopathology in individuals with sexual dysfunction. *American Journal of Psychiatry*, 138:757–763.

Dolan, B., and Coid, J. (1993). *Psychopathic and Antisocial Personality Disorders: Treatment and Research Issues.* London: Gaskell.

Dubé, R. and Hébert, M. (1988). Sexual abuse of children under 12 years of age: a review of 511 cases. *Child Abuse and Neglect*, 12:321–330.

Faller, K.C. (1987). Women who sexually abuse children. *Violence and Victims*, 2:263–276.

Forth, A.E., Hart, S.D., and Hare, R.D. (1990). Assessment of psychopathy in male young offenders. *Psychological Assessment: A Journal of Consulting and Clinical Psychology*, 2:342–344.

Gill, E. and Johnson, T.C. (1992). *Assessment and Treatment of Sexualized Children and Children Who Molest.* Rockville, MD: Launch Press.

Green, A.H. and Kaplan, M.S. (1994). Psychiatric impairment and childhood victimization experiences in female child molesters. *Journal of the American Academy of Child and Adolescent Psychiatry*, 33:954–961.

Grob, C.S. (1985). Female exhibitionism. *Journal of Nervous and Mental Disease*, 173(4):253–256.

Hanson, R.K. and Bussiere, M. (1998). Predicting relapse: a meta-analysis of sexual offender recidivism studies. *Journal of Consulting and Clinical Psychology*, 66(2):348–362.

Hare, R.D. (1980). A research scale for the assessment of psychopathy in criminal populations. *Personality and Individual Differences*, 1:111–119.

Hare, R.D. and Hart, S.D. (1992). Psychopathy, mental disorder and crime. In Hodgins, S. (Ed.), *Mental Disorder and Crime* (pp. 104–115). Newbury Park, CA: Sage.

Hare, R.D. and Hart, S.D. (1995). Commentary on antisocial personality disorder: the DSM-IV field trial. In Livesley, W.J. (Ed.), *The DSM-IV Personality Disorders* (pp. 127–134). New York: Guilford.

Hare, R.D., McPherson, L.E., and Forth, A.E. (1988). Male psychopaths and their criminal careers. *Journal of Consulting and Clinical Psychology*, 56:710–714.

Hare, R.D., Forth, A.E., and Strachan, K. (1992). Psychopathy and crime across the lifespan. In DeV. Peters, R., McMahon, R.J., and Quinsey, V.L. (Eds.), *Aggression and Violence Throughout the Life Span* (pp. 285–300). Newbury Park, CA: Sage.

Hare, R.D., Hart, S.D., Forth, A.E., Harpur, T.J., and Williamson, S.E. (1993). Psychopathic personality characteristics: development of a criteria set for use in the DSM-IV antisocial personality disorder field trial. *American Psychiatric Association DSM-IV Update*, January/February:6–7.

Harris, G.T., Rice, M.E., and Cormier, C.A. (1991). Psychopathy and violent recidivism. *Law and Human Behavior*, 15:625–637.

Harris, G.T., Rice, M.E., and Quinsey, V.L. (1993). Violent recidivism of mentally disordered offenders: the development of a statistical prediction instrument. *Criminal Justice and Behavior*, 20:315–335.

Hart, S.D. and Hare, R.D. (1997a). Psychopathy: assessment and association with criminal conduct. In Stoff, D.M., Brieling, J., and Maser, J. (Eds.), *Handbook of Antisocial Behavior* (pp. 22–35). New York: Wiley.

Hart, S.D. and Hare, R.D. (1997b). The association between psychopathy and narcissism: theoretical views and empirical evidence. In Ronningstam, E. (Ed.), *Disorders of Narcissism — Theoretical, Empirical and Clinical Implications* (pp. 415–436). Washington, D.C.: American Psychiatric Press.

Hazelwood, R., Warren, J., and Dietz, P. (1993). Compliant victims of the sexual sadist. *Australian Family Physician*, 22(4):1–5.

Hemphill, J.F. and Wong, S. (1991). Efficacy of the therapeutic community for treating criminal psychopaths [abstract]. *Canadian Psychology*, 32:206.

Henson, C., Rubin, H.B., and Henson, D.E. (1979). Woman's sexual arousal concurrently assessed by three genital measure. *Archives of Sexual Behavior*, 8:459–469.

Hickey, E.W. (1997). *Serial Murderers and Their Victims,* 2nd ed. (pp. 204–232). Belmont, CA: Wadsworth Publishing.

Holmes, R. and DeBurger, J. (1985). Profiles in terror: the serial murderer. *Federal Probation*, 39:29, 2D34.

Hunter, J.A. and Mathews, R. (1997). *Sexual Deviance in Females.* In Laws, D.R. and O'Donohue, W. (Eds.), *Sexual Deviance Theory, Assessment and Treatment* (pp. 465–480). New York: The Guilford Press.

Hunter, J.A., Lexier, L.J., Goodwin, D.W., Brown, P.A. and Dennis, C. (1993). Psychosexual, attitudinal and developmental characteristics of juvenile female sexual perpetrators in a residential treatment setting. *Journal of Child and Family Studies*, 2(4):317–326.

Johnson, T.C. (1993). Assessment of sexual behavior problems in preschool-aged and latency-aged children. In Yates, A. (Ed.), *Child and Adolescent Psychiatric Clinics of North America: Sexual and Gender Identity Disorders* (pp. 431–450). Philadelphia: Saunders.

Knopp, F.H. and Lackey, L.D. (1987). *Female Sexual Abusers: A Summary of Data from 44 Treatment Providers*. Brandon, VT: Safer Society Press.

Margolin, L. (1991). Child and sexual abuse by non-related caregivers. *Child Abuse and Neglect*, 15:213–221.

Mathews, R., Hunder, J.A., and Vuz, J. (1997). Juvenile female sexual offenders: clinical characteristics and treatment issues. *Sexual Abuse: A Journal of Research and Treatment*, 9(3):187–199.

Meloy, J.R. (1995). Antisocial personality disorder. In Gabbard, G. (Ed.), *Treatment of Psychiatric Disorders*, 2nd ed. (pp. 2273–2290). Washington, D.C.: American Psychiatric Press.

Morokoff, P.J. and Heiman, J.R. (1980). Effects of erotic stimuli on sexually functional and dysfunctional women. *Behavior Research and Therapy*, 18:127–137.

O'Connor, A.A. (1987). Female sex offenders. *British Journal of Psychiatry*, 150:615–620.

Petrovich, M. and Templer, D.I. (1984). Heterosexual molestation of children who later became rapists. *Psychological Reports*, 54:810.

Rice, M.E., Harris, G.T., and Cormier, C.A. (1992). An evaluation of a maximum security therapeutic community for psychopaths and other mentally disordered offenders. *Law and Human Behavior*, 16:399–412.

Rudin, M.M., Zalewski, C., and Bodmer-Turner, J. (1995). Characteristics of child sexual abuse victims according to perpetrator gender. *Child Abuse and Neglect*, 19:963–973.

Salekin, R.T., Rogers, R., Ustad, K., and Sewell, K.W. (1998). Psychopathy and recidivism among female inmates. *Law and Human Behavior*, 22(1):109–128.

Schur, E.M. (1984). *Labelling Women Deviant: Gender Stigma and Social Control*. New York: Random House.

Serin, R.C. (1991). Psychopathy and violence in criminals. *Journal of Interpersonal Violence*, 6:423–431.

Simon, W.T. and Schouten, G.W. (1991). Plethysmography in the assessment and treatment of sexual deviance: an overview. *Archives of Sexual Behavior*, 20(1):75–91.

Smith, S.S. and Newman, J.P. (1990). Alcohol and drug abuse/dependence disorders in psychopathic and non-psychopathic criminal offenders. *Journal of Abnormal Psychology*, 99:430–439.

Thomlison, B., Stephens, M., Cunes, J.W., Grinnell, R.M., Jr., and Krysik, J. (1991). Characteristics of Canadian male and female child sexual abuse victims. *Journal of Child and Youth Care (special issue)*, 65–76.

Travin, S., Cullen, K., and Protter, B. (1990). Female sex offenders: severe victims and victimizers. *Journal of Forensic Sciences*, 35:140–150.

Wakefield, H. and Underwager, R. (1991). Female child sexual abusers: a critical review of the literature. *American Journal of Forensic Psychology*, 9(4):43–69.

Weisheit, R.A. (1984). Women and crime issues and perspectives. *Sex Roles*, 11:7–8.

Wincze, J.P., Hoon, E.F., and Hoon, P.W. (1976). Physiological responsivity of normal and sexually dysfunctional women during erotic stimulus exposure. *Journal of Psychosomatic Research*, 20:445–451.

Witt, P.H., DelRusso, J., Oppenheim, J., and Ferguson, G. (1996). Sex offender risk assessment and the law. *Journal of Psychiatry and the Law*, Fall, 343–369.

Yates, A. (1991). Differentiating hyper-erotic states in the evaluation of sexual abuse. *Journal of the American Academy of Psychiatry*, 30(5):791–795.

14 Serial Offending by Children and Adolescents

Wade C. Myers and Marian J. Borg

CONTENTS

INTRODUCTION

This chapter will examine the phenomenon of serial offending by children and adolescents. Serial crime by juveniles is rare, and some historical cases are included for illustrative purposes. In our review of this area, we have set the upper age limit for youthful serial offenders at 17 years. Most states now define adulthood as beginning at the age of 18 years.

There are various ways to define what one means by "serial" crime (Egger, 1990). For murder, Egger (1984) states that "serial murder occurs when one or more individuals commits a second murder," although the lower limit for serial crimes is more commonly set at three or more. We have used a slightly more liberal definition of serial crime for youth, and define it as occurring when a juvenile commits a second, unrelated crime — but of the same crime category — against another victim or target at a different time. We also required the time between crimes to be at least 24 hours so as not to confuse these actions with "spree" offenses — those committed in different locations with no cooling-off period in between.

Six areas of serial criminal behavior by youth will be covered in this chapter. The first, "generic" juvenile delinquency, while not fitting exactly our definition of serial crime, was included to help provide a framework for the subsequent more specific offenses. The remaining five sections — arson, cruelty to animals, sex offenses, sadistic crimes, and serial murder — do not represent all potential forms of serial crime by youth but do cover the more serious and high-profile types. A more comprehensive treatment of the area might include additional, less serious crimes that nevertheless are serial in nature, such as kleptomania.

SERIAL DELINQUENCY

Studies of chronic delinquents are generally based on two types of research designs. Cohort studies track samples of individuals from a particular birth year over a period of time, documenting their involvement in delinquency. Typically, analyses are based on data from official documents — such as school, police, and juvenile court records — indicating evidence of delinquent behavior and/or contacts with the juvenile justice system. A second type of research strategy uses interviews in which juveniles are asked to self-report their involvement in various delinquent acts. This information is sometimes supplemented with interviews of parents, teachers, and peers. Although each of these research strategies has distinct advantages and disadvantages (Barlow and Ferdinand, 1992; Tracy et al., 1990), and perhaps neither renders a precise count of all juvenile delinquency, both suggest similar patterns regarding delinquent behavior. Two conclusions are particularly consistent. First, delinquency is fairly widespread and common. Most adolescents engage in some sort of rule breaking, usually of a non-serious nature, during their teenage years. Second, a small core of teens is responsible for a disproportionate amount of delinquency, especially more serious and violent offending (e.g., Cernkovich et al., 1985; Gold, 1970; Shannon, 1982; Tracy et al., 1990; Wolfgang et al., 1972). Various terms have been used to refer to this smaller group, including "chronic delinquents," "serial offenders," and "career criminals." Although the precise definition of these labels varies across studies, in general this category pertains to juveniles involved in more frequent offending, over longer time periods, and in more serious types of offenses.

The first large-scale, generalizable cohort study investigating delinquency in the U.S. examined 9945 boys born in Philadelphia in 1945 (Wolfgang et al., 1972). Focusing on the boys' activities between their 10th and 18th birthdays, researchers collected data measuring official police contacts — interactions that resulted in an official report, but not necessarily an arrest — from school records, juvenile court files, and police reports. Over one third of the boys in the sample had a record of at least one contact with the police, and in total they had accumulated 10,214 police contacts. Importantly, the data indicated that a small core of the sample, about 6%, was much more heavily involved in delinquency than the others. Each boy in this "chronic delinquent" group had had a minimum of five police contacts, and together they were responsible for 52% of the total offenses identified in the data (Tracy et al., 1990). Similar results were found in a followup study examining a 1958 cohort of Philadelphia boys (Tracy et al., 1990). Both analyses also found that the chronic offenders in each cohort were responsible for a majority of the very serious offenses. In the 1945 cohort, the chronic delinquents committed 76% of the violent offenses (homicide, rape, robbery, and aggravated assault), and the 1958 serial offenders were responsible for 71% of these crimes (Tracy et al., 1990).

Research focusing on later birth cohorts and in different geographic locations, both within the U.S. and in other countries, has consistently found similar evidence of a chronic offender category (e.g., Elmhorn, 1965; Shannon, 1988, 1991; Snyder, 1988; West and Farrington, 1977). More recent studies suggest a slight increase in the number of chronic offenders since the 1980s. Snyder (1997), for example, examined court records of more than 151,000 juveniles who turned 18 years old between 1980 and 1995. The adolescents all lived in Maricopa County, AZ, a major urban area that includes Phoenix. Snyder found that 15% of all the youth in the sample had been referred to juvenile court on four or more occasions and were responsible for 59% of all serious case referrals in the study sample. Examining different time periods, Snyder found that beginning in the 1990s the proportion of chronic delinquents within each graduating class began to increase, from about 13% during the 1980s to 17% during the early 1990s. Despite this increase, however, the nature and frequency of offending had not changed across the study period examined. In each of the 16 years of data, serial offenders had an average of 6.6 referrals in their juvenile court career. Most of these referrals were for non-serious offenses (4.2 on average) or serious nonviolent offenses (2.0 on average). Still, as a group, the chronic recidivists were responsible for most of the violent offenses in the sample.

Researchers examining gender, race, and social class differences among serial delinquents have reached fairly consistent conclusions. Males are overwhelmingly more likely than females to be chronic offenders, both serious and non-serious (Chaiken, 1998; Hamparian et al., 1978; Tracy et al., 1990; Wolfgang et al., 1972). Although the data are a bit less consistent with regard to race and social class, the majority of the evidence suggests that teenagers belonging to minority and lower socioeconomic groups are disproportionately represented among chronic offenders compared to white and middle- and upper-class adolescents (Elliott and Ageton, 1980; Elliott and Huizinga, 1984; Tracy et al., 1990). This is particularly the case with regard to the most frequent and most serious and violent offending patterns.

While early studies of general delinquency compared chronic and non-chronic offenders, more recent research has called attention to differences among serial offenders themselves. Results of these analyses suggest the existence of two types of chronic offenders, one consisting of individuals who are repeatedly involved in relatively non-serious and status offenses, such as shoplifting, truancy, and running away from home, and others whose law-breaking involves more serious and violent crimes, including burglary, motor vehicle theft, arson, drug trafficking, robbery, rape, aggravated assault, and homicide. The characteristics of each group and their like-lihood of continuing their criminal careers into adulthood seem to be somewhat different.

While most non-serious chronic offenders are male, females comprise a greater proportion of this category than of serious chronic offenders. In fact, most researchers have found that females are much less likely than males to become career delinquents in general, but, when girls are more heavily involved in delinquency, their offending usually consists primarily of non-serious and status offenses (Cernkovich et al., 1985; Shelden and Chesney-Lind, 1993; also see Kelley et al., 1997). And, while the evidence is not plentiful, research examining chronic status offenders vs. other types of repetitive offenders has concluded that juvenile status offenders generally do not escalate to more serious or violent offending. For example, Shelden et al. (1989) concluded that their longitudinal data from 863 adolescents first referred in 1980 to the Clarke County Juvenile Court in Las Vegas, "clearly and unambiguously demonstrate that those first referred to court on a status offense are more likely to return to court for a second or third time than most other offenders. However, if they do return, it will not be for a more serious crime."

In later analysis of the same data, Shelden et al. (1993) focused more specifically on gender and race differences among different types of chronic recidivists. They defined two types of serial offenders: "chronic nuisance offenders" and "chronic serious offenders." While the first group consisted of adolescents primarily involved in status offending, petty larceny, drug and alcohol possession, and other relatively non-serious delinquency, the second group included teens whose offenses involved robbery, rape, assault, burglary, grand larceny, and other serious crimes. About 16.5% of the entire sample were chronic offenders, almost evenly split between the serious (7.5%) and nuisance (9%) categories. When the sample was examined along gender and racial lines, results indicated that boys were significantly more likely than girls to be chronic offenders, in general, and chronic serious offenders, in particular. In fact, among girls who were chronic offenders, almost all fell in the "chronic nuisance" category. In contrast, male chronics were evenly split between the nuisance (9%) and serious categories (10%). Among males, non-whites were more likely than whites to be chronic serious delinquents and to have adult felony arrest records.

The most recent data on adolescents involved in serious and violent chronic offending come from three ongoing, longitudinal studies sponsored by the Office of Juvenile Justice and Delinquency Prevention (see Thornberry et al., 1995, for an overview). Collectively referred to as the Program of Research on the Causes and Correlates of Delinquency, the studies are being conducted in Rochester, Denver, and Pittsburgh and use generalizable probability samples based on 4500 inner-city youth ages 7 to 15 in 1988. The research design includes self-report methods, interviews with adolescents and their primary caregivers, and analyses of school, police, court, and social service records. Some of the key findings from analyses of data through the spring of 1994 pertain to serial offenders, and particularly to chronic serious offenders:

- Consistent with other studies, the Causes and Correlates of Delinquency research indicates that age and gender are the most significant demographic predictors of involvement in chronic offending, in general, and violent offending, in particular. Preliminary data indicate that chronic violent offenders begin their involvement in both general delinquency and violence between 1 and 2.5 years earlier than non-chronic violent offenders (Thornberry et al., 1995). Older teenage boys and young men are much more likely to be involved in serious high-rate offending than girls or older men (Kelley et al., 1997). For example, the highest rate of female violent offending in the Denver study occurred among the 14-year-old girls — 17 violent offenses reported for every 100 girls in this group. In comparison, the 18-year-old boys reported the highest rate of violent offending — 228 violent offenses per 100 boys.

- Although the majority of adolescents in each of the three study areas reported involvement in at least one violent incident, violence in general was concentrated in a small proportion of each sample. Using a seven-point index of violent offenses ranging in seriousness from simple assault to armed robbery and aggravated assault, researchers compared adolescents with the highest involvement in violence (chronic violent offenders) to those with some (non-chronic violent offenders) or no (nonviolent offenders) involvement. In Denver, chronic violent offenders comprised only 15% of the sample but were responsible for 82% of all the violent offenses reported. In contrast, the non-chronic violent offenders represented 36% of the sample but accounted for only 18% of the violent acts (Thornberry et al., 1995).
- The Rochester and Denver results indicate that chronic violent offenders are generalists rather than specialists in terms of their overall offending patterns. That is, most of the chronic violent offenders were also heavily involved in property offending, drug sales, public disorder offenses, and alcohol and marijuana use. They also exhibited a variety of other behavioral problems, including dropping out of school, gun use, gang membership, sexual activity, and teenage parenthood (Thornberry et al., 1995).
- The Rochester data indicate that chronic violent offenders have distinct family, school, peer group, and neighborhood relationships that appear to put them at particularly high risk for violent behavior. Compared to nonviolent respondents, chronic violent offenders report lower attachment to parents, less parental monitoring, greater exposure to multiple forms of family violence, less commitment to school and lower attachment to teachers, greater association with delinquent peers, and a greater likelihood of living in high-crime neighborhoods (Hawkins and Catalano, 1992; Huizinga et al., 1994; Thornberry, 1994; Thornberry et al., 1995).

In sum, both recent and historical research indicates the existence of a small but significant group of juveniles involved in serial delinquency. They are typically male, come from a disadvantaged socioeconomic background, begin their offending at a very young age, and are more likely than other youth to be involved in serious and violent offenses. A good deal of research suggests that negative experiences in the family, peer, and school relationships of chronic delinquents contribute to their high-rate offending patterns.

SERIAL ARSON

In the FBI's annual report on serious criminal offending, arson is defined as "any willful or malicious burning or attempt to burn, with or without intent to defraud, a dwelling house, public building, motor vehicle or aircraft, or personal property of another" (Federal Bureau of Investigation, 1996). According to this definition, 110,000 incidents of arson were reported to law enforcement officials in 1997 (Snyder, 1999). Although the police were able to identify and arrest offenders in only 18% of these cases, the characteristics of those arrested suggest the significant involvement of juveniles in firesetting activities. Of the 20,000 arson arrests made in 1997, 50% were of individuals under the age of 18; among these juveniles, 67% were under age 15, and 35% were children 12 years or younger (Snyder, 1999). In fact, while the rate of juvenile arrests for arson compared to other property crimes is small, adolescents under 18 comprise a greater proportion of arson arrests than they do for any other serious crime measured by the FBI. Furthermore, research suggests that even adult professional arsonists, who are less likely to be represented in arrest statistics because of their skill in alluding law enforcement, often have a history of firesetting as juveniles (Wooden and Berkey, 1984). Indeed, if the focus is expanded to include "firesetting" that is not necessarily "arson" (i.e., ignoring the criteria of criminal or malicious intent), juvenile involvement in this activity is even more pronounced.

While accidental firesetting is not uncommon among young children whose curiosity leads them to play with matches (Block et al., 1976; Wooden et al., 1984), for some this involvement develops into a repetitive pattern of intentional firesetting. Research on chronic juvenile firesetters suggests two common characteristics shared among these adolescents: a disruptive family environment that often includes sexual abuse and numerous behavioral problems that are either symptomatic of high stress levels or are consistent with poor mechanisms for coping with stress (Barnett and Spitzer, 1994; Wooden et al., 1984). These two factors coupled with positive reinforcement of firesetting activity at a young age appear to increase the likelihood that firesetting will become a chronic behavior (Wooden et al., 1984).

The study by Wooden et al. (1984) of juvenile firesetters is consistent with other research on the topic. Their findings are based on analysis of original data from 104 juvenile arsonists apprehended in San Bernardino County in southern California between 1979 and 1983. These data were supplemented with information from a comparison group of non-firesetters and with data from 536 juveniles apprehended over a 7-year period for setting fires on school property. Compared to non-firesetters, the juvenile firesetters in the Wooden et al. (1984) study tended to have disruptive family relationships and to exhibit a range of behaviors suggestive of psychological and mental health problems. Home environments marked by abusive, alcoholic, and/or psychotic parents; divorce, separation, or desertion; and lower levels of marital satisfaction were more common among juvenile firesetters compared to non-firesetters (Kaufman et al., 1961; Nurcombe, 1964; Siegelman, 1969; Wooden et al., 1984). In fact, Wooden et al. (1984) identify "severely disruptive family environments" as the major problem shared by the firesetters in their study. Children who were victims of sexual abuse were at particularly greater risk for becoming chronic firesetters. Additionally, compared to the non-firesetters, the firesetters exhibited a number of problematic behaviors, including truancy, stealing, lying, impulsivity, aggression, hyperactivity, impatience, an inability to get along with peers, poor school performance, and being out of touch with reality (Wooden et al., 1984; see also Nurcombe, 1964; Vandersall and Weiner, 1970). As the firesetters grew older and more chronically involved in arson, their behavioral problems became more numerous and complex. Wooden et al. (1984) suggest that firesetters' need for "power enhancement" is one factor contributing to their behavior: "Feeling a lack of power or control in the home and social environment and with other people, these juveniles turn to setting fires as an expression of their great hostility and aggression, or as a response to parental abuse or neglect."

Based on their data, Wooden et al. (1984) described differences in the behavioral problems exhibited by different age firesetters — young, preteen, and teenager. Within each age category, a smaller number engaged in repetitive firesetting and shared a larger number of behavioral problems compared to the other firesetters within that group. We highlight some of the more significant patterns here. *Young* chronic firesetters, ages 4 to 8, displayed severe mood swings and typically expressed their anger by striking out at objects or people close to them, such as pets, their own toys, their siblings, or themselves. They were characteristically impatient and hyperactive and had a history of lying, disobeying, bedwetting, stuttering, and constant thumbsucking. The more severe *preteen* firesetters, ages 9 to 12, also exhibited high levels of anger and aggression. They tended to project their hostility toward their peers, often fighting with them, were poor losers, and threw temper tantrums. In addition, preteen chronic firesetters were more likely to steal, have sleeping problems, be accident prone, have bizarre speech patterns, and experience anxiety, depression, and stomachaches. The recidivist *teenage* firesetters, ages 13 to 17, suffered from health-related conditions, including vomiting, diarrhea, and constipation, all symptomatic of stress. In addition, the more severe teenage arsonists were likely "to have a history of behavioral difficulties, to be out of touch with reality, to have strange thought patterns such as 'hearing voices,' to express jealousy, to suffer from severe depressions and to have phobias" (Wooden et al., 1984).

Based on these and additional data pertaining to the adolescents' motivations for setting fires and to their family backgrounds, Wooden et al. (1984) suggest a four-category typology of firesetters that is consistent with findings from other studies on the topic (Garry, 1997). While the first of these categories consists of very young children (4 to 8) whose firesetting appears accidental and often results from "fireplay," the other categories involve juveniles who act intentionally and who are more likely to develop into chronic arsonists. "Crying-for-help" firesetters, primarily preteenagers ages 9 to 12, appear to use fire as a means of expressing anger or resolving inner tensions due to jealousy or feelings of neglect or abandonment, as an unconscious strategy to change their family environment, or as a tool for power enhancement. They typically set fires alone and close to home and target objects that symbolically represent the source of their anger or stress. In the Wooden et al. (1984) study, the chronic crying-for-help firesetters exhibited the more numerous and severe behavioral problems of the preteenagers, as described above. Once they received positive reinforcement for their firesetting, whether from parental reaction to the fires, peer approval, or the thrill of seeing the firefighting response, the crying-for-help firesetters were more likely to continue their behavior into adolescence and hence into the next category identified by Wooden et al. (1984), the "delinquent firesetters."

Delinquent firesetters, ages 13 to 18, typically have a history of firesetting behavior and tend to set fires as acts of vandalism, to cover up other crime, to strike out at authority, as a way of seeking peer approval, or simply for the excitement or thrill of destroying other people's property. In the Wooden et al. (1984) study, the delinquent firesetters usually set larger, premeditated fires and were more likely to act as part of a group. The older firesetters within this category typically had records of engaging in antisocial behavior beyond chronic firesetting, as well as histories of poor academic achievement and severe emotional disturbances. In addition, their home environments were disrupted by death, abandonment, conflict, or divorce, and they had often been victimized, particularly by sexual abuse.

The last category identified by Wooden et al. (1984), and the one most likely to include chronic or pathological arsonists, is the "severely disturbed" firesetter. This category was the smallest of the four in their research and included youths of all ages, although most were between 13 and 17 years old. Wooden et al. (1984) identified two personality types among the severely disturbed firesetters in their study: the "impulsive neurotic" and the "borderline psychotic." The impulsive neurotic firesetters exhibited characteristics such as impatience, impulsivity, sleeping disorders, stealing, and destroying their own possessions. The borderline psychotic firesetters displayed such behaviors as extreme mood swings, uncontrolled anger, violence, bizarre speech, and numerous phobias (Wooden et al., 1984).

These personality types are consistent with the findings of other research on chronic juvenile firesetters. Rothestein's study of firesetting children between 6 and 12 years old, for example, suggests that firesetting is used as a way of expressing inner tension among borderline personalities and is related to sexual conflict among neurotic personalities (Rothestein, 1963). Similar to the other categories of firesetters, Wooden et al. (1984) found that the severely disturbed youth had a history of significant disturbances in their family backgrounds, including divorce, abandonment, inadequate parenting, parental abuse, particularly sexual abuse, alcoholism, and parents displaying a higher frequency of mental disorders (Barnett et al., 1994). The severely disturbed youth displayed a more abundant and serious array of behavioral problems compared to the juvenile firesetters in the other categories.

Wooden et al. (1984) concluded that factors beyond environmental conditions likely influence the behavior of severely disturbed firesetters. In the same vein, Siegelman and Folkman (1971) conclude that recidivist firesetters have a greater need for child psychiatric treatment compared to non-recidivists. Studies indicating a history of diagnosed mental disorders and psychiatric care among chronic adult arsonists are also consistent with these conclusions (Barnett et al., 1994).

SERIAL CRUELTY TO ANIMALS

Research examining cruelty toward animals among adolescents, particularly of a chronic nature, is not plentiful. Pertinent studies tend to be based on retrospective data collected from adults and usually include samples or case histories drawn from institutionalized populations, typically imprisoned criminals or psychiatric hospital patients (e.g., Arluke et al., 1999; Felthous, 1980; Kellert and Felthous, 1985). An issue often addressed in these studies is the link between animal cruelty in childhood and interpersonal violence as an adult. MacDonald (1961) first suggested such a relationship when he proposed that a triad of childhood characteristics — namely, firesetting, enuresis, and cruelty toward animals — was predictive of adult aggressive behavior. Most empirical work, including his own (MacDonald 1961, 1968), however, has not substantiated this argument, referred to by some as the "violence graduation hypothesis" (Arluke et al., 1999). Alternatively, the "deviance generalization hypothesis" posits that childhood cruelty toward animals accompanies, but is not a cause of, other forms of later antisocial behavior, including interpersonal aggression and violence. Analyses examining adults with histories of childhood cruelty toward animals and records of interpersonal violence tend to support this interpretation.

For example, Kellert et al. (1985) examined 152 criminals and non-criminals in Kansas and Connecticut and found significantly higher rates of childhood animal abuse among the criminals compared to the non-criminals and particularly high rates of animal cruelty among the most aggressive criminals. While a majority (60%) of their subjects reported at least one act of cruelty toward animals as a child, 8% indicated at least five or more instances of such abusive behavior. The aggressive criminals were significantly more likely to report repetitive childhood animal abuse than others in the sample. Twenty-five percent of the aggressive criminals had abused animals five or more times in childhood, compared to 5.8% of the non-aggressive criminals and none of the non-criminals (Kellert et al., 1985).

The findings of Arluke et al. (1999) in a study comparing the criminal records of 153 individuals with histories of childhood animal abuse to 153 control participants are consistent. The animal abusers in their study, who ranged in age from 11 to 76 years old and 58% of whom were younger than age 21, were significantly more likely than the non-abusers to have a violent criminal record and to have committed other antisocial acts. Those who had records of cruelty toward animals were 5.3 times more likely to have been arrested for a violent crime, four times more likely to have been arrested for property crime, and 3.5 times more likely to have been arrested for drug-related crime. The data of Arluke et al. (1999) also indicate that animal abuse is equally as likely to precede, as it is to follow, other types of criminal offending. Hence, they concluded that a history of cruelty toward animals is often symptomatic of individuals who display a range of antisocial behavior, including interpersonal violence: "Individuals who commit one form of deviance are likely to commit other forms as well, and in no particular time order" (Arluke et al., 1999).

Descriptive typologies of individuals involved in childhood animal cruelty are not well-developed. Kellert et al. (1985) proposed one classification scheme based on the most excessive cases of cruelty reported by 40 of the 152 subjects in their study. The categories are delineated by reported motivations for the abusive behavior. Kellert et al. (1985) identified nine different motivations, although they stressed that the impetus to mistreat an animal is usually multidimensional and that their study participants typically reported a variety of these motivations. The motivations identified included: to control an animal, to retaliate against an animal, to satisfy a prejudice against a breed or species (most commonly cats), to express aggression through an animal, to enhance one's own aggressiveness, to shock people for amusement, to retaliate against another person, displacement of hostility from a person (e.g., a parent, sibling, or adult) to an animal, and nonspecific sadism (e.g., deriving pleasure from causing injury or suffering).

Finally, the data of Kellert et al. (1985) suggest that family experiences play a significant role in the involvement of juveniles in animal cruelty. In their study, the family backgrounds of aggressive criminals who reported a history of childhood animal cruelty were particularly violent, often involving paternal abuse and alcoholism. Similarly, the non-aggressive criminals and the non-criminals in their study who reported childhood animal cruelty had histories of being physically abused as children, frequent fights with their fathers, and parental alcoholism (Kellert et al., 1985).

SERIAL SEX OFFENDERS

Juvenile sex offenders are a heterogeneous group — more so than their adult counterparts — with widely varying etiologies, acts, and outcomes (Kaplan, 1999). According to U.S. Department of Justice statistics (Greenfield, 1997), youth under the age of 18 account for 16% of forcible rapes and 17% of other sex crimes. The typical juvenile sexual offender is an adolescent male with a history of nonsexual offenses as well. In about one half to three quarters of cases, the offender himself will have been sexually abused. A history of impaired family functioning, physical and sexual abuse, deficits in self-esteem and social skills, poor impulse control, psychopathology, lack of empathy, and deviant sexual interests are also common findings (Becker and Hunter, 1993; Shaw, 1999). Victims are usually younger females who are relatives or acquaintances of the perpetrator.

Although the precise number is not known, a significant proportion of youth who commit sexual offenses develops a course of chronic, more serious offending (Hunter, 1999). Working backwards, it is generally held that most chronic adult sexual offenders experienced deviant sexual thoughts and committed sexual crimes as juveniles (Abel et al., 1987; Berliner, 1998). Rubenstein et al. (1993) carried out a followup study of 19 sexually assaultive male juveniles who had been incarcerated for their offenses without treatment. At a mean followup period of 8 years, 37% had reoffended sexually; some had committed multiple sexual offenses. Moreover, 89% had been re-arrested for other kinds of violent offenses and had committed twice as many violent offenses as the violent juveniles who had served as a control group. In contrast, Sipe et al. (1998) followed up a group of 124 nonviolent juvenile sexual offenders after a mean of 6 years, and found a recidivism rate of 9.7%. These authors concluded that we should expect differing recidivism rates by type of presenting sexual offense. Thus, it appears that the violent adolescent sexual offender is at greater risk for becoming a serial sex offender. The following case illustrates this point.

Ressler et al. (1983) reported the case of a teenage boy who committed 12 rapes and rape-murders over a 4-year period. His female victims ranged in age from 17 to 34. The five murder victims were all randomly selected and targeted as they drove into the apartment complex where the offender lived. After stabbing, strangling, or drowning the victims, this youth would then typically collect a souvenir (e.g., a piece of jewelry), drive the victim's car around, and then return home to watch for television or newspaper accounts of the crimes. This offender had begun acquiring criminal charges at the age of 12, although he first murdered when he was 18 years of age. He was of average intelligence but had performed marginally at school. DSM-II diagnoses included adolescent adjustment reaction, character disorder without psychosis, and multiple personality. He carried a reputation as both a "macho ladies' man" and as a "con-artist." All of his rape and murder offenses, with one exception, occurred while he was on probation and under psychiatric supervision.

Rasmussen (1999) looked at factors related to recidivism in juvenile sexual offenders. Molestation of multiple victims, parental divorce or separation, and a history of sexual abuse increased the odds of the youth re-offending sexually. The recommendation was made to address all factors in treatment that may contribute to any type of criminal behavior — not just those that appear directly related to the sexual offending. This recommendation is in agreement with the successful use of multisystemic therapy in a small sample of adolescent sex offenders (n = 8). In this study, those treated with multisystemic therapy had a lower recidivism rate at 3 years (12.5%) when compared with a control group treated with individual counseling (75%) (Borduin et al., 1990).

In general, treatment of the juvenile sexual offender can range from community-based services to psychopharmacology to intensive residential treatment, the latter sometimes requiring two or more years of treatment in certain instances (Hunter, 1999). Treatment programs typically employ some combination of individual, group, family, social skills, behavioral, and educational therapies. Cognitive-behavioral therapy is considered the most useful of psychotherapies for this population. Involving the court system in their treatment is also helpful because it provides added motivation to consistently participate in therapeutic endeavors.

Overall, treatment results for juvenile sexual offenders have been variable, with some cautiously optimistic recidivism rates in the range of 10% at roughly 1 to 2 or more years followup (Becker, 1990; Bremer, 1992; Hunter, 1998). In all fairness, these same outcomes can be just as easily viewed from a pessimistic perspective based on the relatively short periods of time after treatment used to assess recidivism rates. One of the difficulties in assessing treatment outcomes is accurately determining rates of recidivism. Re-arrest rates are spuriously low, as most offenders are not arrested for any given offense. Moreover, self-report measures are dependent on the reporter answering honestly and thus can be unreliable. This is particularly true in a population that has some degree of antisocial character traits, that may not be convinced of reassurances of confidentiality when asked to self-report, and that stands to lose their liberty if they are caught for sex offenses. It is hoped that future research efforts will help define subtypes of juvenile sexual offenders that will allow clearer predictions of treatment amenability and recidivism.

SERIAL SADISM

Krafft-Ebing, in his classic text *Psychopathic Sexualis* (1882), defined sadism as: "The experience of sexually pleasurable sensations (including orgasm) produced by acts of cruelty ... [on] animals or human beings ... [and] may also consist of an innate desire to humiliate, hurt, wound, or even destroy others in order to thereby create sexual pleasure in one's self." More recent definitions offered this century have changed little, defining sadism as a wish to control another person through domination, humiliation, or inflicting pain for the purpose of producing sexual arousal (MacCulloch et al., 1983). The commission of sadistic acts is thought to be typically stimulated by sadistic fantasy.

There are few studies addressing the concept of sadism in children and adolescents; however, there are a number of rich case reports that detail a variety of sadistic fantasies and behaviors by youth. For instance, Johnson and Becker (1997) described a series of nine adolescents who had developed sadistic fantasies. One of the boys had tried to kill others using a knife on several different occasions, and another boy, at the age of 17, murdered an unknown woman with whom he then engaged in necrophilia. Cruelty to animals was common in these youths' histories.

In this section, several abridged case reports from older and more recent literature will be summarized to illustrate the diverse trajectories that childhood sadism may take. These cases support the description by MacCulloch et al. (1983) of sadistic offenders who, in their perverse development, manifest an "escalating sequence of sadistic behavior," from progressively sadistic fantasies to increasingly active "*in vivo* trials" to the ultimate acting out of the entire fantasy. A study addressing the application of sadistic personality disorder in juveniles will then be summarized.

Krafft-Ebing (1882) described the case of "The Girl-Cutter of Augsburg." This offender at the age of 14 was experiencing the urge to cut girls to satisfy his sexual desires. He denied masturbating to these fantasies but admitted to nocturnal emissions during dreams of girls who had been cut. At the age of 19, he could no longer resist these urges and he cut a girl, having an orgasm in the process. Following this first cutting act, the impulse reportedly grew "constantly more powerful." His cutting eventually progressed to stabbing, and he achieved greater sexual satisfaction knowing that the stabbing created greater pain and bleeding in his victims. Until his arrest almost 20 years later, he continued his knife attacks, injuring 50 victims in all. A search of his dwelling revealed a collection of "daggers, sword-canes, and knives." He reportedly felt intense sexual excitement merely when grasping one of his weapons. In adulthood, he had been a wine merchant and was described as having a pleasing external appearance but a "peculiar and shy" personality.

Jesse Pomeroy began his sadistic career in Boston at the age of 11. The year was 1871. His victims were 7- to 8-year-old boys. The first known victim was tied to a beam and beaten until he was unconscious (Phoebus, 1974). Three months later, another boy was lured to the same place as the first attack. This victim was stripped naked, beaten with a rope and a board, and also knocked unconscious — he lost teeth and suffered a broken nose during the assault. Over the ensuing months, five more boys were victimized in similar fashion. Jesse would take his victims to an isolated location, disrobe them, and then beat them, stab and cut them with a knife, and torture them with pins. Jesse was finally apprehended and sentenced to 18 months in a reform school. One month after his release, a 10-year-old girl was reported missing. Two months after his release, a 4-year-old boy was found with his head nearly severed and 31 knife wounds about his body. Jesse was again apprehended and sentenced to solitary confinement for life. The decomposed body of the missing girl was eventually found buried in the cellar of his mother's home.

Russell (1966) outlined the case of a 14-year-old boy who acted on a "sexual urge" by striking a male friend's mother in the back with a knife in order to weaken her so that he could "feel her up." He had committed a similar offense during the previous year and as a result underwent outpatient treatment. Following this second episode, the Court placed him in a psychiatric hospital, where he was treated with intensive inpatient psychotherapy for 9 months. After release, he continued in out-patient treatment for 2 years. His IQ was measured at 129. In high school, he did well academically and was active in sports and extracurricular activities. The psychiatrist who had been treating him as an outpatient believed his illness had gone into remission, and when he was almost 17 years old the Court dismissed his case. Less than 2 years later, he stabbed to death a young adult woman with whom he had been spending time.

Sexual sadism and psychopathic traits among adult sexual homicide offenders are established findings. Myers and Monaco (2000) investigated the relationship between anger experience and styles of expression, sadistic personality disorder, and psychopathy in 14 juvenile sexual homicide offenders whose mean age at the time of their offenses was 15.2 years. Instruments used to evaluate these boys included the State-Trait Anger Expression Inventory (STAXI) and the Schedule for Nonadaptive and Adaptive Personality (SNAP).

The STAXI is a self-report inventory designed to measure two domains of anger: anger experience and anger expression. Anger experience has two scales: State Anger and Trait Anger. The second domain, anger expression, has three scales: Anger-In, Anger-Out, and Anger Control. Trait Anger measures angry temperament. Anger-In indicates how often angry feelings are held in or suppressed, while Anger-Out measures how often angry feelings are expressed toward other people or objects. Anger Control measures how often anger expression is controlled. The DSM-III-R version of the SNAP was used to allow for the diagnosis of sadistic personality disorder. The criteria for this diagnosis refer to a pattern of cruel, demeaning, aggressive behavior, not specifically of a sexual nature.

Those four (31%) participants who met criteria for sadistic personality had significantly higher Anger-Out scale scores than those without the disorder and were also higher on Trait Anger to a marginally significant degree. For the group as a whole, Anger Control was a more prominent style of anger expression than Anger-Out. The authors postulated that this latter result might be related to the finding that over one half of the participants in this sample had admitted to violent sexual fantasies (e.g., raping women at knifepoint, mutilating victims, and removing their organs). Perhaps some of these boys invested their energy in resisting these ongoing sadistic fantasies. Thus, this anger control style may have served an adaptive function for these boys prior to their crimes. Megargee and Mendelsohn (1967) theorize that the "overcontrolled" offender is often responsible for the most aggressive of criminal acts. Additionally, schizoid and schizotypal personality disorder were the most common Axis II diagnoses in the boys, both present in 38% of the group, indicating the presence of personality types prone to reliance on fantasy.

The findings in this study lend support to the validity and utility of sadistic personality disorder as a diagnosis in younger forensic populations. It should be mentioned that this DSM-III-R diagnosis was dropped in 1994 with the publication of the DSM-IV. However, a survey of the members of the American Academy of Psychiatry and the Law found that those who had clinical experience with individuals with sadistic personality disorder believed the diagnosis to be useful for both clinical and forensic purposes (Spitzer et al., 1991). Moreover, the diagnostic criteria for sadistic personality disorder were found to have a high sensitivity and specificity. Other studies have reported on the reliability of this personality diagnosis and its high prevalence rate (33%) in sex offenders (Feister and Gay, 1991; Reich, 1993).

In closing this section, it is important to stress that sadism in children and adolescents is a rare but valid phenomenon in need of further study. Youth may exhibit a wide variety of sadistic behaviors, both sexual and nonsexual in nature. Moreover, juvenile sadism can become serial in nature, progress to serious violence, and even culminate in murder.

SERIAL MURDER

There are few documented cases of serial murder committed by children and adolescents. The FBI calculates that there are only about 35 serial killers presently operating in the U.S. (Holmes and DeBurger, 1985), while others suggest a figure of 100 is more accurate (Wilson, 1988). In either case, serial murder by any age group is a rare entity.

Research suggests that serial murderers typically begin their "careers" in their 20s. In a series of 222 classic serial murderers collected by The National Center for the Analysis of Violent Crime (1992), the mean age of their first murder was 27.5 years. However, it is not uncommon for the first murder of a serial killer's career to occur during their adolescence. Burgess et al. (1996) reported that 10 out of 36 (28%) men who had been convicted of sexual homicide first committed murder as juveniles. Furthermore, the average age of onset for rape fantasies in these men was 11.6 years if they had been sexually abused, and 15.3 years if they had not been sexually abused. Eighty percent of this sample killed multiple victims (Ressler et al., 1988). These findings illuminate the frequent formation of fantasies involving sexual violence during the childhood of the serial murderer.

Several notorious cases of serial murderers from the 19th and 20th century are presented to demonstrate the beginnings of the murderous pattern in childhood. The limited literature that describes serial murder by youth is also reviewed in this section. Finally, several cases of juvenile serial murder are presented.

Peter Kürten, born in 1883 in Germany, was identified by the monikers "The Sadist of Dusseldorf" and "The Vampire of Düsseldorf." He killed 8 or 9 people and sadistically injured many others through stabbings and batterings during his nearly 4-decade career. His reputedly victimized 70+ people and eventually confessed to committing his first two murders when he was only 9 years of age (Phoebus, 1974). One day, Peter was playing with two other boys on a raft in the Rhine River. Peter pushed one of the boys into the river. This boy could not swim, and immediately began to flounder. The second boy instinctively jumped in to help, and Peter purposely shoved him under the raft. Both boys drowned. Peter was not suspected of foul play due to his young age and a lack of witnesses.

Peter Kürten later explained that his sadistic tendencies had not significantly developed at the time of the two boys' deaths. His violent sexual tendencies began to emerge in his early teens, when he displayed cruelty to animals and engaged in sexual acts with them. He had sexual intercourse with farm animals and knifed them to heighten his sexual excitement. He first attempted rape of a human at age 16. A sadistic, alcoholic father who had destructive rage attacks dominated his home environment. During one of these attacks, Peter witnessed him raping his mother and eldest sister. The father served time in prison for the latter crime. As an adult, Peter Kürten was described as a quiet, married, hard-working, vain man who paid excessive attention to his appearance. He had a job as a factory worker, and his hobby was bird watching.

The vast majority of serial killers are male. Mary Bell was a rarity in being not only a female but also a child who killed twice and nearly three times. She was a withdrawn, callous girl who had been rejected by her emotionally disturbed mother at birth. Mary had a chaotic childhood, having been passed around between relatives and foster homes. She killed for the first time on the eve of her 11th birthday in May of 1968 (Phoebus, 1974). Her victim was a 4-year-old boy who was her Newcastle-upon-Tyne neighbor. After this first murder, Mary tormented the family members by asking them questions about whether they missed their dead child and if she could see him in his coffin. She strangled other neighborhood children around this time to the point that they turned purple but was still not arrested. Two months later she successfully strangled another neighborhood boy, this one 3 years old. On the victim's stomach she used a razor to carve her first initial "M." Also during this time, she broke into a school with her best friend and scribbled on the wall, "Fuck off, we murder, watch out, Fanny and Faggot." She was arrested soon after the second murder and convicted of two counts of manslaughter. Her sentence was life in an institution with a chance for release if her "psychopathic personality" was cured. She was freed in 1980 and now lives under an alias. A biography of her life was recently published in 1999, entitled *Cries Unheard: Why Children Kill: The Story of Mary Bell.*

Henry Lee Lucas, a serial killer who was responsible for the deaths of an estimated 40 to 50 victims (he claims to have killed hundreds) in the 1970s and early 1980s, is believed to be the most prolific serial murderer in U.S. history (Peyton, 1984). He killed for the first time at 14 years of age. His victim was a 17-year-old girl he abducted from a school bus stop and later strangled. He had decided that he wanted to see what sex was like with humans. Prior to this, he had been killing animals for sex, typically with a knife (Egger, 1990). He reportedly had developed a fascination with knives in first grade. His second murder, the victim being his mother, did not occur until 9 years after his first killing.

At the age of 15, Edmund Kemper fatally shot his grandmother and grandfather. He explained that he "just wondered how it would feel to shoot grandma" (Strentz and Hassel, 1978). He was released from penal and psychiatric institutionalization at the age of 21, and two psychiatrists attested to his excellent response to treatment. Over the next 8 months he murdered, dismembered, and sexually assaulted six young girls (cannibalizing at least two of them), bludgeoned his mother with a hammer, and strangled one of his mother's friends, bringing his victim total to ten before surrendering to authorities (Hickey, 1991).

Schlesinger and Revitch (1999), in a recent paper on sexual burglaries and sexual homicide, serendipitously documented the case of a serial juvenile murderer. At the age of 15, this youth began regularly burglarizing homes. After 18 months of voyeuristic burglaries, he killed the first of his two murder victims. The victim was one of his teachers, and after breaking into her house and searching for money, he killed her by strangulation. The second murder occurred a number of weeks later. This victim was a 60-year-old woman whom he drowned in a bathtub after gagging her, sexually abusing her, and twisting her breasts. He was arrested one month later while peeping into a home. Of note, the two murders were separated by a sadistic, non-fatal attack on another woman. In addition to sexually assaulting this woman and twisting her breasts, he also inserted objects into her vagina and tortured her.

Although not from scientific sources, several cases of notable serial murder by youth were identified through media and Internet sources. Thomas Quick, referred to as "Sweden's premier serial killer," committed his first murder at the age of 14. He is alleged to have killed at least 10 people in Sweden during a 2-year killing period and also confessed to six killings in Norway. His criminal acts included dismemberment of and necrophilic acts with his victims.

Gustavo Adolfo of El Salvador was charged with 17 counts of homicide and convicted of seven. Like Thomas Quick, Gustavo also killed for the first time at 14 and committed all of his murders as a minor. He raped his first victim, removed her breasts, and threw her into a well to die.

Finally, Craig Price may be the youngest serial killer in U.S. history. He first killed at the age of 13. The victim was a neighborhood woman whom he stabbed to death. At 15, he killed another woman and her two daughters in a similar fashion. He is reportedly suspected in other Rhode Island murders as yet unsolved.

SUMMARY

The intent of this chapter has been to provide an overview of some of the more serious types of serial offending by children and adolescents. Space limitations restrict a more in-depth look at each of the six crime categories covered in this work. The scientific community has only recently begun to address the existence of serial criminal behavior in juveniles. It is hoped that this overview will provide some useful insights into these offenders and help identify specific areas in need of further study. Furthermore, because of the paucity of existing literature, the authors wish to encourage the exchange of research observations and findings among those with an interest in and clinical exposure to serial offending by children and adolescents.

REFERENCES

Abel, G.G., Becker J.V., Cunningham-Rathner, J., Mittelman, M.S., Murphy, W.D., and Rouleau, J.L. (1987). Self-reported sex crimes of nonincarcerated paraphiliacs. *Journal of Interpersonal Violence*, 2:3–25.

Arluke, A., Levin J., Luke, C., and Ascione, F. (1999). The relationship of animal abuse to violence and other forms of antisocial behavior. *Journal of Interpersonal Violence*, 14:963–975.

Barlow, H.D. and Ferdinand, T.N. (1992). *Understanding Delinquency*. New York: Harper Collins.

Barnett, W. and Spitzer, M. (1994). Pathological fire-setting 1951–1991: a review. *Medicine, Science and Law*, 34:4–20.

Becker, J.V. (1990). Treating adolescent sex offenders. *Professional Psychology: Research and Practice*, 21:362–365.

Becker, J.V. and Hunter, J.A. (1993). Aggressive sexual offenders. *Child and Adolescent Psychiatric Clinics of North America*, 2:477–487.

Berliner. L. (1998). Juvenile sex offenders: should they be treated differently? *Journal of Interpersonal Violence*, 13:645–646.

Block, J.H., Block, J., and Folkman, W.S. (1976). Fire and children: learning survival skills. U.S.D.A. Forest Service research paper PSW–119. Berkley, CA: Pacific Southwest Forest and Range Experiment Station.

Borduin, C.M., Henggeler, S.W., Blaske, D.M., and Stein, R.J. (1990). Multisystemic treatment of adolescent sexual offenders. *Journal of Offender Therapy and Comparative Criminology*, 34:105–114.

Bremer, J. F. (1992). Serious juvenile offenders: treatment and long-term follow-up. *Psychiatric Annals*, 22:326–332.

Burgess A.W., Hartman C.R., Ressler R.K., Douglas J.E., and McCormack A. (1986). Sexual homicide: a motivational model. *Journal of Interpersonal Violence*, 1:251–272.

Cernkovich, S.A., Giordano, P.C., and Pugh, M.D. (1985). Chronic offenders: the missing cases in self-report delinquency research. *Journal of Criminal Law and Criminology*, 76:705–732.

Chaiken, M.R. (1998). *Violent Neighborhoods, Violent Kids: What Could Be Done with Boys in D.C.* Alexandria, VA: LINC.

Egger, S.A. (1984). A working definition of serial murder and the reduction of linkage blindness. *Journal of Policy and Science Administration*, 12:348–356.

Egger, S.A. (1990). *Serial Murder: An Elusive Phenomenon.* Westport, CT: Praeger.

Elliott, D.S. and Ageton, S. (1980). Reconciling race and class differences in self-reported and official estimates of delinquency. *American Sociological Review*, 45:95–110.

Elliott D.S. and Huizinga, D. (1984). The Relationship Between Delinquent Behavior and ADM Problems, unpublished report prepared for the Behavioral Research Institute, Boulder, CO.

Elmhorn, K. (1965). Study in self-reported delinquency among school children in Stockholm. *Scandinavian Studies in Criminology,* Vol. 1. London: Tavistock Publishers.

Federal Bureau of Investigation (1996). *Crime in the United States, 1995.* Washington, D.C.: U.S. Government Printing Office.

Feister, S.J. and Gay, M. (1991). Sadistic personality disorder: a review of data and recommendations for DSM-IV. *Journal of Personality Disorders*, 5:376–385

Felthous, A.R. (1980). Childhood antecedents of aggressive behaviors in male psychiatric patients. *Bulletin of the American Academy of Psychiatry and Law*, 8:104–110.

Garry, E.M. (1997). *Juvenile Firesetting and Arson.* Fact sheet #51. Washington, D.C.: Office of Juvenile Justice and Delinquency Prevention.

Gold, M. (1970). *Delinquent Behavior in an American City.* Belmont, CA: Brooks-Cole.

Greenfield, L.A. (1997). *Sex Offenses and Offenders: An Analysis of Data on Rape and Sexual Assault.* U.S. Department of Justice: Washington, D.C.: Bureau of Justice Statistics.

Hamparian, D.M., Schuster, R., Dinitz, S., and Conrad, J.P. (1978). *The Dangerous Few: A Study of Dangerous Juvenile Offenders.* Lexington, MA: Lexington Books.

Hawkins, J.D. and Catalano, R.F., Jr. (1992). *Communities that Care.* San Francisco, CA: Jossey-Bass.

Hickey, E.W. (1991). *Serial Murderers and Their Victims.* Pacific Grove, CA: Brooks-Cole Publishing.

Holmes R.M. and DeBurger J.E. (1985). Profiles in terror: the serial murderer. *Federal Probation*, 49:29–34.

Huizinga, D., Loeber, R., and Thornberry, T.P. (1994). *Urban Delinquency and Substance Abuse: Initial Findings*. Washington, D.C.: Office of Juvenile Justice and Delinquency Prevention.

Hunter J.A. (1999). Adolescent sex offenders. In Van Hasselt, V.B. and Hersen, M. (Eds.), *Handbook of Approaches with Violent Offenders: Contemporary Strategies and Issues*. New York: Kluwer Academic/Plenum Press.

Johnson, B.R. and Becker, J.V. (1997). Natural born killers?: the development of the sexually sadistic serial killer. *Journal of the American Academy of Psychiatry and the Law*, 25:335–348.

Kaplan, M.S. (1999). Juvenile Sex Offenders, paper presented at the Sex, Psychiatry, and the Law conference, January 23, 1999, New York.

Kaufman, I., Heims, L.W., and Reiser, D.E. (1961). A re-evaluation of the psychodynamics of firesetting. *American Journal of Orthopsychiatry*, 31:123–137.

Kellert, S.R. and Felthous, A.R. (1985). Childhood cruelty toward animals among criminals and noncriminals. *Human Relations*, 38:1113–1129.

Kelley, B.T., Huizinga, D., Thornberry, T.P., and Loeber, R. (1997). *Epidemiology of Serious Violence*. Washington, D.C.: U.S. Department of Justice.

Krafft-Ebing R. (1882). *Psychopathia Sexualis* (F.J. Rebman, trans.). Brooklyn, NY: Physicians and Surgeons Book Company.

MacCulloch M.J., Snowden P.R., Wood P.J.W., and Mills, H.E. (1983). Sadistic fantasy, sadistic behavior and offending. *British Journal of Psychiatry*, 143:20–29.

MacDonald, J. (1961). *The Murderer and His Victim*. Springfield, IL: Charles C Thomas.

MacDonald, J. (1968). *Homicidal Threats*. Springfield, IL: Charles C Thomas.

Megargee, E.I. and Mendelsohn, G.A. (1967). Development and validation of an MMPI scale of assaultiveness in overcontrolled individuals. *Journal of Abnormal Psychology*, 72:519–528.

Myers, W.C. and Monaco, L. (2000). Anger experience, styles of anger expression, sadistic personality disorder, and psychopathy in juvenile sexual homicide offenders. *Journal of Forensic Sciences*, in press.

National Center for the Analysis of Violent Crime (1992). *Serial, Mass and Spree Murderers in the United States: Search of Major Wire Services and Publications on Offenders Operating from 1960 to the Present*. Washington, D.C.: U.S. Department of Justice.

Nurcombe, B. (1964). Children who set fires. *Medical Journal of Australia*, April, 577–584.

Peyton, D. (1984). Henry Lucas was a killer at age 14, *West Virginia Herald-Dispatch*, December 16, p. A-5.

Phoebus Publishing Company (1974). Children who kill. In Hall, A. (Ed.), *Crimes and Punishment: A Pictorial Encyclopedia of Aberrant Behavior*. Hicksville, NY: Symphonette Press.

Rasmussen, L.A. (1999). Factors related to recidivism among juvenile sexual offenders. *Sexual Abuse: A Journal of Research and Treatment*, 11:69–85.

Reich, J. (1993). Prevalence and characteristics of sadistic personality disorder in outpatient veterans populations. *Psychiatric Research*, 48:267–276.

Ressler, R.K., Burgess, A.W., and Douglas, J.E. (1983). Rape and rape murder: one offender and twelve victims. *American Journal of Psychiatry*, 140:36–40.

Ressler, R.K., Burgess, A.W., and Douglas, J.E. (1988). *Sexual Homicide*. Lexington, MA: Lexington Press.

Rothestein, R. (1963). Explorations of ego structures of firesetting children. *Archives of General Psychiatry*, 9:246–253.

Rubinstein, M., Yeager, C.A., Goodstein, C., and Lewis, D.O. (1993). Sexually assaultive male juveniles: a follow-up. *American Journal of Psychiatry*. 150:262–265.

Russell D.H. (1966). A study of juvenile murderers. *Journal of Offender Therapy.* 10:55–86.

Schlesinger, L.B. and Revitch, E. (1999). Sexual burglaries and sexual homicide: clinical, forensic, and investigative considerations. *Journal of the American Academy of Psychiatry and the Law,* 27:227–238.

Shannon, L. (1982). *Assessing the Relationship of Adult Criminal Careers to Juvenile Careers.* Washington, D.C.: U.S. Department of Justice.

Shannon, L. (1988). *Criminal Career Continuity: Its Social Context.* New York: Human Sciences Press.

Shannon, L. (1991). *Changing Patterns of Delinquency and Crime: A Longitudinal Study in Racine.* Boulder, CO: Westview.

Shaw, J.A. (1999). Male adolescent sexual offenders. In Shaw, J.A. (Ed.), *Sexual Aggression* (pp. 169–194). Washington, D.C.: American Psychiatric Press.

Shelden, R.G. and Chesney-Lind, M. (1993). Gender and race differences in delinquent careers. *Juvenile and Family Court Journal,* 44:73–90.

Shelden, R.G., Horvath, J.A., and Tracy, S. (1989). Do status offenders get worse: some clarifications on the question of escalation. *Crime and Delinquency,* 35:202–216.

Siegelman, E.Y. (1969). *Children Who Set Fires: An Exploratory Study.* Sacramento, CA: Resources Agency of California, Department of Conservation.

Siegelman, E.Y. and Folkman, W.S. (1971). *Youthful Firesetters: An Exploratory Study in Personality and Background.* Springfield, VA: U.S. Department of Agriculture, Forest Service.

Sipe, R, Jensen, E.L., and Everett, R.S. (1998). Adolescent sexual offenders grown up: recidivism in young adulthood. *Criminal Justice and Behavior,* 25:109–124.

Snyder, H. (1988). *Court Careers of Juvenile Offenders.* Washington, D.C.: U.S. Department of Justice.

Snyder, H. (1997). *Serious, Violent, and Chronic Juvenile Offenders: An Assessment of the Extent of and Trends in Officially Recognized Serious Criminal Behavior in a Delinquent Population.* Pittsburgh, PA: National Center for Juvenile Justice.

Snyder, H. (1999). *Juvenile Arson, 1997.* Fact sheet #91. Washington, D.C.: Office of Juvenile Justice and Delinquency Prevention.

Spitzer, R.L., Feister, S., Gay, M., and Pfohl, B. (1991). Results of a survey of forensic psychiatrists on the validity of the sadistic personality disorder diagnosis. *American Journal of Psychiatry,* 148:875–879.

Strentz, T. and Hassel, C.V. (1978). The sociopath — a criminal enigma. *Journal of Police Science and Administration.* 6:135–140.

Thornberry, T.P. (1994). *Violent Families and Youth Violence.* Fact sheet #21. Washington, D.C.: Office of Juvenile Justice and Delinquency Prevention.

Thornberry, T.P., Huizinga, D., and Loeber, R. (1995). The prevention of serious delinquency and violence. In Howell, J.C., Krisberg, B., Hawkins, J.D., and Wilson, J.J. (Eds.), *Serious, Violent and Chronic Juvenile Offenders* (pp. 213–237). Thousand Oaks, CA: Sage.

Tracy, P.E., Wolfgang, M.E., and Figlio, R.M. (1990). *Delinquency Careers in Two Birth Cohorts.* New York: Plenum Press.

Vandersall, T.A. and Weiner, J.M. (1970). Children who set fires. *Archives of General Psychiatry,* 22:63–71.

West, D.J. and Farrington, D.P. (1977). *The Delinquent Way of Life.* London: Heinemann.

Wilson P.R. (1988). "Stranger" child murder: issues relating to causes and controls. *Forensic Science International,* 36:267–277.

Wolfgang, M.E., Figlio, R.M., and Sellin, T. (1972). *Delinquency in a Birth Cohort.* Chicago, IL: University of Chicago Press.

Wooden, W.S. and Berkey, M.L. (1984). *Children and Arson: America's Middle Class Nightmare*. New York: Plenum Press.

15 Survivors, Families, and Co-Victims of Serial Offenders

Laurence Miller and Louis B. Schlesinger

CONTENTS

INTRODUCTION

No news item evokes as strong a visceral reaction as that of a family member's murder. And few news stories so strongly elicit the dual responses of revulsion and

0-8493-2236-7/00/$0.00+$.50

titillation as serial sexual homicide. Especially in high-profile crimes, it is typically the killer who gets all the attention, with the case almost always referred to, indeed immortalized eponymously, by the murderer's name or call sign: "Son of Sam," the "Dahmer case," the "Boston Strangler."

No less than in the popular media does this focus on the offender appear in clinical and research agendas. Psychologists and criminologists love to interview those fascinating torturers, mutilators, dismemberers, and anthropophagers, while expressing scant interest in their homicidal fodder of dead or violated victims and the traumatized mourners whose lives have been permanently warped by horror. Serial offenders make hot copy for reporters and raise hefty grants for doctors and professors; victims lie mutely and their surviving loved ones pay the medical and legal bills.

This chapter is for the survivors, the families, what Spungen (1998) has termed the *"co-victims"* — the mothers, fathers, spouses, siblings, children, and close friends who become victimized by their loved one's tragedy. This chapter is also for those who help them — the dedicated law enforcement investigators, prosecutors, criminal justice advocates, psychotherapists, and support group peers who try to mitigate the terror, anger, and desperation at different stages of the criminal justice process, and who, in so doing, may become co-victims themselves.

As sparse as the psychological treatment literature is on victims' survivors, rarer still is clinical material written specifically for treating co-victims. Accordingly, this chapter represents a combination of a literature synthesis and our own clinical observations in treating victims of interpersonal violence (Miller, 1994; 1998b,c; 1999a,b,c) and the helpers and healers (Miller, 1995; 1998a,c; 2000a,b) who try to make bearable their extraordinary ordeal.

SURVIVOR REACTIONS AND SYMPTOMS

Murder is the ultimate violation that one individual can inflict upon another, a brutal, purposeful assault forced on an unwilling victim. The murder or serious assault of a family member rakes survivors over the rough and jagged existential terrain of fairness, justice, faith, and the very meaning of life. The especially cruel and sadistic nature of many serial offenders compounds the rage, grief, and despair of the survivors. Unlike the relatively controlled, decorous demise of a relative with a progressive illness, bereavement caused by a sudden and unanticipated violent offense robs the family of the innoculatory balm of anticipatory grief. Added to this is the stark confrontation of the survivors with their own mortality and vulnerability, as the illusion of safety and order in the world is shattered (Bard and Sangry, 1986; Rynearson, 1988; Rynearson and McCreery, 1993; Sprang and McNeil, 1995).

COMMON SURVIVOR REACTIONS

For many survivors, the first news of the offense strikes a mortal blow to the self, evoking their own sense of personal loss. Family members are typically preoccupied with the nature of the injuries inflicted on the victim, the brutality of the attack, the types of weapons used, and the victim's suffering. Families may clamor for information about the identity of the offender, the relationship he had to the victim, and how the victim was first abducted or assaulted. When the offender knew the victim and is known to the family, the family has to cope with their own feelings about their relationship to the offender (Ressler et al., 1988). Unlike death by illness, murder and serious assault always involve a human perpetrator, and the greater the perceived intentionality and malevolence of the offense, the higher the distress of the survivors (Carson and MacLeod, 1997; MacLeod, 1999).

Survivors may be seized with an impulse to "do something." A deep and justifiable anger toward the offender alternately smolders and flares as the investigation and trial meander along. Even after sentencing, the anger may persist for years, or forever. A common coping mechanism for dealing with rageful feelings and impulses consists of ruminating on fantasies of revenge. Actual vengeful attacks by family members on perpetrators are extremely rare, probably due in large part to the sheer impracticability of getting at the criminal, who, especially in high-profile cases, is always seen accompanied by a phalanx of bodyguards and protectors during the trial, and also to the basic moral values and "common decency" of most families, who are not looking to correct one atrocity with another. Most families direct their energies toward efforts to aid in the apprehension and prosecution of the offender, which can be seen as either a help or hindrance by investigators and prosecutors (Ressler et al., 1988; Rynearson, 1988; Rynearson and McCreery, 1993; Sprang and McNeil, 1995).

Even more common than anger, a pervasive "fear of everything" begins to loom in the survivors' consciousness, beginning with their first awareness of the crime and persisting for several years or more. Survivors' heightened sense of their own vulnerability may spur them to change daily routines, install house and car alarms, carry weapons, and refuse to go to out after dark or to visit certain locales. There may be phobic avoidance of anything related to the trauma, including people, places, certain foods, music, and so on. Survivors may experience psychophysiological hyperstartle responses to such ordinarily non-threatening stimuli as crime shows on television, shouting in the street or among family members, or news stories of any tragedy, including non-criminal deaths such as traffic fatalities or fatal illnesses.

The survivors' usual range of territorial and affiliative activity becomes constricted as the home is turned into a protective fortress, strangers are avoided, and unfamiliar surroundings are circumvented. All family members may be outfitted with pagers and cell phones and may have to submit daily schedules of activity, as there develops a compulsive need for family members to be close at hand or reachable at a moment's notice. Older children and adolescents, especially, may resent this "babying" restriction of their autonomy and independence (Ressler et al., 1988; Rynearson, 1988; Rynearson and McCreery, 1993; Sprang and McNeil, 1995).

Survivors may identify or over-identify with the victim and begin sleeping in the dead relative's bed, wearing his or her clothing, and developing a feeling of kinship with other bereaved victims and co-victims of similar tragedy. Many feel like lepers or pariahs, "cast out" of a pre-trauma Eden or state of normal existential comfort that the rest of us "civilians" rely on to assuage our sense of vulnerability, but which no longer is a coping option for co-victims of violent crime: "We know better — the world is a cruel and ugly place." Survivors may have frequent disturbing dreams of the imagined horrifying death of the victim or wish-fulfillment dreams of protecting or rescuing the victim. This may be compounded by guilt, especially in parents, if they feel they should have "done more" to keep their child safe (Ressler et al., 1988; Rynearson, 1988; Rynearson et al., 1993; Sprang and McNeil, 1995).

Everybody's health suffers. Common psychophysiological disorders include appetite and sleep disturbances, gastrointestinal problems, cardiovascular disorders, decreased resistance to infectious disease, and increased anxiety and depression. A significant number of family members die within the first few years of a homicide (Schlosser, 1997; Sprang and McNeil, 1995).

Grief work is the term often used for the psychological process that moves the person from being preoccupied with thoughts of the victim, through painful recollections of the experience, to the final step of an integrative experience (Parkes, 1972). Those who appear to adapt best to stressful experiences in general typically have a range of available coping strategies and resources that permit greater flexibility in dealing with the particular demands of the traumatic event (Aldwin, 1994; Bowman, 1997; Miller, 1998c; Silver and Wortman, 1980).

THE MURDER OF A CHILD

While all murder is tragic, few family victimizations are as ferociously wrenching as the homicidal death of a child (Schlosser, 1997). Rage, horror, and despair all commingle as the survivors struggle for understanding and sense of justice — indeed, for a reason to go on, to "keep fighting," even to keep living. Family adaptation to a child's homicidal death involves the restructuring of all relationships, often straining marriage and extended family bonds to the breaking point (Kiser et al., 1998), and many bereaved families do not survive as a unit.

Special problems arise when a child is killed by another family member, confronting the entire family with the dilemmas of identification, divided loyalties, belief, and trust. Intrafamily murder comprises 25% of homicides and often occurs in families with a long history of instability and dysfunction. In these cases, not only will all the family members identify with the victim, but they are identified with the murderer, as well. These families need specialized, skilled intervention, and even with this care the prognosis for a positive family outcome remains guarded (Rynearson, 1988, 1996).

Ressler et al. (1988) cite Rinear's (1984) study of survivor reactions in a survey of members of the support group, Parents of Murdered Children. The symptomatology began within the first few weeks of the child's murder and persisted, in varying combinations and degrees of intensity, for as long as two years later. The traumatic stress symptoms were consistent with *post-traumatic stress disorder*, or PTSD (APA, 1994), and included, in rank order of frequency:

1. Sleep disturbances, such as early morning awakening, insomnia, and hypersomnia
2. Constricted affect, particularly feelings associated with intimacy, tenderness, and sexuality, as well as depression and "feeling dead inside"

3. Diminished interest in previously enjoyed activities, such as work, church, or social relationships
4. Recurrent and intrusive recollections of the murder, including preoccupation with thoughts of the nature of the brutality and the extent of the suffering experienced by the child
5. Feelings of detachment, estrangement, or alienation from others, who are felt to have "no concept" of what this experience is about
6. Avoidance of activities that arouse traumatic recollections, including any situations that are somehow associated with their child's murder
7. Intensification of post-murder symptomatology — described as "instant replay" — in response to stimuli and events that symbolize or remind them of their child's murder, such as chance remarks by friends, television programs or magazine articles on violence, and so on
8. Recurrent dreams of the murder, which may take one of three forms: (a) wish-fulfillment dreams, in which the child is seen as alive and well; (b) "undoing" dreams, in which the parent attempts to defend or warn the child of the impending danger; and (c) repetitive dreams, in which the parent relives and reworks some particularly distressing aspect of the traumatic experience
9. Cognitive impairment, including difficulty with concentration, memory, or "making decisions," which, in some cases, may result in sick leave and job loss

STIGMATIZED GRIEF

For someone to be acknowledged as a victim means that other people must validate the crime as a crime. People may have considerable ambivalence over viewing an act of violence as a legitimate crime with a legitimate victim if, for example, the victim has had a longstanding relationship or connection with the offender. In such cases, people may have a tendency to place a certain portion of blame on the victim, in the same psychologically self-protective way that we reassure ourselves that we are safe from crime if an assault or rape victim was careless or "asked for it." The stigmatization of the victim may lead to avoidance and isolation of co-victims by the social network just at the time they most need support (Fowlkes, 1990; Ressler et al., 1988; Spungen, 1998).

In a broader sense, American culture is success motivated and pleasure oriented, and people do not like to be around others who are sad, mournful, depressed, or otherwise "bring us down." Society is threatened by the sense of vulnerability imposed by crime, and individuals may go to great lengths to distance themselves from those "tainted" by this type of tragedy (Sprang and McNeil, 1995). This stigmatization response has special relevance in cases of serial crime. Spungen (1998) points out that, while many states have enacted "shield laws" to protect rape victims against harassment by prying questions about past sexual behavior, ironically these statutes do not apply if the rape or sexual torture victim was also murdered. During the criminal trial, the rape-murder victim may be demeaned, defiled, and dishonored, with all manner of facts and speculation dredged up about her sexual proclivities, drug and alcohol use, and overall lifestyle, the defense attorney often attempting to lead the jury to assume that the victim "asked for it." In the process, surviving family members are typically shamed and humiliated, without any judicially sanctioned recourse to respond.

SURVIVORS AND THE CRIMINAL JUSTICE SYSTEM

This raises the larger issue of the retraumatization, or "secondary wounding," that families often undergo as they negotiate the police and court systems. As tormenting as the wait for news can be for families during the investigation, the stress may only intensify once the victim is found and the perpetrator is apprehended. Even where the murderer is aggressively prosecuted, many opportunities arise for repeated retraumatization and secondary wounding of family members (Sprang and McNeil, 1995; Spungen, 1998).

DEATH NOTIFICATION

A frequently neglected step in the criminal justice process is the nature of the notification of family members that a loved one has been killed or that the body of a missing relative has been located and identified. If not for the sake of basic compassion, then at least the practical need to encourage the survivors' optimal cooperation with police and prosecutors argues for extreme sensitivity and support in breaking this worst of all possible news to families.

The best formulation to date of a death notification protocol comes from Spungen (1998), who delineates the following recommendations for notifiers: To begin with, always go in person. Unless there is no other choice, death notification should never be made over the phone. Go in pairs, and decide who will be the lead person, whose job it will be to actually say the words and give the news. The other team member provides backup support, monitors the survivors for adverse reactions, and provides temporary supervision of young children during the notification, if needed. If no one is home when you get there, wait a reasonable amount of time. If you are queried by a neighbor, ask about the family's whereabouts, but do not reveal the purpose of your visit to anyone but the immediate family. If the family does not show up, leave a card with a note to call. When the call comes, return to the family's home to make the notification.

Needless to say, make sure you have the correct family and residence. When you arrive, ask for permission to enter. Suggest that family members sit down face-to-face with you. Get to the point quickly and state the information simply and directly. If the facts are clear, do not leave room for doubt or false hope. You needn't be brutally blunt or insensitive, but try to use straight language and avoid euphemisms. Use the deceased's name or his/her relationship to the family member being informed — for example, "We're sorry to have to bring you this terrible news, Mrs. Jones. Your daughter, Mary, has been killed by a suspect who we're actively trying to apprehend. Mary and her personal effects are at Municipal hospital."

Allow time for the news to sink in. It may be necessary to repeat the notification several times in increasingly clear and explicit terms. Tolerate silence and be prepared for the calm to be broken by sudden explosions of grief and rage. Intense reactions should be restrained only if there is some danger to self or others. In the face of outright denial, be as gentle as possible, but make it clear that the murder has in fact occurred. Answer all questions tactfully and truthfully, but do not reveal more information than is necessary at that time. Repeat answers to questions as many times as necessary. Try to be as calm and supportive, yet comforting and empathic, as possible. Let the tone and cadence of your voice register the appropriate amount of respect and dignity, but do not become overly maudlin or lose control yourself.

Offer to make phone calls to family, friends, neighbors, employers, clergy, doctors, and so on. Ask family members if they want you to get someone to stay with them. Respect the family's privacy, but do not leave family members alone unless you are sure they are safe. High emotionality can impair memory, so give pertinent information and instructions in writing. Provide family members with the names and telephone numbers of a victim advocate, the prosecutor, the medical examiner, and the hospital; try to consolidate all the information onto one sheet.

Explain to family members what will happen next (e.g., body identification, police investigation, and criminal justice protocols). If this is a high-profile case, brief them on how to handle the media. Give family members as much information as they ask for, without overwhelming them. Repeat the information as many times as necessary.

Determine if the family members require some means of traveling to the medical examiner's office, hospital, or police station. Offer to drive them or arrange for a ride if they have no transportation. Be sure to provide a ride back home, and try to assist them with babysitting arrangements and other needs. If the notifying team is made up of police personnel and a victim advocate, the advocate may remain with the family members after the police leave (Spungen, 1998).

BODY IDENTIFICATION

The finality of identifying the deceased's body can have a paradoxically dual effect. On the one hand, there is the confrontation with the victim's remains and the final shattering of any hope that he or she may still be alive. On the other hand, the actual sight of the deceased often provides a strange sort of reassuring confirmation that the victim's death agonies may actually have fallen short of the survivor's imagined horrors and, even if not, that the physical presence of the body at least means that the victim's suffering is finally over (Rynearson, 1994, 1996). Although no specific research has been done with homicide co-victims, outcome studies of relatives after a death from natural causes report longer periods of denial and lower total recall of the deceased in mourners who were unable to view the body prior to burial (Sprang and McNeil, 1995).

Spungen (1998) provides useful guidelines regarding body identification as follows: Unless there is a legal requirement, let survivors make the choice as to whether they want to view their loved one's remains. Some family members may be anxious or intimidated about making or declining such a request or articulating their wishes, so ask them. In cases where it is forensically essential to involve the family in the identification process, as when the victim has been missing for a long time, be sure to provide the appropriate support.

Family members may want to touch the deceased. For some, it may be a way of beginning to accept the reality of the death, a way of finally saying goodbye. If the victim's body is mutilated, dismembered, burned, or decomposed, identification may have to be made through dental or other records. Explain to the family members why this is necessary and give them the choice of whether or not to view the remains. Again, provide the appropriate support (Spungen, 1998).

THE CRIMINAL JUSTICE SYSTEM

There are several phases of the criminal justice process following serial crimes and homicides, and each phase has its own requirements for responsible and compassionate treatment of surviving family members.

No-Arrest Cases

Statistics from the FBI's *Uniform Crime Reports* indicate that many crimes committed in the U.S. are never solved. Officially, no-arrest murder cases are never closed because there is no statute of limitations for homicide, but police know that with each passing day, the trail grows colder and the opportunity for an arrest declines (Spungen, 1998). The situation may actually be different for serial murder, as the repetitive, high-profile nature of the crimes may spur more persistent clue-gathering with mounting pressure to solve the case and prevent the "next victim" from being targeted.

No-arrest cases usually fall into one of two categories: (1) the police have insufficient clues regarding the identity of the suspect, or (2) there is an identifiable suspect, but not enough evidence to make an arrest. The latter situation seems to be more difficult for survivors to accept because they usually do not understand why an arrest cannot be immediately made or more evidence gathered "if we already know who it is" (Spungen, 1998).

No matter how many years have passed since the offense, most survivors never give up the belief that an arrest will be made. After a while, great hopes may come to be invested in this magical event, the arrest representing, literally or symbolically, the redemptive, restorative process that will return their world to normal. Many families, either through misinformation or self-delusion, come to believe that an arrest will automatically bring justice and they are ill-prepared for the tortuous prosecutorial role ahead. As families become desperate, they may ceaselessly pester detectives for news of the case, thereby annoying and alienating the very law enforcement personnel they depend on to solve the crime. Unless and until the offender is apprehended, survivors are deprived of a concrete, identifiable target for their anger. Absence of a perpetrator, or failure of the criminal justice system to prosecute, sets up an "emotional vacuum," impeding the resolution of anger, and potentially leading to helplessness and depression (Sprang and McNeil, 1995; Spungen, 1998).

Families, however, need not be either mute bystanders or obnoxious gadflies in the criminal investigation process. As long as they are in basic cooperation with law enforcement, taking an active role in the case can provide survivors with a productive channel for working out their anger and frustration and can afford a means of taking back some control. Families may hire private detectives to assist the police effort, or they may be able to provide investigators with certain specialized facts and information about the victim or crime circumstances that could aid police in their investigation. The goal for such families is to tread the thin line between making their case stand out among all the other unsolved crimes in their law enforcement jurisdiction and at the same time avoiding being seen as intrusive pests who are muddling the case (Spungen, 1998).

Specifically in multiple or serial murder cases, victims and their survivors may lose their individuality, with each family getting lost in the scale of the horror as the body count rises. It is this kind of high-profile serial murder case that, then as now, has typically been referred to in the media by some tag line of the perpetrator ("Jack the Ripper," the "Railway Killer"), which further seems to mockingly highlight the namelessness and facelessness of the victims and their families (Spungen, 1998).

In high-profile multiple or serial murder cases, certain victims, because of their youth, attractiveness, social position, or intriguing lifestyle, may become the "chosen victims" of the media, replete with yearbook photos and home-movie clips splattered over newspapers and television screens. Other involved families may thereby be afforded second-class status by the media and perhaps even by law enforcement, feeling shunted aside and neglected as the chosen victim becomes the "poster child" for the crime wave. On the other hand, recipients of this special attention may feel abused and violated, as their slain or missing loved one is involuntarily made the object of tabloid "infotainment," while their own homes and workplaces are laid siege by battalions of reporters and gawkers (Spungen, 1998).

Plea-Bargaining

The structure of the criminal justice process does not afford "party status" to family members of crime victims. Most families will never have their proverbial "day in court," as over 90% of cases are handled through plea-bargaining between defense attorneys and prosecutors, in which families have minimal input (Sprang and McNeil, 1995). Often, the police and prosecutor may disagree about the strength of the evidence needed to make an arrest, and their agendas concerning the case may differ. The first priority of police investigators is to close the case, while prosecutors want to be sure that sufficient evidence is collected to secure a conviction or nudge a satisfactory plea-bargain. The final arbiter in this process is usually the more conservative prosecutor (Spungen, 1998; Young, 1988).

The Trial

If the case goes to trial, some of the most difficult feelings to deal with involve the frustration and anger evoked by the often impersonal attitude of the court and its participants. Typically, families want justice; they want the criminal prosecuted and punished. For many families, the majority of their anger, anxiety, and depression can be accounted for by their dissatisfaction with the criminal justice system. Trials sometimes occur years after the crime and, for many survivors, the resolution of their grief and anger cannot be completed until they face that ordeal (Amick-McMullin et al., 1989; Ressler et al., 1988; Sprang and McNeil, 1995).

When the case finally goes to trial, survivors may have to deal with another whole set of traumatic experiences that they are probably ill-prepared for. These include reliving the tragedy through the graphic testimony of witnesses and investigators, as well as the presentation of grisly crime scene and autopsy photographs, torture devices and murder weapons, and other grim exhibits and evidence. The trial may expose families to information about the crime that they were not aware of or prepared for. Families may hear their murdered loved one defiled and calumniated as defense attorneys try to paint a picture of the victim as "asking for it." In the courtroom, families may come face-to-face with the accused perpetrator, whose reaction to the entire trial procedure may range from stony indifference to smirking bemusement. Families that become too emotional may be removed from the court-room (Sprang and McNeil, 1995; Spungen, 1998).

Unless they are actually called as witnesses, the only real input to the judicial process that most families will have occurs in the form of a *victim impact statement* that is filed with the judge, prosecutor, or Board of Pardons and Paroles or may be read in court prior to sentencing. The victim impact statement allows the survivors to express the impact the crime has had on their physical, emotional, social, occupational, and economic well-being, and most victim advocates advise survivors to avail themselves of this mechanism if that is their wish (Sprang and McNeil, 1995; Spungen, 1998).

PSYCHOLOGICAL TREATMENT
OF SURVIVORS AND FAMILIES

Just as there are different phases in the reaction of families to the offense against a loved one, the ensuing investigation, and the criminal justice process, there are different approaches to treatment of survivors during their long road back to equilibrium, sanity, and, it is hoped, justice.

CRISIS INTERVENTION AND VICTIM ADVOCACY

In the immediate aftermath of a serious crime, crisis response is a priority, and the type of crisis intervention and support services provided to families may make all the difference for their subsequent and long-term psychological functioning. Crisis intervention may include support services at the crime scene, hospital, medical examiner's office, survivor's home, police station, or in a court setting. Interventions at this stage may include nonjudgmental listening, provision of basic information, and referrals for other services (Spungen, 1998; Young, 1988, 1994).

Many court jurisdictions assign a victim advocate to victims of violent crime, and some jurisdictions may provide this service to homicide family co-victims as well. The advocate's accompaniment of the survivors to court can provide them with the needed strength and support to deal with the painful and intimidating court proceedings. Unfortunately, victim advocates themselves may sometimes feel frustrated because they seem to be primarily serving the criminal justice system, especially the prosecutor's office and the police, and only secondarily the victims or survivors (Spungen, 1998).

PSYCHOTHERAPY: GENERAL PRINCIPLES

Psychotherapists who work with victims of violent crime and their families need to combine hard-headed, practical, problem-solving approaches with compassion and a tolerance for extreme emotion (Miller, 1998b,c; 1999a,b). The following recommendations combine a selective review of the relevant literature with our own clinical observations.

For the most effective targeting of services, mental health clinicians should form collaborative relationships with victim advocates and the relevant players in the criminal justice system. In most cases, short-term, focused, crisis management-type therapeutic strategies will be the first line of intervention, followed, as necessary, by more interactive and integrative psychotherapeutic techniques. In addition, therapists and patients should plan for follow-up booster sessions, both scheduled and on an as-needed basis, for dealing with the inevitable recurrences of anxiety, anger, or grief that occur at several stages in the criminal trial or later on holidays, during family anniversaries or significant life transitions (weddings, funerals), and so on (Spungen, 1998).

For psychotherapy of traumatically bereaved survivors to be effective, the process of assessing the individual coping skills and other psychological resources of the patient is essential. The particular therapeutic approaches and methods will vary, depending on the needs of the individual survivors and their stage of processing of the traumatic anxiety, anger, and grief (Sprang and McNeil, 1995).

INDIVIDUAL PSYCHOTHERAPY

Sprang and McNeil (1995) divide the psychotherapeutic intervention strategies for victim survivors into several phases. An initial evaluation and debriefing phase occurs immediately following the traumatic event and focuses on crisis intervention and stabilization of the individual's emotional, social, and physical environment. At this stage, the therapist should be careful about challenging the patient's defenses; if anything, self-protective defenses may have to be shored up to forestall complete psychological decompensation. Appropriate interventions include empathic support, validation, and normalization of the patient's reaction to the traumatic loss.

The importance of intact, adaptive defenses at this point is highlighted by the need to prepare survivors for the multiple stresses that follow the victimization of a family member. Therapists should encourage a graded and dosed ventilation of emotion and provide necessary support. Then they should gradually begin to educate family members as to what they can expect and try to dispel unrealistic expectations. Another aspect of this educational process includes providing concrete information about such victim resources as the Red Cross, Crime Victims Compensation Fund, employee assistance programs, and so on. At each step, the therapist should monitor patient reactions to avoid overwhelming them with too much information too quickly (Sprang and McNeil, 1995).

When trust and therapeutic rapport have developed, the therapist should help the patient identify symptoms of distress. These should be explained, normalized, demystified, depathologized, and validated to the patient. Pertinent relaxation, bio-feedback, desensitization, and other effective cognitive-behavioral or psychophysiological techniques should be applied to symptom management. Opportunities should be provided, arranged, or planned for patients to take back some control of their lives — for example, by helping and educating others, running support groups, and so on. Therapists should use transference dynamics as a vehicle for enabling patients to adaptively seek and obtain support from significant others in their social environment (Miller, 1998b,c; Sprang and McNeil, 1995; Young, 1988, 1994).

The patient should be helped to reduce self-blame through the use of cognitive or existential therapeutic approaches. Psychological mastery over the traumatic bereavement can be encouraged by asking patients to describe the future: "If you were not struggling with your grief anymore, what would you be doing?" In the early stages, such a question may elicit incredulous stares by patients who may be bewildered and angry at even the suggestion that there could ever be a time when they were not consumed by unrelenting emotional pain. Accordingly, one sign of recovery may be the ability to even entertain this question. Related to this is the process of helping the patient say a psychological "goodbye" to the slain loved one, realizing that there will always be painful memories, but that the survivors have a right to continue their own lives (Sprang and McNeil, 1995).

An important point here is that the role of the therapist or other caregiver is not to encourage the survivor to "get over it." Co-victims will never "get over" the murder of a loved one and will continue to think about the murder for the rest of their lives. Therapists should not state or imply that survivors "should be doing better by now" or "should be able to stop thinking about the person already." This is unrealistic and can be poisonous to the therapeutic process. It also sets the patient up for failure because patients will never be able to meet the standard of "getting over it." A far more productive therapeutic strategy involves validating the survivors' pain while supporting their strengths and helping them to live as "normal" a life as possible, albeit a life that will be radically different from the one they had before (Spungen, 1998).

A related issue is the question of "forgiveness." Survivors may be told by well-meaning friends, family, clinicians, clergy, or self-help books that for "true healing" to take place, they must forgive the offender. The so-called *restorative justice* movement actually arranges voluntary reconciliation meetings between victims or families and the still-incarcerated offenders. While forgiveness may be a noble adaptive coping strategy for some co-victims, it cannot be overemphasized that this is a choice that survivors have the right to make for themselves; they have no obligation to "forgive" anyone they do not wish to. For many, the unacceptable price of forgiving the offender is a trivialization and dismissal of the victim and co-victims, not to mention the tacit encouragement of future crimes by the notion that absolution is easily bought by a cheap apology. For many survivors, holding onto burning indignation is their only way of coping with the monstrous cosmic unfairness of the crime, and so long as this does not involve overt harm to self or others, righteous anger may have to be accommodated in the therapy process (Safer, 1999; Spungen, 1998; Van Biema, 1999).

Some survivors, especially in the early stages, may have difficulty expressing their pain to a therapist or anyone else; for them, speaking about the victim's death "out loud" symbolically makes it real. For such patients, Spungen (1998) recommends keeping a daily diary or journal and writing down their thoughts and feelings about the crime and its impact on the loved one. This notebook should be portable enough to carry around so that patients can jot down their thoughts as they occur. Another suggestion is speaking their thoughts into a portable tape recorder; these tapes can later be transcribed, if desired. Even if the survivor never reads the diary again, the act of writing itself can be therapeutic; clinicians will recognize this as the technique of journaling. Spungen (1998) has found that some co-victims may create several volumes of such notes before they realize they have made progress. Our only caveat is that this exercise not become a prolonged obsessive preoccupation to the exclusion of other therapeutic strategies and participation in life generally.

FAMILY THERAPY

In many cases of family bereavement, individual and family therapy will slip into one another, as family members show up for treatment sessions alone, in pairs, or in different group configurations. Some particular therapeutic considerations apply to families as a unit.

The effects of successive traumas may be cumulative (Alarcon et al., 1999; Miller, 1994, 1997, 1998c; Weiner, 1992), and therapy may have to deal with unresolved traumatic material from the past, which will almost certainly be re-evoked by the more recent trauma. Also, other aspects of life cannot necessarily be automatically put on hold when the offense occurs, so therapy must address coexisting issues such as school and job problems, marital conflict, substance abuse, or other pre-existing family stresses. This may require some prioritization by the therapist in terms of what are "front-burner" vs. "back-burner" issues (Spungen, 1998).

Throughout the course of therapy, the supportive nature of the clinical intervention and the therapeutic relationship are essential elements in the traumatic resolution for families. The nature of the therapeutic relationship may serve to buffer the effects of the trauma, increase self-esteem, and alter the family's role functioning, thereby helping to mitigate the traumatic impact of the event (Sprang and McNeil, 1995).

Spungen (1998) cites Getzel and Masters' (1984) delineation of the basic tasks of family therapy after bereavement by homicide, as follows: (1) helping the family understand and put into perspective the rage and guilt they feel about their loved one's murder; (2) helping survivors examine their grief reactions and other people's availability to them so they regain their confidence in the social order; (3) helping the family accept the death of their relative as something irrevocable, yet bearable; and (4) assisting members of the immediate and extended kinship system in establishing a new family structure that permits individual members to grow in a more healthy and fulfilling manner.

Figley (1988, 1989) views the basic goal of post-traumatic family therapy as restoring the members to their pre-trauma level of functioning, and his system divides the treatment process into five phases, as follows.

1. *Building commitment to the therapeutic objectives:* Inasmuch as commitment and trust are crucial elements in all effective psychotherapy, it is important to encourage as many members of the family as possible to disclose their ordeal in an atmosphere of trust, empathy, and support. The therapist should convey an attitude of realistic confidence, authority, experience, and optimism about the treatment process.

2. *Framing the problem:* Detailed information is collected from each family member as to their individual experiences, reactions, and conceptualizations of the traumatic event. Particular problems to watch for are unproductive blaming-the-victim responses or, in the case of traumatic bereavement, blaming other family members for contributing to the lifestyle that "set up" the victim to be murdered, providing lax security in the case of a child, and so on.

3. *Re-framing the problem:* The therapist must help the family reframe the individual members' experiences, insights, and conceptualizations to make them generally compatible with one another. The goal is not some form of artificial thought control to force all family members to think alike, but rather to foster enough of a conceptual common ground so that family members are all basically "on the same page" in terms of their understanding of the traumatic event and their own reactions to it. Often, this can only begin when the heavier layers of family denial have been sufficiently excavated (Allen and Bloom, 1994). The goal is for the family to reframe what they had originally regarded as a tragic, insurmountable burden in new terms as a painful challenge that they can work together to overcome.

4. *Developing a family healing theory:* Here, the therapist more explicitly guides the family in the kind of existential reformulation that will enable them to craft some meaning and purpose from their trauma. Developing such a healing family theory (Figley, 1988) or whole family story (Allen and Bloom, 1994) may not be an easy task, especially in families whose cohesion and dynamics were never very healthy to begin with. It is not necessary for all family members to "buy" the healing family theory with equal enthusiasm and in every detail, as long as the basic conceptualization is accepted as a provisional working model that will serve to keep family peace and get the members back to functioning like a whole family.

5. *Closure and preparedness:* As the family healing theory is consolidated and family functioning improves, the therapist begins to prepare the family for the end of therapy by reviewing specific objectives that have been met and encouraging the family members to recognize their accomplishments. Family members should be encouraged to contact the therapist as necessary, but they should be urged to use the skills and insights they have

developed in therapy to try to handle their own problems as they emerge. Followups focus on post-therapy problems that may arise, as well as on "practice drills" that the therapist may pose to help the family generalize its new-found problem-solving skills to future crises that may arise (Allen and Bloom 1994; Figley, 1988, 1989; Miller, 1999a).

Recommendations for individual and family therapy specifically applied to parents of murdered children are provided by Rynearson (1988, 1994, 1996), who cautions against pushing the cathartic narrative too quickly, especially in the early stages. In the aftermath of homicidal bereavement, as a defense against overwhelming emotional turmoil, many bereaved parents and family members may adopt what appears to be either an unnatural flippancy or a hyper-rational "facts-only" attitude, which others may mistake for unconcern or callousness. If, immediately following the homicide, some family members cope better by using the twin emotional crutches of avoidance and denial, this should be provisionally respected by the therapist. Remember, even in orthopedics, the useful and legitimate function of a "crutch" is to support a limb until sufficient healing occurs to begin more active rehabilitation (Miller, 1998c).

When the therapeutic narrative does begin to flow, psychotherapy for crime bereavement combines many of the features of individual PTSD therapy and family therapy modalities. Therapists should inquire about individual family members' private perceptions of death. Nihilism and despair are common early responses, and helping patients and families to recover or develop sustaining spiritual or philosophical beliefs or actions can buffer the destabilizing and disintegratory effects of the homicide. Therapeutic measures may involve exploring the family members' concepts of life and death, as well as encouraging both private meditative and socially committed activities (Rynearson, 1996).

Pictures and other mementos of the deceased can serve as comforting images. In reviewing family picture albums together, the therapist and survivors can try to summon nurturing, positive imagery that may counterbalance the grotesque recollections of the crime. Similar memorializing activities include writing about the deceased or creating a scrapbook. Again, this should not become an unhealthy, consuming preoccupation, although in the early stages some leeway should be afforded to allow the memorializers to "get it out of their systems." If possible, family members should collaborate on these personalized memorial rituals and projects as a way of forging a renewed sense of meaning and commitment within the family structure (Rynearson, 1996; Spungen, 1998).

Once the psychological coping mechanisms of self-calming and distancing from the offense event have been strengthened, therapy can begin to confront the traumatic imagery more directly. Less verbally expressive family members may be asked to draw their perception of the crime or death scene in order to provide a nonverbal expression of reenactment that can be directly viewed by and shared with the therapist. Family members can then be encouraged to place themselves within the drawn enactment to allow the process of abstract distancing to take the place of mute avoidance. In these exercises, family members often portray themselves as defending, holding, or rescuing the deceased (Rynearson, 1996).

Consistent with the theme of finding meaning in tragedy as a mode of self-healing, the family should be encouraged (but not pressured) to serve as a role model to other families needing assistance — for example, in the form of support and advocacy groups, as well as productive participation in the criminal justice system (Brown, 1993; Figley, 1988; Spungen, 1998). When the family is ready, therapists may recommend participation in appropriate local and national support groups, such as Compassionate Friends or Parents of Murdered Children. Peer support is important because, when our traumatically bereaved patients tell us that we can't really understand what they are going through, they are right; we can't — unless we have lived through it ourselves. Of course, lack of personal experience does not rule out our being therapeutically effective, just as therapists who successfully treat brain-injured, schizophrenic, learning disabled, or terminally ill patients need not suffer these syndromes themselves. Empathy-by-proxy that comes from extensive clinical experience with certain classes of patient should enable us to form a sufficient therapeutic connection so that these patients feel understood (Everstine and Everstine, 1993; Figley, 1995; Matsakis, 1994; McCann and Pearlman, 1990b; Miller, 1993, 1998c; Prigatano, 1999).

Finally, the sad truth is that some members of a given family may be more willing and/or able than others to leave the grim past behind and move on; some members just "can't let go." In such cases, family separations may be necessary for some members to escape the stifling emotional turmoil of unhealthy family enmeshment and misery in order to make a fresh start and find their own way back into the world of the living (Barnes, 1998; Miller, 1998c, 1999a).

In this regard, clinicians need to remind themselves of the limited therapeutic goals in most cases of homicidal bereavement. Do not expect families to totally "work through" the trauma of a murdered loved one, and do not tell them they'll "get over it" — they won't. The bereaved family will always maintain an attachment to the slain loved one, especially a child, and it would be a mistaken therapeutic objective to insist on complete detachment. Instead, it is hoped that the bereaved family will learn to maintain involvement with others while always retaining an internalized relationship with the image of the slain child, parent, or sibling (Miller, 1998c, 1999a; Rynearson, 1996).

The therapist's task, then, is first to keep the family members from destroying themselves and one another, and second to restore some semblance of meaning and purpose in their lives that will allow them to remain productive, functioning members of their community. Often, the crucial first step is to get the family members to believe in one simple fact: "You can live through this." In the best of cases, family members may "grow" from such a horrendous experience as the brutal murder of a loved one, but such cases are the blessed exceptions, not the rule, and most families do well just to survive (Miller, 1998c, 1999a).

Bereaved Children

Children may be among the survivors of a serial crime or homicide that seriously injures or takes a parent or sibling. While many of the above individual and family therapy recommendations apply, with age-appropriate modifications, to the treatment of traumatized children, certain special considerations apply to this younger age group of co-victims (James, 1989; Johnson, 1989; Miller, 1999a,b; Spungen, 1998).

The first step involves notification of the child about the family member's death, or victimization, if appropriate. Spungen (1998) cites Beckmann's (1990) recommendation of a supportive but forthright approach in which children are told that the loved one has died, avoiding such euphemisms as "sleeping" or "gone away" which might cause the young child to wonder when the deceased is "coming back" or why the deceased "went away" without saying goodbye.

Young children may ask the same questions repeatedly until they are able to process and understand all the information. Therapists should advise adult caregivers to be patient and respond to the child's questions, in an age-appropriate manner, as many times as necessary (Spungen, 1998). Contrary to the impression of many adults, children often have a more sophisticated notion of the concept of death than is first appreciated (Yalom, 1980). Since same-age children may differ widely in terms of their psychodevelopmental maturity, adults should take their cue from the cognitive level and personality of the individual child.

Due to a combination of developmental factors and response to traumatization, children may have particular difficulty in verbalizing their reactions to the traumatic bereavement. Individual and group therapies with children, therefore, necessarily need to be more participatory and experiential. Worksheets, games, play therapies, skits, puppet shows, music, storytelling, and art modalities should be integrated into the therapeutic program for traumatized children (Beckmann, 1990; James, 1989; Spungen, 1998).

Children should be included in any memorialization activities, at an age-appropriate level. They should be part of both the planning process and presentation of memorial services. Children may write poems or stories, draw pictures, create a scrapbook, plant a tree, or create some other memorial. This can be done either as an individual or family project, or both (Sprang and McNeil, 1995; Spungen, 1998).

Recently, a number of innovative treatment systems have been developed specifically for children who are bereaved by homicide; these may be productively applied to the more restricted population of children of serial murder victims. Temple (1997) describes a treatment program, called *contextual therapy*, that is used with siblings of inner-city homicide victims who, in addition to the expectable bereavement issues, often struggle with feelings of guilt and anger, as well as both internal urges and social pressures toward revenge. The goals of the program are to restore family cohesion and functioning as rapidly as possible, to prevent retaliatory violence by family members of the deceased, and to encourage family members to develop future plans based on honoring the memory of the murdered loved one.

These goals are achieved by quickly and effectively connecting the involved families to as wide a range of practical and supportive services as possible and by encouraging them to support one another. In addition, psychotherapy with siblings focuses on deriving some meaning or lesson from the deceased's life and death and honoring the deceased's memory by both symbolic artifacts, such as scrapbooks and photograph albums, and concrete activities, such as becoming active in anti-violence programs (Temple, 1997).

Parson (1997) describes a program, called *post-traumatic child therapy*, for working with inner-city children exposed to violence, including the murder of a parent. The program consists of several phases. In phase 1, the *pre-therapy* phase, the child is oriented and acclimated to the process of therapy, and the therapist develops an idea of the child's concept of the traumatic event and his or her own reaction to it. Phase 2 is termed *stabilization of biopsychic response* and includes establishing a therapeutic relationship with a stable and supportive adult figure, teaching psychophysiological stress-control techniques, encouraging the use of cognitive-behavioral problem-solving strategies, and using the resulting improved sense of control as the foundation for beginning to explore specific elements of the traumatic experience.

Returning to the psychographic scene forms the basis of phase 3, which includes deconditioning of negative emotionality through the use of systematic desensitization and cognitive-behavioral working through of trauma via play therapy and other modalities. Phase 4 is the phase of *completion,* or moving toward growth and integration. This primarily involves using the relational and transferential aspects of individual trauma therapy to help the child restructure his or her self-view and world-view in order to develop a new post-trauma meaning system. In this latter respect, the goals of Parson's (1997) post-traumatic child therapy come close to those of trauma therapy for adults.

The advantage of Temple's (1997) and Parson's (1997) approaches with children is that they use age-appropriate therapeutic techniques to establish competence and control and thereby pave the way for the young survivor's eventual ability to profit from more reconstructive and integrative techniques of trauma therapy. In addition, note that many adult trauma patients may also present initially in such a regressed, decompensated state that many of these preliminary techniques of arousal regulation and trust restoration are appropriate in the early stages of their treatment, as well (Everstine and Everstine, 1993; Matsakis, 1994; McCann and Pearlman, 1990b; Miller, 1994, 1998c).

HELPERS AND HEALERS: VICARIOUS TRAUMATIZATION

As noted above, this chapter is also for the helpers and healers who, until recently, were largely neglected by the psychotherapy field, either because they were felt to be resistant to psychological intervention (law enforcement personnel) or because the very nature of their work inoculated and shielded them against distress (mental health clinicians). This section discusses some of the challenges and therapeutic approaches that apply to these groups, based on a review of the pertinent literature and our own clinical observations (Miller, 1995; 1998a,c; 2000a,b).

CRIMINAL INVESTIGATORS

Stereotypes of the "hardboiled" detective, both from within and outside the law enforcement profession, have contributed to the under-recognition and under-treatment of post-traumatic stress syndromes in this dedicated group of helpers.

Stresses of Criminal Investigation

Aside from the daily aggravations, challenges, and hassles encountered by law enforcement officers in general (Anderson et al., 1995; Blau, 1994; Miller,1995, 2000a), special pressures are experienced by detectives who are involved in the investigation of particularly brutal crimes, such as multiple rapes and serial murders. The normally expected societal protective role of the police officer becomes even more pronounced at the same time as their responsibilities as public servants who protect individual rights are compounded by the pressure to solve the crime (Sewell, 1993).

Especially in no-arrest cases, and particularly those involving children, some detectives may become emotionally involved with the families and remain in contact for many years. Some detectives become obsessed with a particular case and continue to work on it at every available moment, sometimes to the point of compromising their work on other cases and leading to a deterioration of health and family life (Spungen, 1998).

The sheer magnitude and shock effect of many mass murder scenes and the violence, mutilation, and sadistic brutality associated with many serial killings — again, especially those involving children — often exceed the defense mechanisms and coping abilities of even the most jaded investigator. Revulsion may be tinged with rage, all the more so when "innocent" victims have been killed and the murderer seems to be mocking law enforcement's attempts to capture him (Sewell, 1993).

As the investigation drags on, the inability to solve the crime and close the case further frustrates and demoralizes the assigned officers and seems to jeeringly proclaim the hollowness of society's notions of fairness and justice. All the more galling are situations where the offender is known but the existing evidence is not sufficient to support an arrest or conviction, leading the officers to fear that the perpetrator will remain free to offend again. Stress and self-recrimination are further magnified when the failure to apprehend the perpetrator is caused by human error, as when an officer's bungled actions or breach of protocol lead to loss or damage of evidence or suppression of testimony, allowing the offender to "walk" (Sewell, 1993).

All of these reactions are magnified by a cumulatively spiraling vicious cycle of fatigue and cognitive impairment, as the intense, sustained effort to solve the case results in sloppy errors, deteriorating work quality, and fraying of home and workplace relationships. Fatigue also exacerbates the wearing down of the investigator's normal psychological defenses, rendering him or her even more vulnerable to stress and failure (Sewell, 1993).

Treatment of Criminal Investigators

Sewell (1993, 1994) has adapted a stress-debriefing model of psychotherapy to the particular needs of detectives who deal with multiple murders, serial killings, and other violent crimes. The major objectives of this process are (1) ventilation of intense emotions; (2) exploration of symbolic meanings; (3) group support under catastrophic conditions; (4) initiation of the grief process within a supportive environment; (5) reduction of the "fallacy of uniqueness;" (6) reassurance that intense emotions under horrifying circumstances are normal; (7) preparation for a continuation of the grief and stress process over the ensuing weeks and months; (8) preparing for the possible development of emotional, cognitive, and physical symptoms in the aftermath of a serious crisis; (9) education regarding normal and abnormal stress response syndromes; and (10) encouragement of continued group support and/or professional assistance.

Sewell (1994) finds such interventions to be appropriate for two specific groups and at two specific times. First, the stress of the first responders who deal with the trauma of the original crime scene must be confronted quickly and decisively. Second, the stress of investigators must be handled as needed throughout the course of the crime's investigation and prosecution. In the regular group debriefing sessions, Sewell (1994) recommends that attendance be mandatory for all involved personnel. Where a particular officer needs additional counseling, such visits should be encouraged and supported by the departmental administration (Miller, 1995; 1998c; 2000a).

TRAUMA THERAPISTS

Those psychotherapists who specialize in treating victims and co-victims of violent crime, including murder, have stresses of their own. We are only belatedly coming to realize that taking good care of our patients means taking care of ourselves (Figley, 1995; Miller, 1998a,c; 2000b).

The "Trauma" of Trauma Therapy

The traumatic experiences and reactions of patients can "rub off" on therapists. Trauma workers are regularly surrounded by the extreme emotional eruptions of trauma-inducing events and their aftermath. No matter how hard we try to resist it and how mature and resilient we may be, trauma workers are inevitably drawn into this vortex of emotional intensity.

Figley (1995) has coined the term *compassion fatigue* to describe a particular syndrome of clinical burnout that affects therapists who regularly deal with brutally traumatized patients, including crime victims and co-victims, and he identifies several reasons why trauma therapists are particularly vulnerable. First, empathy is a major resource for trauma workers to help the traumatized. While the process of empathizing with the trauma victim and family members helps us to understand their experiences, in the process of doing so we may be traumatized ourselves.

Second, many trauma therapists have experienced some traumatic events in their own lives, and these unresolved traumas may be activated by reports of similar traumas in patients. Thus, there is the danger of the therapist's over-generalizing from his or her own experiences and methods of coping, and over-promoting those methods with patients. Finally, special stresses accrue from working with traumatized children or the families of child murder victims (Figley, 1995).

The therapist's growing recognition as a trauma specialist inevitably leads to greater numbers of trauma referrals. As the cases mount, so may the therapist's growing burnout and compassion fatigue. The therapist may begin to lose his or her objectivity, to over-identify with patients, and to become increasingly depressed.

The effects may spill over into the therapist's family, as he or she becomes more withdrawn and emotionally unavailable (Cerney, 1995). Other therapists may progressively become "trauma junkies," increasingly reinforced by the lurid thrill of working with such dramatic cases (Yassen, 1995).

McCann and Pearlman (1990a, 1990b) coined the term *vicarious traumatization* to describe the transformation that occurs within the trauma therapist as the result of empathic engagement with patients' trauma experiences. These effects do not arise solely from one or two therapy relationships but are cumulative across time and number of clinical relationships. Pearlman and MacIan (1995) examined vicarious traumatization in 188 self-identified trauma therapists. They found that, while most therapists generally function well, a subset experience significant psychological disturbance as a consequence of their work. The affected therapists tend to have a personal trauma history, to have been doing trauma work for a longer period of time, and to have larger numbers of traumatized patients in their caseloads. Other research (Elliott and Guy, 1993; Follette et al., 1994) suggests that characteristics of the therapist, such as age, sex, personal trauma history, and current personal stress, may interact with exposure to patients' trauma material to contribute to trauma-related symptoms in the therapist.

In a study of staff therapists at a mental health center that provides services to crime victims, Sprang and McNeil (1995) found that therapists who work with crime victims are at risk for vicarious traumatization due to constant exposure to intense suffering and traumatic graphic content. Over time, the therapist's view of the world can become distorted, with tragedy and malevolence seeming to be the rule in life, rather than the exception. The therapist's own sense of safety, control, and existential frame of reference may be transformed by overexposure to the aftermath of violent crime. Many therapists complain that family, friends, and colleagues are often insensitive or do not understand the seriousness of their trauma work; many lose perspective and cannot understand why others are not as outraged as they are about the injustices in the world. Well-meaning friends and family may advise the therapist to "lighten up" or "leave your work at the office." A vicious cycle of alienation may develop as the therapist becomes more isolated and withdrawn from former sources of social support.

Treating the Traumatized Therapist

Several general strategies for the prevention of, and recovery from, vicarious traumatization include the following: (1) maintain a healthy personal and professional balance; (2) apportion out professional responsibilities, such as clinical contact, research, teaching, public speaking, and advocacy; (3) in clinical work, balance caseload responsibilities between trauma victims and "ordinary" patients; (4) respect personal boundaries by planning for time off, setting realistic work schedules, and making time for supervision and consultation when needed; (5) develop realistic expectations and goals regarding clinical outcomes; (6) accept permission to experience fully the emotions produced during the therapeutic encounter; (7) find ways to self-nurture and self-support; (8) participate in activities that promote social or political change; and (9) seek out non-victim-related activities that provide hope, enjoyment, and healthy support (Saakvitne and Pearlman, 1996; Sprang and McNeil, 1995).

A more focused treatment approach for traumatized therapists, termed *psycho-logical debriefing*, has been developed by Talbot et al. (1995) specifically to help therapists who provide crisis intervention and trauma therapy services to victims of bank holdups and other violent crimes, although their model may productively be applied to mental health clinicians who work with survivors of most crime victims. The aim of the psychological debriefing model is to help mental health clinicians in the processes of ventilation, catharsis, and sharing of experiences, in order to gain psychological mastery of the situation and prevent the development of more serious delayed stress syndromes.

Particularly important for psychotherapists is the gentle but forthright explora-tion of their identification with the victim's or co-victim's experience, which enables them to properly assimilate the burden of empathy, to gradually integrate the trau-matic experience, and to make the transition back to everyday life and work. A therapeutic debriefing model with psychotherapists must incorporate not just emo-tional ventilation, but also an integrative intellectual understanding of the traumatic events and of the therapist's role in dealing with victims and survivors (Talbot et al., 1995). In this model, the debriefing of the therapist is attended by two or more psychologists — here referred to as "*secondary debriefers*" — who were not part of the original civilian crisis intervention. The therapist debriefing is held far away from the crisis scene as soon as it is practical for all involved therapists to attend.

The therapeutic debriefing procedure incorporates and attempts to make sense of the crisis event, the responses to that event by the therapists, and the processes occurring in the debriefing itself. The secondary debriefer is dealing with a number of different levels of the crisis: (1) the event itself, (2) the victim's response to the event, (3) the therapist's response to the event, and (4) the therapist's response to the victim. Essentially, the secondary debriefer assumes a quasi-supervisory role to help therapists to reach an understanding of the interventions they made, assess those that were useful, explore possible alternatives, and decide on appropriate future actions.

Because greater psychological knowledge is often associated with more sophis-ticated defenses, the secondary debriefer may need to be somewhat more confrontive with the therapists than clinicians typically are with civilian victims, or debriefers might be with other emergency responders such as police officers or paramedics (Miller, 1995, 1999d). As in a therapeutic session, the secondary debriefer needs to summarize, contain, and make sense of what occurred. Therapists should be able to verbalize what they have learned from working with crime victims and co-victims in that particular crisis.

To continue to function and to grow personally and professionally, psychother-apists need to have a sense of mastery of the experience, as well as the assurance of feeling valued, worthwhile, and positive about themselves and their work. Cog-nitive understanding and adaptive self-insight give therapists mastery of the situation, objectivity, and a theoretical base from which to craft interventions. This is essential in order for them to continue to function as effective trauma therapists (Talbot et al., 1995).

CONCLUSIONS

Working with bereaved survivors of serial crimes or other victims frequently leads the therapist on a tour of the most foul and dank grottos of the human soul, only occasionally penetrated by thin, life-sustaining shafts of light and fresh air. Psychotherapists who can keep their own guiding beams from being sucked into the black hole of cynicism and despair and who can beat back their impending burnout by creatively diversifying their practices and updating their clinical skills represent vital allies of the forces of law and justice against both the commonplace and unusual barbarisms that corrode our civilization. For their part, survivors who find the resolve to move forward, and even try to help others in the process, deserve our support and our praise. At the same time, we cannot afford to abandon those co-victims who, crushed and drained by the burden of their despair, turn over to us the responsibility of speaking and working on their behalf.

REFERENCES

Alarcon, R.D. (1999). The cascade model: an alternative to comorbidity in the pathogenesis of posttraumatic stress disorder. *Psychiatry*, 62:114–124.

Aldwin, C.M. (1994). *Stress, Coping, and Development*. New York: Guilford.

Allen, S.N. and Bloom, S.L. (1994). Group and family treatment of post-traumatic stress disorder. *Psychiatric Clinics of North America*, 17:425–437.

Amick-McMullan, A., Kilpatrick, D.G., Veronen, L.J., and Smith, S. (1989). Family survivors of homicide victims: theoretical perspectives and an exploratory study. *Journal of Traumatic Stress*, 2:21–33.

Anderson, W., Swenson, D., and Clay, D. (1995). *Stress Management for Law Enforcement Officers*. Englewood Cliffs, NJ: Prentice-Hall.

APA (1994). *Diagnostic and Statistical Manual of Mental Disorders*, 4th ed. Washington, D.C.: American Psychological Association.

Bard, M. and Sangrey, D. (1986). *The Crime Victim's Book*. New York: Brunner/Mazel.

Barnes, M.F. (1998). Understanding the secondary traumatic stress of parents. In Figley, C.R. (Ed.), *Burnout in Families: The Systematic Costs of Caring* (pp. 75–89). Boca Raton, FL: CRC Press.

Beckmann, R. (1990). *Children Who Grieve: A Manual for Conducting Support Groups*. Holmes Beach, CA: Learning Publications.

Blau, T.H. (1994). *Psychological Services for Law Enforcement*. New York: Wiley.

Bowman, M.L. (1997). *Individual Differences in Posttraumatic Response: Problems with the Stress-Adversity Connection*. Mahwah, NJ: Erlbaum.

Bowman, M.L. (1999). Individual differences in posttraumatic distress: problems with the DSM-IV model. *Canadian Journal of Psychiatry*, 44:21–33.

Brown, C.G. (1993). *First Get Mad, Then Get Justice: The Handbook for Crime Victims*. New York: Birch Lane Press.

Carson, L. and MacLeod, M.D. (1997). Explanations about crime and psychological distress in ethnic minority and white victims of crime: a qualitative explanation. *Journal of Community and Applied Social Psychology*, 7:361–375.

Cerney, M.S. (1995). Treating the "heroic treaters": an overview. In Figley, C.R. (Ed.), *Compassion Fatigue: Coping with Secondary Traumatic Stress Disorder in Those Who Treat the Traumatized* (pp. 131–149). New York: Brunner/Mazel.

Everstine, D.S. and Everstine, L. (1993). *The Trauma Response: Treatment for Emotional Injury*. New York: Norton.

FBI (1993). *Uniform Crime Reports for the United States*. Washington, D.C.: U.S. Department of Justice.

Figley, C.R. (1988). Post-traumatic family therapy. In Ochberg, F.M. (Ed.), *Posttraumatic Therapy and Victims of Violence* (pp. 83–109). New York: Brunner/Mazel.

Figley, C.R. (1989). *Helping the Traumatized Families*. San Francisco, CA: Jossey-Bass.

Figley, C.R. (1995). Compassion fatigue as secondary traumatic stress disorder: an overview. In Figley, C.R. (Ed.), *Compassion Fatigue: Coping with Secondary Traumatic Stress Disorder in Those Who Treat the Traumatized* (pp. 1–20). New York: Brunner/Mazel.

Fowlkes, M.R. (1990). The social regulation of grief. *Sociological Forum*, 5:635–652.

Getzel, G.S. and Masters, R. (1984). Serving families who survive homicide victims. *Social Casework: Journal of Contemporary Social Work*, 65:138–144.

James, B. (1989). *Treating Traumatized Children: New Insights and Creative Interventions*. New York: Free Press.

Johnson, K. (1989). *Trauma in the Lives of Children: Crisis and Stress Management Techniques for Counselors and Other Professionals*. Alameda, CA: Hunter House.

MacLeod, M.D. (1999). Why did it happen to me? Social cognition processes in adjustment and recovery from criminal victimization and illness. *Current Psychology*, 18:18–31.

Matsakis, A. (1994). *Post-Traumatic Stress Disorder: A Complete Treatment Guide*. Oakland, CA: New Harbinger.

McCann, I.L. and Pearlman, L.A. (1990a). Vicarious traumatization: a framework for understanding the psychological effects of working with victims. *Journal of Traumatic Stress*, 3:131–149.

McCann, I.L. and Pearlman, L.A. (1990b). *Psychological Trauma and the Adult Survivor: Theory, Therapy, and Transformation*. New York: Brunner/Mazel.

Miller, L. (1993). *Psychotherapy of the Brain-Injured Patient: Reclaiming the Shattered Self*. New York: Norton.

Miller, L. (1994). Civilian posttraumatic stress disorder: clinical syndromes and psychotherapeutic strategies. *Psychotherapy*, 31:655–664.

Miller, L. (1995). Tough guys: psychotherapeutic strategies with law enforcement and emergency services personnel. *Psychotherapy*, 32:592–600.

Miller, L. (1997). Neurosensitization: a pathophysiological model for traumatic disability syndromes. *Journal of Cognitive Rehabilitation*, 15(5):12–17.

Miller, L. (1998a). Our own medicine: traumatized psychotherapists and the stresses of doing therapy. *Psychotherapy*, 35:137–146.

Miller, L. (1998b). Psychotherapy of crime victims: treating the aftermath of interpersonal violence. *Psychotherapy*, 35:336–345.

Miller, L. (1998c). *Shocks to the System: Psychotherapy of Traumatic Disability Syndromes*. New York: Norton.

Miller, L. (1999a). Treating posttraumatic stress disorder in children and families: basic principles and clinical applications. *American Journal of Family Therapy*, 27:21–34.

Miller, L. (1999b). Posttraumatic stress disorder in child victims of violent crime: making the case for psychological injury. *Victim Advocate*, 1:6–10.

Miller, L. (1999c). Workplace violence: prevention, response, and recovery. *Psychotherapy*, 36:160–169.

Miller, L. (1999d). Critical incident stress debriefing: clinical applications and new directions. *International Journal of Emergency Mental Health*, 1:253–265.

Miller, L. (2000a). Law enforcement traumatic stress: clinical syndromes and intervention strategies. *Trauma Response*, 6(1):15–20.

Miller, L. (2000b). Traumatized psychotherapists. In Dattilio, F.M. and Freeman, A. (Eds.), *Cognitive-Behavioral Strategies in Crisis Intervention*, 2nd ed. (pp. 429–445), New York: Guilford.

Parkes, C.M. (1975). Determinants of outcome following bereavements. *Omega*, 6:303–323.

Parkes, C.M. and Brown, R. (1972). Health after bereavement: a controlled study of young Boston widows and widowers. *Psychosomatic Medicine*, 34:449–461.

Parson, E.R. (1997). Post-traumatic child therapy: assessment and treatment factors in clinical work with inner-city children exposed to catastrophic community violence. *Journal of Interpersonal Violence*, 12:172–194.

Pearlman, L.A. and MacIan, P.S. (1995). Vicarious traumatization: an empirical study of the effects of trauma work on trauma therapists. *Professional Psychology: Research and Practice*, 26:558–565.

Prigatano, G.P. (1999). *Principles of Neuropsychological Rehabilitation*. New York: Oxford University Press.

Ressler, R.K., Burgess, A.W., and Douglas, J.E. (1988). *Sexual Homicide: Patterns and Motives*. New York: Free Press.

Rinear, E.E. (1984). Parental Response Patterns to the Death of a Child by Homicide, unpublished doctoral dissertation, Temple University.

Rynearson, E.K. (1988). The homicide of a child. In Ochberg, F.M. (Ed.), *Posttraumatic Therapy and Victims of Violence* (pp. 213–224). New York: Brunner/Mazel.

Rynearson, E.K. (1994). Psychotherapy of bereavement after homicide. *Journal of Psychotherapy Practice and Research*, 3:341–347.

Rynearson, E.K. (1996). Psychotherapy of bereavement after homicide: be offensive. *In Session: Psychotherapy in Practice*, 2:47–57.

Rynearson, E.K. and McCreery, J.M. (1993). Bereavement after homicide: a synergism of trauma and loss. *American Journal of Psychiatry*, 150:258–261.

Saakvitne, K.W. and Pearlman, L.A. (1996). *Transforming the Pain: A Workbook on Vicarious Traumatization*. New York: Norton.

Safer, J. (1999). Must you forgive? *Psychology Today*, July/August, pp. 30–34; 70–72.

Schlosser, E. (1997). A grief like no other. *Atlantic Monthly*, September, pp. 37–76.

Sewell, J.D. (1993). Traumatic stress in multiple murder investigations. *Journal of Traumatic Stress*, 6:103–118.

Sewell, J.D. (1994). The stress of homicide investigations. *Death Studies*, 18:565–582.

Silver, R. and Wortman, C. (1980). Coping with undesirable life events. In Garber, J. and Seligman, M. (Eds.), *Human Helplessness* (pp. 279–340). New York: Academic Press.

Sprang, G. and McNeil, J. (1995). *The Many Faces of Bereavement: The Nature and Treatment of Natural, Traumatic, and Stigmatized Grief*. New York: Brunner/Mazel.

Spungen, D. (1998). *Homicide: The Hidden Victims. A Guide for Professionals*. Thousand Oaks, CA: Sage.

Talbot, A., Dutton, M., and Dunn, P. (1995). Debriefing the debriefers: an intervention strategy to assist psychologists after a crisis. In Everly, G.S. and Lating, J.M. (Eds.), *Psychotraumatology: Key Papers and Core Concepts in Posttraumatic Stress* (pp. 281–298). New York: Plenum Press.

Temple, S. (1997). Treating inner-city families of homicide victims: a contextually oriented approach. *Family Process*, 36:133–149.

Van Biema, D. (1999). Should all be forgiven? *Time*, April 5, pp. 55–58.

Yalom, I.D. (1980). *Existential Psychotherapy*. New York: Basic Books.

Yassen, J. (1995). Preventing secondary traumatic stress disorder. In Figley, C.R. (Ed.), *Compassion Fatigue: Coping with Secondary Traumatic Stress Disorder in Those Who Treat the Traumatized* (pp. 178–208). New York: Brunner/Mazel.

Young, M.A. (1988). Support services for victims. In Ochberg, F.M. (Ed.), *Posttraumatic Therapy and Victims of Violence* (pp. 330–351). New York: Brunner/Mazel.

Young, M.A. (1994). *Responding to Communities in Crisis: The Training Manual of the Crisis Response Team*. Washington, D.C.: National Organization for Victim Assistance.

Index

Index

vaginal pulse rate (VPR), 268
Vampire of Düsseldorf, 15, 302
vampires, 5
vampirism, 9, 14–15
Verzeni, Vincenz, 5–7, 12
vicarious traumatization, 329
victim advocacy, 318–319
violence
    borderline psychotic firesetters, and,
        296
    brain injuries, and, 191
    delinquency, and, 293
    neurochemistry of, 144–145
    psychopathy as predictor of, 281
    six risk markers for men in intimate
        relationships, 172
    stalking, and, 175
violence graduation hypothesis, 297

violent offenses, five categories of, 141
voyeurism, 13–14, 18–19, 106, 108

W

war, violent acts and, 19
Wechsler Adult Intelligence Scale-
    Revised (WAIS-R), 267
Wechsler Memory Scale, 149
werewolves, 5
Williams, Wayne, 138
Wisconsin Card Sorting Test (WCST),
    149
Wuornos, Aileen Carol, 280

Z

zoophilia, 267